AMERICA AND EUROPE.

BY

ADAM G. DE GUROWSKI.

NEW YORK:
D. APPLETON AND COMPANY,
346 & 348 BROADWAY.
M.DCCC.LVII.

CONTENTS.

America, the progeny of Europe, differs from the generator in many of the most salient features of her social and political organisms, differs in public and domestic life. To point out these dissimilarities, to ascertain their sources, is the aim of the following pages.

A rapid and succinct view of human affairs and events, as far back as the dimmest light of history extends, shows that the diversified aspects of civilization have been successively elaborated through different people and at different eras. It demonstrates that the civilizing impulses have been inherent, inborn in man, of almost all historical races and nations, and in various regions and climates. A higher principle has inspired, mightier laws have presided over the destinies of mankind, than the exclusively physical law of races. Humanity soars above races and nationalities. However active, and at times, however seemingly all-powerful may have been the agency of the law of races, it has never been paramount.

In the progressive development of man, in the march, the oscillations of civilization, the law of races, now scarcely perceptibly, then more distinctly but well-nigh uninterruptedly, has receded before the more elevated, nobler, and more truly humane principles and incentives of man's mental faculties, aspirations, and actions. In America these principles and laws have been put in action with a fulness unwonted and impossible in the old world, generating here a social state and evolving institutions almost unknown to the past.

The social and historical standpoint reached by America, solves several problems, which up to this time have been distinctly regarded as nearly insoluble, from epoch to epoch, from generation to generation.

Man as a unit, in the free untrammelled development of his individuality, has been more or less thoroughly absorbed in various aspects and ways for the benefit of the whole; and was so even in the freest ancient or European communities and states. In principle and in fact, individuality has been and is still limited, circumscribed, compressed. This is the case in the still surviving social structures, as well as in the ancient and modern theories of initiators, innovators, socialists, reformers, of whatever name and principle, with a few rare exceptions. For the first time in free America, man's individuality has been normally fixed and established, its rights asserted and realized. Fourier's theories of association, hitherto abstract and unrealizable, but wantonly and ignorantly confounded with what is commonly called socialism—these theories alone reveal a higher, more scientific, and therefore fuller scope and guarantee for the developement of individuality, for the play of its moral, mental, and physical powers and activities. But America fills the present, throws effulgent rays into the future.

Authority and liberty have always struggled for pre-eminence and leadership over the historical development, and the domestic hearth of nations. The past has witnessed countless centuries of the reign of authority, religious, political, social, and governmental; and comparatively, only lightning-like flashes of that of liberty. The former always endeavoring to recover the lost ground, to seize the supremacy over man's mind and his social economy. Moralists, men of genius as Dante, philosophers, statesmen, have continually attempted to conciliate the two antagonistic principles and forces, to modify or reduce their extremes, to bring them into peaceful juxtaposition, to find in their combination an equipoise for society. Some way or other, however, authority gets the lion's share in theory as in practice. Here the relations of authority and lib erty to each other and to man have received a new and elementary realization.

The principles from which the institutions of America have been evolved, form the source of her material prosperity. It does not enter within the range of this work to detail the giant steps of her progress, nor to present statistical comparisons. Statistics, even the most detailed and complete, never axiomatic and conclusive in themselves, serve only to elucidate and verify the soundness and potency of a dominant social and governmental system. And the universally admitted prosperity of America, wants not a statistical confirmation.

Generalizations always embrace all existing or presumable exceptions. To specify these, would have been tedious or altogether impossible. For good or for bad, for large or smaller contingencies, exceptions are implied in the generalizations, which constitute the strictures of comparison between America and Europe, or relate to customs, manners, habits, and usages. A few scattered mountains or hills do not constitute the general physiognomy of a country, a few warm or cold months do not make a soft or a rigid climate, a few brave men or cowards do not make an army fight, win, or run. The same axiom applies to social and political conditions, to the appreciation of the most various and minute public or private relations, to the moral, social, and domestic character of a land and its inhabitants.

AMERICA AND EUROPE.

CHAPTER I.

RACES, POPULATION.

A LEADING social feature distinguishes America from the European nations. This is the union of the utmost individual independence and equality with a well-regulated social and political organization. This radical difference already existed in the germs out of which sprang the ancient, the European civilization, and this new world. In both cases, the embryo was different. Different was the historical process of formation. A principle begot the American society; force and conquest were the parents of the ancient one.

To the various characteristics of races are nowadays ascribed the various manifestations of social structures and civilizations, in their progressive unfolding. Such characteristics, wholly physical in their nature, are set up as exclusive and omnipotent agencies in the development of human destinies. They are supposed to constitute the power of man to elevate his existence, to elaborate the various conditions of his social culture. To those characteristics are subordinated all the other incentives and inspirations, which stimulate man's unappeasable activity; nay, they are said to constitute his mental and moral essence.

By the oscillations which mark the development of the world's history, the centre, the focus of civilization, became displaced from South to North. Now a verdict contrary to historical evidence proclaims the so-called southern races of every region, of each hemisphere, to be deprived of initiative, of active powers, in the labors and struggles for social amelioration. On account of the climate, and of certain presumed anatomical dissimilarities, they are declared to be too weak morally for freedom; too weak physically to be its supports and sanctuary.

In man, however, as in the universe, every thing is wonderfully united. In all regions and in all conditions, he is endowed with the germs of similar passions, inclinations, tendencies, aspirations. Their development and play, actuated by the events and conditions which surround and press upon him, carry man decidedly astray at times in a special direction, or keep him more fully under the influence of his purer and indestructible essence. This law —if positive, well-defined laws are to be recognized—is human in its nature, all-embracing, and more elastic and expanding than that which, according to the variety of races and of their dwellings, distributes their participation and significance in the eternal epos of our social destinies.

Societies, nations, and states move, act and live by the combination of facts and events of the external world with internal human impulses and propensities. Sometimes the higher human powers succumb under the pressure of external, and merely material circumstances. Herein the true cause is to be found, amidst many explications, of the fluctuations of civilization, of its slow march, of its difficult expansion even in one and the same nation, dwelling in the same region. Moreover, because, by the fortuitous concourse of events, a nation, mostly forming a small branch of what ethnologically is called race, and favored by peculiar combinations, has often become a leader of a given epoch, such ascendency was not predestined nor permanent. There have been several Ionic States, but only *one Athenæ*, and the Beotians were likewise Greeks. The same phenomenon is reproduced in the development of all the cardinal and secondary races.

The lights which illuminate the orbits of the human race were not enkindled simultaneously, but one by one. They radiated in various directions. Neither North nor South, neither this nor that primordial race, nor any branch issuing therefrom, has been, in ancient or in Christian times, the exclusive and predestined holder of the sacred fire. So neither the man of the North nor that of the South, is exclusively endowed with the love of liberty, or with exclusive mental and physical powers to secure and to sustain it. There is no social or historical law by which a special race is intrusted with the highest gifts which alone constitute the supremacy of man over the inferior creation. The tendency to happiness is common to all, as well as the efforts for amelioration. These tendencies manifest themselves differently, and at various epochs among various nations. They are evoked by accidents of human character, and constitute the brightest phenomena in the ascending movement of humanity. Their investigation unravels the laws by whose action nations appear and march on the stage of history.

And if there is an absolute historical law, revealed by the uninterrupted labor of the human race, by its struggles with nature and with itself, by the bloody as well as the luminous pages which fill history, by the efforts for ameliorating the moral and material state wherein consists civilization, by the religious and philosophical speculations enkindled in the succession of ages, by the multifarious manifestations of the human spirit in literature, in refinement, in arts, in industrial, mechanical, and agricultural pursuits—it is the law of the successive appearance of races and nations in the course of history. It is the law of transmission from one to another of the sacred fire of civilization; it is the succession of nations to each other on the foreground of the events of ages. Not simultaneously in all places, and by all races and nations, but in succession is civilization to be elaborated. When the time had arrived for calling a people to light and truth, it mattered not whether it lived amid the snows of Scandinavia, or on the burning plains of India. The cause of this law has hitherto been hidden, unexplained, but the law speaks to the mind from all the pages, from all the events, from all the evolutions of history. There is no absolute reason why the light of civilization should not have spread simultaneously over the plains of Iran and over those of Germany—especially as branches of the same stock, of the same family or race, extended, moved, lived, worked, suffered and enjoyed over this space. But perhaps more than forty centuries elapsed before the light, already shining and evoking a higher life south of the Himalaya and along the Indus, reached the Rhine and the Atlantic. And in that space and time, how many, and how variously endowed actors, how many fertile ideas, and mental and social manifestations, what various utterances of the human mind have filled the ages, succeeded to each other, all of them in turns initiators and initiated into the great, mysterious and nevertheless luminous sanctuary of human development and progress. In this succession, each race or nation, in its time, brought its offerings, elaborated one or even many ideas, according to its own peculiarity, according to special data and conditions. But the impulse, the aspiration towards progress and amelioration, the ethereal sparks of this life-giving fire, how different its manifestations; it was and is glimmering in the mind, in the bosom of man in all regions, all climes, and all physical conformations. A luminous current of culture runs throughout the whole history of the race, and constitutes its development. Sometimes rapid and broad, then at times slow and dimmed, but never interrupted. The tyranny exercised over historical and philosophical studies and comprehension, by the narrow-minded, one-sighted classicisms,—a tyranny resulting in a blind confidence and devotion to the axioms and verdicts of Greek and Roman writers,—overclouded the judgment of sound, impartial reason. Thus, on Greek civilization and philosophy was bestowed a power of virtual originality and self-creation unjustified by the investigation into the history of human development. In our times, another tyranny prevails and overshadows the mind; a tyranny more exclusive, because concentrating in one race all the better and higher endowments of man, endowments constituting the higher essence in which consists the culture of our time. It is presumptuously asserted, that only northern races are enabled to achieve civilization, in all its various mental, social, and material manifestations; that only a few northern nations are the exclusive bearers and the agents of the culture of the globe. Thus the modern post-Roman civilization—according to this haughty verdict—is exclusively worked out by the German mind, the German race. On this continent, freedom, democracy, activity, those highest goods and conditions of the happiness of man, are to form in their turn, preëminently, if not exclusively, the lot of a single family—the Anglo-Saxon one. How little history justifies all this sweeping range of assertions, can be shown by taking the evidence even at random which is amply scattered over its pages. History demonstrates that neither climate nor certain geographical conditions enervate mind and body, disabling men from mental and industrial laborious activity. It shows that man is subject to these powerful external influences, that under their action the events of his life are variously combined and manifested. Man reacts on all nature or the medium wherein he moves and works. Every thing in creation is subject to reciprocal action,—stagnation is death. Man is the centre, the focus of the universe; in him nature or matter reaches the highest combination with mind. Thus he reproduces and reflects all the countless variety and combinations of those two essences, their modifications and graduations, their affinities, repulsions, attractions. Thus he is versatile in his utterances and actions, in his modes and methods, in his ways of shaping out the fruits of his mental and plastic productivity. For this reason, in certain conditions, under certain combinations of events and of influences, under the inward impulse of faculties and propensities, some of them may acquire greater fulness and power of expansion than others; these in this manner becoming crushed, crowded out, remaining in an embryonic state. So in inorganic as in organic nature—from various proportions and combinations of rather a small number of chemical elements, come forth an innumerable variety of ores and stones, of colors, flavors, tastes, of forms and powers in the vegetable and in the animal realm.

The greatest, the most crushing and difficult material works and labors have been accomplished in the hot regions of Asia, at epochs when man did not possess such various scientific means and tools to bridle and master the reluctant elements of nature. There at remote times was first accomplished the hardest, the rudimental task of civilization. To-day a blast of powder severs immense blocks of granite; machinery cuts, separates and carries them to various destinations. But are the first inventors in mechanics not even more astonishing than those who inherited the results of their efforts, and of their successful or frustrated attempts? The man who understood and applied the first rudiments of mechanics, probably spent as much power of observation, combination and calculation as did Fulton, for whom the former prepared and smoothed the path. And so with all other sciences, inventions, industries and productions. Daily experience shows how unconquerable and deadly to man is the exuberant vegetation of hot and tropical regions, how difficult in those regions to subject nature to the power, to the will, to the handling of man. Far more in the Southern clime does nature resist and defend itself than in that of the less reproductive and moderate North, where now civilization shines more brightly. But the plains of Egypt, Syria, and of the Indus, cut by canals, watered by art, highly cultivated and nourishing millions and millions at the remotest times, those regions covered then with rich, powerful and monumental cities, swarming with industrious, enterprising and therefore skilful and intelligent populations, bear witness to the falsehood of the assertion concerning the inability of the Southern races for hard labor, and of the absolute enervating influence of climate. What an immense amount of labor, skill, industry, invention were spent, used up, before those regions reached that high state of culture which they enjoyed forty or fifty centuries ago. The gigantic ruins of the Egyptian civilization show a high degree of development in the mechanical and architectural arts, as well as of others. And the Brahminic remains? Energy, industry, refinement flourished on the Indus when Greece was probably occupied only by savage barbarians, when the man of the now proud North had scarcely a hovel wherein to crouch, or the skin of a wild beast to cover his shivering body. In their times those Southern tropical regions were the seat and representatives of the highest degree of culture and civilization, which man was to reach in a given epoch; in the same way as the man of the Northern regions represents it now. Corresponding mental culture of course was the twin, or rather the incentive to material progress, and mental culture, as reproduced in a higher comprehension of social duties in social organization, manifested itself in the past, in the remotest antiquity. Love of country, the extension over all members of a given society of the means of information, the absence of social privileges of caste can be traced out to nearly immemorial times, even beyond the boundaries of the Indo-European family.

The antiquity of the now slightly treated Chinese civilization is not ascertained. But for the whole period of positive history, this civilization seems to have made little if even any progress, having at that remote epoch already reached a remarkably diversified and eminent development. It is still an unsolved historical problem, whether the Chinese received civilization from Egypt or India, or transmitted it to those regions. Such an antiquity proves at any rate an inventive and exertive power of the Turanic or Altaic race. When the proud Indo-Germans were shrouded in torpidity and savageness, the Chinese cultivated the soil, the arts; had various manufactures, had mental development; the art of writing was familiar to them. The society of the ancient, as well as of the European world, was and is based on distinctions and privileges of castes; was and is construed out of social superpositions. Slavery under various forms existed among all the nations. No traces of either of these evils exist in the Chinese social structure. Castes, privileges and slavery are still the great chains obstructing, impeding the free development of the Christian, as they did that of the ancient world. The whole social history is the reproduction of the struggles and of the attempts of men to free themselves from those troublesome deformities. The highest conception of social advancement not yet attained even in our epoch, is the recognition of the position of the individual in society, not according to inherited privileges and accidents of birth, but according to his individually acquired mental and scientific distinctions and accomplishments. On them, however, has depended social position in China for uncountable centuries, and nowhere are to be found traces of existence of social, civil or military slavery. There are, to be sure, many black spots and deficiences in the Chinese social state and civilization—many wherein they are greatly inferior, but from the other side the above-mentioned phenomena throw many of our boasted superiorities into the shade. Knowledge, such as exists in China, is brought within the reach of the whole population; and with all our facilities for printing and diffusing of letters, we are left far in the background by the Chinese, among whom for long centuries the habit of reading is as general among the masses as any other function of daily life. Books are at a price lower than the smallest alms. The whole Empire forms a leaf, covered with written sentences and axioms of their moralists. Schools accordingly existed there for the masses of the people at a period when European nations did not even dream of the availability of learning. Printing, that great engine of modern progress, was probably known to the Chinese when Harlem was a wilderness. The use of powder was undoubtedly brought to Europe from China. In India the education of the people through public schools, the universal knowledge of reading and writing, date back from a time when neither of these accomplishments was thought of as a necessary element in the existence of the masses. They were not judged indispensable even in Greece and Athens; nor even for long centuries afterwards in Europe, where even now more than half of its population is wholly illiterate. The Mahometan conquest and the English dominion ruined the Hindoo people, destroyed schools, destroyed arts and industry. Oppression and the turn of human events enervated and debased these regions, and in every way exerted over them their baneful influence.

The facts which constitute civilization, are scattered here and there over various regions and various nations. Times and circumstances are seemingly confounded. But there is a wonderful chain stretching over the course of centuries, enclosing the world and accommodating itself to the ebb and flow of human affairs.

Many civilizing rays warmed Greece, reaching there from the East, and to those the Greeks and the Romans added again their own products. When the men of Northern Europe made their appearance in history, they became initiated into a new life; a light was at once transmitted to them, and however feeble were its morning rays, they alone quickened the germ of modern civilization. The love of freedom, the attempts to establish society on great democratic foundations were neither the specialty of German races, nor did they originate with them. Both were pre-existent in history; they grew to maturity under the combined action of Christianity and human events; and the indestructible and eternal element in the essential destiny of man.

Two races especially emerged out of the ruins of the Roman Empire and inherited its civilization. The one, the Celtic, was already partly interwoven with the Roman civilization, and had early received the Christian vivifying teaching. From the Celts emerged the Romanic nations, as they are now called. The other race, the German, broke forth furiously and savagely, and establishing itself upon the Roman ruins, extended a dark and heavy shroud over the dissolving fabric of society. The labor of centuries was required to reinvigorate its remaining and feebly smouldering sparks, which were again to warm and stimulate and fertilize the minds of the Northern barbarians. But as they are the last comers and actors, they proclaim themselves the originators and creators of all the good in modern civilization. Invoking the fallacious and superficial evidence of craniology and physiology, they assert that the comprehension of freedom and of equality was exclusively located in their brains. But history overthrows the condemnatory verdicts, and teaches that the fact was the reverse, and restores to their due share the disappeared, wasted and withered races and nations.

Paleontology teaches that in the animal kingdom, genera and families disappear after having fulfilled their time, or become transmuted and further developed in others, called more perfect. The so-called monsters of the antediluvial world were as perfect in the condition of their existence, as can be the actual living animals, created among different vegetations, a different state of the earth-crust, different combinations of air, gases, atmosphere, and the thereby stimulated productivity of the soil. Animals of the last creation, man included, would have been unable to live when our planet was in the jurassic or even diluvial condition. The animals of every kind belonging to those bygone epochs, were as perfect in their way as the conditions of life and existence required and allowed. An animal world disappeared in revolutions of the globe, revolutions covering it with new strata, and fostering new creations.

The present animal kingdom is subject to the same absolute conditions, but modified or adapted to new combinations, appropriate and adapted to the so-called higher forms and functions.

And so it is, in a higher philosophical appreciation, with races, nations, and even individual families. Their work done, or transmitted to successors, they retire into the background, or even,—above all the so-called historical families—they die out. New ones succeed them in the ascension of an infinite spiral. During the periods of their vital activity those races, nations and individual families, answered fully to given and existing conditions, and in given epochs they constituted the acme of general life. For right and for wrong, even dynasties and families embodied, influenced and directed human events during long spaces of time. Now the race enters a new era. The actors of the past disappeared and disappear from the world's stage, in accordance with the same laws that ruled the disappearance of the animal creations of the antediluvian world.

The aspirations for freedom, the struggles for social equality, and even for democratic organization, were familiar to other races as well as the Indo-European or Germans, and fill the history of the past as they do that of the present. The Hebrews belonging to the Semitic or Aramaic stock, represent the most ancient republican and democratic society, with Jehovah for president, and judges for administrators. No social privilege or distinction prevailed among the tribes, excepting that one derived from religious functions, as in the tribe of Levi. Nowadays the Hebrews are held up as deprived of warlike courage and gallantry;—but the times of the Maccabees elevate them to a level with the most glorious military deeds of any nation whatever; and the defence of Jerusalem against the Romans remains unrivalled on the records of devotion and patriotism. So events give character to men and nations. Modern pride cannot too often be reminded of the Hebrew origin and the humble condition of the teacher of love and humanity, and thus of its highest redeemer. Love of liberty, heroism and civilization do not depend on the phrenological conformation of certain angular depressions in the cerebral cavity; and the races who, to-day, direct the events of the world, shine in more than one respect in a lustre transmitted to them by preceding ones.

Greece and Athens will remain for eternity the brilliant stars in the history of the mental and social development of men. The Greek mind does not yield to any other in power, boldness and depth; in many of its productions and conceptions it remains unrivalled; and nevertheless it borrowed many features of civilization from the East, and above all it borrowed therefrom that speculative philosophy, wherein consists one of its greatest splendors.

The Christian cardinal dogma of which many acknowledge the influence on the modern mental and ethical civilization; an influence as powerful as the exclusively moral precepts taught by Christ himself; this dogma derives its essence from the conceptions of divinity prevailing in the East long centuries before Zoroaster's doctrine, which embodying the conceptions of a distant epoch, in a purified form, marked the transition to Christian theology. This last emerged and received its complement from the holy fathers, those disciples of the New-Platonic, and essentially Eastern philosophy.

The claims of the German races to superiority, to having originated out of their individual and special essence a new culture, a new social idea, pregnant with the germs of a higher social maturity and development, and foreshadowing exclusively the actual tendencies, and aspirations of Europe, and the republican democratic organization of this country—these claims contradict the eternal movement of history, and are not substantiated by her records.

The German destroyers of the Roman world gained dominion principally over the Celts in Gaul, Spain, and Italy. But first of all, those invaders, establishing themselves in the regions which they had conquered, carried there a new political organization as a natural result of conquest; but in the lapse of many centuries, they scarcely produced any effect on the prominent features of character belonging to the conquered.

The Frenchman of the last ten centuries, as well as of our own days, is the same as the Celto-Gaul, who, during the first centuries of the Roman republic, promenaded from the Seine to Asia Minor, ravaged Italy and Rome under Brennus, and boasted that he was able to sustain on his spear the falling roof of heaven. Notwithstanding the admixtures of various German races, as the Franks, Goths, Burgundians, Normans, the Gallo-German-Frenchman, who sprang from the combination, did not lose his ancient bellicose and reckless propensities. Now, as of old, he plunges into a war for the sake of fighting for glory rather than for positive results. In the frozen solitudes of Russia, as recently under the walls of Sebastopol, the French have shown the ancient Gallic character.

In the same way, the Spaniard of our days, notwithstanding the Gothic admixture, is the Celto-Iberian of the times of Carthaginian and Roman domination. The same terrible, cold contempt for his own life, as well as that of others, as described by Pomponius Trogus, was evinced in the murders of the inquisition at home, and in those perpetrated in the Netherlands; it echoes from national habits in tragedies and songs, and the same character was finally delineated by Chateaubriand. Saragossa recalls the memory of Saguntum and Numantia, and the guerilla-warfare practised against Napoleon reminds us of Sertorius and his patriotic struggle against the Romans.

Nearly all the German invaders left their footprints on Italy, some of them, as the Longobards especially, establishing a domination for a couple of centuries. And still the Italian features, the Italian mind, the Italian character in all its variety, from the Alps to Tenarus, has not the slightest resemblance to that of the Germans. If, in some eminent features, the Italians of the Christian centuries differ from the ancient Romans, they nevertheless have nothing in common with the Germans. The remains of these various invaders became quietly absorbed, overflowed, dissolved, decomposed by the powerful creative exuberance of the Italian soil. Circumstances, various events, variously acting, and a peculiar run of human affairs for about twelve centuries, shaped out the characteristics of the Italians.

In their political organism and internal struggles, for twelve centuries the Italians proclaimed an insurmountable repulsion to centralization, to becoming fused and condensed in one single State. All the efforts of the Papacy stranded against this innate repulsion, as now-a-days the efforts of devoted patriots strand equally against it. Only the iron grasp of ancient Rome subdued this centrifugal proclivity of the various Italiots* tribes and municipalities. But when once that iron band was broken, Italy burst asunder, returning almost naturally to the former state of decentralization—and thus at the distance of

* Italiots are called the inhabitants of ante-Roman; Italians those of post Roman times.

nearly twenty-five centuries, the social propensity of the ancient Italians is vigorously salient in modern Italy.

Imagination has surrounded the advent of the German races with an epic nimbus, but sound critical and philosophical appreciation destroys the assumed poetry, and dispels the charm. This is always the result of the cool application of science. Before it, disappear all the fanciful images and adornments which poetry has created. Thus science has denuded nature of its mysterious poetical sounds and images. We now know too well what material causes produce the soft murmur of a brook. Even the nightingale in the handling of science, is nothing more than a mechanical instrument, and destitute of any romantic feeling. So in the history of our race, science and sound sense destroy the phantasmagorical. Not that true poetry should be blotted out from our destinies. The life of our race is, was, and will for ever remain the most sublime epos. More truly so when it embraces humanity, than when it is limited and woven around the accidents of one race, nation, and family.

The various German tribes emerged to daylight from the dark mist surrounding them, by virtue of the historical law, which pushes onward on the scene, successive races and nations. According to widely-spread assertions, the Germans were predestined spiritually and physiologically, by higher will and impulse, and by craniological construction, to become the true exponents of Christianity, to disenthral the world. A new culture, a new civilization, social and political freedom, elevating the mass of men to a higher and general level, or to true democracy: these were the gifts of which the Germans, to the exclusion of all others, have been the chosen bearers and agents from the moment of their first appearance on the stage. To be sure, these savage invaders were incited by the passionate love of personal independence, breaking with impetuous ferocity the bounds of civilization which they encountered. But this fierce sentiment of personal independence is not the germ or embryo of rational and social liberty; it is common for the most part to all savages; it is the state which approaches nearest to the condition of animals. The fiercest among them have the strongest passion for individual independence. Contrary moreover to the assertions of phrenological and craniological science, this sentiment is not even the result of a higher animal conformation, or a superior volume of brain, as birds endowed with a less volume of brain than quadrupeds, have a more violent instinct of independence. Fishes, comparatively brainless, are more indomitable.

Not this savage sentiment of personal independence was pregnant with the social and mental freedom to which gravitates the human race, for which it works and toils. And if this should be the distinct mental specialty of the German race, in all its ramifications down to the past or to the modern Anglo-Saxons, raising them in this manner above other races and nations, their colaborers and competitors in the social arena, this specialty would rather class the Germans with a lower mental degree. Modern science ascribes to the Celtic race the desire for social equality. If this is the case, then in psychological appreciation the Celtic race would be the exponent of a higher social and mental endowment. Equality is of higher psychological origin than the merely animal craving for individual independence. Animals have not the feeling of equality, and the weaker keeps at a respectful distance and avoids crossing the path of the stronger. There is an end to individual independence. But a man relying on the equality of rights, raises his head boldly and proudly in the face of mere physical force and superiority. Events and history, show to the utmost, that social liberty and equality are fruits of association and culture; that they were stimulated and developed by the run of human affairs—and began always to ferment among those nations, which possessed a comparatively higher culture and civilization. History shows sufficiently, that neither of these germs was brought, or exclusively developed, by any of the branches of the German race.

Further, the ulterior fate of the Christian world, of the Christian creed, was secured by the northern invasion. But Christianity was already firmly rooted in humanity, otherwise it would not have resisted the furious attacks of those formidable pagan invaders. The spirit of Christianity as well as its dogmas was developed in its utmost plenitude and purity in the first centuries of its existence, and therefore by men of the southern and Semitic races. To them belong all the holy fathers, and the north has not augmented their number by a single name. Even Luther preached the return to the original principles of Christianity, the return to the so-called primitive church. The primitive Christians suffered martyrdom for mental or religious, as well as for social emancipation. They suffered for not recognizing gods in the Roman Emperors before whom the whole world trembled, at whose bidding men with their own hands shortened their lives. Emperors were even more adored than gods. The poor Christian refusing to sacrifice to the Emperor, shook the Imperial structure at the basis, aimed a blow at the head of society, and thus committed a religious as well as a social revolt; and so it was considered by those most interested in the preservation of the past, by the pagan Emperors, and by the pagan society. For them the Christians were religious and social subversionists. Those who publicly scorned this Imperial worship, on which reposed the social structure, who by thousands and thousands were murdered for this act of revolt, were the first martyrs in the cause of liberty. German races have the smallest number of the like martyrs. The tribes who overran the Roman Empire, received the Christian teaching from Celts, Latins or Greeks; and to those who remained on their primitive soil, Christianity was afterwards brought and preached principally by Celtic and Latin apostles. The German races produced the smallest number of such primitive missionaries. But the German races, as soon as they asserted themselves in history, and began to participate in a more regulated way in the movement of events, were the first in the West who politically identified church and state, thus inaugurating the greatest aberration and adulteration of Christian or Catholic, and virtually spiritual organization. The German races, or kings, the Franks, the Carlovingians, the Saxons gave fixity to the power of the Popes and submitted to it. They were its defenders. A German emperor, a Hohenstauffen, burnt the Italian Arnold of Brescia, who, in the 12th century, contested the temporal power of the popes. In one word, without the powerful aid of German races and sovereigns, papacy would not have taken such a firm hold of Europe at the very beginning of the middle ages.

Born in rigorous climates, crowding on each other by their rapid increase, unacquainted with agriculture, or averse to it, and on these accounts obtaining with difficulty the means of subsistence, some of these German tribes saw before their eyes, others knew by report, the abundance and the luxuries of ample, well cultivated regions. They were at the same time urged on by extreme want, and strongly excited by the presence of plunder. Such were the reasons which, at the distance of several centuries before, urged and attracted the German hordes of the Cymbri to Italy at the time of Marius, who, previous to the Cæsarean wars, stimulated the Helvetians to abandon their Alpine hollows and peaks, and to descend upon the more cultivated Gaul. The German tribes pressed on each other, and the nearest to the boundaries of civilization were continually wedged in by the pressure of others. To repulse this pressure, Cæsar was obliged to cross the Rhine, and the Roman emperors to push further and further into the interior of Germany the boundaries of the empire. Hence the mostly imaginary wrongs complained of by those savage tribes. The Franks who first invaded Gaul, penetrated into Spain before the epoch of general irruption; they were bands of robbers united under a chief, leaving behind them all the family ties; attracted, stimulated by the thirst of gold and wine, and going on a mission of bloody massacre and fierce destruction, as is the case with all the beasts of prey. After this attempt of the Franks, other savages for nearly three centuries invaded the empire; and gorged with plunder, they burned, ravaged, murdered, destroyed, for the sake of destruction and massacre. There was no higher or better impulse in their breast than the fierce pleasure of playing amid the chances of the world and life with power and liberty; at the utmost the indulgence in the joys of activity without labor. Such was the romance which inspired those invaders. Thus out of murder and rapine emerged the present Europe. Out of individual hardships and toils, out of the sweat of the brow, expressed not in battling with civilization, but in breaking the virgin soil, and enkindling the light of culture, out of the labor of the first settlers along the Alantic shores, emerged America, the land of promise, and the revelation of higher and broader destinies.

The German invaders were the bearers of the corruption, the vices, the crimes inherent in savage races. Robbery, murder, rape, theft, were practised on a large scale in the newly subdued lands, just as they were practised by and among them, in their primitive forests. When those conquerors established themselves in a fixed position, they began to collect the legal customs, or common laws, as they asserted, which prevailed among them of old, and they condensed these customs in written codes. Very naturally those codes re-echo what was observed by the German tribes in their primitive state, and they give an idea of their morals. The laws of the Francks, the Goths, the Burgundians, the Anglo-Saxons, and the other German tribes, dwell principally on the above-mentioned crimes. Robbery and similar offences are ever constant themes of the capitularies of Charlemagne. Among the Germans, from remote times murder was atoned by a composition under the name of weregild, and paid by the murderer to the relatives of the murdered. This of course does not give an elevated idea of the feeling of individual honor and dignity which could have been satisfied with money or its equivalent. The ferocious vendeta as practised by other races, is less degrading, more natural in the men of primitive state, and shows more manliness and dignity. Civilization, Christianity have softened among us the feeling of revenge. We may forgive—but even the meanest will not accept a composition for the blood of a parent, a brother, a sister or a child.

This peculiar way of atonement used by the barbarian Teutons previous to their irruption over the world, was not a result of weakness, as it does not prove their humanization. The comparative mildness with which crimes were punished, is the best proof of their frequency. When in a society, assassinations, mutilations, and other similar attempts are very rare, they are regarded with horror, and the perpetrators are severely punished. Where certain actions—in a society of whatever character—are considered as heinous offences, the legislator, the public opinion, expressed in common law or usage, will reverberate the public conscience. But when crimes are frequently committed, they insensibly lose their enormity; not only those who commit them, but the society—whatever it may be—becomes accustomed to them, and bears them with indulgence.

Such were the German races when history began to throw light upon their doings, and such they must have been for centuries before,—in the times of Tacitus. His enthusiasm for them was the counterpart of his manly indignation at the effeminacy of Rome. He embellishes them purposely. He contrasted with Rome the savage Germans, by whose bravery he was dazzled, and with whose usages and domestic life he was not and could not have been as thoroughly acquainted as we imagine. Sidonius, who lived among them after they had already been for a long time under the soothing influence of Christianity, exclaims: "Happy the eyes who do not see them, happy the ears who do not hear." Very likely Tacitus exalted the Germans for the same reasons which incited Rousseau, St. Pierre and others, to endow the fancied primitive man *l'homme de la nature*, with all moral perfections. The fierce, treacherous and thieving Indian, who abhors every kind of culture and civilization, was held up as a model of purity and simplicity not only by sentimentalists, but by minds as positive and clear-sighted as that of Jefferson. And even according to the testimony of the enthusiastic Roman, the Germans, like the Indians, were more fond of plunder than of labor, and he likewise mentions some tribes that were subjected to the most debasing despotism.

The husband and father among the Germans had as absolute dominion over the wife, the daughter, and the son, as he had among the Romans. He had the power of life and death over his family, and could sell them. By the common law and usages of England, the Anglo-Saxon right to such a traffic still exists, or has only lataly been erased. The German wife espoused the quarrels of the husband, fought at his side; so did the Gallic, the Celto-Iberian women—precisely as in given circumstances, the same acts of devotion have been shown on all parts of the globe. The chastity of the German woman, and the fidelity of the man, which Tacitus so highly extolled, clash singularly with the above-named tenor of the laws derived from usage; and at any rate they must have disappeared very soon, and gone the way of all flesh. Monogamy was not absolute in the German forests. Cæsar says that Arivistus had two wives, and Tacitus speaks of other Germans who had them also. Beyond romance there exist no proofs in the German customs and manners, to justify the assumed assertion that the position of the woman was elevated by them to its natural purity and virtue. The Germans did not surround woman with the reverence due to her purer devotion. The women of the Germans were domestic slaves, performing the hard field or garden labor, as they do still in Germany, and as is still customary among all savages, as well as among Christian nations of a lower degree of civilization. In this respect, material progress and labor-saving inventions will alone fully emancipate woman and restore them to softer functions. The German women, wife, and daughters, had no civil rights, no property. The Roman daughters had a dowry; their rights in this respect were under the guarantee and the guardianship of the law. The German husband could punish publicly or privately, with the utmost severity, even by death, the infidelity of the wife; but among the Germans, as among all past and present nations, the wife has no rights and no legal method to punish the infidelity of the husband. Whatever might have been the degradation of the woman in antiquity; the mother, the true matron, was honored and respected. Xenophon's Economics bears testimony that it was so in Greece. The matrons of the better centuries of Rome were surrounded with respect and deference by the usages and the laws; and these matrons are among the loftiest adornments of Roman history.

The chaste and pure priestesses of Ceres in Athens enjoyed an elevated social standing: and in the privileges which surrounded the consecrated Roman Vestals, the highest worship was paid to chastity, even by a society in which the comprehension of morals did not extend to sexual passions. Among the Slavi, women were honored in the remotest times, in those of their ante-historical existence. Monogamy prevailed in their usages, the women stood in high consideration, and exercised great influence. This fact is alluded to so far back as Nicolas Damascenus, a friend of King Herod.

The most sublime phenomenon of our civilization, the purification, ennoblement and elevation of woman, is altogether the work of Christianity. Christianity taught man that woman ought not to be his slave, but his equal, his companion. The atrocious right of life and death was destroyed. Christian charity purified the manners, and thus elevated woman, whose dignity is incompatible with corruption and licentiousness. Christianity is the source whence this powerful, salutary, and generous influence emanated. This is the origin of the dignity and honor of woman in Europe. Women were the most ardent and devoted apostles of Christianity among the barbarians. The sacred ties of marriage united the barbarian to the Christian woman. Thus Clotilde Christianized the fierce Clodwig or Clovis and his Franks; Dombrowka brought Christianity to the Poles; Olga and Helen to the Russians, and the same way of propagation prevailed among nearly all the various Northern tribes.

The Southern nations invaded by the Teutons, were already Christian. Thus woman was already purified and honored among the nations of Celtic, Latin or Romanic descent. From them the Germans received the initiation into the purer and loftier appreciation of woman in domestic and in social life. Chivalry found woman for centuries purified, raised, surrounded with veneration. It surrounded the womanly charm with inspiring illusions, with passionate, religious gallantry and devotion. And the poetical source of the legends of chivalry lies not among the Germans—still less among the Moors of Spain, whose houris are the opposite of Christian virgins and unblemished wives—but among Celtic Britons.* The most violent, ungovernable and reckless passions, in their most unsocial manifestations, prevailed among the Germans in their forests, as well as when by their victories over other countries, they found themselves in a new situation. If they were bearers of new germs, those germs were of such a kind as to stifle society in its cradle; and this they did in reality and for centuries. The Germans in their forests not only made slaves of their prisoners of war, as did all the nations of antiquity, but often gambled themselves into slavery. All the vices and crimes that form the special characteristics of a savage state of society, were common to the various German tribes, who under various

* Arthur, Launcelot, and the whole legend of the Round Table belong to Brittany.

names, one after another, or at times simultaneously, for centuries poured into the Roman empire. Destruction was the watchword for all. The differences of caste and of class, nobles and villains, which (according to the testimony of Cæsar and Tacitus) existed among them in their forests, were brought to the countries which they subdued. The ancient nobles, chieftains and princes, being for the most part the leaders of the invaders on the battle field as well as in the division of the conquered lands; those military distinctions soon acquired even a new and stronger fixity than they had in the original German countries. Nowhere, not in a single case, are to be detected among these tribes, the germs or notions of social equality. "Legitimacy of royal races among European nations is a Germanic idea," says Ranke; and so was that of the military nobility, which had been partly already brought from the German forests, and partly sprouted out from the new social conditions, into which the conquest over men, soil, cities and vast uncultivated lands, had put the conquerors.

The Goths overran the greatest part of the Roman empire. They broke in, East and West, and finally took possession of some of the most beautiful portions, as Italy, the South of France, and Spain. It is believed that their domination extended previously from Scandinavia to the Danube, at least under Hermanric, one of their greatest leaders. Others pretend that the Goths are not of a German stock, but are the direct descendants of the ancient classical Getæ. This doubt is based on the historical fact, that the Goths alone among the German races, did not compound for murder by a fine or weregild. At any rate they are now counted among Germans, who received from them a written language, in the translation of the Scriptures, by Ulfila, a Gothic bishop. They received architecture, moreover, and many rudiments of refinement, which the Goths themselves learned from the Romanic nations which they subdued. The Goths entered the civilized regions under the leadership of their royal races, of the Amali and the Balti, and both, according to their national creed, of superior half godlike origin. The Gothic nation was divided by various social privileges; they had the *Capelleti*, or long-haired, and the *Pilefori*, distinguished by wearing caps in the presence of the King and at the divine sacrifices. To wear long hair was a kingly and nobiliar distinction among other German tribes. The *Pilefori* formed a supreme theo-aristocratical class, and had the power to elect a king or a reigning dynasty. When the Goths became Christians of the Arian creed, the privileged class of the *Pilefori* perpetuated itself, absorbing in its members the dignity of bishops. The same was the case when they subsequently melted into Romanism under the reign of King Recarede. This is the origin of the great power and influence of the Westgothic Bishops, as shown in Toulouse, and above all in Spain during the Westgothic rule. The celebrated councils of Toledo, held by Gothic bishops, legislated for the kingdoms; by the decree of bishops, King Vamba was dethroned. Montesquieu as well as Guizot, was puzzled to find the origin and the cause of this power exercised by the Gothic or Spanish bishops; as no other Roman Catholic nation at that time submitted to the power of the clergy to that extent. The source of the power was in the ancient caste of the Gothic *Pilefori;* as therefrom likewise comes the right of the Spanish Grandees to remain with their heads covered in the presence of their sovereign.

Social gradations and nobiliar privileges, partly as the perpetuation of their primitive social state, partly deriving their strength from the nature of such a military establishment, as was in its origin and beginning the German conquest; these were implanted and extended over Western Europe by the Germans. Therein was the origin of feudality,—an organization natural to all nations conquering and extending under the leadership of chiefs and dynasties. Thus at the dawn of history, when the Iranic or Arrian races made an irruption over the ancient world, encompassed in the then known circle embracing Asia from the Indus to the Mediterranean, a part of Greece, and Egypt; this immense Empire was for several centuries of its existence propped up on feudal dynasts or magnates. Out of those feudal dynasts were the Median, Bactrian, Afghan princes, Nebuchadnezzar of Babylon, and Cyrus himself. Darius Hystaspes put an end to this ancient Eastern feudal regime, which was reproduced after long centuries in the West, and evoked by similar causes, by the current of affairs and events, similar to each other, at least, in their general outlines. None of the above characteristics of the German conquerors could in any way have been pregnant exclusively with democratic germs.

Old Cato spoke of Greece as "mendax in historia." Niebuhr, Arnold, and many modern writers on Roman history, show to what an extent it is necessary to be distrustful of Roman historians and annalists. Grote, who, of all historians, has rendered the most eminent services to the comprehension of the beneficial workings of the democratic principle; Grote has shown how prejudiced, partial, and unjust in several respects to their country, to their eminent men have been the Greek writers, full often from a heinous spirit of party. All these short-comings are fully reproduced by German writers. Notwithstanding their unequalled erudition, as soon as in any way it concerns Germanism, the spirit of historical justice vanishes; their judgment is overclouded. History, facts, and events are twisted and forcibly wedged into a preconcerted scheme. By such a process, the invading German races were surrounded by a poetical halo, and endowed with all the highest social characteristics. What events, circumstances, affections, passions, relations, contact with other nations, and with their different modes of life brought forth,—what the Germans received or learned from others,—all this was absorbed in behalf of the German race in comparison with all others. And thus modern civilization, with all its social and mental manifestations and variations, was to be exclusively the work of the German world.

The influence of human affairs on social development,—as well as the fallacy of distributing the highest human attributes according to races, or to physiological, and craniological conformations, is most strikingly elucidated by throwing a rapid glance on the Slavic neighbors of the Germans, and from whom the latter at the commencement of their historical existence, learned several rudiments of cultivation, and among them the plan of communal organization.

It can be said, that from the remotest times, the tribes known in history under the name of the Slavic race, occupied the same portions of continental Europe in which they now dwell. They were undoubtedly the first agriculturists in the North, between the Rhine and the Volga. Although savages and barbarians similar to the primitive Germans or Celts, the Slavi early attached themselves to the soil; no traces of nomadic or roaming life are to be detected among them. The dawn of history finds them living in villages as agriculturists, under simple communal institutions, with elective chiefs, and judges, or administrators. A special fact elucidates their social usages; in those remote times the Slavi alone among all nations recorded in history—the Chinese excepted—never transformed their prisoners into slaves, but after one year's detention allowed them to return to their own country. The enslaving of conquered enemies began among the whole race only in Russia, and this very likely with the establishment of the Romans or Variagues. Subsequently, certain human events, which it is not necessary to enumerate here, created slavery and serfdom, nobility and princes among the various Slavic tribes,—and German example, German influence, can be counted among the foremost. And now, serfdom on an enormous scale still exists among the Slavi; serfdom strengthened by circumstances and by events, it crushes down a branch of the human family; the only one which, in the cradle, was free from this social curse.

In the course of centuries, by wars, conquests, and German migrations, the Slavi became involved, mixed with the neighboring Germans, and Slavic sprouts extended in different directions into Germany. Thus in various ways they taught the Germans agriculture and horticulture, previous to the introduction of Christianity into the German forests. They introduced into Germany the culture of rye, which was unknown before to such an extent to the Germans, that Charlemagne in one of his capitularies especially enjoins its culture upon his German subjects. The Slavic tribes extending along the Baltic shores were daring navigators. According to the Chronicler Saxo Grammaticus, and the historian Sismondi, they united in the predatory excursions into Britain and Gaul with the Angles and Saxons, and with the Danes. And when the communal and municipal organization, suppressed by the German rule, began again to give signs of life in the south of Europe in the eleventh century, according to the authoritative testimony of the erudite and truthful Muratori, it was in the Slavi city of Ragusa among the Slavic

Dalmatians that took place the first municipal elections, as recorded by history. Circumstances, to a great extent, destroyed the communal and municipal as well as the other liberties among the Slavi, as circumstances evoked them from smouldering ashes, gave them life, virtuality, and force among the other contemporary nations.

Where the Germans permanently established their dominion, they also in various ways established servitude, serfdom, and slavery among the conquered, including the burghers, the rural populations, the artisans and the laborers. They themselves despised every kind of peaceful occupation. Neither industry nor agriculture had any attraction for them. All this was abandoned to the indigent. In Italy, Spain, France, and Britain, the conquerors, spreading over the lands, settled not in cities, but outside of the walls, erecting strongholds and castles, or burghs. They divided the whole land into cities and populations according to certain tenures, which, in their various applications, constituted the feudal system. The cities, the trades paid revenues to the new lords, the lands were tilled by aborigines, of Celto-Romanic descent. In the course of time, the descendants of the common soldiery among the conquerors, whose services were rewarded with the smaller lots or freeholds, became impoverished; then willingly or by force they were turned by the mightier knights and barons into rustics, and became subject to predial servitude equally with the natives. Others among them retired to cities, and increased there the number of laborers and workingmen, still remaining dependent on the lords. But this kind of influx into the cities could not influence or modify the character of the natives, who were far more numerous. The question therefore of the rekindling of culture after the terrible night which continued through centuries of invasion, the question of the first efforts for disenthralment and emancipation from the tyranny exercised by the feudal nobility, those questions are still pending between the Celto-Romanic and the Germans. In Germany proper, serfdom, oppression, and slavery were established, not by conquerors over the conquered of different origin, but over a people of the same blood. This was principally done after the example of what was previously consummated on the ruins of the ancient Empire. Germany proper was the last in turn to receive feudalism; she was last in turn in the effort for disenthralment, last in turn in enkindling civilization. For every thing, Germany, for centuries, went to school to Italy and France.

Throughout the whole extent of the ruins of the Roman Empire, the half burnt and desolated cities were peopled by the remains of the ancient inhabitants. After the frightful confusion of centuries began to subside, the cities little by little began to recover; industry gave feeble signs of vitality; and for its products as well as for money the inhabitants were enabled to buy from their masters, if not a recognition of rights, at least some small temporary liberalities or concessions. In the cities and among the natives were preserved the feeble traditions of previous municipal rights, the almost expiring sparks of once flourishing cultivation. What Savigny has proved and firmly established concerning the Roman law, can with safety be applied to the preservation and continuation of the overthrown civilization. If the Roman law was never wholly suppressed, nor ever disappeared from use in the darkest and most confused times; in the same way there was nowhere a total suppression and extinction of ancient civilization. This feeble spark was preserved of course, and not by the brute, unlettered, savage conquerors, but by the natives. The clergy, moreover, a powerful and softening agency, formed a connecting link between the old and new elements of society, and the clergy belonged principally to the Celto-Romanic race.

During the early part of the mediæval epoch the darkness was the thickest, the confusion the greatest; right and light were downtrodden, suppressed; arbitrariness and recklessness were the general rule. The German races alone were the exponents of the state of society as well as its exclusive leaders. Only the clerical robe enjoyed some immunity and respect, and was sheltered from outrages. But even this was often a feeble, insufficient shield. It was, however, natural, that, feeble as this protection was, individuals among the oppressed natives should seek quiet and refuge under it. Thus the monasteries became the exclusive asylum of such remains of the ancient mental and material culture as could be preserved from total extinction. In the monasteries, therefore, not only letters were preserved, but the rudiments, or rather the remains of arts and industry; and even the culture of the soil. The arts of healing, of architecture, with all their belongings, were then almost the exclusive possession of the clergy and the monks. Those belonged every where to the conquered Celto-Romanic race.

Feudality soon invaded the Church; the abbeys became rich in aristocratical feoffs and investitures; the conquerors began to enter the orders, and the abbots were selected from among the privileged, noble German class. The chronicles of most of the monasteries mention violent and often deadly strifes between the monks and the abbots; strifes originating generally in the difference of blood and descent.

Through such a state of things—through such a bloody mire—was society dragged for centuries by the Germans. Traffic and commercial intercourse, that elastic, indestructible agency of humanization; that stimulus to industry, and the consequent to peaceful and orderly occupation and activity of intellect and of mind, was preserved, and carried on by the natives alone. Orderly activity, that all-embracing hearth of civilization, manifested itself exclusively at first among the Celto-Romanic inhabitants of cities, where the German element either did not exist at all, or was mixed in a comparatively imperceptible proportion. The German, still clad in steel, was familiar only with the use of the sword and of the battle-axe:—even the poorest one among them, who tilled his own freeholds, considered mental, industrial, and commercial pursuits, as unmanly and mean.

During this whole terrible and protracted epoch, the Eastern or Greek Empire was the seat where culture, arts, industry, trade, studies, refinement existed, and comparatively flourished; parts of Italy recognized the supremacy of Byzantium, and maintained an uninterrupted intercourse with the then capital of the civilized world. This intercourse contributed to a great extent to preserve in Italy the smouldering sparks of culture. By the combination of those various tutelary and nursing agencies, these sparks were kindled, light began to dawn, to spread, to radiate. Slowly strengthening and increasing these remains of ancient culture, in Italy, in Spain, in the south of France, on the Loire and Seine, along the Rhine, every where among the cities it successively embraced, warmed the Celto or Gallo-German regions of the North, and was forwarded to Germany itself. Generally the German rulers, especially after Charlemagne, as soon as they began to comprehend the benefits of culture, erected cities which served either as so many asylums for the natives, or as centres for the slowly-reviving industry and commerce. In this slow-paced march towards the North, one country and city transmitted culture, vitalized the other.

As soon as prosperity began to give vitality and strength to the cities, the spirit of independence began to revive, and the cities began to strive against the tyranny and oppression exercised by the surrounding lords and barons. The first raising of cities was made in Italy, and in Italy the municipal and communal institutions then began to be recalled into life. The Italian cities began to be emancipated before the time of the crusades, at which time they already formed independent corporations and municipalities, some quickly transforming themselves even into powerful sovereign States. Venice alone survived the terrible conflagration caused for centuries by the irruption of the barbarians, alone preserved independence and liberty. Venice, the asylum for the martyred and conquered race, Venice, which never recognized the conquerors as masters, might have been a powerful stimulant for the other Italian cities to imitate her example. In the tenth and eleventh centuries, the cities of Lombardy, of Liguria, of Tuscany, began successively to break the yoke of the feudal barons. Uniting sometimes with the rural populations, they attacked the frowning nests and abodes of the nobles, by which they were surrounded, took or destroyed them, and forced the nobles to settle within the walls of the cities, to submit to common rule. Thus the nobles or descendants of the Germans came within the action of civilization, and began to be warmed by it. Moved by similar reasons, the French and Walloon cities afterwards took the same course, and the last in this work of disenthralment were the cities in Germany. Thus the first move for disenthralment was made in Celto-Romanic lands, the first feeble cry for social liberty was uttered by Celto-Romanic voices.

This struggle of cities or of the middle classes, first

against nobility and then against royalty, extended to our own time. It had various manifestations and forms—at times violent, then under some cover of legality. Thus it was sometimes carried for the preservation of certain privileges; finally it was carried by legists, and was called then a parliamentary one. It played an eminent part in the history of liberty, and for centuries its principal leaders on the continent were France and Flanders. During its continuation, the influence of cities or of the bourgeoisie steadily increased, until it became almost omnipotent in the great French revolution of 1789, as the mass of the people had their turn in 1792–93. Although, in the course of time, the combination of various events and affairs gave moral and material fuel to the contest, it can, nevertheless, be considered as an uninterrupted effort of the descendants of Celto-Romanic stock, against the descendants of German conquerors. The burghers, as a class or as individuals, were continually recruited in France, as every where else, from among the rural population; and thus was sustained uninterrupted and almost unadulterated the primitive distinction of blood between the privileged oppressor and the oppressed.

Hand in hand with the attempts at liberation from the petty tyrants, with the revival of industry and of commerce, hand in hand and in the same regions began the dim revival of mental culture. The cities and their inhabitants, the burghers, were its agents, its disciples. This revival at first took place in Italy and in France. Aside from the clergy and the monks, the middle classes alone, rarely the peasantry, furnished scholars, teachers and disciples. From them were the professors of various sciences, the philosophers, the theologians, the jurists and lawyers, and the physicians. All these pursuits and professions were despised for centuries by the conquerors, those ancestors of the nobility. Originally the clergy served them as amanuenses, and thence is derived the appellation of a clerk for inferior officials, doing the harder mental and written work. For ages following the conquest, the nobility throughout all Europe showed the same aversion to mental pursuits. Those who did otherwise were exceptions. It is on account of this ignorance of the nobles, for centuries the rulers and administrators of society, that the jurists and lawyers, who all belonged to the middle classes, acquired thus early a preponderating influence in the administration of the affairs of state and of justice. In France the nobles formed the judicial courts. There they judged and decided about various matters between themselves and the natives. Charlemagne principally organized such courts of the Reichembourgi. The same custom prevailed among the Longobards in Italy, and the Anglo-Saxon conquerors of Brittain. But the ignorant nobles were obliged to have their amanuenses at their side. Originally those clerks were seated in courts each at the feet of their master. By slow degrees their significance and influence increased; the nobles were glad to throw on them the burden of affairs; the clerks became permanent judges. Thus originated the gentlemen of the long robe, and in France the celebrated provincial court of parliament. Early in the second part of the middle ages France stood at the side of Italy, and was foremost in the orbit of civilization, as it then existed. Not the French, not the Spanish or Italian nobility, nor the German, was instrumental in this slow and difficult dispersion of darkness and of ignorance. Every where the nobility kept aloof from the burgher class. For long centuries intermarriage with burghers was considered dishonorable, was considered as contamination of the purity of blood. In Spain until the time of King Riceswindus, any intermarriage of a Goth with a native was punished with death; this prejudice was perpetuated there as by all the nobles of Europe, and transformed into a horror of mixing with burgher or ignoble blood. Thus when the most difficult, because the first steps in the road of culture were made, the nobility nowhere participated in them either as a class, or through the mixture of blood; and the palm for having nursed the feeble sparks of culture throughout Western and Southern Europe, belongs wholly to the lower or not noble classes, that is, to the descendants of Celto-Romans. Undoubtedly intermarriages between conqueror and conquered were contracted, and this might have been the case even to a large extent in Italy and France as well as in Britain. But according to the usual process where social distinctions prevail, it was the man from the superior position who married a woman from the inferior one, and very seldom the reverse took place. The children of such marriages followed the condition of the father, enjoyed all his privileges and shared all his prejudices. In Italy, when the cities forced the nobles to live within the walls, they thus brought them within the focus of civilization, and bestowed upon them the possibility of warming themselves at its vivifying fire. The nobleman could receive tuition in schools, could follow the labor of professors, for the reason that the Italian nobles were the first in Europe who became polished and distinguished by superior mental accomplishments. But every where else the nobility lived as it does now in castles and burghs, and for a protracted period, for centuries, nourished the old prejudices of their ancestry, the conquerors, against light and culture. Not with them were filled the halls of professors and of universities when those were created. Not nobles were professors, nor to any considerable extent were they pupils in the first period after the establishment of the University of Paris, that Alma Mater of all the universities north of the Alps. This was entirely filled, used and profited by burghers, those direct descendants of the conquered natives.

The Germans in Germany received the initiation from Italy and France. Coming last in turn, they afterwards penetrated into some parts of the domain of mind and of knowledge to a greater depth than their previous masters. But it was not the Germans that enkindled the culture of Christian or modern Europe, nor the Germans that were the first to strike for freedom and break down tyranny. Therefore not from the Germans exclusively did the post-Roman or Christian world receive its higher and purer character.

Circumstances and events aroused the Celto-Romanic nation to action far previous to the Germans, either Franks, Saxons, Anglo-Saxons, or any other branch of the great stock.

Events alone transformed the Germans as conquerors into oppressors, and the conquered into oppressed. Thus what in history is called the darkest epoch of the middle ages, was exclusively the work of the German race. It extended an iron net over the whole Christian Western world. The knights and nobles were independent of any superior overmastering power, they lawlessly carried out their arbitrary will. Italy, Germany, above all, France, were transformed into nearly as many independent suzerainties as there were nobiliar families, strongholds and castles. The sovereigns were impotent and poor, nearly deprived of power, without revenues, and leaning willingly on the cities, who proffered them money and means to curb the reckless feudality. The movement for emancipation on the continent of Europe was however not at all democratic in its nature. The paramount question then was, to secure the nearest available good, and to get a respite from the immediate oppressor. The royal power was a more sure support than could possibly be obtained from the people at large, the rural masses, enslaved by the nobles. The primitive movement for emancipation in Europe, England included, had nowhere the broad democratic character of securing rights to all; this era was inaugurated by the American revolution. The European cities tried to obtain and secure privileges. These privileges in themselves were deductions from eternal principles, but at that time the principles were only dimly comprehended and by a few persons, and not positively asserted. The question was to obtain security and guarantees, and any one was welcome who could procure and defend them. In this manner originated on the continent a kind of understanding between royalty and the cities, and the burgher classes were thorough monarchists. The legists who issued from the middle classes, finding in the Roman law a forest of axioms in favor of the absolute will of the sovereign, became its violent and decided partisans. Stimulated by hatred of the nobility, from the middle classes issued the boldest supporters of absolute authority. These, and the like events, were arbitrarily construed in proof of the love of absolute power by the Romanic nations. But nowhere for centuries did the German races show any decided or exclusive tendency, or move in a democratic direction; nowhere is to be detected among them a recognition of the pure democratic principle. Events subsequently disengaged and extricated the principle from the meshes wherein it was entangled; events to whose development contributed proportionally the Germans, as well as the Celtic, Gallic and Romanic descendants.

When ideas find their way into the world and become

facts, they are modified by external circumstances, by special relations corresponding to the mental and political state of society. Their availability and the ease of their extension depend upon the state of society, upon the demands, the aspirations, and the readiness to accept the new comer. For this reason ideas, longings and needs, more or less generally felt, were often suddenly seized, at the most propitious time, appropriated and embodied by a special nation rather than a race, which was in a more favorable condition for the new task or mission.

In the course of ages Romanism became all-powerful, oppressive, endangering the destinies, the mental and political progress of the European, or Christian Western world. Society in its mental life as well as in its political government and civil relations, was to be detached forcibly from the Vatican for the sake of preservation. In various ways Europe longed for emancipation, for freedom of worship or of conscience, for separation of church and state, or for giving to every church a national organization independent of Rome. Previous to the 16th century, the papal temporal power had as many friends as violent enemies in Italy. Arnold of Brescia, mentioned before, was one of the martyrs of this idea. The small Celto-Romanic tribe of the Albigenses and Waldenses never submitted to the Roman papal spiritual power, and the wholesale murders of these populations, carried out by fanaticized Franks, directed, sanctioned by popes, saints, bishops, and by all kinds and degrees of the priesthood, will for ever remain in history as the true exponents of Romanism. The Bohemians, the Moravians, all of Slavic stem, fought and suffered for the independence of teaching, and the free construction of the Gospel, as proclaimed by Huss. They extorted from the papacy and from the imperial power, which was subservient to it, the right to administer the

Lord's Supper in both kinds, before the Reformation firmly established this order of worship. Even the celebrated Thirty Years' War, which established Protestantism on fixed foundations in Germany, was started not by Germans, but by the Bohemians.

Thus in different lands and at different times, the idea of emancipation from Rome burst out and kindled into a flame. It was, however, suppressed previous to the apparition of Luther.* The time for its easier expansion approached, and the soil was moved by the previous mental as well as positive attempts. The reform of the 16th century was in all minds. Luther applied the spark to the mine. He embodied the general longings that were confusedly felt. The religious reform may justly be considered as having contained within its womb all the subsequent reforms and revolutions of Europe, as having produced or facilitated not only the religious and mental, but likewise the social and political emancipation of society. But as to Luther himself and his immediate supporters, friends and disciples, it can be said that all of them were the decided enemies of political reform ; they did not wish to touch in the slightest way the social and political organism. Luther's sole idea was to put an end to the power of Rome over the dogmas, the worship, and the organization of the church ; to emancipate the individual reason in affairs of conscience. Otherwise he was wholly devoted to the existing organization of society, to the power of sovereigns or princes. There was no more stanch supporter of the absolute, nay, the divine power

* About the year in which Luther was born, died in Switzerland a fugitive Dalmatic bishop, who was pitilessly persecuted by Rome, for proclaiming the necessity of the same reforms which afterwards were preached by Luther. See in Joh. v. Müller's History of Switzerland.

of the emperor than Luther, even to the extent of not opposing his authority even if he used violence against the Protestants. When Francis Lambert, a Frenchman, attempted to instil into the reformation a revolutionary and democratic spirit, Luther strenuously opposed it. The German peasantry, galled to the quick by the reckless and arbitrary oppression of the nobles, embraced in their minds the union of the two reforms, the religious and the political, but they found in Luther the most bitter and decided enemy.

It must not pass unobserved, that the rising of the German peasants against the nobles, was far posterior in date to the French Jacqueries, and to the war against the nobility, or the battle of spurs in Flanders; occurrences in which the original Celto-Gauls attempted to break down the yoke under which they suffered. All those insurrections of the people in France, in Germany, as well as that of the Kentish boors, prove that similar reasons and causes produce similar results in this or that race, nation, or form of government.

Luther and most of the Lutherans were not moved by the grievances and the projected reforms of the Saxon and Franconian rustics, who in a short but brilliant strife, for a moment forced princes and nobles to accept and sign the submitted reform. Four centuries back those simple men, those genuine democrats, put the German question on more tangible and practical grounds than did the science and statesmanship of professors in 1848. The peasants moderately demanded the cessation of all kinds of tithes, and of every other species of grinding injustice. They asked for the introduction of a uniform currency, and of uniform weights and measures, the abolition of serfdom, of internal custom houses and duties, the abolition of privileges of caste, free popular courts of justice, bails for imprisonment, etc.; in one word, their demands embraced all the fundamental and not subversive principles of a free and well organized state. To all this Luther answered, that "A pious Christian should rather die a hundred deaths than give way a hair's breadth to the peasants' demands. The government should exercise no mercy; the day of wrath and the day of the sword was come, and duty to God obliged them to strike hard as long as they could move a limb. Whoever perished in this service was a martyr of Christ."

Altogether the first Protestants or Lutherans in Germany stood on the side of legitimacy. "Cujus regio ejus religio," said Luther, transferring thus to the sovereigns the power over the church that had been wrested from the popes, and investing the princes with the exclusive power of the reformation. The Lutherans further maintain, that God alone sets princes and sovereigns over the human race. They insisted upon the duty of submitting to unjust and censurable sovereigns. The English or Anglo-Saxon reform carried out by Henry VIII., as the Episcopal Church, was the most faithful to the spirit of Lutheran principles. If, therefore, the spirit of reform is analyzed and classified according to certain predispositions or aptitudes of races, the spirit originally evinced by the German race with all its branches, the English or Anglo-Saxon included, was a conservative one in all social and political questions. From another language, from another race came the breath, by which the spirit of reform acquired its full, all-comprehending signification and fulfilment. The social, democratic ideas of Lambert were taken up by Calvin to the great dislike and repugnance of Luther, and of the immense majority of German reformers. Without Calvin a Frenchman, the reformation would have preserved its monarchist character. Calvinism gave to it the republican and democratic one; to Calvinism belongs the merit of having thoroughly reinvigorated and renovat ed the Christian world. Calvinist writers, as Languet and others, maintain that the people make a state and not the sovereign; that the states can exist without the prince, but not without the people. Such principles were professed by the French and Flemish Huguenots, and brought to Scotland by Knox. The Scotch presbyterians and puritans, not by any means the descendants of Anglo-Saxons, but Huguenot and Flemish refugees, introduced these principles into England. There they fructified in independents and puritans, those founders and inaugurators on this continent of a new evolution of humanity.

Democratic in principle was the life of the primitive Christians, sustained and animated by fraternity and equality. The example of the primitive Christians, the principle of election prevailing among them, moved to imitation the Calvinistic and puritan reformers, and not the inspirations resulting from a distinction of race. Even in the Catholic hierarchy a shadow of democratic principle was preserved; as dignities were conferred by a kind of election, and functions bestowed according to mental capacity, and the people likewise originally participated in the election of Bishops. Democratic tendencies were spread and working, previous even to the reformation, among the Italians. Rienzi Savonarola proclaimed the principle of the sovereignty of the people. Even the Jesuits, those stanchest apostles of absolute power, and of legitimacy, in cases of need paid homage, in their peculiar manner, to the principle of the supremacy of the people. Parsons, Allen in England under Elizabeth, Bellarmine in Italy, and many others of these fathers wrote and asserted: "That God has not bestowed the temporal or worldly power and authority on any one in particular,; whence it follows that he has bestowed it on the masses. The authority of the state is lodged therefore in the people, and the people consign it sometimes to a single person, sometimes to several; they perpetually retain the right of changing the form of government, of retracting its granted authority, of disposing of it anew." In this spirit wrote Suarez. Above all, the Jesuit Mariana elaborated the dogma of the sovereignty of the people. True it is, that for these Jesuits of the sixteenth century the principal object was to prove, that Elizabeth, and Henry IV. could be deposed by their Catholic subjects. But to establish this they were obliged to bow before the absolute principle of the sovereignty of the people.

The principle, albeit not in its absolute purity and vigor, became generalized, reinvigorated, and established as an indestructible fact by the spirit of Calvinistic reform. Switzerland alone formed an exceptional case. The establishment of the Swiss republics, of which only those of the three primitive cantons were then democratic in principle, resulted from events perfectly human in their nature, and not out of any specialty of race, as both the oppressed and the oppressor belonged to the German one. Thus likewise, in the struggles of the sixteenth century, the confluence of events brought that to pass; albeit the populations of the French language, wherein Calvinism spread the most vigorously, had the greatest number of victims murdered by Charles V., Phillip II., Alva, and the Papal or Roman inquisition. Those of the German tongue succeeded in finally overthrowing Romanism and despotism, and in establishing the Dutch republic.

Nowhere therefore in the development of modern civilization, in what by some is called the modern social and political comprehension of liberty, does the German mental or ethnological element prevail to such an extent as to give to it a peculiar character. If even the domain of abstract speculation or metaphysics is by common fallacy assigned almost exclusively to the German mind, it was yet a Frenchman, Des Cartes, who laid the foundations of modern post-scholastic metaphysical philosophy; it was Spinosa, a Hebrew, who laid those of the modern rationalistic system. In all the struggles of our epoch for liberty on the continent of Europe, the Celto-Romanic nations struck before, and more boldly, than the German ones. The great French Revolution led the van. In 1822–23 Italy and Spain attempted to establish constitutional governments, while the Germans were still speculating; and so in 1848, the first shock came again from Celto-Romanic descendants. Those Romanic nations rose repeatedly, imperiously urged and spurred by events, and events alone influence and shape out the destinies of the human family.

The invaders of Britain, the Angles, the Saxons, and the Jutlanders were a branch of the German race, issuing out of the stem which extended over the greatest part of the North, and to which belonged the Scandinavians, the Frisons, and some others. These Angles and Saxons dwelt between the Eider and the Elbe, where now is Holstein—and even now the Holsteiners can be considered as the original and pure root. The primitive mode of life, the customs and characteristics of the Anglo-Saxons were common to them, with the great majority of the whole German family, as were common too all the myths, and the divinities, and the legends. It would seem, however, that in destructiveness and ferocity the invaders of Britain surpassed all the other kindred tribes. Fire and sword was their law. The natives retired before them to the North and to Wales, and about four hundred cities, the remains of Roman culture, were destroyed. This Anglo-Saxon invasion was not, however, similar to that of the tribes who poured into the continental Roman world, moving with whole families to the West in search of new homes, wholly abandoning their former seats, and leaving behind them a solitude open to the invasion or occupation of a new tribe, or of a new race. Not the whole tribe moved from the banks of the Elbe, but bands of rovers, leaving behind them all the family ties. The same thing was done by the Scandinavians, the Danes, the Normans. They could not encumber their embarkations with women or children, to face the dangers of the stormy sea. For their predatory purposes they wanted hands rather than mouths. These expeditions accordingly were wholly different from migrations. When a portion of land was already subdued and secured, then only succeeding expeditions carried with them women and families, but never in sufficient number, and the majority of the conquerors would naturally, therefore, be induced to take wives from among the natives. The scarcity of women is the prevailing feature of all colonizations. The same was the case with the first settlements in this country, although made under pacific and well regulated conditions. American history records how this scarcity of women was felt, and by what curious methods it was often supplied. In those distant barbarian times, the same mode of supplying the want could not take place, nor did there exist cities filled with such a marketable produce. Therefore, when the Anglo-Saxons began to settle in Britain, they must have united with the native women. Those women, already born and brought up in a certain culture and refinement, naturally charmed and attracted the rude barbarians. That is a common and general occurrence, and can be considered as an unavoidable as well as a logical law, in the play of human passions. In this way, by intermarriage with the native women, even in the first generation, in the first years of the conquest, a considerable adulteration must have been made in the purity of the Anglo-Saxon blood. Subsequently the Danish and the Norman invasions produced new amalgamations. The Normans, brought originally from the same stem as the Anglo-Saxons, had been modified for centuries by the influence of new combinations and events, by the settled mode of life in Normandy, and by contact with Western culture. Thus thèy brought with them to England characteristics new and wholly different from those of their Scandinavian and German ancestry.

Out of those various combinations and crossings came forth the Englishman, whose character and features are thoroughly different from any of the German stocks and tribes from which he is ethnologically descended. The English character was formed under the action of special combinations and events, and the institutions framed out and developed by the action of time, were the result of special historical circumstances. If these institutions can be exclusively ascribed to a special mental Anglo-Saxon and therefore German qualification, why did they exist neither in Holstein nor in other parts of Germany, where the source ought to have been preserved in its unaltered purity, and where there was no contact whatever, no mixing with the ancient, declining world?

Some rough traditional customs were very likely preserved; but new emergencies, new modes of life, new creeds, claimed new solutions. Therein and not in the distinctness of race, lay the germs of the future English nation. The English history bears eminently the marks of events, and not of any special predestination.

The Anglo-Saxon laws and customs, wherein some, with unabated pertinacity, look for the germs of political liberty and democracy, are more or less similar to those of all the other Germanic tribes of that epoch, and therefore neither are marked by a special spirit of liberty, nor by the recognition of equal rights to every individual member of the State. The much spoken of Witenagemote, were councils of the elder or Ealdorman and kings, that is, of the more influential and powerful of those who were entitled to it by the personal privilege of birth or of social position. Bishops participated therein. Besides that, such councils are common to the rudest state of society, and they were in use among other tribes. The meetings of the Indian chiefs and sachems to discuss their affairs had the same bearing, and in principle the same origin. Not these Witenagemotes contained the germ of the representative system subsequently developed in England. In ancient republics—always municipal—each citizen having political rights, exercised them in person by vote. The same was the case with the Germans. They had their March and May meetings. When they settled on conquered lands, became scattered over extensive spaces, and formed large States, their domestic habits became more fixed and orderly. These gatherings became more necessary and more frequent. The new mode of social life begat more numerous and various interests, and complications increased. The administration of justice at the outset of society was almost exclusively in the hands of the Germans. This obliged the knights, who were scattered over waste territories, to appear in person in cities where courts were to be held. But a peaceful residence in cities was repulsive to the majority of the knights. It seems that under Charlemagne they already preferred to delegate their powers and the duty of participating in the courts of justice to such members of their body as inhabited the cities, or as were more willing to sojourn in them for a time. This might have been the beginning of the representative system, originating in new social combinations, habits and necessities. The same or similar causes might have existed in England; but the time of its commencement, or the positive causes which brought forth this system, cannot be ascertained with historical certainty. When the Norman barons called the cities, the inferior knighthood, and the yeomanry, to participate in a limited manner in the administration of the State, the cities, which were incorporated bodies, and the country gentry, very naturally could not appear in mass, but only by their mandataries or representatives, as some centuries before was practised in France under Charlemagne, and perhaps even earlier. The subdivisions into privileged classes was even more strongly marked among the Anglo-Saxons than among the other Germans. The social body was composed of the high aristocracy or Ealdorman, wherefrom the earls, of gentry or Thanes or Thegons, of the free yeomanry, who stood under the patronage of the powerful, called *Hlaford* or *bread-giving patrons*, and the slaves. All these classes were separated and distinct from each other, by a proportional gradation of the rights which they enjoyed. The composition or weregild existed among the Anglo-Saxons, and was proportioned to the social order of the victim. The same was the case among other German tribes. The oath of an earl was equal to that of six Thanes, and so down proportionally. An offence committed against a woman of noble birth was punished sometimes with death, which same offence against one of lower origin was atoned for by a proportional fine. So much for Anglo-Saxon democracy. Feudality was the cement of Anglo-Saxon conquest, and of the division of the subdued lands.

The constitutional liberty of England is the work of the Norman barons, who could no longer endure the oppression exercised over them by the kings. The move ment originated not with the Anglo-Saxon part of the population, nor was it an outburst of a higher principle. The kings injured, in various ways, the rights, the material interests of the barons, and they rose to defend them, but not because they were moved by an abstract love of freedom, or urged to action by preconcerted ideas. The agencies in the English movement of the 13th century were wholly different from those which previously acted throughout the continent. On the continent, burghers and even villains united with kings against the nobles; in England the nobles were the first to strike against tyranny, and called in and admitted the commons. This was a stroke of good policy, by which the king was prevented from drawing the cities to his side, a policy taught to the barons by the events of the continent. The movement for emancipation on the continent was effected when the Anglo-Saxons, that is, the mass of the people, trembled at the bidding of Norman barons and sovereigns. These barons are the fathers of the English liberties. After the battle of Lewes, Simon Montfort, a French nobleman, and the other barons called the commons to their parliament; they did it in order to strengthen themselves against the arbitrary action of the king. For a long period those commons—the only genuine Anglo-Saxon element, if there be any—the knights, the gentry and yeomanry; all of them very reluctantly and even against their will participated in the parliaments. This is illustrated by the fines which were continually imposed upon them for non-appearance. So much for the innate Anglo-Saxon love of self-government and of liberty.

The movement against King John originated in the lesion of interests. The barons wished to submit no longer to arbitrary taxation, to the arbitrary disposition and administration of feudal estates, to unlawful wardships over minors, and above all they wished to have the free use of forests. The rest of the nation, who were equally injured in property and security, responded to their appeal. All this is perfectly in accordance with the common course of human affairs, and no proof of a special predestined exclusive mission.

The division of the districts or counties into the *thungs* and *hundreds*, was the result of organic necessity in a population principally living on scattered farms and country-seats, in a land having then few and poor boroughs rather than cities. In the necessity of organizing originated the division of the population and of the city under the Roman, Athenian and other republics and municipalities. The tens and hundreds might likewise have been made in imitation of the Slavic communes, as the Anglo-Saxons were of old the neighbors of the Slavi. A continual intercourse existed between the two tribes; they united in predatory excursions, and some of the Slavi very probably participated in the conquest of Britain. The division of the Slavic communes into tens and hundreds, for administrative purposes, can be said to be immemorial. It still prevails in Russia, and no traces of such a division are to be detected in Germany the fountain head of the Anglo-Saxons.

The emancipation of cities is thus described by Hallam: "The progress of towns in several continental countries, from a condition bordering upon servitude to wealth and liberty, attracts attention. * * * Their growth in England, both from general causes and *imitative policy*, was very similar and nearly coincident. Under the Anglo-Saxon line of sovereigns we scarcely can discover in our scanty records, the condition of their inhabitants. * * * But the burghers of some towns were already a distinct class from the ceorls and rustics, though hardly free according to our estimation."

The cities in England were oppressed, and in England, as every where else in the ancient and the modern world, it was oppression and arbitrariness which evoked emancipation. The oppression of the feeble and poor by the rich and powerful gave birth to the laws of Solon; the same causes produced the Tribune in Rome, gave power to the crushed plebeians, and were the principal agencies in framing and developing the immortal *jus civile.* Oppression, as has been pointed out already, aroused Italy, Spain, France, brought the Norman barons into arms against royalty, and resulted in the initiation of the commons into political life. Material interests were at the bottom of all these movements, and Hallam says with truth, "that in the further development of English liberties, these liberties were purchased by money." If any special characteristic of the Anglo-Saxons is perpetuated in the Englishman, it is the deferential respect paid to aristocracy, a feeling which penetrates the English people to the core. Events evolving from new combinations, different from those of the Anglo-Saxon epoch, framed out the English institutions. The conquest of the Anglo-Saxons by the Normans, is one of the easiest recorded in history. What history calls the Norman times, gave and marks the mettle of the English character.

The institution of the jury is claimed to be specially Anglo-Saxon. If so it is specially German. As such it ought to have existed in Germany as well as among the original Anglo-Saxons on the Elbe, and other northern branches of the same stem. It cannot be expected that the contact with the Roman civilization destroyed there the original German judicial habits. Such an assertion can be applied with some plausibility to the Franks, Goths, Burgundians, Longobards—but is of no avail in respect to the immense majority of the German race.

The method of settling disputes and litigations by councils, composed of the oldest of the tribe or of the community is, it may be said, inherent in the rudest social state. It has prevailed from time immemorial, and among various nations, and to it can be traced with certainty the origin of what is called juries. Thus the Amphictyons were a kind of jury. The Roman law, nearly from the beginning of its development, used a kind of jurors in civil matters, jurors whose opinion on a given case was submitted to the prætor. How this judicial custom became obliterated does not belong to the present discussion. In criminal matters, in Athens and Rome, nearly the whole people composed the jury and the judge.

The primitive Germans had certain judicial observances for the investigation of material truth, more or less resembling those of other tribes. The so-called jurors of the Anglo-Saxons served as means to investigate and find out the material facts of the case, but not to give any opinion about its validity. The circuit judge or functionary, an earl, or a count, called the nearest neighbors of the litigants to give evidence according to their knowledge of facts. Under the Saxon kings no criminal cases were submitted to the deliberation of such witnesses, or to that of any body of jurors selected from among knights or yeomen. The kings themselves, or their mandataries decided all such cases. Not the Saxon epoch therefore can alone be considered as having been pregnant with the great judicial institution. The historical development of the institution of the jury in England, out of Anglo-Saxon, Norman and Roman judicial elements is very complicated. It took place under various political and social combinations and conditions, which it is impossible to compress within a brief outline. A jury in criminal cases, and above all for political offences against the monarchy and the State, can be traced no farther back than to the reign of Henry III., an epoch completely Norman. The barons insisted always on being judged by their peers, according to the universal privilege of nobility and chivalry all over Europe. This privilege was extended over the nation, together with all those constitutional liberties, into which she was initiated by the Norman barons. The last but the most beneficial of liberties, that of the free press, was for nearly three centuries wholly unknown and unnecessary in England. The cradle of the liberty of the press was Holland, after it became a republic; and from Holland it was transplanted in the 18th century to England, and radiated successively over all Europe.

Human events, by whose diversified influence various European evolutions and changes have been carried out, as well as the liberties of England, nursed in their infant development, those eternal principles which have given to America her lofty position in the history of social progress. As the Englishman has no physical or special mental resemblance to the German or the Anglo-Saxon, so the American has only few and very dim features in common with the Englishman, from whom he descends. Not Anglo-Saxon, therefore, is the character of the Americans, and not to this assumed origin are to be traced the faculties and qualifications which mark the American political and social institutions. Neither history and physiology, nor psychology and logic justify the favorite American theorem, that their freedom and democracy are the fruits of their Anglo-Saxon descent. It is, however, the property of fallacies, in proportion as they extend, to run out into what is absurd and illogical.

Statistics show that in the early periods, when the English began to settle on this continent, two other nations composed the British Empire. The Irish and the

Scotch—both of Celtic origin—migrated to America in such large numbers as to immediately produce a new physiological amalgamation. Various kinds of oppressions expelled them from their native lands; freedom and more equal social organization attracted and fused them in America. Scotch and Irish poured in freely in the seventeenth and eighteenth centuries. Buchanan and other statisticians assert that from 1691 to 1743, 263,000 Irish emigrated to America. This emigration was occasioned partly by the stagnation of the linen trade, partly by political and religious oppression. According to the same authorities, during the eighteenth century down to 1829, about a million of Irish and a quarter of a million of Scotch came to America. The Dutch element in New York, and that of the first French settlers in the Carolinas must likewise be taken into account. All the various elements of population were cemented together by religious and political liberty, embracing every one, and admitting him to equal rights in the community, and not on account of his former descent or nationality. Under the combined action of climate, new habits, new necessities and hardships, new daily pursuits and occupations, new and more intense mental and intellectual activity, the Americans became in a short time totally unlike the English in all external and internal characteristics. Even in the heart of New England it is nearly as easy to point out a genuine Englishman, as to point out a Frenchman, an Italian, or a Hebrew. The elongated, sharp, dried-up features of the American have nothing in common with the round, slightly turned-up, and juicy-faced Englishman. The long-necked American has not his type in England. Similar divergencies extend to the hair, and to the whole frame. The English phlegm is directly the opposite of the febrile American, who with reckless impetuosity hurries his pursuits, and uses up his own life. In proportion as the American character is active and expanding, these differences become more numerous, salient, and puzzling. All these changes were effected by the paramount action of combined physical and mental events, and their all-powerful and uninterrupted influence and activity reveals itself in the various geographical and political sections of the Commonwealth. Not only the man of the Southern States descends originally from the same English social class—for the cavalier descent from English nobility assumed by the Southern planters is not sustained by history—as the man of the North, but New England has to a large degree peopled the Southern States. The Southerner, however, of the present day, has no resemblance in character either to the Englishman, or to his countrymen in the East and in the North. A gulf separates them in mental, social, and moral respects. The language is the only common tie. Two absolutely ethnologically different races of the old world, could not present a deeper contrast with each other.

The American world was not called to life, and is not circumscribed by the narrow, blind, fatalistic physical laws of race. Amidst ups and downs, in smooth and in thorny paths, at times overshadowed and then brilliantly luminous, the American world has been the bearer of the all-embracing, truly human manifestation of principles. They inspired the Puritans, and to save them they abandoned the old world with its oppressions and prejudices. Races and tribes are already fully represented in history. Each specially has given the last solution, the last word, if in reality a law of races has presided over human progress. To initiate man into a higher sphere, America issued out of nothingness. The right of reason watched over her first steps. Carried as he is here by the current of time, and of circumstances, man is to make a worthy use of the principles, and the mental and intellectual qualifications with which he is endowed. Then only they lead him to freedom. Freedom is the mass of all our physical and mental powers. It is the final aim of their combined efforts. It is at once development and consummation. Thus comprehended, freedom has reached its highest expression in the institutions of the American free States, and freedom has carved out and has given the peculiar mark to the character of the man and to the citizens.

CHAPTER II.

CHARACTERISTICS.

The character of an individual or of a nation is the result of a mass of variously combined inclinations, affections, volitions, dispositions, convictions, determinations. They are all general and special, and the traits or characteristics determined by them are common, human, or individual, when evoked by the agency and play, in and upon us, of special conditions. Thus nearly every individual, and every nation, aside of what is in its character human and common with others, has certain peculiar features of its own. And so have the Americans. The differences in character between the inhabitant of America and that of any other country whatever in Europe, are as salient as are the differences of their social state, of their political development, of their pursuits, habits, and comprehension of life. Those differences are related to many causes at once; their impartial appreciation explains and solves naturally, and therefore easily, the so-called enigmatical peculiarities of the Americans.

New and powerful interests and strivings have evoked an unwonted and special current of activity, and with it new and diversified manifestations of man's nature. Therein is to be found the source of certain characteristic dissimilarities between the man of the new and of the old world. And the American people absolutely ought to have certain characteristic traits of its own to fulfil the task before it, to elaborate this task by a new and special process, and to perfect its own destinies and those of the part of the hemisphere adopted and appropriated for such an end. The character of the American, with all its sunny and shady sides, was not to be throughout the reflection of the European one. Sameness is repulsive to nature, indefinite multifariousness is the everlasting manifestation of her creative power. Man was placed here in new moral and material conditions and needs. Out of the fathomless depth of human nature these agencies evoked to the surface, that is to life, to activity, new characteristics in the individual and in the people.

Political and social institutions often give an indelible mark to the character of a people, and as often again they are its reflection. History is full of the evidences of this fact. In America the character of the people and the institutions have acted reciprocally on their development; a case of very rare occurrence in the history of nations and of their political and social evolutions. No nation, no people now existing is so thoroughly and intensely identified with its institutions as is the American people.

With sacred jealousy the American people watches over the national honor, over its relations with other States, over national independence. Being in possession of the highest goods, no sacrifice can be too great for their defence and preservation. No invasion from whatever quarter, no conquest, no overthrow of the existing order, could ever be successfully carried out. Not the presumed Anglo-Saxon blood, but the genuine American feeling, pouring out from constitutive principles as from a fountain-head, is the repelling force. Patriotic, exalted devotion is not an effort, but a natural lineament of character, a simple but inherent element of national life.

The love of social independence, of domestic liberty, and their fullest enjoyment, produces in the American character that unbending quality which disables the individual from becoming a permanent denizen of other powers, of other States. There may be a few rare exceptions. It is almost impossible to imagine an American becoming a servant of kings, subservient for ever to social caste. Soon his better nature must revolt; but numbers of Europeans, from all social orders and positions, assimilate themselves easily and in a short time to the state of things prevailing here; they become identified with it to the core. To an Americanized, and therefore a reinvigorated European, a return to the past worn-out conditions of existence would prove unbearable.

Whatever shadows and shortcomings may be discovered in individuals, or in the mass of the people, as manifested in their domestic, internal complications—shadows and shortcomings mostly inseparable from our nature—a public spirit animates the whole people, and is forming here a public general characteristic, unrivalled in history.

Such is the prominent and decided feature deeply carved out in the general national character. It breaks out with such a fulness and vitality, that definitions could only impair its comprehension.

Not that patriotism in itself constitutes a dissimilarity between European nations and the American people. The virtue of patriotism is a patrimony of human nature. But here it has a different source, a different essence, and thus its workings and manifestations are different from those of other nations. Their domestic gods differ. The gods of old nations are local divinities; those of the American people are all-embracing, pure and elevated principles.

Tradition surrounds the one with its venerated halo, which is often stifling and obfuscated by narrow prejudices, by indurated hostilities; the American lares emit a life-expanding flame. Its action is quickly penetrating. Out of a social commingling issues the American people. It derives its lineage from various nations that are traditionally hostile to each other. On this soil fusion operates, ancient hereditary alienations melt and evaporate. One common patriotism embraces and inspires them all; reason, freedom and humanity are its watchwords.

Not less salient and peculiar than the public spirit, and created by the same or similar causes, is the characteristic of the American mind manifested in the thirst for knowledge, for information. It imperatively urges the individual with a pertinacity and generality not to be met with in any other nation on the globe, to satisfy this noble mental irritation, to satisfy it by sacrifices of the time and means, whether large or small, at his disposal. It is thus the most brilliantly projecting feature, and an individual property of this people. Not the wealthy, not the better circumstanced are principally the expression of these urgings, but it is rather special to the laborious masses. Not outward worldly leisure produces or evokes it, but an inward impulse. That is one of the cardinal differences between American and European populations. This craving results from the radical recognition of equality of rights in every individual, inspiring him with self-consciousness, with self-respect, and opening before him the bright horizon of nobler purposes and aims. It is not a transmission by blood, nor the result of certain liberal concessions, called in Europe liberal institutions. In the English people, the nearest kindred to the majority of Americans, and living under liberal institutions, this spontaneity is not awakened, and the mass still gropes its way in a self-contented ignorance.

Neither is this craving incited by an admonition exercised from above, by the efforts of a government, by the prevalent suggestions or example of a so-called superior stratum of society. This American phenomenon strengthens the faith that the human race is to bask in floods of light, that enlightenment is the essence of man's nature, although its effusion may have been benumbed for uncounted ages. This characteristic trait redeems at once the broadest and most truly democratic comprehension of a people, from the cavils heaped on it by the apostles of an absolute supreme authority, which, according to their assertions, is to hover providentially above the masses, to take the initiative and to direct their mental development.

Extremes seemingly prevail in the American character. It is a combination of violent, nervous, feverish excitement and sturdy quietude, of calculation and daring, of cautiousness and swiftness in decision and action, of steadiness of purpose and recklessness in pursuits. It is stubborn and mobile, impressible and cold, cunning and straight-forward. Often inflated with immense pride and self-conceit, now soundly appreciating ones powers, and then humbly underrating them.

Excitement is one of the most powerful springs in the American. It is so contagious that new comers, after a comparatively short residence, are affected and carried away by it. Easily excited, the American cheerfully, nay enthusiastically, greets the object which for the moment satisfies this necessity of his temper; and no efforts of his own invention are spared to endow this object for the moment with all imaginary attributes. Neither age nor sex is exempted from this intoxicating pleasure. He pays willingly and with the best grace for the moment of satisfaction, and raises the idol to the skies. But when the excitement is over, he lets it slide, unceremoniously, or often drops it roughly, careless where it may fall, to run the next moment after another.

The people at large, as well as the various circles in which sociability divides society, all equally whirl in this dervis dance; sometimes in common around a so-called public character, a literary, artistical, or any other often adventurous celebrity; then around the *deos minorum gentium*, thrown in their way by chance, or whom often their own excited fancy adorns with imaginary distinctions.

Many and various are the causes accounting for and explaining this peculiarity. The nervous irritability lying at the bottom, most probably is produced by the influences of a trying and changeable climate. This turn given to the character at an early epoch has become now hereditary. The uniformity of the ancient colonial life, the rigidity of the Puritans and of their imitators, might have contributed to form it. Human imaginative nature revolts against uniformity, compression, against turning in one and the same circle. Single-track routine in life is repugnant, and any object or event is welcome which breaks such tiresome evenness. After contraction follows relaxation in some manner or other. So the imagination eagerly and indiscriminately seizes upon any provender with which to appease its cravings.

Even now, although new and more diversified elements are mingled in American life, a certain sameness still pervades it. The circle extends, the horizon enlarges, and nevertheless monotony dominates the whole. It becomes the more painfully sensible, as the multifariousness of the world from without, and the longings from within excite, attract, and tickle the Americans. What therefore seems to offer a momentary interruption of monotony, excites and carries away, and often overpowers the better and cooler judgment.

During the colonial or embryonic period, the colonists were separated from the events of the world. The gloominess of such an isolation was only cheered up by arrivals from Europe, from the mother country. The communications were rare, and thus whatever could give a new turn to the monotonous existence, must have been heartily greeted, as a link connecting the Americans with the general, social and civilizing movement. It was an echo from a distant, fairy land, and even its feeblest or most discordant sound must have deeply moved, strongly excited and affected those whom it reached. For domestic as well as for social reasons, any accession of new comers, settlers or visitors, must have been felt as increasing the moral and material worth and significance of the colonial existence. By all these accumulated reasons, as well as by the physical conditions so powerfully acting on the nerves, on the frame, on the temperament of the inhabitants, excitement became almost a second nature. And what among the society of Europe is only a rare and transient outburst, becomes here almost a normal condition.

Often by superficial observers, as well as by the Americans themselves, excitement is confounded with enthusiasm. But enthusiasm has its hearth in the mind and in the heart. Its sacred, ever-glowing fire pours from within, warms and inspires; excitement blunts the imagination, or at the best reflects only a delusive mirage. And for the honor of human nature, below the froth of excitement, lies in the American breast the deepest enthusiasm for all that is grand, generous, and noble. Enthusiasm generated their history, enthusiasm inaugurated their political existence; and among all the nations they alone emerged from such a sacred source.

The great reproach made by Europeans to the Americans, and one which has become proverbial among themselves, is the excessive love of money, the fact that they are a money-making people. Undoubtedly money-making has eaten itself deep into the American character, but the love of money, although considered a moral disease by all the moralists of antiquity and of our times, has been and is now the most deeply-rooted passion in human nature. Under one or another shape, in this or that manner, money has ruled the world at all times. Neither is the love of it less violent, less intense among the immense majority of Europeans than among the Americans. If among the latter money-making seems to form the main object of existence, it is the effect of various causes, intrinsic and normal, and explained as such by their history, by the concatenation of peculiar events and circumstances, which have surrounded them from the cradle.

Money and commerce were the only ties between the colonists and the mother or any other country. The colonies of modern Europe have been exclusively mercantile enterprises. Mercantile speculation sent out the first settlers, and even the Puritans looked to trade as the sole means of maintenance, and of preserving the imperatively necessary intercourse with the old world. Mercantile relations therefore formed the pivot on which turned the existence of the colonists and of the colonies. Thrown upon their own scanty resources, the colonists could only obtain for money or money's worth, all the necessaries of life, the implements and requisites whose possession alone could preserve them from destruction when they first exhibited themselves on this soil. All this was to be paid for, in some way or other. Thus almost before the first immigrant took a firm root in the soil, money-making became the absorbing object of his activity, as upon money depended his domestic, his family, and his social existence. His entire social position and significance depended upon his commercial means. The colonist, his toilsome labors and sweat, must have been the object of greedy speculation in the mother country. Every thing therefore powerfully urged and contributed to develop in him from the start the money-making propensity, and to make it paramount to all others. It was his defensive weapon and his salvation. So from infancy every thing stimulated, nourished and developed this passion.

Since the Americans elevated themselves to the dignity of a nation, the character of the American community is even more industrial and commercial than it was of old. Their growth, their increase, their prosperity, are indissolubly connected with the extension of their mercantile or industrial operations. Thus money-making becomes more intense and all-absorbing, as the love of money is more inherent in commercial occupations than in any other, and in America every occupation runs out into a commercial one.

Only a prosperous nation can be considered as truly civilized, as enabled and prepared to enjoy democracy and self-government. The prosperity of such a nation consists in the prosperity of the whole population. It is the duty of every individual to devote all his faculties to securing this blessing to himself, and in this way to the community. Money-making, in its true sense, is the reward of intelligence, labor, and toil; it was and is the road to individual and to general prosperity. It is an inborn and noble pride to be the artisan of one's own position and independence. It is one of the noblest manifestations of the consciousness of human dignity. The possession of wealth has always been among the most powerful incentives to action; money-making by industry, enterprise, speculation, is the only legitimate and honorable way to reach the goal. And of such a nature is the money-making, which engrosses an immense majority of the Americans. It continually extends the area of culture. It conquers the rugged face of nature, transforms the wilderness into a habitable and cultivated soil. It is this which pushes the American to cross torrents, cut his path across primitive forests, disembowel the earth, people solitudes. He tries to make money out of the rough forces of nature. The sons of farmers, artisans, operatives, as soon as their faculties are developed, look forward to the means of securing their independence, of making money. They leave home, plunge into distant regions, and into hardships, privations and toils. They try to discount, to turn them into money, that is, into their own well-being and prosperity, and that of their families. Money-making has given the unparalleled expansion to American industry and commerce, covered the ocean with American bottoms, the land with prosperous cities, with nets of railroads, with mills and factories. In proportion as prosperity increases and expands, increases and expands general civilization. The genuine Yankee, that is, the man of the East and his kindred in other States, is considered the most sharp in this feverish pursuit. But they have the best and most numerous public schools and scientific establishments, buy the most books, and subscribe most generously for all public establishments and objects, as well as for alleviating private miseries and sufferings. True it is, that this all-absorbing fever has likewise its morbid results. But when the good and the evil are summed up, good comes out victorious.

All conditions being equal, consideration will always

attach itself to wealth. Agamemnon became the leader of the Greeks in the Trojan war, because, as Thucydides says, he was the wealthiest among the confederated kings. The starting point of the colonists was nearly alike, as was also their aim. The one who first reached it honestly must have enjoyed consideration, the more so as in the colonial life there existed few other distinctions. Almost all were in one way or another devoted to trade, and the so-called ancient families derive their pre-eminence from the fact that by successful labor or trade, they acquired before others a proportional independence. The distinctions are therefore only chronological questions; their source, their origin are alike. Those who first acquired wealth, and there was no other way to do it than by money-making, became benefactors of their community, establishing and endowing various public establishments. It was only by acquiring wealth they were able to satisfy their nobler impulses.

The sneer at Americans for their money-making propensity does not become Europeans. As mentioned above, to this propensity the country owes the major part of its greatness. What is done by governments and sovereigns in Europe, is done here either by private individuals or by communities rendered prosperous by their own exertions. European society had its origin in the absorption by one class of the labor of another, and this still continues to prevail. The European social organization contains various social parasitical existences, not less greedy to acquire and make money; only the greediness is overlaid by certain conventional definitions and incrusted prejudices. If the European aristocracy, if the world of leisure, the official world do not make money themselves, in the same way as the Americans, these European classes make money by oppressing millions, and living upon their labor, or upon the taxes. European society has various social inherited distinctions, to which it pays due, or oftener undue deference. American society, from the start a commercial one, very naturally paid and pays deference to the successful money-makers. It may be that nowadays wealth enjoys in certain cases too much of consideration. But even this is paid to it rather in social and private relations, than in political ones. However desirable it might be to have this current modified at least, if not changed, still it is not absolutely to be condemned in itself. It is in human nature to pay deference to success. In the great events of the world, success is considered as God's verdict. In a society constructed like the American, moving in such an orbit, generally devoted to pursuits of a commercial character, success crowned with money is easily appreciated, understood, and felt by society at large. By such a success society is mostly benefited. A man who has made his fortune by honorable means and enterprise, of whatever kind or nature, such a one, however deficient he may be in general culture, has nevertheless given proofs of certain eminent faculties of intellect; powers of judgment and of combination; ability, in seizing hold of the opportune moment; endurance, skill, activity, energy; and so he deserves consideration. A fool or an imbecile will never become rich—never be able to make money.

With all the numerous and dark drawbacks of this propensity, it does not generate avarice in the Americans. If generally they are infuriated in the pursuit of money, they spend it as freely as they make it. If they are called men of the dollar, at any rate they are not hunters of cents. Parsimonious economy is not their characteristic, and in general the racing after dollars, the thirst for gain, does not make them contemptible misers, or callous to others. The celebrated axiom, "Help yourself," signifies that every one ought to make his choice independently, and build up his position by personal exertions; but it is far from including any egotism, any cold indifference to his neighbor, to the efforts of any one undertaking a difficult path in life. Americans are generally the most cautious persons in the world, in giving free advice, in going direct to the point. They shun the responsibility of deciding for another—of disillusioning him, or of interfering with a contrary advice or opinion. Thus when asked a question, they mostly answer in generalities. But if the choice is once made, the pursuit or object selected, then they stand by with counsel and action. The settler in a new and strange land, is heartily supported in his toils by his neighbors. A foreigner or native, starting in any honest undertaking finds support and credit, this mainspring and soul of a commercial society, and nowhere so largely and liberally conceived, or carried to such an extent, as in America.

Comprehended in a broad national sense, money-making, a result of the combination of events that have pressed upon Americans from the start, and amidst which they still live, is neither reprehensible, nor abject, nor mischievous, as it is commonly represented. That this propensity belongs originally to human nature, and that here it is stimulated by special and peculiar circumstances, is evinced by the fact, that the Europeans, continually pouring into this continent, do not yield in any respect to the native Americans in the heat and the eagerness of the race. Among the largest fortunes may be counted those made by Europeans, and great numbers, especially from the commercial class, immigrated here exclusively for the purpose of money-making, unmoved by any other broad interest. Further, without the money-making and money-spending Americans, European industry must burst of plethora, or come to a stand still. Unacquainted as I am with the whole nature and manipulation of articles of this kind, I judge and appreciate the general results. The general character of commercial and other business transactions, seems not to be impregnated with so much dishonesty as is often witnessed by England. Aside from the astounding forgeries and bankruptcies which have recently burst over that country, foreign merchants, above all those in the East, complain of frauds perpetrated upon them by the English manufacturers, and others of the commercial brotherhood. Although such occurrences, almost inherent in the nature of commerce, of intense money worship, and forming the dark side of both, might happen in America, at the same time as much integrity, honesty and rectitude is to be found there as in any country in the world. Undoubtedly, in individual cases more or less numerous, money-making degenerates into a degrading and coarse passion; but such cases do not prejudice or stamp the national character. With many who entered the race early in life, this passion has subdued or absorbed all the other faculties of intellect—it has become a second nature.

As almost every body is obliged to run the gauntlet, one that stops even for respite, is soon overwhelmed. The whirlwind seizes and carries them away. Money-making becomes an unquenchable thirst, an object of love, an attraction similar to that which art or study exercises over the artist or the scholar. It is a power and a distinction. Then money is made not merely for the sake of becoming independent and rich, of enjoying both, but from habit—on account of finding any other congenial occupation impossible. It becomes an intellectual drilling, and a test of skill. It becomes a game, deeply combined, complicated—a struggle with men and events, exciting, captivating, terrible, hand to hand, man to man, cunning to cunning. The socially passionate life in Europe, diversified, and full of various enjoyments, gives to a successful winner, new scopes, attractions and pleasures, such as society does not proffer, allow or create in this country. An American can with difficulty if at all turn in another direction, plunge in another passion, or activity, seek around for new and different drastic or soothing pastimes, to quench this ardor which for the greatest part of his life has been concentrated in money-making, and has been urging and directing his course. Thus where the European can stop or divert his attention to other objects, an American once in the middle of the torrent must go on, spurred by habits, by the force of events; as even to preserve an accumulated fortune, becomes in itself another race, another almost deadly strife. Such is the exclusive money-maker, but he is not the type of the general character,—he has no hold on the people at large, his dens are in large cities.

No nation is equally sensitive and impatient of criticism as the Americans. They often become irritated not only by the finding fault with their character, customs, manners, habits, institutions, or culture, but find it disagreeable when climate, soil, fauna or flora is judged inferior to those of the old world. Various causes provoke this sensitiveness, and it can be accounted for in various ways. It results from both pride and diffidence. The Americans are well aware of their deficiencies, but they feel the sting of injustice done to them by those foreigners who obtrude themselves as unrelenting judges. Generally the faults are overrated, and the people are lashed by scorching and undeserved ridicule. The American, the last comer into the family of nations, is continually on the alert—not to be treated or considered as a parvenu, not to be slighted or disparaged. Youth is generally susceptible and irritable before it enters manhood. The more so, when occasional shortcomings are maliciously pointed out, when the intrinsic good is almost overlooked. The taunts of English travellers and writers, of the English press, have principally provoked this irritation, and made it nearly chronic. Such authors, taking a superficial glance at the country and at its inhabitants, have misunderstood, misrepresented what they saw. Without investigating the cause of certain effects, by which their genuine or assumed fastidiousness was offended, they deliberately calumniated by wholesale, for faults committed by some. The European standard, when forcibly applied here, must necessarily wound and be faulty, the two states of sociability differing wholly from each other.

Boasting is often carried by certain Americans to the extreme. Often however it is a reaction against slights, an effort to veil deficiencies, an effort made by a people aware of them, but on the other hand conscious of having accomplished in two or three generations what it took other nations centuries to perform. Generally, human nature revolts at taunts, at arrogant reproof, at undervaluation. Experience and time alone teach a becoming equanimity. European nations bear scoffing more patiently because they have thrown it occasionally for centuries at each other's head. Like old war horses accustomed to the roar of battles, they remain cool and self-possessed. There is on the American surface much to be rubbed off and rounded. Rude angles are to be softened, ease, flexibility instilled. Time must do the work. Refinement is a fruit slowly ripened by ages. And in America the whole people, not a class, is the tree on which the fruit is to be borne. In the people at large reposes soft mould below the apparently coarse crust, and in due time, the plastic virtue of nature will cast it into congenial and sociable forms.

CHAPTER III.

DEMOCRACY.

AMERICAN nationality has two hearth-stones—democracy and self-government. The origin of all other nations and states, past or present, was different from that of the American commonwealth. America was evolved from a fruitful social element and principle. The authority of one exercised over the many, acquired by traditional influences, by superior physical or mental force, or by voluntary submission of individuals, forming one and the same race, family or tribe—such in all ages was the beginning of societies. Nimrod, Zohack, Saturn, Japhet, Danaus, Cadmus, Theseus, Romulus, Odin, Pharamond, and all those heroic legendary founders of nations and states, bore the same character, acted under similar circumstances and conditions. Conquest and the individual authority of one over all, or afterwards of few over many, begat classes and castes. And so to the present day, whatever may have been the changes and modifications, European society, like that of the ancient world, is composed of three principal elements. The one, which under different names rules and legislates; the second, which shares in the power, in the spoils, prominently executes the laws, defends, fights and upholds the privileged state; the third, on whose shoulders reposes and presses the whole structure.

Not one of these elements existed at the outset of American communities. No hero or chief, implanting his sword or banner, marked out around the foundations of the city the boundaries of an empire. No submissive companions or subjects were the pillars of the genuine American structure, nor was it cemented by any authoritative will. Democracy was the vital essence of this new society, and democracy was cradled and nursed by the combination of events which brought it into existence. And not one of the facts, axioms and theorems, which for ages ruled the old world, had any bearing on the new one.

Identical convictions, aims and purposes, attracted and united the primitive settlers. Therein was encompassed social equality. Those among them who might have belonged in the mother country to a superior or privileged class, at the start gave up all such distinctions, doing it either by conviction, or by force of circumstances. The first administrators or directors among the settlers, were freely elected by them. Their fitness, their mental superiority were the qualities which influenced the choice, and not any recognition of privileged aristocratic superiority. Besides, no social supremacy or distinction can be transfused from an anterior condition, or built up in colonies, with such beginnings as those on this northern continent, and above all those of New England. However socially mixed might have been the first body of settlers, necessity would bring them at once under the rule of equality in rights and duties. Each colonist was to carve out his own path, to work for himself. Mutual assistance could only have been accorded by the principle of association, and not by that of any obligation deriving from social inferiority. The first commune or village was composed of equals, socially and politically. From such a germ the whole society was developed. No masters nor lords obliged others to work for them and obey. Neither the functions in the community, nor the economic occupations, pursuits, labors, separated its members into different classes or stamped them with inferiority or superiority. All were equally necessary, useful, and therefore honorable; pulpit, office, trade, artisan, workman, daily laborer, were equal, closely interwoven and connected with each other. A log cabin was their original abode, was the common cradle.

The old and the new society are as two streams issuing from two wholly different sources. And in their whole course the original difference maintains itself and prevails.

The states of antiquity all began, as Cicero justly says, under the kingly form of government. The king or hero founded and ruled a city; the city was the state; time, events, revolutions, transformed cities into republics. America began in settlements, in cottages, in townships and villages, and when cities were formed, no social or political privilege elevated their inhabitants above their brethren in the country. Modern Europe at the outset bristled with menacing towers, strongholds and castles, overawing the ancient cities, the ancient civilization. Shadowed by the banner of the all-powerful lord, the boroughs, the villages and hamlets filled with serfs and slaves, crawled timorously before him. The church, the curate, the parish, leaned against the walls and battlements of the stronghold, and the helmeted lord was the founder and protector of the house of God. A school for master or serfs was not thought of.

A church or meeting-house, a school, a common hall, formed the hearthstones of the first American settlements, cementing, enlivening the log cabin, the cottage, the village, the township. In all this there was no germ, no basis, no fuel for an aristocracy. No special privileges or liberties to localities or cities, no corporations, guilds, handicrafts, or any such subdivisions, classified the population, creating interests opposed and hostile to each other. The embryo of the future State and nation was unadulterated by any of the antiquated elements which prevailed in the social and political composition of Europe. Not a tradition, but a broad principle was sown in the American soil.

Charters were granted by English kings. But they did not create any special privileges for special localities, or bestow certain rights upon a small number of inhabitants; they related to the colony at large, embraced its whole population. The proprietors of certain large grants, as Baltimore, for example, followed by conviction or necessity the general impulse—as they would not have found settlers if privilege for some of them had been substituted for general democratic equality. Penn realized the purest conception of spiritual and social fraternity, and not out of such germs could grow and unfold the creeds of privilege.

All aristocracies have germinated under royalties, which they have subsequently overthrown, stepping into their place. Such was the origin of almost all the republics of the old world. Warfare has been the life-giving element of all societies; it was the source, the nursery of aristocracies. The better armed man, the possessor of a horse, were the principal founders in Greece and Rome. Not for war and conquest, but for peace, agriculture, industry and commerce, did the primitive settlers, the colonists, provide themselves with arms. War and strifes with Indians, or the warring in the interests of the mother country, were accidental and accessory events, and not in view of them were founded and organized the various colonial communities. After the cities of Europe had become successively chartered, enfranchised, or had fought out their liberties, the mass of the people still remained in fetters. The immense majority of the European population was deprived of rights, deprived of every pulsation of political existence. So the burghers formed a third or a middle class between the nobility or aristocracy, and the villeins or the rural populations. Here in America, there was no above and no below, and thus no distinct invested or innate rights of one above the other. And for the same reasons that America at the start had not the germs of an aristocracy, there did not exist any elements to constitute a genuine political middle class, burghers or bourgeoisie; a class so preponderating and influential in the historical throes of Europe. On the contrary, if an eminence could in any way have been given to a special pursuit or to a special position in the community, it must have been to that of the agriculturists, the farmers, who constituted the villages, those cradles of American society, and whose axe and plough hewed out its solid foundations. Even the temporary bondmen, after having served out their time, became equal to the other colonists in the enjoyment of political rights.

The ancient monarchies and republics, as well as those of modern Europe generally, received their organization, their laws from one, either a hero, a founder, a king, or a lawgiver. Historians, political philosophers, with remarkable obstinacy draw therefrom the conclusion, that no spontaneity can be ascribed to the masses at large, to humanity itself. If a whole nation gives up its former settlements in search for new lands, in the opinion of annalists, of philosophers and poets, it is some hero, who, to illustrate his race, starts and founds a new empire. If new manners, new customs are established, it is some legislator who initiates them; his fellow-citizens forming only more or less malleable materials for the thoughts and the conceptions of one man. But to discover, to explain who in reality created a new institution, or even a new enterprise, it is necessary to consider who were the persons that wanted it. To them belongs the first suggestive idea, the determination to act, the power of evocation, the largest share in the execution. *Is fecit cui prodest*, is an axiom admissible in history, as it is in justice. The social beginning, as well as the successive development and history of this country, reintegrates spontaneity to the masses.

The first regulations and rules for the settlers, upon their organizing into a body politic, were the result of mutual deliberation and consent. Afterwards all colonial laws had the same common popular origin, and the same spirit acts now. The initiative comes always from the people. Not a chief or leader called the first Puritans together, and established here the first free communities. Washington, who for the sublimity and equipoise of his character, stands alone and unrivalled in history, Washington did not call the nation into life; he did not evoke the events; but the colonists arose; the events brought Washington on their waves; independence was asserted; a nation was born. Washington in his civil career was an adviser, a tutor, but not a legislator. Laws in America had been hitherto evoked by a necessity felt by the people, and were framed in view of such a demand by the people themselves. Contrary to all the organic legislations of the old, of the European world, laws were not made in American communities to correct the abuses of a power, to stop oppression exercised by a single ruler, or a class over the rest of the nation. Laws were not enacted here, evoked by the necessity to limit, circumscribe, or curtail the abuses which were called the rights and privileges of a portion of the community and State; laws were not made here to protect one class, and are not directed against another. They were not imposed either by a class legislating for its special use and advantage, nor by tribunes or Solons, acting in the defence of oppressed masses. The laws here have the common consent, because they are framed by the common will, urged, evoked by common necessity. They did not originate in the attempt to crush one class for the benefit of another, and thus they have not been looked on or accepted with distrust and hatred, as have been most of the laws of the ancient and of the modern European world.

The primitive social and organic seeds of American communities were of the purest democratic nature and origin. These communities were born democratic; European nations gravitate across hardships, toils, frustrated attempts, towards democracy. For Europe it is a question of a social transformation from an antecedent opposite state, into a new one. But transformation necessitates the dispossession, the annihilation, or destruction of a previously existing social form or state. A cardinal difference therefore marks and separates the two democracies,—the American and the European. The American was at the outset, and still remains, constructive; the European, by the force and combination of events, is reduced preeminently to a destructive action.

European democracy, in order to breathe freely, to come to daylight, to acquire and enjoy rights, was of old, in Greece or Rome, as well as in modern times, forced to uplift, to pierce and break through a thick and heavy social crust pressing over it. European democracy must question, attack, break down and destroy her masters and oppressors, whatever their name, or their influence. So it was of old, so it is now. The space, the soil, as well as the moral convictions have been and are occupied by the enemies of her existence, of her principles. Democracy to get air must necessarily destroy the superincumbent structures, clear away the rubbish, and thus only is she enabled to act freely, and to generate a new social organism. Thus European democracy is absolutely, exclusively militant in idea, in conception and in action; in order to be, she must be aggressive, or she is nothing. Imperatively, she must be born in revolutions. Her present existence and action is a whirlwind. She has no clear insight, no clear conception of the future. Destruction of what exists, what presses upon her, what crowds her out of life, is and can only be her fixed purpose. The actual European democracy can only prepare the soil for the future; but what structure, what social form shall become inaugurated, is an enigma to be solved by time.

In America the democratic elements are normal, and no other ever existed or exist now in society. American democracy was not born from a social struggle; it is the growth of an original social germination. In America a man is born a democrat, and from childhood breathes democratic air and sucks in invigorating, constructive democratic ideas. In Europe democracy must be taught to the people; from a theory it must be transformed into a fact. Its principles and notions must be explained to those most interested; they must be admonished, aroused from slumber. The genuine people must be told and taught that they are men; that they have primitive, imprescriptible rights; that they ought to claim and conquer them. Thus —in strict appreciation—in Europe the impulse to emancipate, to inspire self-consciousness into the democratic social element, this impulse always comes from above. Ideas are to be inoculated, instilled by certain inspired and devoted personalities, originally separated from the masses by their education, their pursuits, their mode of life, and who as leaders try to penetrate the masses with their ideas to raise them, to become one with them. Contrary to what prevails in America, democracy in Europe does not find its true comprehension within the people,—at the utmost, is only latent. The immense majority of European populations are not accustomed to act freely by themselves, scarcely even to think about objects intimately connected with the sphere, the action of a government. In emergencies they look right and left for personification, for leaders mostly beyond their class, from whom they are to receive direction, intuition. The masses must be concentrated, governed in the strictest application of this term, even if it is in the name of the democratic principle. Events different in their origin and nature, from their having been engendered in America, events having their causes in a variously combined and complicated past, these preside over the destinies of European democracy. At present it cannot and ought not to be compared, judged, or a verdict issued, according to the strict American standard.

As has been already stated, American democracy was not born amidst the convulsions of a social struggle; she came neither violently, nor painfully and laboriously to life, amidst the death rattle of castes, social classes, or political parties, warring for opposite and deadly antagonistic interests. The conditions of its political and social existence and activity do not depend on the violent depression or subjugation of an irreconcilable social enemy. The European political writers and statesmen seem not clearly to comprehend this primordial character of American democracy. They seem to confound the purely political nature of internal parties, and their influence on the legislative and administrative action and play. For them the names of whigs and democrats seem to represent two hostile social parties, bent upon the destruction of one another. The European publicists do not comprehend their issues. The whigs in their judgment represent an aristocracy or a conservative party, similar to the same party in European States. The party calling itself democratic, has alone in their judgment the character of democracy like that of the European or philosophical conception. But neither the question of State rights, nor that of strengthening the federal power, nor that of free trade or protection, of internal improvements, and others of the same purport, on which the two parties differ, have the effect of changing or deteriorating the constructive democratic principle which is common to both. If the strict construction of State rights, as claimed by the democratic party, may appear to be more in harmony with the pure democratic idea, it is only in the form and not in the substance itself, for since the organization of these political parties and issues, the so-called whig States have been and are more progressive, more absolutely devoted to the principles of equality, more averse to arbitrary power, to slavery, to all oppression and lawlessness, than are those enrolled under the political denomination of democracy. All this seems to be misunderstood by European publicists, and above all by those of France, even by those generally belonging to the democratic creed. They cannot discriminate between democracy, as the name of a political party, and democracy as the only social constructive element in American communities. Those well-intentioned writers repeatedly implore and exclaim, *Might democracy only not be oppressive of the minority.* In their appreciation, this presumed minority is the relic of a caste or of a class dispossessed of power, averse and hostile to democratic elements, to democratic institutions. They suppose, therefore, that the party which holds the reins of legislative and administrative power, has nothing so much at heart as to legally oppress the minority, to avenge ancient social wrongs, to disable the dispossessed from doing any mischief in the future. But as there does not exist in the American social state any such stratum to be absorbed, destroyed, or even to be hemmed in, the enacted laws cannot under any circumstances have such a coercive and personal aim. The laws are made for general needs and interests, without any reference to parties, and democrats and whigs are equally bound by them. Finally, if a legislative oppression has followed and results from the struggles and frictions of the two political parties, it was by the force of a well concentrated organization, that the democratic or slavery-sustaining minority enacted laws distasteful, repulsive to the humane, honest and generous feelings of the immense majority of the American people. In general, the application of the name of democratic to the political party known under that term in America, is a monstrous misnomer.

The divergencies between the modes of the European and American democracies are cardinal,—divergencies resulting from different circumstances and events. Although the essence is alike, and the aims to secure the happiness and the enjoyment of inborn rights to every individual are the same, they differ now, and very likely will differ in the future, with regard to the methods which the European democracy will be obliged to adopt and try successively, previous to becoming a fixed social fact.

It is amidst the revolutions and changes to be effected in the foundation of society, that the democracy in Europe can alone make its way. She must assail, and the assailed will make, step by step, the sturdiest resistance. The European democracy is and will be opposed in the field of facts and in the region of ideas, of convictions. She must meet physical, mental and moral enemies with at least equal if not superior weapons. The struggle or revolution out of which the American nation was born, was of a different character, as was, is, and will be that of European revolutions. Comparisons are continually made between the American war of independence and the French revolution, as the representative of all European revolutions; but when impartially examined, the terms of both those events are to such an extent of a different kind, that in justice such comparisons ought not to be started.

A whole social order was to be unhinged in France, as it is to be unhinged in Europe. The American colonies rose principally against administrative oppression, and the injustice of a royal government, incited, supported by the parliamentary pride and the omnipotence of the mother country, unwilling to concede to the colonists certain political rights which bore principally on their participation in the internal administration of the finances and the right of taxation. It was a contest between nearly the whole colonial population and a government denying to it certain rights that were enjoyed by the rest of the English nation. It ended not in changing the internal social state of the colonies, but in constituting them an externally independent nation. It was not an upheaval from below, a rising against domestic oppression, exercised by castes armed cap-à-pie, in privileges and exemptions. The colonists took up arms, not for the purpose of overthrowing such a privileged class, or avenging hereditary wrongs, which had crushed them for long centuries. George III., after all, was the expression and the agent of the majority of parliament, without which his government would have been unable to enact the stamp duties, or levy war on the colonies. There existed in the colonies no obnoxious aristocracy, whose head was the king. Democracy was already socially and legally established in the colonies, when the war burst forth.

It was the normal state. With the exception of the financial questions, the colonies enjoyed the benefits of self-government. The American tories who preferred dependence on the mother country, to forming a distinct nation, did not enjoy any distinct social position which raised them above the rest of the citizens. When the colonies became a nation, the democratic principle, which was inherent in them, acquired more fulness and expansion. It acquired space to manifest its miraculous, creative, organizing and constitutive qualities, but it was not the result of the revolutionary war. The pre-existent democratic institutions alone secured the final success of the war, and without their pre-existence, most probably a new nation would not have risen on the horizon of history. In one word, the American revolution was made to preserve, secure, sustain, to give more air and space to a democratic element which was already active, and not to evoke it from nothingness to life.

France was externally an independent nation. Internally it was subdivided into social classes, and the genuine people, the masses were crushed by those centennial superpositions. The people were to be disenthralled, reintegrated in its imprescriptible rights. Castes and privileges were to be destroyed and disappear. The problem was to erect a new social structure on the spot occupied by the ancient one. Democracy, that is, the people, was to assert its social and political rights and existence. It could not do this otherwise than by breaking the massive superpositions which pressed it down. The king was attacked and destroyed, not for any special arbitrary measure or vexation, but as representing an odious principle, as being the keystone of an edifice, the head of a social order, against which were directed the efforts of the democratic element. Ruins and rubbish were to be cleared away, as impeding the new organization. Centuries had accumulated these structures and privileges, beneath which lay compressed a mass of explosive forces. They struggled for life and daylight until the moment of explosion came.

The ideas which prepared the French revolution, were already in fermentation for a long time previous to the American revolution. The ideas of the 18th century, of which France was the principal laboratory, acted even on the colonies, on the principal men of the American revolutionary epoch, stimulated their ardor, and gave, to a certain degree, a consecration to the democratic ideas already transformed into facts in the colonies. Revolutionary ideas had been brooding in France, in the public mind, in philosophy, in literature, previous to any revolutionary manifestations in America. And this must have been so, as all these ideas were directed against social oppression, against castes and classes, evils of which the colonists could not complain. Rousseau was the boldest and most earnest revealer of the new era, and his voice resounded in the minds, in the hearts of the masses of the people. The American struggle and success laid the sparks to the mine, accelerated explosion; but undoubtedly the explosion would have occurred even without the previous emancipation of the country. The declaration of rights made by the American Congress, to be sure, will remain for ever in the history of humanity, as the most luminous and sublime inauguration of a new era; as the first social assertion of Christian civilization. It vibrated in France, because the people were partly, at least, prepared for the work of regeneration.

The impediments to overpowering their enemies which the two revolutions had to combat, were likewise of a different kind. The struggle, the energy, the exasperation, the mode of destroying their enemies, must have necessarily differed in the two countries. In America, the whole contest was almost entirely reduced to a purely military strife. It was an invading enemy which was to be repelled. In France the object was to upturn a whole existing social order, which had been taking root for centuries. The French revolution therefore must have taken a bloody and destructive course. In America, the enemy was only on the battle-fields. Arrayed as an army in France, he was in the pre-existing institutions; he had hold of all the positions; he covered the land; he possessed physical and mental power and influence. He was to be ferreted out in all his windings, and destroyed. If the English soldier, representing the power of England, was justly shot, destroyed as the tool of oppression, as an impediment in the way of national development, how much more dangerous to the French people were royalty, nobility and priesthood! Their existence rendered any new social order impossible; their destruction was therefore a fatal necessity. The mode of warfare must therefore have been different in America and in France, as it will be in every European nation which shall strike for regeneration. Hence the comparison between the mildness of the American revolution, and the bloody violence of the French is not just. They had different enemies to destroy, and were obliged to make use of different means and weapons. What in America was the rifle, in France was the guillotine. The purport of the American revolution was at the outset misunderstood in Europe. No social danger, at least no immediate one, for the old order of things, for royalty and aristocracy, was anticipated by those who were the most interested in the event. Kings and aristocrats throughout nearly the whole of Europe, applauded heartily the efforts of the colonists. They saw therein only the means to weaken, to reduce the overbearing English nation. But at the first move in France, old Europe was shaken. The news of the convocation of notables in 1787, was received with rage by all those who rejoiced at the proclamation of American independence.

Previous to the war of independence, the American communities had already begun to develope within themselves the absolute principles of a superior social organization, and in this respect they had surpassed the English, then the only European nation enjoying liberal institutions. If the germs of such institutions were brought by the colonists to America, they became refreshed in the democratic essence which filled the minds of the Puritans. They grew vigorously, and with more fulness than they ever could have done in the old world. No historical associations adulterated them; no social privileged excrescences impeded or distorted their growth. The Magna Charta, the Bill of Rights, was rather the offspring of oppressed and injured interests, and by no means an assertion of absolute rights. It was made to correct certain abuses, and to render their repetition difficult or impossible. The Magna Charta is a transaction between king and nation, evoked by previous acts of arbitrary power; it was called out by grievances, and thus may be considered to a certain extent as accidental in its nature, since, without grievances, there could not have been a Magna Charta. This accidental character is preserved in the successive development of the English constitution throughout centuries. The initiative comes not from a broad principle, but from a wrong previously experienced, to prevent which for the future, is the aim of the constitution. It is an uninterrupted compromising with various interests, a strain of concessions, compacts and checks.

In America, at the outset, with the first cry of life

by the colonies, the broad, absolute principle was asserted, and from it the laws, the institutions, the legal and political habits were deduced and developed. The body of liberties for Massachusetts, as the mould wherein have been successively cast all the institutions and constitutions of the American states and communities, and of the American nation; this body of liberty ascends immediately to the fountain head of social life. In 1641 the colonists enact for *the fruition of such liberties, immunities and privileges as humanity, civilization and Christianity regard as due to every man*, etc. The English Magna Charta does not embrace the people, but speaks of kings, lords, bishops, knights, commons, leaving the mass of the people without laws or security. The colonial body of liberties asserts the principle of freedom and equality in every man. The Magna Charta and the English constitution is rather a pact concluded in a business-like manner, and for special purposes. The Massachusetts bill treats all the business objects as deriving from principles. And thus the colonists led the van before England, in many special enactments and measures concerning the personal liberties of individuals, and the private interests of the community. Thus the liberation of heritages and lands from fines and from all governmental exactions, as wardships, liveries, etc., was established twenty years before the like was done in England under Charles II. The right of petition and remonstrance was guaranteed in America nearly half a century before it was thought of in England. The guarantee of personal liberty, as embodied in the habeas corpus, this highest pride and costliest jewel of free institutions, was established in America forty years before the act was promulgated in England. The right of a person charged with a capital offence, to have counsel aside from the simple discussion of points of law, was recognized to the accused in New England more than a century before it was admitted into English courts.

Various ameliorations respecting juries were introduced independently of the influence of the mother country. More than two centuries ago the position of the wife, of the widow was secured by the law; the wife was sheltered from domestic tyranny, while the English law scarcely begins even now to humanize its statutes in this respect. So also were recognized .the rights and claims of children. The German, Saxon, English and feudal right of primogeniture was eliminated at the outset in the colonial legislations; and aristocratic longings—if there were any—were nipped in the bud. Daughters inherit with the sons as copartners, while the English law scarcely and exceptionally preserves them a parcel only in the inheritance.

All these rights and guarantees, constituting a superior social and legislative organization, emanated exclusively from the spirit which at that time already animated the colonists. This spirit descended upon them, not from their connection with the mother country, not from affinity of blood, but from the essence of absolute social truth. Animated by it, the colonies, previous to becoming a nation—above all, those of New England—elaborated higher solutions to great social and legislative problems. The above-mentioned guarantees and laws are therefore of genuine American origin. They evolved from new and purer conceptions, new events, new combinations. At that time England did not give, but received the impulse from the colonies, where the rights of man were recognized as being the paramount social agencies. The English constitutional laws, born out of special exigencies and complications, were mostly framed and conceived by statesmen, clergy, legists; the colonial domestic rules were made chiefly by simple-hearted men, inexperienced, unlearned in legislation or statesmanship, but whose minds and hearts had been warmed by pure humanity and civilization. Men who deduced rights not from precedents and parchments, but from the ever-pouring fountain of the better human nature. Only true democracy developes in man those transcendent and vigorous mental capacities and qualities, on which depend the progressive destinies of communities, of nations and of the human race.

The colonies became a nation. Democracy, which lighted and warmed their domestic hearth, became a luminous phenomenon in the world's history. Independence gave it a new impulse, opened a broader horizon, and secured henceforth its untrammelled and full action in all directions. Independence completed and perfected the primitive elementary condition.

What was germinating in secluded and quiet domesticity, became developed in mighty social and political institutions. A new and complete polity—the child of new events—and hitherto unparalleled in history, began to expand outwardly. By the assertion and establishment of democracy in substance and in definitive governmental forms, the comprehension of the relations of men to each other, of the individual to the state—the comprehension of his social standing and rights, of his political rights and duties, acquired a clearness and vastness hitherto unprecedented. In the states of antiquity, in those of Christian Europe, the individual was considered as existing exclusively for the benefit of the state, or for that of the power or powers which held and embodied it; in America, for the first time, a state and states were formed for securing the happiness of the individuals.

The colonies struck for independence, because nearly all the previously existing conditions of their existence were endangered. Charters and privileges that had been once granted by the royal power, and were now violated or annulled, together with certain guarantees of the mode of the internal government, embraced and secured the main conditions of colonial existence. The colonies, principally, nay exclusively, pivoted on labor. The whole colonial population was in principle and in fact a productive one. Assiduous application to labor, to enterprise, to industry, to business of every nature, and security for what was thus acquired, formed the essential and paramount terms which constituted the individual as well as the integral existence in the colonies. Labor was the only way of being useful to oneself and to the community. Privileged social drones could not subsist in communities, which started in life in the manner of the American colonies. It was therefore not the privilege of unproductive consumption, of useless unoccupied existence, which was to be defended against the encroachments of power. It was the emancipation of labor and of its products from fiscal and arbitrary control, from lawless oppression and political disregard, which necessarily formed one of the principal purposes in the rising for independence. It can therefore be asserted, that the condition of labor was at the bottom of the various causes of the revolution. Mental and physical labor became finally and positively ennobled. All who took up arms were exclusively laborers of various kinds, and the revolution was to emancipate labor. This aim was the natural result of pre-existent causes; it was contained in their essence. Labor is the soul of a democracy; it is the cardinal agency of progress and civilization; it is the most binding cement of every solid and rational social structure.

The principles laid down by the American people at the foundation of their political systems and constitutions are for the most part simple and therefore elastic and all-embracing. Such also are human rights; they are one and the same for the whole human family. The American constitutions do not take cognizance of artificial rights and positions, and do not need them for their practical operation. They are not based on certain interests at war with certain others, all of which are to be perpetually adjusted, equilibrated, kept in check, and which continually threaten to encroach upon, to overboil, or to break through the artificial boundaries surrounding them. American constitutions do not recognize or relate to abuses or privileges embodied in a few, and thus they neither create nor confirm abnormal situations, antagonistic to the interests of the majority of the population. For nearly half a century, several European nations have attempted and still attempt to implant, acclimatize, and adapt the English constitution, considered as the model for every European liberal government. All those attempts have ended and still end in failures. This is as it ought to be. The English Constitution is a special home-grown product. In order to prosper, it needs certain special conditions of the soil. It cannot operate with ease, without certain distinct, separate social bodies or classes; it must have at least three springs or social powers, acting on, attracting, and at times repelling each other. The Constitution is rooted in the life, in the notions, in the habits of the English people, of whom an immense majority, for instance, look with as much pride on royalty, and above all on the parks, the castles and their inmates, as could possibly be done by the lords themselves. The Constitution grew up line by line, step by step with the nation and its various evolutions; it forms therefore a necessary complement in the existence of every Englishman. It is an edifice to whose erection each century contributed bricks and mortar, whose partitions were built one by one according to the exigencies of the moment, in whose windings generations grow up, and every Englishman finds himself at ease. But for other nations such circumstances and conditions no longer exist. The internal conditions are different, and the English frame never can be adjusted to them. At times too narrow, at times too loose, this frame hurts here and there, and neither royalties, aristocracies, nor the common people which compose the Continental nations, understand how to move and operate therein. Moreover, the spirit of a new age breathes over the European nations. Their dim aspirations are for a future, wholly unconnected with the past, their efforts are directed to getting rid of those centurial encumbrances. The European nations are every where undermining the ancient structure, with its compounds of royalty and aristocracy. These exist as material facts, but they have lost all hold over ideas, convictions. Royalty, aristocracy have no faith in themselves but only in brute force. They are rotten, decayed to the core. And such is the substance of the two principal ingredients which are expected to give vitality to the Anglo-European constitutional system.

On the other hand, the American constitutions, simple and uncomplicated as are vigor and health, can be safely imitated in substance, and applied to every nation. They embrace uniformly all social conditions, and do not need artificial supports. Every individual, rich or poor, can live with ease, untrammelled in his pursuits, according to his inward impulses, his nature and his choice. Democracy does not deny to any body his human inborn rights; all enjoy them equally, all are amenable to the same equal laws. The American constitutions procure and bestow the greatest possible freedom and space to each individuality. The American people, the American democrat, the American citizen enjoys individually more freedom, security and power than is possible in the best fenced aristocracy, which, on account of its abnormal condition, and of its constituent privileges, must always be on the alert, always on the defensive, always prepared to repel an assault, or to carry one out.

For the first time in history, the democratic principle, in full growth and purity, became embodied in the American commonwealth. For the first time society and states were born, became developed, and exist and operate with uniform, simple and normal social elements. A past did not transmit to them any dusty relics, but only those eternal, indestructible ideas which constitute the moral life, the civilization, the progress and the happiness of men. All the ancient and European republics, when compared with the American, can be considered only as outbursts, as attempts on behalf of social and political freedom, as indications that the democratic principle is at the bottom of the destinies of the human race. The ancient republics at the best were only the forerunners of a new and complete initiation. Not even the brilliant Athenian democracy was a pure realization of the principle. Its origin was already adulterated. The Athenian democracy wrested life and power from the aristocracy, which remained among the constitutive elements of the republic, with the exclusive tendency to destroy democracy. The origin of all Christian republics was similar to that of the republics of classical times. Nowhere were republics begotten by democracy. The so-called Florentine democracy was born and operated under conditions similar to those of the Athenians. It came not from the people; it started in opposition to a pre-existent power, and was amalgamated, and even directed, organized by the Guelfs, who were no less nobles than the Ghibellins. All the past republics limited the exercise of political rights by privilege and exclusion. Liberty in Europe had never equality for her parent, was always surrounded with graduations and modifications. The use of political rights was always only a privilege; in America for the first time it was an inborn right, a social duty.

The privilege was lodged in cities, and then in corporations and guilds. Cities established republics over the world, and as such ruled over the land or country. Whoever was outside of the walls of the municipality, did not participate in the privilege of exercising political rights, enjoyed no sovereignty. In America at the outset, liberty was a right settled in the individual, not in the locality. The rights accompanied the man. Wherever he put his foot, he bestowed them on the soil; carried and spread them over the land; and equal rights dwelt in a log cabin, as well as within the walls of a city. The American republics have no privileged central power to rule over the rest; wherever the people meet for deliberating and deciding, there was and is the centre.

As has been often mentioned, the cities began the movement for emancipation in Europe. It was therefore a privileged spot, a privileged class that acted, and not a whole people. Cities and corporations led in the war, and bore the principal brunt of the struggle. The three primitive cantons of Swiss, Uri, Schwytz, Unterwalden, make an exception. In all the other cantons, the cities represented the republican power. In Holland, the cities struggled against the bloody tyranny of Philip II. And only cities in the past were enabled to rise. They were the only regularly constituted organic bodies, when the country, the peasantry was in vassalage, serfdom and dependence, without any rights, without any means of combination. Nowhere existed a democracy, and the popular element was seldom and feebly represented in cities. In the Dutch Republic the supreme power was not in the people at large, not in the States General, nor in any kind of Congress; nor in the legislatures of states or provinces, but in cities. And again, in those cities the power was not in the whole community, but in the hands of a local, closely corporated supreme aristocracy. These conditions were the consequences of historical causes, of a special concourse of events. The cities conquered franchises and certain political liberties, principally by struggles with the knighted aristocracy or nobility. After having subdued the nobles, the burghers imitated their laws and habits. Liberty was not based on natural primitive rights, but only a part took possession by force and enjoyed it. The rural populations, the laborers, the working men were regarded by the burghers with nearly as much pride and disdain, as they were once regarded by the nobles. The burghers never thought of sharing political and social rights equally with the people. It can be said that all these republics were a modified feudality. Against those privileges of the burgher class, the people, who were excluded therefrom, revolted. Thus in Holland, under the son of William the Silent, and in Switzerland, in the course of the present century. With all his civic virtues Barnavelt of Holland was the champion of the burgher class, of the burgher privileges.

Humanity and democracy are one and the same conception. If man is the image of God, then the divine emanation animates not a certain few, but all; thus men are equal, and have absolutely equal rights, equal destinies. In whatever way their functions may differ, in the all-embracing association and combination of various activities and interests, their virtual condition, their dignity and rights as men are not thereby affected or altered. In the whole creation every thing is submitted to general laws; their various combinations constitute certain differences, but nowhere is to be found a privilege raising any created being above the action of general laws. Nothing privileged exists in nature, and all its forces, essences and elements are for the use of all her creatures, according to the special conditions of their existence. The inspirations of genius, that sublime force which raises the mind and opens the secrets of the creation, these inspirations or discoveries are beneficial, and become the property of the whole race of mankind. Genius does not limit its creative action to the benefit of some privileged few, and thus its pure nature is therefore democratic or all-embracing.

The history of the culture of our race bears evidence of the unrivalled superiority of the workings of democracy. Democratic was the social and political organization of the Hebrew tribe, and it accordingly overrode time. The Hebrew law still exists. Among the ruins of forty centuries it still has life. No other social organization relating to things, castes and classes, has reached us so vital and indestructible.

Athens eternizes the blossom of the Grecian civilization. Without Athens, Greece would have been overpowered and subdued by Persian kings. She would have been ruled by satraps or dynasts, as were the Grecian cities in Asia. Not the spirit of oligarchical Sparta, but that of democratic Athens saved Greece. Democratic Athens gave the lofty and unlimited expansion to the Greek mind; it enkindled a light which shall radiate for eternities. The Athenian democracy, during its brief existence, works more in the development of the spirit of our race, than the most dazzling reigns of monarchy, than all the monuments erected by them—dead stones in the path of nations.

What remains from the conquests and victories of Rome? The gigantic republic, the more gigantic empire, is a heap of mould and dust. But the Roman civil law is still a living fountain of jurisprudence. And the Roman law is the product, not of the rugged, inflexible and narrow spirit of the patricians, but its clearness, its omnipercipience are due to the accession of the plebeian or the democratic element, to the full citizenship of Rome.

All-embracing, all-elevating Christianity can only receive its completion in democracy. Christ teaches that all are equal before God. The Gospel is spiritual democracy. But the spirit realizes itself in social forms. These must be of an adequate kind. There ought not to subsist an antagonism between the outward world and the spiritual one. If Christ left untouched the political and positive social relations, it was because he was to regenerate the internal, the spiritual man. This accomplished, the regeneration of social relations was to be made by man himself, in harmony with the moral truth, which had been revealed to him.

Among the greatest deeds in history, we must count those in which a whole people or populations, exalted by terrible emergencies, have risen to action, repelled invasions, or in the defence of the domestic hearth, of a country or city, in defence of conscientious convictions or of faith, have cheerfully sacrificed life, families and earthly goods. The people, generally deprived of their rights, and not enjoying any privileges, have more than once in history saved their rulers, their oppressors, who appealed to them imploringly. And these oppressed masses every where constitute the unadulterated democratic element, redeeming the faults of their oppressors.

Europe, however slowly, gravitates towards democracy. No cavils and objections can arrest the movement. The Anglo-European constitutional forms of government, with all their deficiencies and shortcomings, are after all the first initiatory steps. These constitutional governments continually raise the bolts and admit more and more from the people to the enjoyment of political rights. Popular education, although in a wretched state among the immense majority of European populations, nevertheless stirs up the mind and creates longings for the amelioration of the political organism. The increase and the more equal distribution of material prosperity, awakens self-consciousness in the masses. Large communities and nations slowly but uninterruptedly become more and more intelligent. And even Aristotle, not at all friendly to democracy, who witnessed the decay of the Athenian one, nevertheless concluded that when communities become very large, it is perhaps difficult for any other than a democratic community to exist. Lord Brougham prophesied that the English monarchy must end in democracy and a republic. Enemies pay homage to democracy, dreading its advent, and nevertheless recognize its all-powerful, creative vitality. So does Guizot, Thiers, Montalembert, Balmes, and others; even so do the kings, who set themselves up as representatives and defenders of the rights of the people.

The freshest and most recent despotism, that of Napoleon III., is in its way a recognition of the democratic principle as paramount to all others. Louis Napoleon recognizes and tells to the French people, that he holds the power, not by legitimacy, not by the grace of God, but by the popular choice, by the popular will. Thus, notwithstanding the political oppression, the chaining of all kinds of liberties—of which the masses of the people enjoyed less than the burgher class—these masses become accustomed to consider themselves as the source of power, as the social kernel. This is what is principally wanting, and hence, even this degrading despotism can after all be considered as a social and democratic progress. It is a mental schooling of the people at large, and however vicious and defective it may be, it is better than nothing. So in learning the rudiments of reading, even a bad schoolmaster is preferable to none, and a vicious spelling is more satisfactory than total ignorance. At any rate the idea is stirred up, the impulse is given, and the people at large become familiar with the regular operation of the institution, even in its present falsified state. The people will no more be dispossessed of the notion, and a short time will teach them to handle the power more thoroughly and normally, and hence more efficaciously.

Thus in Europe democracy is a rising tide. It rises slowly but uninterruptedly. It overflows, carrying away, one after another, the barriers and impediments erected to arrest or suppress it. It is not organized, not constructive; it tears every thing down; it has hitherto been a black tornado, approaching nearer and nearer, but its final outburst will be terrific. The fears, as well as the concessions of its most inveterate enemies are the best evidences of the all-powerful working of the democratic principle, of its eternal right, of its incontestable supremacy. Rulers and partisans of the right divine, of exemptions and privileges, speak continually of the just claims of the people, of necessary concessions to the spirit of the age, and other similar objects—all of them satisfactions given to the democratic principle. All this is a first vacillating step, but by the invariable laws of logic and dynamics, the next must follow. Customs, manners, social pursuits, level conditions, bring men together and mix them continually. The means of mental development and culture are daily enlarged in Europe, and are accessible without distinction. Not difference of birth, but poverty shuts any person out from using and being benefited by them. True it is that notwithstanding all this, the past with most of its niches, hooks, social compartments, stands there upright, overshadows and impedes a healthy, normal growth. But this past no longer fructifies European life, and its representatives are useless to themselves and to society. So the centennial oak of the forest, eaten up at the heart, barren and leafless, overtops the new and vigorous vegetation. But its branches, its roots are dead, storms break them away, and finally the giant falls, uprooted and prostrate.

For ages democracy has been variously assailed as a principle, as a civilizing and social agency, as a political and governmental institution. No cavils have been spared against her. All social evils are attributed to her. . Since the establishment of the American commonwealth, the old flaws are diligently reproduced, and large telescopes and highly powerful microscopes are directed for the purpose of discovering new ones. These accusations are as diversified as the human passions, and the perpetrators of them now as in all times, in all epochs, belong to the class or political party dispossessed of power by the democracy.

Among the foremost reproaches brought against democracy, is that of instability in political and social institutions ; instability in aims, workings, and ways. Democracy is represented as destitute of all respect or veneration for time-hallowed axioms, theories, institutions. But instability and not veneration of the past, not deference to opinions, to facts, and to results of different conditions: instability is the principal agency and condition of progress and of development. Nature is an eternal creation, life and motion. The embryo, the kernel, throw away their first shapes and forms, put on another, and are uninterruptedly in a process of transformation. What logical or moral reason or right has the past which is a corpse, to fetter the life, the motion, the activity of the present? What right have defunct generations which lived, moved, acted, amidst certain different circumstances, impulses and exigences, to tie and enchain those succeeding them, and placed or thrown in conditions new and diverse? Nearly every scientific progress or discovery is made under the law of instability. If the existing conceptions on all scientific subjects had been religiously upheld and maintained, all the immense developments which have so rapidly succeeded each other, would have become utterly impossible. Why should social and political institutions and forms alone constitute an exception? or by what obligations are the successors made to wear forcibly the gear of those who lived before them? America shows in its rapid progress, in its wonderful development, that man can successfully upturn and erect, destroy and construct, and that materially and socially, new edifices, as new institutions adapt themselves easier to men, assure his power over nature, develope the resources of the soil, and render it more fit for the comfortable support of life. Every generation has the right to build up its own dwelling. Old edifices and castles are admirable to look at, but generally uncomfortable to live in. They do not answer to a changed or modified condition of life, to new notions, habits, occupations. Modern existence, modern generations require air and light in streams. In the same way it is more considerate, from the financial and economical stand-point to invest less capital in walls, and not construct them for centuries. A house, an edifice might be constructed at the cost of one hundred or fifty dollars, and be equally suitable, substantial, and adapted to the principal purpose. The one might last centuries, the other a few decades. But the surplus of the cost economized on the second building, can be invested in a productive way, and enable the next successor to build with it a suitable new house. That built up for centuries, deteriorates, loses in value, impoverishes the owner, and does not in reality contribute to private or public comfort or good. The same to a certain degree is the case with social and political institutions. Not that every conception, idea or structure of the past should be absolutely pushed aside, condemned and declared to be useless. There is an uninterrupted chain of mental and physical transmission running through and cementing generations. But the living one has unlimited power to select, to make its own choice, to preserve and reject what it judges and recognizes as proper or useless, to live according to its own chances, will and decision. When a life-giving, all-embracing and fruitful principle reposes at the bottom, when in its development and free action it shapes out society, embraces it and penetrates it in all its fibres, then the instability on the surface is neither dangerous nor destructive. Instability is the manifestation of health and vigor—stimulates man's creative powers. In new mental, social and material productions, man constantly attempts to reach higher regions, to give more perfect solutions; to improve, embellish his existence, his social and domestic relations.

Besides, a man born in 1856 is chronologically and arithmetically older than one born one thousand or two thousand years before him. To call the past the older time is logically a misnomer. The present is older than the past and wiser too; it inherits the experience, the discoveries, the sum of activity of bygone times. Bacon, the great utterer of axioms for the concerns of practical and every day life, was the first who, with his wonted clearness, assigned in this respect to the past its true relation with the present. As the result of instability, destructiveness is largely put to the account of democracies. It is declared to be innate with them. So democracies are accused of having by intestine discords accelerated the downfall of Athens, Thebes, and other smaller Greek republics, and in Christian times, of having been the occasion of the destruction of the Florentine republic. It has already been mentioned who are the accusers. The storms, the dissensions which beat thus furiously on the ancient republics always originated with the aristocratic parties attempting to reseize the power. Democracies once in normal political motion, that is. when no violent, treacherous impediments are thrown in their way, are neither vindictive nor aggressive, but elastic, confiding, unsuspicious, good-tempered, that is to say, aiming and wishing to enjoy life, and let others do likewise. Democracies in their normal state are the everlasting youth of humanity. Such was the Athenian democracy after the Persian war, and for years under Pericles. Such to a great extent was the Theban under Pelopidas and Epaminondas, and the Florentine without their Medici and their Palleschi. Every where the aristocracies conspired, created internal convulsions, stirred up discontent, calumniated, threw all kinds of impediments in the way of the regular functions of the republic, betrayed, invoked foreign intervention or influence. Such was the case in Greece during the Peloponnesian wars. Democracies have never, not on a single occasion, betrayed a country. Corruptions have been almost a specialty of oligarchies and aristocracies, from Sparta down to our own times. Aristocracies, not democracies, join invaders and foreign enemies. Aristocracies create anarchy and bring final destruction. Not the plebeians, but the patricians of Rome received gold from Jugurtha, and so it has always been in history.

Aristocracies have formed and still form always egotistical, unsubmissive minorities, usually preferring the destruction of the state rather than to submit to the general rule, to submit to laws equal for all. Because aristocracies, when wielding power, did it for special aims, always prominently legislating for the good of their class, always dividing the state, the nation, in various antagonistic and violently opposed interests. Egotism has been the moving soul of monarchies as well as of oligarchic and aristocratic communities. Whatever may have been the dark spots, the true or artificially projected shadows on democratic communities, their political nature makes it impossible to enact exclusive special laws for one part of the population, and directed against another. Internal disorders and even intestine wars were always provoked by aristocracies, whose haughty unprincipled members, always ready to violate the laws, to show their contempt for existing power, to tread down public and private morality, studiously invoked popular animadversion. Such was the case in Athens and Greece, such was the case in Rome. Whatever could humiliate or exasperate the people, was always perpetrated by the patricians, by the Tarquins, as well as by a son or grandson of Cincinnatus. Sylla, not Marius, provoked domestic war. The same was the case in the Italian republics; so in France with the *jeunesse dorée.* In private as well as in public matters, offence, provocation, open or surreptitious contempt or violation of general laws, have nearly always been perpetrated by aristocracies.

It is generally asserted that all democracies have a peculiar tendency to identify themselves with a single individual, and thus to become tools in the hands of ambitious schemers and intriguers. This is considered as one of the most dangerous breakers for the existence of democratic states or communities. True it is that to a certain degree history justifies these assertions. The few democracies which have appeared on the horizon, have been always headed by one man, instead of acting self-consciously. But in substance, not even the thus movable democracy of Athens submitted wholly to the leadership of Pericles, one among the greatest and purest patriots and statesmen on the records of our race. Besides, the origin, as well as the character of the few democracies of the past, have been such as to lead necessarily to such-like personifications. Born from internal tempests, generally with the help of some prominent individual, their existence was continually tempestuous. A single spot, a single city, agglomerated the whole democratic element; there was the centre of the system. There it performed its functions, always in the public place. Attacked, teased, or exasperated by the lawlessness, the taunts, the uninterrupted opposition of the aristocracy, their deadliest enemies, these democracies of the past were nearly always in a feverish state. In a perpetual and violent struggle for existence, it was difficult to reason with calmness, to consider the most vital questions in all their relations. Leaders easily got hold of a people who felt the necessity of being commanded, for the sake of resisting an external enemy, or a still more dangerous domestic one. There was no public press to bring important topics under debate, to enlighten and cool the judgment of the masses, concerning the characters and the value of leading personages. In modern democracies, especially in that of France, the masses of the people form a "rudis indigestaque moles." They have no self-consciousness, no distinct comprehension of their position, of their needs, of their future. For this reason, they submit to be headed or embodied in one, whom they trust, as knowing their feelings and their wants. They require some one to think for them, to act in their behalf, to defend them from their enemies. The masses are not accustomed to exercise self-government, this most important completion of democracy. As was the case with Athens and the other ancient democracies, the modern democratic attempts in Europe likewise find it necessary to have nurses and tutors, to facilitate the first steps on an agitated soil. But the American democracy, being of a normal and natural self-growth, exercising its functions regularly, covering the whole land, and not concentrated in cities, cannot run out into an individualization, as did its forerunners. Already the press forms a powerful panacea against it. In one word, none of the conditions which in other democracies either facilitated, or even rendered unavoidable the personification of democracy in some leader, have existed in the American commonwealth. Doubtless, even for the most regulated action based on the concurrence and combination of such various functions, a kind of head is imperatively necessary. Such a standard-bearer—as he is very properly named in America—serves rather to rally the various scattering forces, but is neither the initiator nor the leader. He receives inspiration, impulse, direction, for good or bad, from those grouped around him. In other democracies the ductile masses were animated, vivified, electrified, or stimulated by the ideas, and still more by the personal forensic influence, by the voice of a passionate patriot, or of a daring, gifted, but mischief-brewing politician. So Pericles or Demosthenes could move them as quickly in a moment of excitement, as could an Alcibiades. Criticism, discussion, on the broadest scale, are the cardinal substances of American public life, and hence sham heroes, and hero worship must in the long run become impossible.

Ingratitude is freely ascribed to republics, above all to democracies, to the people. The American commonwealth is not exempted from this reproach. But in the commonly accepted signification of gratitude and ingratitude, history shows that monarchies and monarchs are no more grateful than republics. Moreover, in sound philosophical criticism, the influence of individuals on the destinies of the world is general, and accordingly does not preponderate, as is commonly believed and asserted, on those of states and people. The great majority of rulers, and of other great and influential men, merely co-operate in a movement, which would have probably pursued its pre-appointed task as rapidly and as completely as if they had never existed. Their work is more or less well done, but if they had not been on hand, then it would have been carried out by some one else. A few prominent men, whose genius, talent and energy have been aided by fortune, have been able perceptibly to accelerate or to retard the progress of events. If, for instance, Cesar had sided with the patricians, the Roman republic would have lasted until his death. Feudality would have taken deep root, would have covered Europe, and would even have finally organized society without Charlemange. The greatest service rendered by Napoleon, was the promulgation of the Code, which undoubtedly would have been promulgated by some one else. The principles of it were fixed in the national life, were fructified by the French revolution. Humanity generally has far fewer benefactors among great historical individuals, than among the great explorers in the limitless field of science, among the men who tear from nature its secrets, who unveil the scientific, the moral, the social laws.

Generally the services rendered to republics are rewarded according to prevailing habits and notions, besides that the individual is surrounded spontaneously by respect and gratitude. Rare are the examples to the contrary. The example of Miltiades is held up as a reproach to the Athenian demos. But Miltiades, divinized as the victor over the Persians, was punished because his subsequent life and actions were such as endangered and offended his fellow-citizens. Past good actions do not compensate for new mischief-brewing ones. The ostracism of Aristides stands there alone without justification. Glory crowns the heroes in the end, whatever may have been the conduct of citizens and contemporaries, and unfrequent are the cases of decided and direct injustice. Society gravitates more and more towards a state, where heroes and benefactors will be useless. At the utmost, their task, their mission has been needed in primitive, unsettled societies; as soon as the movement becomes regulated, and society settled on a firm basis, the time of heroes passes away.

The obligations between those who render the so-called services, and the served, are wholly reciprocal. The one is scarcely more bound by it than the other; and a man who in any way serves his country fulfils only his duty towards the community. The country proffers and procures to him occasion and space to unfold his qualities and capacities, to give them higher scope and full play, to rise over others, to win name and consideration. Without this pedestal, this space, the greatest names which resound through centuries would never have emerged from nothingness. Even the great and justly revered name of Washington, would not have acquired the eternal glory which surrounds it without the revolution, without the sufferings, the sacrifices borne by the people. Without this, Washington would have disappeared in the smooth current of common, daily life.

The American commonwealth or people is upbraided by foreign and domestic political sentimentalists for not electing its most eminent men to the presidency. Such an election is considered as the last aim of an honorable and legitimate ambition, and as a gift always at the disposal of the people, for the crowning recompense of a faithful servant by the highest civic distinction. It is, however, not intrinsically the fault of the people at large, if such men are not elected, but it results rather from certain complicated wheelworks in the process of election, by whose handling and shifting, in each political party, eminent men, out of jealousy, neutralize and defeat each other. The organization of parties often acts on and overpowers the will, the better impulse of the masses. Further, the succession of mediocrities, heading the governmental machinery of the United States, has served to prove emphatically the perfection of the system, which can easily be overlooked, directed and taken care of, even by the most inferior mediocrities. Truly, it is neither a rotten nor a faulty system which resisted, and was not broken or disordered in the hands of a Pierce, the lowest in the ladder of thorough incapacities.

After all, the presidential dignity ought not to be considered as a reward to be bestowed by the people for certain past services rendered to the commonwealth. There is no reason why a general successful on battle-fields, should be equally fit to direct the governmental machinery. The example of Jackson cannot establish a law. The great leaders of political parties, who for years in speeches, parliamentary and stump debates, move, excite and carry with them the public opinion; those men necessarily acquire certain habits of mind, contract certain passionate, imperious dispositions, which unfit them for the methodical and regular functions of national affairs. In extraordinary emergencies, an iron will, based on pure convictions, might be necessary at the head of the national chariot. But in the normal ordinary current of affairs, such so-called eminent men might become, if not dangerous, at least injurious, as very likely for the love of glory and immortality, or by concert, they would be bent on carrying out their special whims or conceptions, despite the exigencies of the moment, or contrary to the real interests of the nation. Honesty, strong common sense, thorough knowledge of the principles on which reposes the governmental structure, are the cardinal needs in a president for ordinary times. Institutions of the nature, character and composition of those of the American republic, can only prosper and operate orderly in normal conditions. Not by jerks and shocks, not among extraordinary combinations, not in the heated atmosphere of passion, can the American institutions unfold and blossom. Reason, calmness, regularity, forethought, and the equitable adjustment of various seemingly antagonistic interests, form the prominent conditions for the prosperous and healthy working of the American body politic. Such conditions can only be secured in normal, undisturbed times, in an air not charged with inflammable or explosive gases. And it is not such a serene atmosphere which propitiates the growth, or evokes to action those personages, whom history usually loves to surround with the halo of greatness.

The enemies of American democracy throw at its head the disorders occasionally perpetrated by unruly mobs, and attempt therefrom to infer that, loosening the strong iron bridle of the government, democracy unavoidably generates violence and lawlessness. Such disorders occur principally, if not exclusively in large cities, those receptacles and shelters of the most degraded characters. The immense majority of such tumultuous agglomerations, is composed of individuals who never received a genuine democratic training and education, who have not grown and lived in a genuine democratic atmosphere. This moving population is composed of discordant and heterogeneous elements, poured out from the old world, destitute of any notion of right and self-control, but always accustomed to feel over them the heavy hand of governmental police. For them liberty is not order and harmony, not an association and deliberate submission to established and equal laws; but a struggle with existing society. Those men were born and brought up in conditions in which law and right were synonymous in meaning and in application with injustice, oppression and exactions; and they cannot at once comprehend the difference which prevails here. Democratic America absorbs uninterruptedly masses of human beings, who are destitute of any feeling, or spark of manhood; without any comprehension of mutual relations of duties and rights. Morally and physically depressed, embruted, they must be washed, cleansed in body and mind, and restored to humanity. Their moral and social education is to be begun and completed. The scales must be torn from their mind's eyes. They must see and learn that freedom and equality are not an opposition to oppression, but a normal, healthy, social condition. They are to learn and to experience that true, genuine democracy is not a battering ram to crush and destroy, but a constructive and cementing element. They are to comprehend that the consciousness, the assertion of individuality does not consist in encroaching in any way on that of another, but in peacefully combining both, for the realization of social, orderly aims. For men who never had a true mastership over their persons, nor over their notions, the first steps on such a path are often difficult; the way of progress remains for a long time unintelligible. For the first time they become seemingly uncontrolled masters, and their time, their labor are enjoyments unknown to them in Europe. What wonder if persons like these, so long unmanned, violently abuse the blessings bestowed upon them by American democracy?

In free action alone, man acquires the consciousness of

his inborn dignity, of his elevated destinies, of his moral manhood. Democracy alone can secure to him this condition of his higher, purer life. In free action, man recognizes that he has inward powers and various resources. Here man becomes unfettered mentally and physically. Large numbers, nay millions, doomed to servitude, to ignorance, to darkness, become redeemed. This process of social purification and of the inoculation of manhood, is unprecedented in the world's history. It is a special and constituent element of American democracy, and marks its superiority over the republics of the past and of the modern world.

Hitherto democracies have been shortlived, and there are not wanting prophets who forebode a like fate to the American republic. But all other democracies were born and lived in abnormal conditions. All of them had a powerful enemy inside, gnawing at the root. This was the aristocracy, always and every where pre-existent to democracy. The reverse has been the case in this country. The American commonwealth cannot therefore run out into aristocratical institutions, become cramped with aristocratical governmental forms, and see a genuine, powerful aristocracy emerge from the actual social organism. Never were aristocracies begotten by democracies. It is an impossibility, historical as well as logical. Aristocracy has for its source and foundation the originally uncontested possession of power; she fills the space, possesses the soil, the land, the localities. All those advantages, acquired beforehand by conquest, or pre-occupancy, have received the consecration of time and usage. Aristocracy must be built up simultaneously with the first boundaries of states, or with the first tracing out of cities. Those who with Romulus dug the earth for the first walls on the Latin hills, were the founders of Rome, were the kernel of the Roman patriciate. Those who first took possession and made their abode in the Venetian lagunes, laid the corner-stones of the Venetian aristocracy. No aristocracy was engendered in America, either by the possession of power, or on battle-fields, or by the primitive erection of cabins, log houses, and villages. Now it is too late. Wealth alone is not the source of a powerful political aristocracy. The possession of hereditary power, the possession of land, secured by exemption and privilege, by law as well as by usage, are the vital conditions of aristocracy. In America, laws as well as customs, convictions as well as habits, do not favor or procure a single particle of nutriment for an aristocracy. There is no solidity in the soil, no stability in the power of wealth. All is moving on sand, wherein will be always engulfed any attempted aristocratic structure. No dykes can arrest the rapid democratic current, which undermines, dissolves and carries away whatever may be thrown into it, for the sake of obstructing its course. Should there be the seeds and embryonic elements—which in reality is not the case—for such an excrescence, they will be destroyed, dissolved before taking root, before being able to give signs of existence. Nowhere could be found even the rudiments for such a structure, aristocracy being antagonistic to the institutions, the notions, the feelings of the immense majority, nay even to the habits of life of those who attempt to play that childish and ridiculous game. Aristocracies must be created by primordial events. Aristocrats must be born with faith in their predestined superiority. Aristocrats cannot be formed from one day to another by grants and parchments. They must be born to command, to assert their right as rulers, overarch the state, and the people underneath must be so degraded as to believe that they are born to crawl and obey. Nothing of this kind has existed here, and such relations and conditions can neither be reproduced nor created. It can be said that God's omnipotence would be insufficient to give the sanction of the dust of time, wherein consists the true value of aristocracy. God's omnipotence could not now create in America such a social and political, privileged, all-powerful body. There appear on the surface, here and there, bubbles, which short-sighted observers consider as atoms, wherefrom in future an aristocracy is to aggregate. But these transient sham existences have no substance whatever, no hold upon the people, no influence upon the run of affairs; their existence is more factitious and shorter than that of those brilliant insects, whom one summer day sees appear, flutter and die. Those aristocracies which ruled, oppressed, betrayed and destroyed states and republics, were not the creations of parlors, drawing-rooms, and church pews. Before they removed into castles and palaces, they literally put the hand to the erection of cities and empires. But no power whatever, no combination of events can be imagined that is able to carve out aristocracy from the American social and political conditions. Whatever therefore may be the breakers ahead, or which surround democracy here, aristocracies cannot be counted amongst them.

Anarchy, dissolution and the consequent despotism of an individual, are pointed out as the necessary terms of popular governments. Rome ended in this manner. Not the plebeians, however, but the patricians, were the most demoralized and dissolute, and their factious combinations rendered the further existence of the republic impossible. The Greek republics, whatever might have been the internal anarchy which distracted them, did not die in domestic discords. No Athenian, Spartan, or Theban despot seized the power and overthrew the republics. Philip of Macedon was a foreign conqueror. The Roman republic excepted, almost all others succumbed to foreign conquest, and not—as the enemies of popular power assert—to domestic anarchy. Florence was overpowered by the pope and the emperor. The ambition of the Medici and of other nobles, and the hatred of a popular form by Charles V., sealed the doom of the democracy and freedom. Holland, Genoa, Venice, albeit not one of them was constituted by democratic elements, ceased to exist by subjection to a foreign conqueror. Not their domestic dissensions, but the overwhelming power of France, facilitated the conquest. The American commonwealth has no such conquering neighbor, and never can such a one exist. No European power could in any circumstances whatever, in the most distant future, dream or attempt the conquest of America, even if an intestine war should rage on her soil. Such speculations on improbable probabilities, are beyond the limits of sound reasoning, beyond the deductions authorized by common sense.

A domestic despot, a Cæsar or a Napoleon might emerge, and put an end to the democracy, to the American republic. Such are the forebodings of those who, from one or two historical facts, deduce an absolute doctrine for all times and for all nations. But they forget the absolute dissimilarity existing in the constitutive elements and principles, in the organism of the government, in its official functions, in the political habits and customs, in the character of the people of Rome, France, and of the United States. In both cases the political and governmental centralization facilitated the work. Rome and Paris were the head, the heart of the two republics. Any one who seized the power there, paralyzed the nation. The people, accustomed to receive impulse and direction from those centres, opposed a doubtful resistance, if any, to the new and violently established power. Cæsar, Octavius, in securing Rome, had already a powerful prestige in their favor, secured a pivot, a centre, when their enemies, on the contrary, were wandering about the earth, dispirited and scattered. In France the possession of the capital, with all its centralized, political and administrative powers, together with the command of the army, secures by a single well-aimed blow any political change. The people, the nation is beheaded or stabbed in the heart in Paris, and submit more or less reluctantly to their fate. The same is and will be nearly always the case with all other European states. Every where, even in England, feeble as it is, centralization deprives the rest of the nation of the energy necessary to resist any usurper of the supreme power. In America every such move and attempt will meet insurmountable political, social, governmental and geographical hindrances.

It can be said, that time and space will be against such a usurper. The American commonwealth, it can be said, has comparatively no standing army. Should a kind of anarchy, precursory to despotism and usurpation, contribute to give force and consistency to a military power, a military leader could never acquire the same influence over the minds and the devotion of the soldiery, that was possessed by the military chiefs of the ancient and European world. The elements of which such an army could be composed here, must be perfectly different from those of the old nations. The men who might enlist under this banner, originally independent citizens, would always have within them a moral repulsion, an undisciplined spirit, which must oppose the absolute will of the leader. Armies identify themselves with their captains by long years of warfare, by the recollections of conquest, glory, and of hardships. But here no such conquest, no such recollections can render possible this incarnation of the spirit of the chief in the whole army. All the European states, monarchies as well as republics, Rome or France, even of 1794 or 1799, have been essentially and traditionally for centuries, a kind of military and militant societies. The American republics have not this character; it is not engrafted in the institutions, in the spirit of the people, and never can be. The man of the people, the masses will fight themselves, but will not submit to have armies of hirelings.

But admitting even at the worst that such an army could exist with an ambitious leader, having in him the stuff for a traitor to liberty. He seizes upon the capital, as is Washington, he corrupts the members of Congress, and brings them over to his side, or seizes, imprisons and disperses them. In either of these cases, having possession of the capital, he has only in his hands a city, wherefrom no threads or administrative nets extend over the country. Having in his hand the members of Congress, he will have some individuals only, but not personages, whose decisions or doom could in any way influence and seal that of the various States. Each state, each district, nay nearly each township and village must have been filled with partisans of the usurper, must have been separately and literally conquered. The independent self-government of states, the self-government of the people must have been eradicated, abolished previous to the establishment of the power of an usurper. From Washington, or any other like centre, no strong governmental rays could carry his biddings, and find or enforce submission to them. Such an administrative current of electricity does not exist in America, and the utmost anarchy is the last way to create and foster it. Each separate state, with its well-ordered administrative and legislative wheelworks, will at once oppose without effort the acts of the usurper, or those of a Congress siding with him. Parliamentary omnipotence is not among the recognized principles of the constitution of the American political structure, and still less is it ingrained in the notions or habits of the people.

In Rome, as in France, there prevailed and still prevails an inborn subserviency, a mental and political servitude in the provinces, the country, in their relations with the capital. The European capitals are in reality not only administrative and governmental centres, but the great and almost exclusive foci of light, and the dispensers of culture for the whole nation. Thus it is natural that the people should follow whatever impulse comes therefrom. But the capital of the American federation is not such a centre for mental culture, or for administrative power. To facilitate the work of usurpation, it would be necessary that an extensive conspiracy should extend its meshes over the whole country, entangling not only individuals, but the temporary holders of the administrative power. Such a supposition, impossible in itself, could not even then advance the work, the aim of an usurper. The threads would break on account of their extension. In one word, considered from whatever point of view, the usurpation of power by one—according to the occurrences and the experience of past times—has no tools to work for it here, no chances in the existing facts and in the material means, and can obtain no possible hold of the country over the minds of the people. A wholly new combination of moral and material events would be necessary to facilitate the course, and bring forth an usurpation. A protracted intestine war, destroying the prosperity, the institutions of the country, destroying whole generations, and breeding in their place new ones, embruted, debased, wholly disconnected with the spirit, with the notions of the past; such is the only possible way to prepare and accomplish the overthrow of the republic. By such a war alone the path for an usurper could be cleared. Such a fearful combination of events lies beyond human forethought, beyond logical probability. It would be the victory of evil over good, of the spirit of darkness over light. Such an event, if evoked at all, would be not the work, not the result of the democracy, but that of the most hideous and treacherous aristocracy that ever darkened and blotted the pages of history, or endangered the free and normal onward march of society. The poison, the anarchy, the curse of America is in the slavery-breeding, slavery-sustaining States, and in their accomplices among the free States.

It is not only difficult but wholly impossible to admit, that a people like that of the American free communities, inheriting for generations the enjoyment of its rights, in a fulness unprecedented in history; that such a people could give them up under any circumstances and combinations whatever. No European people ever existed in the same social conditions, or possessed an equal degree of culture and of political independence, and thus never lost what in reality it did not possess. Inferences from the stages traversed by the ancient or modern European nations and governments, can in no manner be applied to America. Here every individual exercises spontaneously his judgment and his powers, and thus millions of free, untrammelled forces are at work for the well comprehended individual good, and therefore for the public good. The democratic development of America realizes what in Europe was, and is still, considered as a speculation or a utopia. It shows distinctly that humanity henceforth is not a word but a reality, a force in constant action. It shows that the fullest and brightest manifestations of the spirit which animates our race are not concentrated in the few, and that the destinies of masses are the best worked out by themselves. Such a state of society cannot run into anarchy, and be consumed by despotism. Where a people is accustomed to watch over its own interests, and to handle them practically, the power and the right can never be wrested out of its hands.

The beginning, the origin, the growth, the development of the American society and body politic, in all their cardinal phases, is wholly of a different character from those of other nations and states, as well as republics, whether oligarchical, aristocratic, or democratic. Whatever may be the destinies reserved for America, their course and final issue must unavoidably differ from those catastrophes which marked the existence and the doom of other states. The social and political birth, growth, and progress of America refute all the established axioms, that are deduced from the history of pre-existing societies. American society cannot move in the circle to which philosophers have hitherto limited the destinies of the race. Whether Hobbes or De Maistre, Bossuet or Vico, Herder, Lessing, Rousseau, or Haller, Ballanche, Hegel, or Comte, they have all seen only this circular orbit, and assigned to the course of society in its mental, moral, and political march, the same or similar phases for the future. Authority under various manifestations or characters, but always the authority of one, be it patriarch or king, lawgiver or hierophant, is said to have been the starting point, and whatever forms society may have successively run through and lived, it is to return to absolute or modified, but always to a superior authority, or by decay and anarchy, even to despotism. American society, the American nation was neither engendered nor brought into action by the authority, by the influence of a supreme moral, mental, or political leader; it is the offspring of a principle. Admitting therefore even the value of the established axioms, they cannot be applied to America—and she is not to run out into monarchy, anarchy, and despotism. Sociology, with all its various theorems, is at fault, and America does not adjust itself to its frames. All societies began in a synthesis, religious, mental, philosophical, as well as in a social or political unity or authority; and after traversing various phases of activity and development, they run out into the epoch of analysis, subdivision, research, science, and criticism. America, religiously or philosophically considered, is the creation of analysis, and accordingly of that phasis in which other societies have terminated; politically and socially, America personifies the combination of free individuality with association, in a self-conscious democracy—a combination hitherto unknown in the history of nations. The problem before America is therefore different from those which other societies had to solve. She has therefore emphatically to reconstruct a new and higher synthesis, out of the negation, criticism, and analysis, which generated and gave her birth. America, it may be, is destined to lead the ascension on the spiral, and by her example relieve society from the vicious circle in which it has hitherto been imprisoned. And as in the dialectic process, a lower, inferior term dissolves in one of a higher and more general order; of the same ascending character ought to be the solutions which are evolved from the social existence and functions of a genuine democracy. The present state of America is considered an experimental one. Be it so. To a successful experiment succeeds generalization.

CHAPTER IV.

SELF-GOVERNMENT.

Self-government is the absolute and necessary complement of democracy. Together they constitute the highest term of social development and organization, in fellowship and equality. They reciprocally fulfil the ultimate training of man as a social and moral being.

Self-government, as conceived, understood and realized in America, excludes emphatically a priori, and annihilates that notion of government which has hitherto been considered as among the cardinal constitutive elements, as well as cements of a well-organized and well-developed society. Self-government is the negation of authority, of initiative, of direction to be exercised from above, under any title of supremacy based on grounds assumed, artificial, and delusive. Self-government confirms the emancipation of reason, judgment, and will in the individual, from subjection to any kind of moral and physical compulsion, to the reason, judgment and will of another. It is the practical consecration and realization of the indestructible rights of man. It is limited only by voluntary association, with the aim of securing the general welfare of the whole, at the least possible sacrifice of individual freedom.

Authority, as the founder of society, and its consequent exclusive intiatory, directing, or governing power, was inherent in all ancient and European nations. Even the freest among them always recognized in some conception, form or manifestation, such an authority lodged above the mass of the people; authority as aristocracy, patriarchate, etc., giving a moral or positive legal sanction to the exercise by the people of political rights, incompletely as those rights were enjoyed. Such rights were wrested out or conceded. Thus the idea and the fact of the existence of a supreme authority vested in one or several individuals, became almost indestructible. The partial self-government in ancient societies, was always intermixed in some way or other with such authoritative interference from above. In European republics there were always castes or classes, guilds or corporations, exercising authority over the mass of the population; of which, even in those republics, only a small part enjoyed political rights, or was occasionally consulted—but did not decide—about the internal management and husbandry of domestic daily concerns. Communal institutions and subdivisions, as partially enjoyed in Italy, Germany, Spain or France, relating to administrative objects, always acted under the sanction, the direction of a distinct, superior centralized governmental authority, encircling and penetrating society, whatever might be its form or name. In France and Germany, the mayors of the communes are nominated by the government. Absolute, constitutional monarchy, republic, all equally as states and governments, encircle and penetrate, with their anaconda-like folds, the most minute and distant recesses of the governed. In England, authority from above lies at the basis of the constitutional liberties and institutions. The government concentrated in royalty has the major right of initiative, of direction, and interference, has the creative attribute. Out of the three elements composing the political society, two of them, the royalty and the lords, are inborn, superior authorities and privileged powers, the lords being the creation of royalty, and only the house represents, and up to this time represents only in part—the English people. Thus in this tripartite compound, two are direct negations of self-government, and the third is only its imperfect assertion. Communal institutions, to be sure, have been developed for centuries in England, in a fulness unknown to the European continent. But they do not repose on universality of rights and duties, even as regards the administration of their internal concerns, they do not expand as freely in all directions, as in America. However slightly, there is always present and felt the action of a government above them, a centralization overhauls them. And finally in the functions of these communal institutions in the country, if not in cities, there is always felt the moral or de facto influence and the presence of a distinct social class. The nobility, the gentry, the squires personally and by their patronage, exercise a direct action on the smallest commune.

Centralization is an unavoidable corollary of a power, which is exercised by an authority from above. Decentralization goes hand in hand with all the evolutions and ramifications of self-government. The European populations are so thoroughly penetrated and imbued with deferential respect for centralization, they have been so thoroughly trained and drilled for ages of their existence, by sovereign authority, acting from a centre in all directions; that whatever might be the transition to a new order, they would be unable to go through the one or enter the other, without centralization and a superior direction. The present state of Europe may be regarded as a symptom of the epoch of an exhausted political evolution. A higher social order is to succeed. Such inauguration will and must be prompted, accomplished by the ancient governmental process, by an action from above—and not by a spontaneous impulse of the people.

The community, composed of free and equal men, was the fountain-head, the corner-stone of American society. Self-government lay therefore as the exclusive kernel of a future development. The township was the primitive state from which the start was made. The township therefore still remains in its function, the generating power, the foundation, the nursery of self-government and of American social order. On the self-government of townships reposes the freedom of the state, and from it is evolved in wider and wider, all-embracing circles, the whole existing political structure. A township forms in itself a free and independent state, perfectly organized for all purposes. It legislates for taxes itself, and executes its own enactments, without any interference or sanction of the so-called general government. It is connected with similar embryonic states, by the cement of the law; is amenable only to the courts of justice, and these laws the associated townships frame and enact by legislatures, representing the whole people moving in these social cradles.

Although originally these communal habits and notions were brought here by the settlers from the mother country; events and new conditions gave to them a vigorous and complete, and hence almost a new expansion. The first settlements in America, and especially those of New England, being private individual undertakings, were not under any immediate authoritative, governmental direction. The first colony formed a community of equals, who deliberated upon and decided all necessary questions and measures. All these objects were of more vital importance for the new colony than any events occurring in the mother country. Almost daily new emergencies occurred, and the topics for debate and decision acquired more significance. Here at once all the cares of a regularly acting government devolved upon the settlers. So the first settlement or community realized at once self-government in its plenitude. With the increase of the population, new townships and villages, or cities, were raised by men enjoying equal rights, and were thus independent in their action of any direction or submission to any superimposed power, which might have been invested in any privileged locality, in an individual, or in a corporation. Thus decentralization grew out of every step of the extending colony.

Every individual participated in the deliberation, apprentices and servants—the last few in number, and rarely met with—excepted. The decisions became enacted into obligatory laws. The individuals chosen for their administration, were only delegates of the power, which resided originally and uninterruptedly in every one of the members of the community. The persons elected were there to fulfil not their own will, nor that of any superior independent authority of government; but to fulfil the will of their constituents, the people. It can be said that no other human society, nation or state has had a similar origin. This constitutive and absolute character of self-government remained unaltered. It was the main spirit which penetrated the whole body politic, in all the formations of separate states, and which now prevails in the political union of these distinct and independent bodies.

The governors of the colonies, originally named by the English government, served as a kind of administrative link between the two countries, but had no power to organize, to direct, or exercise any authoritative and independent supremacy. Different was the power of the Roman proconsuls and governors, and of those who, in the name of European monarchies or republics, ruled over cities, provinces, districts or other dependencies. It was almost as absolute as the supreme authority which delegated it. The governors of the colonies had no right of initiative, but only of suggestion to the deliberative bodies, which under various names were chosen directly by the colonies. The governors administered and executed the laws and regulations that were enacted by the colonists. Thus at the start, even in the colonial state, self-government, equality and decentralization operated in America with a completeness unknown in the mother country.

The minds as well as the habits of the Americans, were thus daily schooled in the art of self-government, at every step in their social life. The revolution, the conquest of independence and nationality did not create self-government, but only gave to it a broader sphere, and pruned away certain impediments in its normal function and development. Decentralization, which already existed before the revolution, was no hinderance in resisting the aggressions of the mother country. Not the example of cities, forming capitals and centres, as is the case in Europe, inflamed and drew into action the rest of the country. The consciousness, the knowledge of political rights animated every cottage, plantation, hut, and equally in New England as in the Carolinas, inspired every individual to resist arbitrary outrages. Boston, in its resistance to stamp and tea duties, was cheered and encouraged by the population of the whole State.

Centralization is inherent in every European nation. All England in case of emergency will look to London, to the omnipotent parliament, for impulse and decision. America has not now, and never did have such a centre, previous to or during the revolution. Centralization in Europe is, however, a two-edged sword. If it concentrates in the hands of the monarchs an immense power of action and defence, it facilitates likewise the work of revolutions. If the revolution succeeds in the centre, if it seizes the power, then as a general rule success is assured. Any movements on the circumference will always prove unsuccessful. The people, accustomed to being directed, governed, feels no power of initiative within itself, but is always ready to receive an impulse. In one word, although centralization forms the safest stronghold of despotism, it likewise forms the most efficient battering-ram for its destruction. The new social organizations which are to be erected on the ruins of the pre-existent powers, must be aided in their action by centralization, using authority as a principal cement and constitutive element. Self-government, as it operates in America, could not be inaugurated at present in any European nation whatever. Difficult, almost impossible it is to eradicate what ages have consecrated, to change the current of ideas, conceptions, and social habits, which have changed and deteriorated human nature.

Few if any European political philosophers or social reformers have placed self-government and decentralization at the bottom of their theories. Few if any of those who make the institutions of this country the special object of their studies, comprehend to what an extent decentralization and self-government are positive, orderly realities, forming the nutritive elements, as well as the nerves and the muscles of the American political organization and existence.

In the American republics the constituted powers, emanating directly from the people, remain with it, and no delegated body or individual is in any way fully intrusted with the supreme power. The people never divests itself of all its rights, by transferring them to the hands of its delegates, under whatever name those delegates may act, according to the commonly adopted theory of European representative governments, even of those attempted by republican and democratic reformers.

What in Europe is represented and acts as government, with more or less complete attributes of direction, authority and initiative, in strict construction does not exist at all in the American organism. The American Union, the American States are not governed, but only administered in the same way as every township and village. The elective chief of the State, or Governor, and the President of the United States, are only chief administrators. Neither the Governor of a State, nor the President of the Union, possesses the power of initiative. He executes laws framed by the legislative bodies, with or without his advice, with or without his assent, as the veto opposed by him disappears before two-thirds of the legislative votes. The executive of the Union watches over the execution of the laws, and over the general security and the relations with foreign states as well.

The power invested in Governors or in the President, of vetoing the laws enacted by the legislative bodies, is derived from a principle wholly at variance with that in which it is exercised by a monarch. In the king it is the last echo of his supreme authority deriving from above, from God; it is the remains of his once unlimited power, of his function as the fountain-head of right and law, the dispenser of justice, the absolute and uncontrolled ruler of the nation. In the American republics, the veto is exercised by an immediate offshoot of the people, elected for the purpose of wielding for a certain period the power of the people, and as the expression of its supreme choice.

The checks imposed upon the principal branch of the executive, that is, the Governor of a State or the President of the Union, differ in their nature, origin and action from those which surround the constitutional powers in Europe. Royalty, upper and lower houses, whatever may be their denomination, represent different and antagonistic social elements and social interests. They derive their origin either from social and politic excrescences, or from fictions. Royalty, upper houses or senates repose on privilege, represent individual interests, which, under the newly created name of conservatism, are to act in opposition to the rapid and all-embracing movement and interests of the people at large. As if in a well-ordained and healthy society or nation, there could or ought to exist certain separated interests, directly opposing the interests, the well-being, the progress of the masses. The checks imposed upon the constituted powers in American republics, are destined to arrest the abuse of the delegated power contrary to the interests of the people. All these bodies have one and the same origin. It is a democratic self-governing people, administering its general or special affairs through delegates. The President of the Union and one of the houses of Congress are the direct emanations of universal suffrage. The Senate is not a corporation, is not a separated body, but likewise mediately issues from the self-governing people. All these functions stand there, unprecedented and unequalled in the political history of nations. The Senate of the respective States is elected by the people on the same principles as the House of Representatives, only by larger colleges or districts. The Senate of the United States is neither an aristocratic nor conservative body. The Senate represents a higher principle, and occupies a position far superior to that of the senators of Rome, of the councils of Venice, of the houses of lords, or of any upper houses in European governments. The Roman senators represented a social class and caste, represented families, but not the people, and not the whole Roman republic. The same is the case with all hereditary modern constitutional bodies. The Senate of the United States represents independent sovereignties, watching through the senators over those rights which the people of the sovereignties give up partially for the sake of association and of general welfare. It is a position far more elevated than that of the *patres conscripti*, or of modern lords. The Senate confirming all the principal nominations made by the President, for various offices, shares with him the supreme attributes of sovereignty, and by confirming the treaties concluded by the President with foreign countries, it also preserves and represents in the Union the supreme sovereignty of each of the confederated States.

In each of the supreme branches administering the separate republics and the Union, there is always omnipresent, not only the abstractly recognized sovereignty of the people—as for instance in England—but the self-governing people itself through its delegates. All these constituted powers reflect the kernel of society, the internal organization of the commune or of the township, an organization widening according to exigencies, but unchangeable in its nature. This fountain-head of the political organization of the American commonwealth, seems to have escaped the observation of European writers; to such an extent is it new, unwonted, contrary to all received and current ideas.

European publicists have also hitherto generally misunderstood the character of the Union, and the nature of the power of the President, formations opposite to all past political and governmental conceptions. Events combined with the generating principle of American society, gave birth to these political organizations and subdivisions of power, all of which bear the stamp of originality and self-creation. These institutions emerged from the American soil, fructified by equality and liberty. These institutions alone constitute a real progress of the human race, while all the European constitutions are only, under various forms, consecrations of the privileges of a few, against the rights of the many. The American institutions have no precedents in history. Not to Greece or Rome, not to England, not to past European republics can we look for comparisons and for a measuring scale. The township, the State, the Union have nothing in common with what existed in the past, whose authority is not applicable to America.

The intrinsic character of the United States is that of an aggregated nation; in its existence a nation composed out of a triad, never previously known or realized in history, namely, the separate States, the whole people, and the United States. The third is the last born, and the two first are its generators. The United States have no absolutely imperative conditions of existence, but only those which are secondary, incidental, and derivative. The United States emerged out of the concourse of events. Previous to a certain positive chronological epoch, as the end of the revolutionary war—or as more definitively constituted in 1789—there existed no such complex nation as the United States. They were formed, together with their constitution, for certain positive ends. The elements of their formation were the concession and the abandonment of certain, well-defined and specified sovereign rights, inherent in the individuals, in the people in general, and in the separate States. The people, as so many sovereign individuals or units, accepted the constitution which gave birth to the United States. In the logical and moral development of the principle of self-government, the origin of power and the spirit animating the constitution therefore reside in the parents, and not in their offspring. Certain rights not conceded, and equally sovereign in their nature with those given up and absorbed in the United States, for the sake of association, remained with the people and with each State. Those State rights consecrate and preserve the sovereign right of the people, and are the surest guarantee of independence, the firmest barrier against centralization, that deadliest enemy of self-government. They are thus inherent in the political development of America, so normal in their nature and action, that every attempt to strengthen the central or federal power at the cost of State rights, and the consequent diminution of the rights of the people have failed, as antagonistic to the fundamental principle, and therefore illogical and inadmissible.

The Congress can only legislate upon objects distinctly defined in the constitution, but not upon those, by far more numerous and important, which the people of each separate State has reserved for itself. The Congress can in no way interfere with the municipal rights of States and localities. The Congress has no parliamentary omnipotence, like the parliament of England and the legislative bodies of European states, modelled on English constitutions. In the whole of this political and federative structure there runs a broad and luminous line, which marks the difference between the institutions of the past and those of the American commonwealth. It can be asserted that if Greece, or in Christian times, if the cities and small republics of Italy, among others the cities of the Lombard league, could have realized such a kind of association, based on logical combination and compromise of rights and interests, Philip and Alexander would not have disorganized and subdued Greece, and Italy would have been centuries ago a free nation, undesecrated by kings, popes and foreign oppression.

Jealousies between states dug the grave of Greece and Italy. The combination which produced the United States, prevents the germination of similar jealousies. No one special state is the head and the leader, but all are united on rights and prerogatives equal in principle. No one state exercises any special supreme power or influence, as did Sparta, Athens and Thebes, or for acquiring which contended with each other, the Italian, the Lombard cities. Jealousy against each other armed Genoa, Pisa, Sienna, Florence. And again, neither Congress nor the President, even in the name of the Union, is invested with powers and rights, which lessen or endanger those of each state. Thus the President, while wielding the supreme executive power of the collective people, has no official influence over the executives of the separate States. Neither has Congress any right to legislate for the internal affairs of the States. A decentralization of powers preserves the general independence. The President is the medium through which foreign countries enter into legal official intercourse with the United States as a whole, each single State having given up this right of intercourse. The Swiss republics, although confederated, could each contract separate treaties with foreign powers, as can be done by the members of the German confederation.

Except the cases enumerated in the fundamental constitution, and relating to rights conceded to the Union, the central power wielded in the name of the whole people, by the President and Congress, does not press as such on a part of the people, who form a separate State. So the individuality as a State preserves its rights, as it is sacred in every member of the community. As previous to the organization of the Union, the people and the respective

States exercised full attributes of sovereignty, and the combined mass accordingly could never press on a part; so after the construction of the Union the parts remained protected against the abuse of an undue interference of a combined majority.

In all the political structures existing in Europe, either absolutist or constitutional, there is recognized a supreme, an executive, legislative centre and authority. Even the socialist schools, in their projects and theories, uphold the idea of a central organizing power, absorbing all others, and legislating for all. In America a vital difference exists between the purport of laws enacted by Congress, and their bearing on the immediate social condition of the people, and that of the laws enacted by special State legislatures. The laws enacted by Congress are general in their bearing, and relate only to certain general governmental administrative questions, as well as those of external policy. The action of the State legislatures bears directly on social developments. All the questions of vital importance to society, all the radical reforms in legislation, jurisprudence, those connected with domestic life, with the morals of the people, form the exclusive objects of State legislatures. Thus slavery, temperance, the relations and the state of property, the position and relations, the rights and duties of the family, all the great principles on which society is based, are all in the domain of State legislatures. Their action therefore is the mainspring of all social evolutions, and on them really depends the democratic and self-governing progress, the future of America. The State legislatures represent the degree of the morality of the people, as they represent the immediate needs, tendencies, and culture of the populations. The practical, physical, and mental necessities and interests, by which communities act and develop themselves, find their expression and satisfaction in these legislatures. Congress deals with political, the State legislatures with radical social questions and solutions. In Europe the importance and the influence of these legislatures on the condition of American progress is neither understood nor even conjectured.

Like every single individual, the constituted bodies, wielding the delegated power in their variously complicated actions, may encroach upon, may come in various ways in conflict with each other. It is therefore of supreme importance to observe and to know what a people—in the almost unbounded exercise of its individuality and rights—recognizes and fixes as limitations on the reciprocal enjoyment of freedom. These rights are marked out and guaranteed, and the manifold private and political relations between persons, between communities and the State, as well as between the separate States themselves, are determined and put under an efficient safeguard. It was and is of the utmost importance for a society founded on self-government, to secure a regular untrammelled action in all its parts and branches, to secure each from wilful encroachments and violations. All the powers and rights, those inherent in each individual, as well as those delegated and intrusted for the advantage of the association, are to be so regulated and controlled that one cannot expand at the cost of the other. The nature of this supreme controlling authority, its moral comprehension and its positive action and interposition in society, is of the greatest significance in the constitutive organism of a self-governing people.

In ancient societies and states, the people in the forum or in comitias—or oligarchical and aristocratical councils, under various denominations, but with supreme attributes—royalty, personally, or by its lieutenants—and in limited or constitutional monarchies, the omnipotent parliament exercised a supreme regulating power over the laws, and over social guarantees, as well as over the rights of whole bodies, and over individual liberties. If not in the highest executive, as the sovereign, then in the political bodies was invested the supreme power. In America this supremacy is intrusted by the people to the existing law, and to the judiciary as its presumed faithful and conscientious administrators. The supremacy of the law has been nowhere recognized to such an extent and with such a plenitude as by this self-governing people. At every step, in every emergency, in every collision, private or political, in every action of single individuals, communities and political bodies, of legislative and executive branches, every thing is subjected absolutely to the law and to its decisions. The judicial courts in many respects are paramount to all other constituted and existing powers. The judiciary decides in the last resort, when either the executive of the Union or the government of States has transcended the constitutional limits, and declares all such proceedings void. Thus the judiciary arrests the arms of either government, when it would overstep the prescribed boundaries, and encroach upon the precincts of another. The Supreme Court of the United States decides disputes between the various powers and States, and can annul any law of Congress by declaring its unconstitutionality. A similar power is exercised by the supreme courts of each State over the respective legislatures and administration. All matters concerning disputed jurisdiction between the various branches of the administration are decided in the judicial courts. The law is the supreme authority. It interposes its decisive action in all questions, binding together and regulating the motion of all the social particles, the smallest as well as the largest. No conflict whatever can arise which could not be settled by the courts. The decisions of the court can often solve knots which were left unsolved by the elective action of the people.

The English courts would not dare to question the constitutionality of a law enacted by the parliament. Nor could this be done by the supreme court in France. In European states administrative conflicts are decided by the executive. The councils of state which surround the monarchies in Europe, are executive and administrative wheels in the governmental machinery. Neither the supreme will of a parliament in England or on the continent, however oppressive it might prove for political parties, administrative branches or single individuals; nor the personal will of a sovereign, however arbitrary might be its action, could find a curb in the judicial powers. In the historical records, of pure monarchical states especially, rarely do we find the evidences of respect for laws given by the master, and of the confidence of the subject in the integrity of their distribution, like that shown by the miller of Potsdam, who answered Frederick the Great, *that there are judges in Berlin against royal whims;* an answer which remains as the purest ray of glory in the reign of this philosophical absolutist.

The efficacy of the judicial power, which in its nature is rather moral than physical, reposes on the inherent respect of each individual for the law and its decisions. In some exceptional cases the law might be pushed aside in the momentary fermentation of passion, or when its administration was wilfully desecrated; but the immense majority of the population submits to the enforcement of judicial decisions, with a confidence and ease unknown and unthought of in Europe. Every truly free man here recognizes without hesitation, the judicial power as the supreme regulator of society. The American communities, the American self-governing people, in their homage to the law, stand unique in history. The voluntary recognition of the supremacy of verdicts issued in the name of reason, justice and equity, is the highest manifestation of social culture which society could attain in its present stage. It evidences the deliberate effort of a free people, legislating for itself—and not receiving the law from a founder, a sovereign or an individual legislator, in order to defend itself against outbursts of excited or virulent passions. The judge who speaks, is presumed not to speak under the inspiration of his individual will, but to utter the words of a positive existing law; he is enlightened by its cool and discriminating spirit. The supremacy conceded to the judge over the legislator, has a psychological character, and results from the supposition that legislative assemblies might act under the impulse or the pressure of violent excitement; that the spirit of party, or momentary enthusiasm for a notion or a reform, might carry them too far, cloud their appreciative faculties, and result in enactments at variance with previous laws, and with binding constitutional compacts. The judicial courts, as the constituted guardians of the existing laws, represent the sober second thought, the purified conscience of the community.

In many cases, experience has shown that the supremacy accorded to the law, and to its organ, the judge, is wise and salutary. It is one of the noblest features of the system. It is the highest homage rendered to the power of reason. Often, where in Europe brute arbitrary or military force intervenes and settles disputes in blood, in America the calm, fearless decision of the law determines irrevocably, tranquillizes passions, prevents violent conflicts among powers, as well as among individuals, and is intended even to rectify or to arrest the influence of passion in the legislators themselves.

But this subordination of the legislator to the judge, or in other words, of the ever-living spirit to the dead letter, has its dark shadows. Judges as well as legislators, can take an active part in the interests of life by which they are surrounded, can be acted on and carried away by passions. In such cases their decisions clash with the better, generous tendencies of the people, of the majority. The judges act in the name of the past, they sustain the past to the detriment of new conceptions, derived from new wants and conditions, from the moral progress and amelioration of the community. Often the judge, with Mosaïc rigidity, adheres to the letter, excluding the spirit, which alone can reinvigorate society at whatever stage it may have reached. Thus in the temperance question, the people of various States legislated to protect itself against the temptation of crime. The majority of the courts overruled this noble attempt, annihilating by technicalities the inspirations of morality.

Further, the omnipotence of the courts and judges, however conservative of society they may be considered, degenerates, like every kind of rigid, lifeless conservatism, into a kind of despotism. But despotism of whatever nature or name, exercised by a sovereign or by a judge, is antagonistic to regulated and healthy progress. The despotism of tyrants leaning on bayonets, or of judges abusing the construction to be put upon laws, both demoralize society. Courts and judges, overruling by their verdicts the laws which have been enacted by legislatures, and issuing directly from the people, substitute the will of the few for that of the many. The judge publishes his individual opinion, and construes the law according to the comprehension of his individual intellect. So after all, a judge exercises in theory, as well as in certain contingencies practically, as much of absolute power as can be exercised by a sovereign prince. It is true, that the judge acts within certain limitations and forms, but entrenched behind them his power is as irresponsible as that of any absolute ruler. Thus slavery-sustaining influences have more than once polluted the judiciary, and foiled the confidence of society in the impartiality of the distributors of justice. An unprincipled judge becomes as remorseless as the most bloody despot.

There is the most remarkable analogy between the conduct of Judge Kane, in the celebrated case of Williamson, who, according to existing laws, instructed a slave in his rights to freedom, and aided him in their legal recovery, and that of Francis I., of Austria, towards the Lombard patriots of 1822, who were imprisoned in Spielberg. Maroncelli became sick; Francis refused permission for the martyr to be visited by a skilful physician, replying to all entreaties, that the governor of the dungeon was to take care of the health of his prisoner, who finally paid by the amputation of a leg for the ferocity of the Hapsburg. So Judge Kane replied to all solicitations on account of his prisoner, that the United States marshal had to take care of the good health of Williamson. The pressure of public indignation forced the judge to open the dungeon, but he displayed as much ferocity as was allowed by the state of society wherein he lives. Francis I. was a despot, born and educated in the idea that his will was superior to the laws, and that he could deal with men according to his pleasure. The American judge deliberately abused a power, freely intrusted to him by society, for its own well-being and security. Which of the two is the greater criminal?

Self-government developes self-consciousness in the

private individual as well as in the whole people, or rather in spirit as in application, they act on, fructify and reciprocally support each other. In this intimate relationship and fusion, true self-government as the outward manifestation, requires and is based internally on a higher and purer morality, than can be possessed by any people, nation or community, submitted to a recognized superior power, tutored by the will of one or of a few, directed, ruled by kings or prophets. A blind faith is no faith at all, and not such a faith, but perception, reason, constitute manhood, make the man a moral and good being. Thus self-government is the highest assertion of the dignity of man; it is the most powerful agency of human culture, is the most powerful stimulus of a productive, orderly activity. The rapid, well-regulated progress and development of American society in various directions, is the fruit of self-government and of its corollaries and complements. Those communities and States of the American commonwealth, in which self-government is operative in its normal conditions, are far superior in morality, in culture, in mental and material productiveness, in the spirit of order, to those communities where self-government, under the baneful influence of slaveocracy, has degenerated into violent and reckless self-will, or dwindled down to a sham, to a social lie. As light and warmth generate higher productions and vegetation, so self-government and self-consciousness generate higher comprehension and appreciation of mutual relations and duties. They melt down stupidity, evoke action, enterprise, stir up the initiatory creative powers of a people. They are the cardinal conditions for individuals, as well as for a nation, of a vigorous, healthy, and thus of a superior activity.

In no previous state and form of society, in no nation, has self-government constituted so fully as in America the cardinal element, the active spirit of political union. But even its imperfect application and the deficient attempts at its realization, made in European republics, have always evinced its superiority to the absolutely authoritative mode of conducting society. Notwithstanding all the deficiencies and aberrations from the absolute principle of self-government, in republics ruled by oligarchies and aristocracies, by corporations and guilds, the arts, mental and material culture, industry, commerce, evoked as by a spell, have taken an instantaneous start and growth; while under the centralized power, where the tuition of the people has been carried out by the government, where authority, as the constitutive conception, prevails and rules, the process of culture and of civilization is toilsome and slow, Free communities and states—in spite of all their imperfections—in general have accomplished an extensive progress in as many decades, as in the case of the other required centuries.

Self-government, self-consciousness, necessitate a higher culture, and furnish motives for its spreading and expansion. They are the healthiest incentives of the energies of the individual and of the people. They alone convey the various powers of intelligent activity to various and congenial channels. All the so-called paternal regimes, all the strong centralized governments, seizing and appropriating to themselves the right of initiative, often pervert the faculties, falsify their nature and tendencies, and divert them forcibly from normal developments and pursuits. All such governments are apt to decide rapidly on mischief, but are sluggish in introducing ameliorations, in initiating new conceptions, in carrying out beneficial measures. Thus when a government hesitates, and its hesitation is occasioned by narrowmindedness, by conceit, by the spirit of envy, by the misunderstood tendency of self-preservation, by utter inability to disentangle itself from the meshes of ancient routine; a self-governing people invents, creates, acts, selects, applies, makes experiments, arrives at results and marches onward without respite. The initiative, as well as the execution, is in the brains, in the might, in the hands of every member of the community. A government watches and controls every pulsation of intellect, regulates and therefore hinders and cramps every spontaneity and impulse, throws impediments in the way of every enterprise. Governments resemble lamplighters who maintain through their lampposts a scanty and limited, vacillating light; in a self-governing people it pours out freely from the aggregate mass of intellect; radiates warmth in all directions, making darkness recede and ignorance disappear.

Every thing great, beneficial, useful in America, is accomplished without the action of the so-called government, notwithstanding even its popular, self-governing character. Individual impulses, private enterprise, association, free activity, the initiative pouring everlastingly from within the people, are mostly substituted here for what in European societies and nations forms the task of governments. Governmental or legislative action in America is limited to giving, in required cases, the legal formalities to associated or individual undertakings, or to using the public resources and administrative wheelworks, for ends pointed out, demanded and ordered by the will of the people. But by far the larger number of monuments, works and useful establishments, for industry, trade, for facilitating and spreading tuition and mental culture, universities, schools and scientific establishments, are created and endowed by private enterprise, by private association, and by individual munificence. As there is no government in the strict European sense, or according to philosophical definitions, neither individuals separately, nor the aggregated people look to the government for such creations; private association and enterprise—those corollaries of self-government—untrammelled by governmental action, have covered the land with railways and canals, and when under the most enlightened government of Europe, that of Napoleon I., the scientific academy of France rejected the discovery of Fulton, it was seized and realized by private enterprise in America. Private enterprise has constructed iron tracks, and covered the soil with their networks at a time when the governments of Europe scarcely dared to make some few trials of this new mode of communication. And all this was accomplished against heavy odds, in a country without sufficient hands to labor, with insufficient capital. Hands and capital were provided, imported by the unrelenting energy of private enterprise. All this could not have been miraculously carried out, if the American people had been accustomed to look to a government for the initiative, instead of taking it themselves. Without the self-governing impulse, America would be materially and socially a wilderness.

The superiority of private enterprise over any so-called governmental centralizing action, is daily evidenced here. In many branches of administration the government remains behind what an individual enterprise fulfils. Thus the carriage of letters and the whole branch of postal administration, is successfully rivalled by private expresses. Many other administrative branches seem destined in the course of time, to be superseded by private enterprise. A time may come, when even armaments and armies may be levied on the account of states, but by private individuals. Armories and navy docks would to-day be better managed by private than they are by governmental administration. Even external relations are better secured by the numberless threads of private interests, between America and Europe, which extend and cross each other, than by official representatives, or by the stipulations of treaties and conventions.

Self-government harmonizes with one of the most salient and all-absorbing features of the popular character. Americans are spurred on by what may be called a devouring mobility. Domestic ties, the affections of home and hearth, are powerless over the immense majority. Action carries them away, and they change with wonderful facility spots, abodes, regions, and states. Most individuals on starting in life, have no attachment to this or that place, and plunge into the wilderness and distant solitudes; establish there homes and change them again. Without this restlessness, America would not have expanded and become peopled, nor would civilization, culture have been spread over primitive forests, over prairies and valleys. But only among a free, self-conscious, self-governing people could this mobility, from beneath whose steps spring up communities and states, have had such beneficial significance; as it is only in self-government that such characteristics of a people could find the adequate conditions for a free, untrammelled play. Mobility urges the American incessantly to work, to undertake, to spread, create, produce. He could not wait for the permission or sanction of those urgings by a government, or submit to receive advice, or move in the leading-strings of governmental directions. All this is wholly incompatible with the nature of the American, with his mental habits, as well as with the combination of circumstances around him. Events urged the first settlers not to attach themselves to spots, not to be soldered to them, but to extend, spread uninterruptedly farther and farther, to work and subdue lands and regions. Thus at the start was shaped out this feature of character, and it was strengthened more and more in each successive generation. Self-consciousness was the natural compass of this mobility; they are intimately blended; and mobility, thus creative and productive, forms one of the most vital nerves of self-government.

The constructive action of self-government, its living force, its self-organizing power, and its active spirit of political communion, its superiority in practical execution over theoretical conceptions and schemes, were evidenced in the organization of California. Nearly contemporary events in Europe showed, that men schooled in the self-governing townships of America, possess more constructive aptitude for organizing society than the theorists, the reformers, the leaders of the European revolutions of 1848.

The gold sands of California attracted at once the most reckless and adventurous characters from all parts of the globe. *Auri sacra fames* stirs up, even generates the worst passions. This incendiary, centrifugal conglomeration, repulsive to all organization, became a body politic, formed a state, a constitution, enacted laws for jurisprudence and administration with the greatest ease, although surrounded by various impediments and difficulties. The men who constructed and organized this new commonwealth, had been practically trained in their old states in this social architecture; men mostly without names, unknown generally, and not trained in what would be called in Europe, the higher statesmanship. In 1848 France and Germany attempted a renovation, a reinvigoration of society. In both countries the people, called for the first time to use its rights of suffrage, selected all prominent capacities in different departments. In Germany, as in France, statesmen, politicians, savants, reformers, men representing the most advanced social conceptions and theories, were intrusted by the people with the task of erecting a new social and political structure. Learning, skill, experience and higher mental accomplishments were called out. To be sure, California was a virgin soil, on which any structure could have been easily raised, while in Europe various and antagonistic elements were thrown together, and the social soil was encumbered in many ways. But at the start, in the first days of these revolutions, memorable for their miscarriage, the impediments were by no means so great; the incapacity of the architects and builders gave them time to grow, to increase, to extend. In the first moment, the panic-struck representatives of the past, the kings and their retinue in Germany, were ready to yield to every demand, even to give up their power, and an immense majority of the French and of the German people, was prepared to carry out sternly the decisions of their representatives. There was originally little if any resistance, little if any retrograde pulling, and it could easily have been overpowered by a prompt, constructive action. But the renovators of society at once lost themselves in a labyrinth of theorems and discussions, losing precious time, and the prostrated enemy recovered spirits and strength. In France the masses slid out of the hands of the revolutionary leaders, because these showed an utter incapacity of satisfying their direct interests and aspirations; because they were unable to erect a new, social and political edifice, well adapted to the well-being of the masses. The same, to a far greater extent, was the case in Germany. And by the way, it may be observed, that the whinings of the men of 1848–49, in both countries, about treason by their opponents, were childish and ridiculous. Kings, absolutists, conservatives of every hue, Bonapartists, royalists remained true to their nature, and did not belie it. It was childish to expect from any of them to co-operate sincerely in a social or political renovation. This they never could do. They were at war with the new and generous ideas, which were hateful to them; they were on the defensive, and used all the tricks, stratagems and means in their power to crawl upon, and then to crush, to strangle the enemy. The worse for the simple-minded, who trusted them, who rose to grapple with forces and events, while unequal to the task, destitute of promptness in conception, destitute of energy in action. Europe therefore was groping in indecision and in darkness. The Americans go directly to positive, fixed solutions, evolving from a broad, normal principle. This enables them to found communities, and erect states as easily as houses. Europe vacillates between various principles and theories, and does not possess a fixed mode for their execution; but nations exist through positive solutions, and not through uncertainties.

The American social and political world possesses in its self-government a mode of solving all future questions, whatever may be their purport, nature and complication. As the present political union was the creation of the self-government, so, by a new evolution, a new formation may evolve out of this fruitful principle. Political forms, social organizations, are progressive and perfectible, as is every thing belonging to the mental and intellectual manifestations. The creative power of the human spirit is inexhaustible, and in freedom, self-action, self-consciousness, man realizes himself in the outward world. Only the tendency to progress and perfectibility, is eternal and limitless in the race; the scientific theories, the political forms and solutions are temporary, and subject to be altered, rejected and made afresh. In the field of natural science, new discoveries enrich the human mind, increase the human power and welfare, change and improve man's conditions of existence, remodel or create new bases for the scientific comprehension of the creation. Social sciences are subject to like laws, and their solutions are not definite. What is considered as an *ism* in a century or rejected as such by a generation, becomes often a social or scientific truth, a theorem and fact for the following one. Christian Europe has more than once changed her political forms, her internal domestic social economy, her current of conceptions, of ideas. But all such changes, evolutions and transitions, were accomplished with more or less violent eruptions, commotions, and amid bloodshed and destruction. The normal and ordinary action of a rational self-government is sufficient to carry out and to accomplish in an orderly manner, any future changes and evolutions, marking the ascending social development and expansion of America.

Social equality, the facility to acquire by individual exertions a social standing, the public and political life, open and accessible to every one, whatever may be his situation, his precedents, or occupation—provided he succeeds in winning the confidence or the partiality of his fellow-citizens; all this combined, in free communities, creates a powerful stimulus to personal ambition. Self-government more than any other political form, widens the horizon and smooths the path for ambitious longings.

Moralists and philosophers have been of old wont to represent ambition as one of the cardinal sources of all the evils which spread over and gnaw at humanity. But this passion is primordial, generally innate in our nature. It was and will remain one of the most powerful incentives of human action. It is indestructible, shoots out and reveals itself in various ways and modes. Only hypocrites can pass absolute condemnation upon what is intrinsically rooted in man. Society ought to be organized in a manner not to debase and pervert, but to purify and regulate, to combine harmoniously and bring to an equipoise the innate passions which stimulate the diversified, all-absorbing activity of man. Society ought to procure ample scope for their normal expansion. Then ambition, as all other passions, innoxious in principle, will become beneficial and fruitful for social relations. In self-governing communities this balance and accord of certain passions, at least, if not all of them, is nearer approached than in any other political form. In them even that kind of distorted ambition, which forms the subject of accusations and complaints, is rendered less dangerous, less menacing, and less subversive. The organization of society makes it impossible for political ambition to crawl long in the dark, and approach its end by crooked ways, to seize by surprise upon the masses, to drag the people, the nation forcibly, as an unconscious clump. Whatever efforts it may use to maintain secrecy, such an ambition is always detected. Daylight exposes it. It must act under the eyes of all, under the argus-eyed publicity. It is to meet public opinion face to face; it is watched and controlled on every winding and by-way. When words and actions are appreciated, judged and scrutinized publicly, and by all who are willing to do it, the power of exercising blind attraction and sway is weakened and soon destroyed. Whatever may be the anthropological or social appreciation of the baneful or beneficial influence of the passions, unquestionably they are more easily regulated by expansion than by compression. Ambition in a free community necessarily moves in a purer air, and thus becomes less corrosive. Competition rubs off the venomous sting, hollowness runs rapidly through its course, breaking in pieces by its own emptiness. Public life—the possible lot of every one—evokes ambitions from all sides, and these check each other. The more openings for ambition, the easier the outlet, the less danger of violent explosions, or of dark, secret, corrupting dealings and designs.

Ambition in itself, in its normal state is a lever and a ferment, whose action benefits humanity. Ambition and love are almost inseparable. Intense love of any object whatever, makes the individual bent on success, desirous of elevating this object above all others, makes him ambitious. Love and ambition for science have inspired all the great discoverers of the laws and of the forces of nature. Ambition urged Columbus to penetrate into unknown immensities of space. Love for the good, and ambition to be benefactors of their brethren, illuminated the moralists. Whoever has the consciousness of powers of whatever reach and nature, is ambitious to produce them, to make them creative and useful, to win acknowledgment. Whoever has faith in himself, in his convictions and principles, has the ambition to make them prevail. Whoever feels himself capable of doing good, will have the ambition to obtain assent, and by it the power to carry out his conceptions. Whoever acts and produces, aims uninterruptedly at reaching a superior degree, is ambitious of perfection, and thus of surpassing his equals, his competitors.

In a distorted social state, ambition, like most other passions, has its weak, shadowy and dark sides. It often takes root in an impure soil. When pouring out from a muddy fountain, then its course poisons or tarnishes. History bristles with evidences of those unscrupulous, accursed ambitions, which have so often imbrued her annals in blood. Such an ambition does not aim at winning convictions, but at depraving them; it aims at subduing to its will the will of others. But in communities based on reason, on publicity, on culture, on self-consciousness and self-government, the subterranean furrowings of such ambitions are less dangerous, and their final supremacy is to the utmost degree difficult, if not wholly impossible. Ambitious but depraved politicians in republics, appeal to and stir up the most degraded passions and appetites; they evoke to the surface, to action, what was slumbering or hidden under self-conscious shame. Thus they succeed. But their success is generally short. Their course runs rapidly through. The evil perpetrated by them prepares their fall. If the people becomes for a moment charmed by the conjurer, it soon recovers self-control. The better nature wins the upper hand, and the ambitious schemer preserves influence only over the refuse of the community. Such ambitions are sooner or later dissolved by the rays of light, in the crucible of publicity, among populations used to investigate, analyze and judge every member of society. In those republics which have been centralized in one single city or spot, an unprincipled, ambitious leader could seize at a stroke, and delude the masses in the forum, deciding in a state of excitement. So he could extort from them their assent, and involve the country in complications, overthrow the laws, change the form of the government. But in the thoroughly decentralized American commonwealth, such surprise of the public conscience, such success is mentally and materially impossible. The ambition of a despot, of a monarch, of ruling oligarchies and aristocracies, have been always mischief-brewing, as action succeeded to secret decisions, without discussion. An ambitious adviser or minister can seize upon the willing ear of the monarch, and shake the corner-stones of his own and other countries for personal elevation, but not thus easy is the task of politicians, who are surrounded by publicity, and depend on the assent of many. In the American communities, ambition must exclusively recur to the use of mental rather than material means. She must bribe by flattery, if not by conviction, rather than by material advantages. The ambitious must convince the intellect, or corrupt it, a work easy with few, but rather difficult with masses. Here ambition cannot reckon on the support of stupified tools, on that of brute force, on that of legionaries or bayonets. Even if the masses of people are momentarily carried away, intoxication evaporates, and self-interest restores the balance. A Pisistratus, a Cæsar, a Napoleon, even a Cromwell could not succeed among the American centrifugal communities. Generally the eyes of the people, though they might be easily dazzled for a moment, see clear on a cloudy day.

Self-government in its full action and development fosters ambition, nay, makes it necessary and unavoidable. But it possesses within itself the most efficient correctives, neutralizing aberrations, stopping, levelling and drying up the devastating current.

Various are the social and external influences which bear and press upon the holder of power, upon the government, and which share it directly or indirectly with the monarch, limited or absolute. In oligarchical and aristocratic republics some families preponderate, and have generally divided between themselves the cares and advantages of supreme rule. The same elements surround the thrones, and they influence the supreme decisions, the administration of enacted laws, and make their interests prevail supremely over that of the rest of the subjects. The landed or financial wealth of the country, that represented by commerce, industry, manufactures, all of them in some way or other group around the power, centre in the capital, as are attracted and absorbed by it, the various intellects, those representatives of the mental expansion of the country. Thus the seat of government is surrounded by the most eminent and preponderating compounds of the nation, by various concentrated interests, and receives from them inspiration, impulsion. The European capitals, forming the foci of the various resources and powers of the state, react on the government in the same proportion as they in their turn are materially and socially affected by the personality of the sovereign, by that of the court, of the officials, of the aristocracy. The ingredients thus combined and fermenting surround, to a great degree, and control the decisions and actions of legislative bodies. The various interests concentrated in the capitals, use the centralization in the same way as the governments. Generally all of them, but above all the aristocratic and the financial, combine with and support each other. The elective franchise every where, even in England, is for the most part absorbed in or directed from the capital, by the like combinations. By various ways and means the decisions of the centre, of the capital, are conveyed to the country, the elective bodies receive the password, and elect individuals pointed out to them either by the government or by the opposition.

In the formation as well as in the practical operation of the administration of the American commonwealth, and also in the formation of the legislative bodies, such influences, such modes of action are wholly impossible. Here the great cities are generally commercial emporiums, but often are not the capitals of the respective States, nor the seat of the government and of the legislatures. Those legislatures represent in immense majorities the country, its population, opinions and interests, and remain wholly independent of the pressure exercised by large cities, and by interests concentrated therein. Worldly social coteries—as is the case in European capitals—cannot therefore seize upon the representatives, circumvent them, and make them subservient to special ends. The administration and the legislature thus operate with more ease, are, so to speak, in a purer atmosphere, are not controlled and commanded as in Europe; and generally the interests of the country, that is of the majority, of the genuine people or nation, are paramount in the governmental and legislative action, overruling in case of conflict, the special interest of large cities.

The public service is coveted by aristocratic, by rich and influential individuals in Europe, on account of its stability of influence, and of other material advantages as well as on account of the social elevated distinction which it confers in societies, where the government and the ruling power form their keystone, their superior stratum. Public life, official position satisfy the cravings of vanity, clear up the existing social or conventional inequalities, and procure access to the highest social circles. Thus many of those who by a successful and industrious activity, have become artisans of their fortune, and secured wealth and independence—or those who by mental productiveness have rendered their names illustrious in science, arts, literature, aspire finally to public life, considering it as the supreme consecration of their laborious career. Through it they acquire influence, standing, ballast and consideration in a society still constituted out of aristocratic elements, still divided and classified according to certain positive, well defined and formal distinctions. In America, where the mass of influence is scattered among the people, and not condensed in a caste, in a civil hierarchy, or in a class, incentives and attractions, similar to those which prevail in Europe, disappear. Decentralization operates beneficially again in this, preserving the administrative branches from many contaminating influences and contacts. The cities or capitals of States are thus brought more directly under the influence of the country, more into a social and sociable intercourse with it than with the great commercial metropolis. Thus even the city of New York, one of the greatest centres of the civilized and commercial world, influences very slightly, if at all, the government of the State, or the population. Government in the American republics is not a power capable of conferring any stable social distinctions which do not exist in the political structure. Thus men who have acquired fortunes by commerce or industry, rarely take a direct and decided part in public affairs, although they participate actively in the general current of political life. They do not come before the public because they feel their incapacity for a new career, and want those special gifts required to secure popularity with the masses. Thus, contrary to what takes place in Europe, American legislatures rarely count among their members those representatives of argyrocracy, the only real superiority in the social conditions and gradations; and these bodies are thus less easily vitiated than the representative houses in Europe. The general and various elements, interests and occupations are really represented by artisans, operatives, farmers and professional men, and this to the fullest extent—a case rare and almost exceptional in Europe, even in England, where the nobility and gentry still form in parliament a large disproportion over the other classes and positions.

As in America only individuals residing in reality in the townships and districts can become elected to legislative functions, the elections cannot fall into the hands of committees such as are generally formed in European capitals, and impose their choice on the choice of the people. The American law and mode presents, therefore, one more barrier against centralization, one more guarantee of self-government. Members thus elected represent really the various needs, opinions and interests of their constituents, who make their choice with full knowledge of the elected, guided by their own judgment—for which in Europe is often substituted the bidding of a party, directing from one centre the popular decision. Thus the influence of a party, of a coterie, is often substituted for the free manifestation of the popular choice; and the elected representatives often support the interests patronizing them, instead of the true interests of the masses. Every one is familiar with the mode of proceeding and of vitiating the immediate expression of the popular will which is used by political parties in England. In France even during the short democratic exaltation of 1848, the central influence over the suffrage of the people was not given up, and the centralization preserved its hold. The celebrated admonitory circular of Carnot, then minister of public instruction, advising the rural population to elect for the national assembly members immediately from among themselves, was received with general animadversion by politicians and statesman, and was even condemned by the most decided reformers and apostles of the rights of the people. It was considered as a political crime, what in American communities is a natural result of democracy, decentralization, and of self-government.

As the capitals of the various States are not composed of the same ingredients as those of Europe, in the same way the capital of the Union, Washington, the seat of the Federal Government, bears no resemblance to the capitals of European states. It exists and depends wholly upon the Union, that is upon Congress, and thus receives materially and mentally its vitality from without. As a capital Washington is wholly subject to the influences which congregate there from all parts, and represent the opinions and social functions of the whole nation. The political as well as the social tone is given by the national representatives, and not by caste grouped eternally around the ruling power. Wealth again is scarcely represented in Congress. The composition of Congress corresponds to that of the State legislatures, as those for the most part form the stepping-stone for the former.

The various influences pointed out above as bearing upon the government in European states, are superseded in America—above all around Congress—by that of the so-called politicians, a plant of special growth, a sprouting out principally from the fermentation of free institutions. These politicians are the levers, the channels, but as often the managers of the public spirit. They correspond to the misused and common denomination of demagogues. Their existence in the present operation of democratic institutions is however unavoidable. If evils they are, they are necessary evils, canvassers and conveyances of the public wishes, of public opinion, which often they stir up, awaken, stimulate, and as often falsify. They are the real or presumed leaders of opinion in townships, districts and States, but they again depend upon the opinion, upon the good will, the confidence of those whom they lead. However baneful often may be their influence and doings, still the origin, the source, is democratic, and therefore unstable, and can be easily changed and overthrown,—and from this point of view the politicians can never demoralize or pervert a government or the people to the same extent, as can be done by the open or secret machinations of a hereditary deep-rooted aristocracy, the burrowing of the roots of absolute power, or the corrupting breath of the concentrated moneyed corporations, bankers, brokers and exchangers.

The working of self-government is an uninterrupted trial. Over the deep and firm principle, the fluctuations of opinion rise on the surface. They are incessant, they seemingly change, modify or transform the surface, carrying away individuals and masses. Stability reposes in public-mindedness. It is therefore the vital atmosphere; without it self-government must dwindle and die out. And public-mindedness and an intense interest in general affairs animates the masses, as well as the most of those whom the turn of fortune has elevated above the general level. If even the immense majority of the men who possess wealth do not directly try to enter upon a public career, they nevertheless are interested more or less deeply in public policy, in general questions. The most eminent intellects, the most cultivated minds, not only do not keep aloof from the general current, but often contribute to throw light upon questions of general significance and interest. The existing political *blases* are only poor, exhausted, narrow-minded individuals, who, under this assumed affectation of disgust or apathy, cover disappointment or mental deficiency. Some European writers seem to be under the impression that in general, political activity is abandoned by the so-called superior minds to turbulent, unprincipled, impure meddlers—that better men shrink in disgust from the doings of a popular government. This state of apathy has not seized however upon spirits of real vitality and power. The immense majority throughout all the various social conditions,—rich and poor,—feel too well that states become truly great and powerful when each single individual considers himself a link and an active member in the great whole, and does not avoid or even hesitate to bear individually his part of the public burdens, to contribute in a special way to the work which aims at the good of the community.

Nowhere in the political and governmental structure of the American commonwealth, any more than in social and mental development, are to be met the centres which attract and keep together the people by mental and material chains and links, like those in other states and nations, directing, and giving impulsion, nay even absorbing the various activities of the population. Upon such centres depended and still depend the societies of the European world; these centres have various names and functions; they form the authoritative pivots on which turn and group the whole system of social forces. They are the foci of light, the hearts or the heads of the social bodies. Society and its philosophers still firmly believe in their unavoidable necessity. It would seem therefore that the American communities ought to dissolve, being continually under the centrifugal action of those atoms of independent, individual sovereignty. But as attraction is the all-powerful, albeit invisible band of the sidereal and planetary creation; so the free association and combination of forces, of interests, of rights and of duties,—and the generality of mental culture, those fruits of freedom—are the invisible cements of the American communities.

Self-government is the healthy, everlasting maturity, is the full manhood of man in the social state. All faculties and powers develope themselves therein to a vigorous activity. Youthful not senile maturity is the cardinal condition of progress and growth in the mental as in the material world. On youthful maturity therefore depends the mental development, as well as the destinies of society. All the great actions in history, as well as nearly all great ideas, conceptions, discoveries, the loftiest inspirations in arts and poetry, have been accomplished in the prime of years, and before the turn, the approach to old age. Self-governing society alone can, so to say, arrest and perpetuate the duration of this pithy and rich social and mental productivity; an epoch for man as well as for society, of lofty and generous impulses, of high creations and noble and salutary decisions. Senility in man or society produces diffidence and pusillanimity, conceit and inactivity, extinguishes faith in ideas and convictions, and attempts to arrest movement and progress, to bring the world of ideas and of creative productions, together with the social development, to a stand-still, to reduce all in nature to a routine. Senility alone despairs of the efficacy of self-government.

The pliancy, elasticity and expansiveness of self-government render it eminently adapted to self-development and to higher progressive solutions. Thus already the new States growing up in the West, in many of their constitutive structures and institutions, show a progress over their models in the East, adapting them to new combinations and conditions. These Western States, the purest offshoots of national self-consciousness, assert their origin more boldly than their generators. They have no other traditions, no past, no historical connection with the colonial state of dependency in political, any more than in mental and material relations. In the West, therefore, is to be given the fullest expression and solution of all the mental and social terms and combinations evoked, created by the inauguration of this new epoch of pure self-governing democracy. No definitive progress or amelioration hitherto marks any of the liberal European institutions, modelled either on the English type or on that of the French era of 1793. And the reason may be, that those imitations are always introduced ready-made, and introduced authoritatively, either by kings or by social or political reformers and theorists, without direct participation of the people, of the public reason and sense. But each new constitution of a free self-governing State, framed by the direct action of the people, is generally a marked amelioration, and contains a broader conception of wants as well as of conditions, than did the older preceding ones.

Self-government therefore, in the succession of ages, considered as an effort of humanity for the advancement and amelioration of her social structure and relations, is the highest product, soaring above all its preceding forms; forms more or less vital and inherent to society, and all which in given epochs served to facilitate or protect its growth and development. Self-government stands firmly the test of philosophical analysis, answers the most transcendent speculations. And if humanity is to be modelled according to abstract types, self-government is its present most perfect typical form. It stands the test and the trial of practical execution and application, as well as that even of the most practical and direct availability. It may have its epochs of terrible and dangerous probation, of tension and even of crepitation; but such menacing epochs—a common lot of vigor and life—will find in the principle itself the soothing cure. Its imperfections and deficiencies disappear when compared with the pre-existent social forms, and can only be found salient when compared with a new and higher standard, and thus for the time a relatively ideal one. All the other social constitutive ideas of the past are exhausted, effete, worn out, degenerated, disordered, honey-combed through and through, and finally powerless and unproductive. All of them look up from below to the American system, expecting from it a higher solution and salvation, all—whatever may be the conceit and the hypocrisy of their representatives and mouth-pieces—acknowledge that the American original self-governing system has already reached regions of higher purity and serenity, and accordingly more favorable to the health and development of the human race.

CHAPTER V.

SLAVERY.

It is the lot of the American Union to represent man in his highest and nearly typical social development, by the side of the most appalling degradation. It is the lot of American institutions to evince that the noblest realization of freedom, the purest conception of manhood hitherto known, can be marred, distorted and prostituted. At the side of the highest solutions attainable by society in its present stage, as manifested in democracy, in self-government, in the elevation and consecration of labor in its all-embracing sense, as the loftiest social function, there stands Slavery, with its degrading, agonizing contradictions. There it stands, bidding defiance to the moral sense of humanity, to religious conceptions, to civilization, to social progress;—bidding defiance to the universal condemnation transmitted by past ages, and repeated more and more loudly by the European, that is, by the civilized world. There it stands, perverting and debasing all the cardinal notions of American social and political association; notions which alone constitute its intrinsic worth. There stands slavery, poisoning in the substance the promises anticipated by our race, from the fruition of seeds which have been here scattered broadcast by reason, conscience and freedom.

Slavery, as now maintained in the States of the Union, as it has eaten itself, not only into the political and municipal institutions, but into social, domestic and family life, into the mind, the conscience, the judgment, the reasonings, the religion, the human and animal feelings, the comprehension of the rights, obligations, and duties of a man, of a citizen, of a member of society, as it has permeated those devoted to its growth and preservation;—in one word, this modern American slavery differs wholly from what, under a similar name, has prevailed during past ages in Asia or Europe. It bears no resemblance to the slavery of antiquity, nor to the slavery and serfdom known in Europe. From the legendary or historical origin of society in the remotest antiquity, from the primitive formation of nations and empires in the East, down to Greece, Rome and modern Europe, never has slavery been made the paramount condition and question of social structure, of political and domestic economy. Nowhere has slavery so fully overloaded and absorbed the political atmosphere as in the American Commonwealth. Nowhere does its hideous spectre face the investigator, the observer, on every step, in every political move, development or complication. Nowhere has slavery been the source, the reason or the occasion for struggles between states, friendly or inimical. Never has it formed the main attraction for obtaining the supreme power, or has it been the final object for the direction of the internal and external affairs of a nation. The conquerors of the past, from the mythical Nimrod to the last of the Roman Emperors, those who tower over the history of European nations, did not levy wars and imbrue the earth, did not overthrow empires, subduing nations and territories, for the sake of extending domestic and municipal slavery. In all times, in all nations, in all religions, in all theories, slavery has been considered as a painful sore in the social body and organism; for the first time in the history of the race, slavery is hailed as the substance of all human, social, and political relations.

Not in the anti-slavery or abolitionist literature, not in the various anti-slavery utterances and manifestations, did I study and become acquainted with American slavery. That literature is wholly unknown to me, as are personally unknown the foremost leaders of the abolition party. I have scarcely ever been present at any abolition or even anti-slavery lecture, oration or meeting; and never has slavery formed a subject of my conversations with Theodore Parker, Sumner, Phillips, or any of the persons to whom I have been attracted by a congenial turn of mind and feeling, by similar convictions, studies and pursuits. Mr. Calhoun's Works and Speeches have been the object of my conscientious study. As far as possible I have tried to master the pro-slavery literature. Political speeches, statistical, philosophical, historical, economical, pro-slavery disquisitions, sermons, orations, tracts, reasonings, justifications, defences, explanations, are the sources in which I have studied American slavery. The legislative enactments, the laws of the slavery States, the pro-slavery press South and North, the actions and tone of political men, have been for me the exponents of the working of slavery.

Neither in any way do I intend to advocate an immediate, direct, absolute emancipation of the enslaved race. Such a violent passage from a domestic state on which reposes the economic husbandry of the southern part of the Union, and with which agricultural and commercial interests are thus variously intertwined and connected together, a passage without previous preparatory measures, without a gradual transition, would produce inexpressible evil, ruin and destruction. Even for the enjoyment of orderly liberty a previous apprenticeship ought to be made. The more so, when millions of men are to be reinstated in rights, after having been for generations systematically degraded to a condition scarcely above the brutes, which scarcely recognizes in them any human and social qualities. But if the disorder is not at once curable, its corrosive character and influence ought the more to be exposed.

Reason, religion, morality, knowledge, study, the sciences, history, economy, the social, domestic and family relations, all converge to one focus. All are valued only so far as they authorize or justify slavery, in the conception and appreciation of its apostles, supporters, and disciples. Its corrosion gnaws equally at the products of mental and material labor, and the intellectual domain is blighted by its theories in the same degree as the earth's surface. This mental distortion strikes not only individuals, but is chronically rooted in generations, and thus stretches far out into the future. The normal healthy state of reason on the subject of slavery is affected for long years to come. Thus logic, learning, conscience are twisted, put on the rack, to extort from them evidences in favor of slavery. Unwillingly one touches and stirs this mental and intellectual putrefaction.

The African race is doomed to eternal slavery, maintain the theorists of bondage; and this, they assert, is proved by the inferiority of that race, by its historical insignificance throughout the whole existence, throughout the whole history of the human family.

But the African kept in bondage in America, was not conquered by his present master on his own soil. The African was sold to the white man into slavery as a victim, as a prisoner of war, by another victorious African. In the same way slavery has been established and maintained throughout the world, from the remotest times. All the races and tribes of Asia and Europe, for long centuries, have thus had their periods of slavery; all were conquered, and the prisoners of war, nay often whole cities and districts, were sold by the victors into slavery. And from these facts and partial events, which have occurred repeatedly, the conclusion might have been drawn that the white race, or some of its branches, have been at those remote epochs likewise doomed by an absolute law to slavery.

The destinies, the qualities, the mental capacities of the African race, in equity as well as in logic, cannot be comprehended, judged, and appreciated from the part of it which is kept in bondage, transformed into chattels on this continent. Those are debased by slavery, and thus find themselves not only in an abnormal state, but in one which at once destroys manhood and the mental capacities. Slavery forcibly reduces them to a condition far inferior to that of the animals. Not from crippled nature can be drawn the criteria of its power.

If the absolute mental inferiority of the African race should be even an incontestable fact, established by the history of this branch of the human family, there are many reasons for which this inferiority ought to be considered as transient and not definite. Those who admit the aims and the direct interference of God in the management of human affairs, ought not to have left unobserved the following facts. According to their creed, God distributed men over the earth, and assigned to races, families, tribes, various and distinct continents and regions. In this distribution, he has given to the black race for their special use a great and rich continent. For uncounted ages the other races, above all the white one, either Semitic or Japhetic, or Indo-European, have attempted to conquer and get hold of Africa, invading it on all sides; and still this invasion remains limited mostly to the outskirts of that part of the globe. Only in the northern strip have the invading races succeeded in getting a firm footing, in establishing themselves definitively. The European takes hold and domiciliates himself over the earth, penetrates and subsists in all climates, nearly under the poles and under the tropics, on the equatorial line of Asia and America;—but hitherto Africa is his tomb. In the same latitudes he has subdued the aborigines of Asia and America; but in Africa the natives as well as the soil resist him. Nature or providence seems to watch jealously over Africa and say to the European, "Do not penetrate here under pain of death." The aborigines of the American continent, the Australians, the Polynesians, and other primitive occupants of various points of the globe, disappear, melt before the advancing European, before the white race. The African preserves and maintains his rights, his patrimony. If God therefore husbands the destinies of races, then this impenetrability of Africa, this indestructibility of its inhabitants, is not accidental;—it is the result of higher designs, inaccessible to man's penetration. Time will disclose them. Time will draw aside some of the folds of the curtain which veils the future destinies of the human family. History has in its recesses inexhaustible events and apparitions. Allusion has already been made to the cardinal historical law, that of the successive appearance and development of races, families, nations, and states. The future of the African race may be protected by that law. The blacks are now, and have been, as it is commonly maintained, for countless centuries brutes and savages. But what is this period even of forty centuries in the infinite course of the ages? Thirty, and even twenty centuries ago, portions of the Celts, Germans, Scandinavians, Saxons, who made human sacrifices to their deities, were in a state not very different from that of the

Africans. They drank from the skulls of their enemies; some Caledonian tribes were anthropophagi, and all of them were savages, murderers, enslaving each other, pirates, and robbers. It may be doubted if the African tribes surpass all others in savagery, through which the human race passed, previous to appearing in history, previous to entering in part on a new and superior stage. Italy was once inhabited by anthropophagi. Two thousand years ago darkness prevailed over Germany, over the north of Europe; and two thousand years hence Africa may probably shine with civilization.

Those who see in the Scriptures something more than a fragment of the oldest historical records, deduce from the progeny of Ham the whole African or black race. But the same scriptural records establish, and the primitive legendary recollections of the East confirm the fact, that these descendants of Ham founded the first empires and cities, and thus, it can be said, originated polity and civilization. The Hamites or Cushites extended over Asia Minor, Syria, Persia, along the Persian Gulf to the Indian peninsula. So speak myths, analogy, and the roots of names of places and ancient cities, and the most remote traditions. Nimrod and his progeny were Hamites, and around the mouth of the Tigris, of the Euphrates, down to that of the Indus, originally dwelt the black, or, as now called, the African brotherhood. The Persian Gulf was called in remote antiquity the Ethiopian Sea. There the Cushite ruled over the whites and intermixed with them; und the great Eastern founder of the first empire, whom the dim Eastern and Persian legends call Zohack, was in all probability at the utmost a mulatto, Semiramide, his mother, being of the white, then the subjugated stock. This immense empire was subsequently overthrown, conquered and superseded by men descending from the southern slopes of the Paropamisian Range, now Hindoo-Rosh or Himmalaya, from the table-lands of Iran, and bringing with them in the conquered regions their Pehlvi and Sanscrit language, the mother of all European dialects. Those conquerors were the Indo-Europeans, the common ancestry of the European nations. In times so remote as hardly to be reached by positive chronology, this first conquest is to be discerned. These Arrians subdued nations living along the Euphrates and the Indus, nations already enjoying culture and civilization, while the invaders were savage hordes. The Chinese records mention this event, and their testimony confirms the physiological differences of the two races. They call the Indo-Europeans or Arrians horse-faced, on account of the oval form of their face. The Cushites who inhabited the slopes of Himmalaya along the Indus, and whom the Arrians invaded, are called by the Chinese the monkey-faced. The Mongolian or round-faced, or, as others call them, Turanians, aided the Arrians in their conquest. These Chinese records coincide with the remotest Persian traditions.

The Cushites were likewise the inhabitants of the Nile, as were the Ethiopians. The ancient Egyptians were not of Semitic origin, nor does their language or civilization connect them with any of the aboriginal Asiatic races. The descendants of the Egyptian colonists planted in Kolchis by Sesostris or Ramses, preserved for long generations the characteristics of the African race, dark complexion, and black, crisped hair. The kings of the eighteenth and nineteenth dynasty have a decided negro type, as shown in the statues of Tutmes III. and Amenophis III. preserved in the British Museum in London. Besides, the testimony of Herodotus is paramount for me to all others, and every modern historical discovery and research always confirms the veracity, the authority of the father of history. And Herodotus says "that the Egyptians were black, and had short, crisped hair, and that the skulls of the Egyptians were by far thicker than those of the Persians; that they could scarcely be broken by a big stone, while a Persian skull could be broken by a pebble." All these characteristics mark principally the African or the Negro race. Subsequently the continual influx of Asiatics and Europeans, as was observed by Volney, might have modified or changed the populations of Egypt, and produced a mongrel creation.* Under the Persian kings of the lineage of Achaemenes, blacks as ministers, satraps, ruled and exercised a powerful influence over the great Persian empire. A black eunuch, Bagoâs, put on the Persian throne Darius Codomannus, vanquished by Alexander. A black, Batis, governor of Gaza, was the only one who, by his military skill and courage, defeated some time and arrested the conquering career of Alexander, the greatest military leader of past or modern times.†

The predestination of the African race to eternal slavery is based in pro-slavery theories on the fact, that the African populations are enslaved on their own soil. But such has been the lot at various epochs of nearly all

* Numbers of Jews have the greatest resemblance to the American mulattoes. Sallow carnation complexion, thick lips, crisped black hair. Of all the Jewish population scattered over the globe, one fourth dwells in ancient Poland. I am therefore well acquainted with their features. On my arrival in this country I took every light-colored mulatto for a Jew. Could not these Jewish mulattoes have descended from some crossing between the Jews and the Egyptians at a time previous to the Exodus?

† Alexander was superior even to Napoleon in foresight, as well as in having won not only pitched battles, but taken by siege cities whose fortifications were by nature and art the strongest known, of their kind. Napoleon, with the exception of Toulon, never directed the siege of a fortress.

the other races on the earth, and above all in Europe. They likewise, as are now the Negro tribes, were for generations and centuries kept in bondage by rulers and masters of their own kind, or by others conquering and subduing them. So, after the overthrow of the Roman Empire, the populations of Italy, Gallia, Spain, were enslaved by the conquerors. Slavery existed among the German races, among the Anglo-Saxons before and after they conquered Britain. Very likely the greatest part of the ancestry of the settlers and actual slaveholders were once slaves, and wore for generations the iron collar, with the name of their Saxon—kindred in blood—masters; or as boors and villeins were treated with the same cruel contempt by the Norman conquerors, as the blacks are treated here by those descendants of once oppressed serfs. History does not generally sustain the pretensions of the southern oligarchs to their descent from Cavaliers. For centuries the nobility of all the European nations considered as impure and contaminating the blood, any connection or alliance with burghers or peasants, to whom, according to European classifications, belong the white inhabitants of the United States. A southerner cannot feel more repulsion to alliance with a black, than was felt once by a haughty nobleman, careful of his purity of blood, to an affinity or connection with an ignoble family. There still exist many aristocratical families in Europe who nourish this prejudice.

The African despots sell their subjects or their prisoners into slavery. But, as has been already mentioned, such was the custom from uncounted ages in the ancient and in the modern European world. The Elector of Hesse sold to England his subjects to fight against America. Is it to be inferred that Hessians are predestined to eternal bondage?

To the enslaved race on this continent are denied the higher faculties of the mind and of the soul, which are common to the other inhabitants of the globe. If it should be really so—which however is not the case—it is the bondage which has crushed, rooted out or nipped in the bud all the germs of those faculties. The mental inferiority of the African does not differ much from the inferiority in which groped and lingered all the other races and families, before their turn came to issue from darkness. The African has latent all the powers with which man is endowed. If those germs are not active, or are inferior in intensity and expansion, nevertheless they exist. The African speaks, thinks, believes, loves, hates, reasons, comprehends, and therefore he is capable of being initiated into a higher life. However distant the hour of initiation may be, strike it will for the African race. Impartial scientific men, who do not theorize for the support or justification of slavery, who have investigated and observed the African race on its own ground—all these thinkers, physiologists and pyschologists, recognize in the blacks the germs of all the faculties of mind and heart, only differently proportioned from those in the Caucasian. Some recognize in them a greater intensity of affection than in the white race. Not one classifies them on that account—as is done in pro-slavery science—as an intermediate link between brutes and man. Even in their degradation by American slavery, the Negroes alone modify to a certain degree the gloominess of the country. The Negroes alone have minstrelsy and melodies of peculiar intonation and beauty. They alone re-echo American original songs, which are adopted as national by the white race.*

* When a foreigner asks and inquires about national melodies, he is unanimously directed to hear the so called *negro melodies.*

Further, like the white man, the African loves his native land, fights for its independence, resists as he can invasion—although fearful odds are against him. The African, degraded and enslaved, loves liberty, understands how to conquer it, as was shown at St. Domingo. The transition to a better social state on that island is seemingly slow. But it ought not to be forgotten from what a state of slavish abjection the black race there emerged; that scarcely a second generation is in possession of human rights; that after the conquest of independence, the emancipated have to make a thorough and most detailed apprenticeship in order to become men again; that their contact with civilization was and is difficult, and often impossible; and finally that Europe, for centuries the hearth and laboratory of civilization, has still in its bosom masses that are nearly as ignorant and degraded as the Haytians. Slow and toilsome is the work of humanization. In the English West Indies the work of emancipation was not the result of violence, bloodshed and destruction, but was brought forth in an orderly way, by tuition. The internal economy of these islands became recast, large plantations were divided into small farms. Very naturally this transformation for a few years must have reacted on the culture of the soil, and lessened its production. The emancipated were to make the mental and material apprenticeship for their new condition. No apprenticeship whatever is immediately productive. But already the new generation, grown under liberty, compensates for the lost time and for the losses occasioned by the economical revulsion. Recent reports and statistics show that the culture and the productivity of the British West Indies are continually on the increase, as is the prosperity of the newly formed free, and therefore laborious men.

Carelessness, heedlessness, want of foresight, laziness,

disposition to lie, and all the like vices, attributed to the black race in America, even theft, are not inherent in the African nature, but their germs are to be found in humanity in general. Slavery, degradation, developes them; they are the rich manure which propitiates an exuberant growth; and the like vices have been and are common to the white slaves and serfs, and to otherwise degraded, although even free and independent, but corrupted members of the best cultivated society.

The principal psychological inferiority attributed to the African race is based on the assertion that it never could elevate itself to a spiritual conception of Deity, and that fetichism prevails in Africa. But fetichism under various kinds was more or less known to other races, even to families of the Caucasian race. In primitive races, fetichism is always the forerunner of polytheism and of the worship of nature. And have not for centuries the most spiritual religious conceptions been debased and stained by fetichism in the midst of Europe?

The physiological differences, brought forward by pro-slavery science, as conclusive of the absolute inferiority of the African race, are not sustained by truly scientific and disinterested men. Owen, Flourens, Pritchard, Miller, Bachmann, Humboldt, and a host of other genuine savants, find in the physical conformation and structure of the negro as well as in the laws of hybridity, quite different phenomena, and no such cardinal contrasts to the white man, as the pro-slavery physiologists assert. The same researches, observations and analogies give, therefore, different results, according as they serve impartial science, or become diverted for a peculiar purpose. The naturalist, St. Hilaire, maintains that the white man, equally with the negro, in the animal ascending concatenation, proceeds from the ape. But even the sense-sharpening instruments seem to work diversely in Europe and in America. Thus the microscope represents different minutiæ there and here. In the United States the microscope discovers that the negro is covered with wool, while the lens of a Haenle, the founder of microscopical anatomy, shows beyond doubt that the hair of the white man and that of the negro is of one and the same kind. The pro-slavery microscope distorts or changes the form of the cellular tissues of the muscles, the epidermis of the blacks, while the truly scientific instrument shows that the black and white tissues are alike. Here it is decided that the pigment which darkens the skin of the African is a speciality to him; but Simon, a celebrated microscopic anatomist in Europe, together with other men of science, demonstrates beyond doubt, that the dark circle surrounding the nipple of a white woman contains precisely the same pigment which universally colors the skin of the negro.

The physical as well as psychological differences which exist, are not of such weight as to fatally reduce the African race to an irredeemable inferiority. But should even this be the case; on no human, moral, or social grounds can it be justifiable to depress the race still more; to debase it; to deprive it, by slavery and by unparalleled systematic oppression, of the feebler attributes of manhood which it has received from nature. If even the negro should be unable to use his powers with the same vigor as the white man, he is not therefore to be transformed into a chattel.

But these statements and assertions remain unsustained by science or by history, which shows that the branches of the Hamitic race were the first founders of states, of polity, and of cities, and thus the first inventors of useful and mechanic arts, without which no culture of the soil, no construction of walls and dwellings, was possible. The cardinal distinction and pre-eminence of the Caucasian, Indo-European, or Japhetian race, consists not thus absolutely in the power of invention, or initiation. This faculty is the lot of the Asiatics among the descendants of Shem and of Ham, by whom the Japhetian, the Arrian, was initiated into the rudiments of material and mental civilization. The peculiarity of the European consists primarily in the boundless power of expansion, in the impulse, the inclination to sow to the right and to the left, to scatter and implant his ideas, to extend his activity in all directions. Easily impressible, and urged by inward impulse as well as by external events, more sensitive to their action than the other members of the human family, the European became the *anima movens* of the globe. But he disavows those of his race who on this superiority base the right to transform into eternal brutism their less fortunate, or even their apparently less endowed fellow-creatures.

The absolute necessity in America of maintaining the colored population in bondage is supported by an axiom, very unskilfully twisted out of general history. It is asserted that whenever a superior race comes in contact with an inferior one, the second must inevitably become enslaved by the former. Never was a greater fallacy brought forward. Its concoctors are bound above all to clearly establish wherein genuine superiority consists. Whether it is civility, advanced culture, and diversified mental and material development, that constitute a superiority, or only daring, physical force, warlike propensities, military organization and discipline. Nearly all the conquests, and thus the contacts, of different races recorded in history, were made by nations inferior in civility, by mere barbarians, over others more developed. The Medes and Persians of Cyrus were far inferior in every kind of culture to the Lydians, Assyrians, Egyptians, and all the other flourishing states of Asia Minor. These states were subdued. The prisoners of war, the populations of cities taken by storm, became transformed or were sold into slavery; but nowhere have whole races or nations been subjected to domestic bondage. The Macedonians of Philip and Alexander were thorough barbarians, when they subdued Greece, and they did not enslave the Greeks, but on the contrary, they were civilized, grecised, by them. Neither were the Romans of the first centuries after the founding of the city superior in culture to the Samnites, the Etrurians, and the Greek population of Italy. Having extended their domination over the peninsula, the Romans did not make chattels of the Italiots by the wholesale. The Roman conquest in Gaul, as over the world as then known, was not for establishing domestic bondage over all the various subdued races. The number of slaves increased principally by the warlike process above pointed out.

When the races of the North overran and destroyed the Roman Empire, they were barbarians. These invaders to be sure enslaved the populations on whose necks they established their dominion, more generally than any former conquerors recorded in history. As a race, the Germans issued from one and the same root as those whom they enslaved. They had the same origin, whether considered as descendants of the Japhetians, of the Caucasians, or of the Indo-Europeans. The enslavement was the result of events, and not of any absolute law ruling and regulating the destinies of the human kind. And, as it has been pointed our in another chapter, all these northern conquerors in the course of time became humanized, civilized, absorbed, assimilated, recast by those among whom they settled, and over whom they ruled. The character of the French, Spaniards, and Italians, has no traits in common with that of the Germans. The Normans conquered the Anglo-Saxons, and partly enslaved them, although both Normans and Saxons descended originally from the Scandinavians. And the original character of these sea-rovers was almost completely changed by contact with the civility of France, and with the nations among whom they settled. These Normans, although considered by some as forming a superior race, and appeared as such in the eleventh and twelfth centuries, mixed, blended, and assimilated with peculiar facility with the populations among which they established themselves; and thus in new conditions and conjunctures soon changed their original character. What a difference between the English and French Norman! The nobility of Sicily and Naples descending from Tancred, Robert Guiscard, and their followers, in the next generations lost nearly all traits of resemblance to the Normans of France, and to those of England under the Plantagenets. The fierce Arab-Mahometans were modified by the Syrians in Bagdad, Aleppo, Damascus, etc., as well as by the Moors in Africa. The Tartars, as conquerors, were absorbed by the Chinese; and, as races, both belong to the Mongolian stock.

Few, very few, are the contrary examples, where the barbarian conqueror resisted the absorbing influence of the more civilized conquered, and preserved over him the absolute sway of physical force. And in such cases oppression was never transformed into absolute domestic slavery. The Turks are the most salient illustrations of this in their relations with the Greeks, Slavi, Armenians, and other Christian populations. But will any one maintain that the Turkomans are a superior race to the others? The religious hostility of the Moslems to Christianity alone placed an insurmountable barrier, and prevented amalgamation and relaxation of oppression.

Should the historical evidences be all in favor of the pro-slavery axiom, even then they could have no bearing whatever on the relations of the white with the colored man in the United States. The European came in contact on this continent not with the African, but with the Indian. It is therefore the Indian who was to be enslaved, if that fallacious axiom has any meaning. The African was imported here by stealth, by robbery, by a most infamous traffic, not as a nation, but as an individual, already a victim of brute force. To justify and logically confirm their theory, the advocates of this axiom, as well as the supporters of American slavery, ought to fit out a great expedition and make a descent upon Africa, meet the negro face to face, conquer him, and establish their beloved slavery in his native land.

In our epoch the conquests made by European nations over really or apparently inferior races or tribes, and the establishment of European dominion over them, is not followed by domestic slavery, or even by any kind of serfdom or villanage. France does not enslave the Arabs and Bedouins, but raises them to civilized life, confers upon them equal civil rights with Frenchmen. England, notwithstanding the bloody fiscal pressure upon the Hindoos, does not deprive them of civil rights nor of culture, but propagates amongst them civilization, erects schools, and treats them as human beings. England does not enslave the Australians or the Papuans, nor deprive them of human and civil rights. Russia, although serfdom prevails in her bosom, does not extend it over the conquered tribes, whether settled or nomadic, pastoral or roving. And thus, by an extraordinary anomaly, those weaker, inferior populations enjoy more human rights than even the immense majority of the domineering race.

In this sacrilegious way the annals of our race are ransacked to bear evidence of the necessity or of the blessedness of slavery, although they teach on every page that the ancient slavery was different in origin and in principle from the American bondage. It was not based on any physical or psychological inferiority or difference in one race that was doomed to serve another, but it resulted from one paramount fact, war and conquest. The Spartans, those fierce oligarchs of the Grecian world, who cultivated no arts whatever, conquered the Helots, the descendants of the Pelasgi, the first civilizers of Southern Europe, and not at all an inferior race to the Dorians. They brutalized their victims deliberately and purposely by every vice and crime, and above all by fostering intemperance among the Helots, to keep them enslaved more easily. In great dangers the Spartans bestowed on the Helots the right of citizenship. Often cognate and mostly kindred races, tribes of the same family and language, enslaved each other. The slaves mentioned in the Scriptures and possessed by the Jews, were of the same Semitic race as the Hebrews. So were mostly all the slaves of the ancient nations, often their previous neighbors. So Greeks possessed Greeks as slaves. Plato was once sold into slavery. Philip of Macedon destroyed thirty-two Chalkidic cities, and sold their inhabitants into slavery. Alexander, after destroying Thebes, sold all the population into slavery, and the purchasers were mostly other Beotians, kindred of the Thebans. So Romans made slaves when at war with other kindred Italiot populations. At one time Roman citizens could be sold into slavery by their creditors. And yet slavery among the Romans and its influence on the fate of the Roman republic, form the principal pivots on which American slavery is theoretically propped.

The power of the Roman master was absolute, was that of life and death. It was pitilessly and cruelly exercised. But absolute and tyrannical was the power of the Roman father over his wife and over his children. The Roman moral tone in all conditions and relations, was in general stern and cruel. The Romans did not consider slavery as a social corner-stone, without which liberty could not exist. The Roman legist who resumed in short sentences the antique sense of morality and justice, calls slavery emphatically a state contrary to nature—*contra naturam*, as did before him Aristotle, Plato, and others. How different from our southern Papinians and Tribonians! The servile origin of the manumitted disappeared at the farthest in the third generation. But in the South the stain is eternal. The material interests of a slave, his earnings or *peculium*, were under the protection of the Roman prætor. Adrian, the Antonines legislated for the protection of the slaves. The Roman law punished with death any one who unlawfully enslaved a freeman. Slaves in antiquity were not grown, bred specially for the market, as is the case in Virginia; the masculine by far outnumbering the feminine slaves. The children of slaves were instructed in schools, in arts and sciences. Slaves have been architects, physicians, authors, actors. Nearly all the monuments which have survived the destructive force of time, had slaves for architects, for constructors. According to some historians, Vitruvius, whose architectural writings are still authority, was a slave. Many Greek rhetoricians, grammarians, philosophers, were Roman slaves. The purest moralist of antiquity, Epictetus, lived many years the slave of a bad Roman master. And shall any body assert that the Greeks were an inferior race?

History teaches that in proportion as slavery increased, the spirit of ancient Rome became faint. With the extension of slavery, the free yeomanry was either destroyed or reduced to a degraded social state, like that of the southern free-white laborers and small cultivators. Not slaves but Cincinnatus himself ploughed his farm, when the deputies brought him the news of his election by his fellow-citizens to the dignity of a dictator. When in the course of time the soil of Rome was owned by wealthy patricians, and worked all over with slaves, Rome had no more the Fabii, the Horatii Cocles, the Scævolæ. Roman virtue vanished before slavery, and Roman demoralization went hand in hand with its increase. In the first centuries of the republic—the blossoming period of Roman virtue—slaves were made in war alone; and if the prisoners were not ransomed, then hereditary birth in bondage constituted the status of a slave. In the age of the degeneration of the republic—in those of the dissolution of the spirit and laxity of the laws, the husbandry of estates by slave labor was carried out by systematic hunting for men. What for America was Africa, for Rome at that time was Asia Minor. Pirates or slave-traders, principally from the island of Crete and from Cilicia, stole men in the Greek Archipelago and around the eastern and southern shores of the Mediterranean. It is said that at the great slave-mart of Delos (the American New-Orleans), on one day ten thousand slaves were bought and sold.

In the pagan world, divines, moralists, philosophers and statesmen did not exalt slavery. No one represented it as an idyllic state of society, or sang its praise and blessedness. Orations and speeches were not made to the Roman or Greek people to exalt bondage. Pliny, Seneca, Plutarch spoke of it in mild and extenuating language.

The Roman world fell. The destruction was not occasioned by the relaxation of slavery—a favorite assertion of the American pro-slavery philosophers. On the contrary, the extension of slavery was an efficient and primary cause, among many secondary causes, of the downfall of Rome. Slavery deprived Italy of vigorous, devoted, intelligent, energetic and active citizens. Large estates worked by slaves, deteriorating the soil and its culture, reduced the population. Poverty, misery was at the basis, and above it hovered the wealthy, effeminate, debased, immoral and luxurious slaveholder. The *amor patriæ* had been long consumed to cold ashes. The most unbounded and sordid egotism filled the mind and the heart of the people.

The Roman world fell because a new light rose upon mankind, a light which the ancient pagan religious and social institutions could not stand. Because the materialized conception of God and man was to give way before a higher, spiritual one. The time of the pagan civilization, with all its religious and social ideas, was accomplished. The human race received a new password; it was to be impregnated with a purer and subtler essence. A new and loftier order was to prevail. Higher aspirations were to inspire man, and the past was to be blotted out or changed. The past was doomed to destruction. The idolatrous worship of the living Cæsar could not exist by the side of the worship of the crucified Christ. Rome fell because the *civis Romanus*, the highest human dignity at that time, was superseded by the higher one of *civis Christianus*, which signified brotherhood, love and self-denial. The Roman world fell, because mankind was to be initiated into union, and could not move further, as it was forcibly encompassed in material unity. The individualism of the ancient world was to make place for humanity.

Slavery survived the Roman world, maintains southern philosophical science, and European Christian nations based their existence upon it. The most superficial insight into history shows that feudal slavery was in no way considered as a social constructive element.

The inhabitants of the Roman Empire, slaves or free, became enslaved by the new conquerors. The conquered remained attached to the soil, which they cultivated for themselves and for their masters. Villanage went hand in hand with bondage. They could not be detached from the earth. They also preserved the right of family, and families were not separated. At the commencement of the mediæval epoch, therefore, slavery did not possess this fierce feature which it has in America. The conquered were not sold in markets, neither could the master carry his slaves into any other region or land, as is done by the American planter in his migrations in search of a better and virgin soil.

The slave-trade and slave-markets existed at that epoch in various spots of Europe,—in France, above all in Lyons; in various cities of Italy, especially in Venice and Rome; and in some cities on the Baltic. But the marketable slaves were exclusively prisoners of war, or persons carried away by depredatory invasions of the Normans, Berbers and others. In the South and the West of Europe the slave-trade was principally supplied by prisoners taken from the Moors in Spain and other Mahomedans of the Mediterranean shores, and in the East and North, by those made by the Germans among various Sclavic tribes living between the Baltic and the Adriatic Seas. In the thirteenth century this traffic in slaves wholly disappeared from Europe. Since that epoch serfdom, villanage likewise, became successively softened. In royal domains the serfs were put under the jurisdiction of common tribunals. In general the serfs could acquire property, litigate, appear as witnesses in civil and criminal cases, even against their own masters. Thus Western Europe successively relieved itself from this curse, and history teaches that, in proportion as serfdom, villanage, was modified and destroyed, European nations emerged out of darkness; culture, arts, industry, commerce, prosperity, extended in wider and wider circles. Not in slavery was concentrated the patriotism, the honor of the chivalry, of the feudal knights. In the epochs of the most direful feudal oppression, the master hunting an escaped serf was scorned and nicknamed a *man-hunter*. The fugitive serf, if he was not caught in the lapse of a year and one day, acquired his liberty. In Italy, and above all in Germany, the free cities scattered over the land served as a secure refuge for the fugitives. For these cities, as well as for a nobleman, to deliver up one of these fugitives was an infamy. Knights combated rather than commit such a felonious action. Many were the bloody feuds between cities and barons that were occasioned by the refusal of delivery. Nay, if a fugitive, once admitted into the refuge of a city, was caught in some way by his previous master, the city considered it as a violation of her rights and made it an occasion for war. The free city likewise considered it as a violation of her territory and of her rights, and avenged it, if a fugitive serf was in any way molested within her limits. Woe to a nobleman who fell into the hands of the offended burghers. In the city of Reval, in Estonia, a city once belonging to the Hanseatic association, there is still preserved the sword with which one of the mightiest barons of the province was beheaded, for having carried away his fugitive serf from under the walls of Reval.

The misery, the degradation and the ignorance of the European proletariat is held up in comparison by the defenders and upholders of slavery, with what they call the happy and prosperous condition of the slaves. True it is that the masses of the daily laborers in Europe drag out an existence full of desolation. True it is that pauperism gnaws at the core of European society. The original source of this evil was social. It dates from the times when slavery, serfdom, villanage, oppressed the masses. Nowadays, however, the cause is purely economical. It results from the distorted organization and combination of labor and capital. It results from the disproportion in remuneration and in the share of profits, due to the original and immediate creator of wealth; it results from a faulty and imperfect co-ordination of man, and of his intrinsic powers, faculties and propensities. True it is likewise, that this deeply rooted disorder is powerfully alimented by the division of society for ages into castes and classes, in virtue of which there are accumulated in the upper social strata various dead-weights and drones, turning the scales on one side, absorbing the results of the labor of the mass of the people, and rendering difficult its free ascension and normal expansion. But the proletariat is not a distinct race, decreed by those above it to an eternal degradation and servitude in idea and in fact, or retained therein by laws as well as by brutal force. A noble or any other once prosperous person, when impoverished and destitute, merges in the proletariat; he wades into the mire of pauperism. The proletariat reposes not on the principle that it is an indelible stain, an unchangeable condition excluding social and civil rights. In all the European nations, however slowly, there continually emerge from the proletariat, from among the poor, individuals who ascend, acquire comparative wealth, position, and all the advantages of the world are thrown open to them. The proletariat, the poor, their progeny, are not surrounded, like the man of color—slave or free—by an insurmountable barrier separating them from civilization. The so-called middle classes, the wealthy, the aristocracy, was and is recruited from that mass. English aristocracy is in the major part composed of what once was an impure, a villain blood. The poor of Europe are not deprived by laws and observances of the right of religious worship and association, nor of marital rights, nor of family protection and ties, all of which the master of slaves severs according to his own will and pleasure. The civil rights of the proletaries, of the poor, are absolutely equal to those of any other member of society. The slave has none, and the free-colored man scarcely the shadow of any in any State, Louisiana alone excepted—and there only as the remains of ancient French and Spanish supremacy. In Europe political rights depend upon material property; and if the poor can acquire it, he enjoys political rights in all their plenitude. In the European nations there are different codes for the different social compounds. The life, the domestic occupations, the domestic hearth, the time, the labor of the proletariat, are not at the discretion and will of masters and owners. The proletariat, the poor, are adequately protected by the same laws with all other members of the community or of the State. The poor man has the right of litigation against every body. The criminal code is the same for the man of the so-called superior class, as for the proletary, the poor. In Russia, where nobles have real privileges, where serfdom exists, the criminal code is even more severe towards a noble, on account of his social superiority, immunities, and advantages. In the slave States, justice, crime, and its penalties, vary in their tenor, definition, application, according to their bearing on the slave, the man of color, the white man, or the master. What the moral sense, as well as the laws, of every civilized and humane society condemn and stamp as a crime, as "maiming," "killing in undue heat," or "undue correction," in the criminal legislation of the South is scarcely considered as an offence. Laws and regulations exclude not the poor, the proletariat, from "mental instruction," as is done by the laws of the slave States. No government or law of any European country imprisons and fines a teacher for teaching the children of the poor; while the laws of the Carolinas, of Georgia, of Virginia, and of all the other Slave States, Kentucky, Maryland, and Delaware excepted, prohibit under heavy penalties the teaching of the colored race, enslaved or free.

Neither the sovereigns nor the aristocracies of Europe consider the preservation of misery, ignorance and degradation among the masses as a social necessity. The uninterrupted tendency and efforts of European rulers, of the European superior classes, of legislation and administration, tend towards assuaging the evils of pauperism, to lessen it, to educate the poor, to open to them issues, to soften the misery, to alleviate the social burden pressing on their necks. Governments establish schools, and desire to instruct and enlighten. European rulers and the socially privileged of every class, do not prize the blessings of pauperism, but redden in shame or shudder at it. The legislation of the slave States increases from year to year in stringency, ferocity, and contempt for the claims of humanity. They aim uninterruptedly at making darkness darker, the yoke heavier, the chains tighter, the oppression more shocking, bondage and chattelhood more inhuman and indestructible. The aim of their legislatures is to destroy all the germs of human feeling and capacity in the slaves. For this the equitable foundation of human relations is legally, authoritatively subverted. Severance of families, disruption of ties, laceration of affections, which are common even to animals, are sanctioned by their legislation.

To compensate for all these curses, it is asserted that the slaves are better fed and clothed than the proletaries, the daily laborers, living in freedom; that their physical wants and necessities are cared for; that diseases and hunger are averted or healed by the attention of their masters.

It is probable and even well-nigh certain, that plantations can be found scattered over the region of slavery, in which the chattels are treated more carefully, in which some allowance is made for their human origin. Undoubtedly, likewise, the majority of masters try to avoid tyranny and harshness as far as possible, or as far as their own interest requires it. But the majority of slave owners cannot spend their material resources in procuring to the slaves —even on a small scale, comparatively—a real, material prosperity. According to the avowal of the slave owners, slave labor in itself is expensive, and in the smaller estates, by far more numerous than the larger ones, scarcely covers the cost. The owner has barely enough to satisfy decently his own wants and those of his family, and no one will refuse any thing to himself and to his children, for the sake of his chattels. Those are kept just above starvation; the physical forces are alimented enough to enable them to fulfil their daily tasks. The desolated huts —those abodes of slaves, according to impartial witnesses, in an immense majority over the South, do not give an idea of sheltered, prosperous, and well-kept inmates. For one working chattel, well-fed and tolerably dressed, there are necessarily hundreds and hundreds covered with rags, fed on the scantiest and coarsest allowance. Like causes every where produce like effects. In certain general outlines human nature is the same all over the world; as an ancient adage says: *natura humana semper sibi consona*; and slavery or serfdom in husbandry, in economy, in household administration, works now in the same way, shows the same phenomena that marked it among the Romans, that marked it over Europe, that marks it still, however mitigated it may be, in those European countries where serfdom prevails, or where, although serfdom being abolished in principle, custom, habits, tradition, idleness and degradation surround the large land owner, the once master, the nobleman with numerous burdensome retainers, if not chattels. Such was the case for a long time among the Irish and Scotch clans; so it is in Sicily, in the kingdom of Naples, in Hungary, in the Slavonias, in the Danubian Principalities, in numerous households of Poland and of Russia. Every where and always such retainers are often worse treated than favorite animals, as horses and dogs.

But admitting that the physical condition of the enslaved population in America is really as prosperous as it is represented, that all slaves or the majority of them are fat, well-nourished and decently clad; this after all would be nothing more than what is done by every sensible husbandman for his cattle and domestic animals, which must be nourished and well-cared for, on account of the labor which they perform. Every good husbandman attends to and cures his crippled or diseased oxen or horses, and so does the owner of the slave, who after all is the most expensive domestic animal, and one that is renewed or procured with the greatest difficulty. The apologists of slavery, reducing this question to that of food, of physical maintenance, as forming a compensation for all the destruction of manliness in their victims, prove how under the influence of slavery the comprehension, the feeling of manhood is lowered in the master himself.

Finally the question between a well-fed slave and a

lean freeman was settled about eighteen centuries ago, by the celebrated Roman fabulist Phædrus, in the fable *Lupus and Canis*, beginning with the words—*Quam dulcis sit libertas breviter proloquar;* to which I refer the partisans of slavery.

Neither is it true that the enslaved populations are satisfied, and cheerfully support their bondage. Even if it were so, it would justify once more an ancient axiom, and one confirmed by all ancient and modern observers of human nature, that oppression, slavery, destroys manhood to that extent, which makes the slave insensible to the highest good, to freedom. Thus we often meet with hardened criminals, to whom virtue, honesty, honor, become totally incomprehensible. So a distorted organism often rejects the efforts to bring it back to a normal condition. How often an individual affected with an internal chronic disease, or with some external excrescence, dreads the cure, refuses to submit to it, and prefers infirmity to health and vigor.

But innumerable and various facts give the lie to the assertion that the American slave loves slavery. He submits to it, as says Alfieri of all oppressed:—

. . . . . servi siam' si;
Ma servi ognor frementi.

If the chattels are thus satisfied with their condition, what necessity evokes the almost daily framing of violent, ferocious laws, to defend, preserve and strengthen bondage, to make the chain more indestructible? If the chattels are so fond of bondage, whence comes the dread of the masters to see them run away? What urgent necessity was there for the atrocious fugitive slave law? How is it that the Southern papers from all the States contain repeated advertisements of runaway slaves, with rewards for their delivery, alive or dead? Why is it that others of these papers, from time to time announce that possessors of bloodhounds are ready to hire them out, and hunt the fugitives for twenty-five dollars the job? Strange evidences of the felicity and satisfaction of the oppressed. What need of the cudgel, the whip, the gag, the thumb-screw, the bell, and various other implements of refined torture, which stock the household armories of the plantations? Must the devotion of the chattels be shored up with terror? All this so much trumpeted kindness of the masters notwithstanding, thousands and thousands of these human chattels often envy the treatment, the nourishment of the favorite dogs of their owners! And those murdered in their attempts to recover liberty, the mothers destroying their offspring, rather than to see them slaves, redeem the atrocious aspersion on the colored population, as if it were blunted to the sense of liberty. Vainly is it maintained that such cases of utter despair are few and isolated. Few and isolated are the self-devoted martyrs of any oppressed people, but the blood and deeds of the martyrs bear evidence against the tyrants.

Slavery as practised in the States of the Union, civilizes, ennobles the colored race, raises it above its kindred in Africa. These nefarious assertions are uttered as the crowning justification. The coarse varnish of tameness with which slavery glosses over its victims is not culture; servility is not civilization. This varnish, corrosive in its action, eats up, destroys in the slave the dignity of manhood, which makes the savage superior to the enslaved. Civilization is then only genuine and beneficial when she preserves, nourishes, developes, purifies and raises higher and higher the manly germs implanted by nature in the breast, in the mind of man. Such civilization alone ennobles, but such is not the lot of the slave. Such is not within the range of slavery. The taming of the black or the mulatto to serve the wants, to fulfil the biddings and the whims of the white man, is a desecration of the essence, of the principle, of the name of civilization.

The colored race is not alone degraded by slavery. Fate in its equitable retaliation blights the white man with the deleterious exhalations. Nearly three-fourths of the white population in the Slave States do not own any property in man. The condition of the immense majority thereof, according to the accounts published by the defenders of slavery, is most deplorable. This population is subject to material, intellectual and moral privations, is reduced to the most miserable degradation. And this state, according to the same source of information, is yearly growing worse. The younger portion is less educated, less industrious, more wretched, physically and morally, and the evil increases uninterruptedly. The habits of application to close labor is lost among them, and they "while away existence in a state but one step in advance of the Indian of the forest." They grow up without mental and moral instruction, as without any apprenticeship in mechanic and operative skill. Slavery shuts against them all issues. Slaveholders possess the best lands, and slavery is not creative or propitious to the arts, industry or mechanical skill. The whites find no demand, no employment for their labor, nothing spurs them to order, to regulated activity, to progress, and the development of their faculties. The South does not possess towns, villages, and townships like those which compose the Free States, and above all New England, the first among the civilized countries of the Christian world. The germs of liberty, of culture, of progress, of comprehension and firm adhesion to human rights, of their regulated reasonable exercises, are nursed and brought forth in these villages. On them prominently reposes the prosperity, the freedom, the future of American destinies. These villages are so many foci of light and morality, of intelligent, orderly activity. Out of these villages and townships, pours forth uninterruptedly the radiant stream of life, whose innumerable rivulets carry and spread civilization over America, whose halo coruscates brilliantly in the history of our race.

All is darkness and desolation in the Slavery States. The reports and messages of their Governors resound with complaints of poverty, exhaustion, record the decreasing productivity of the land, the increasing ignorance among the mass of the white population. According to those official reports and messages, there are scores and scores of thousands who can neither read nor write in each State. Schools are rare and are maintained with difficulty. Townships often belong to some few of the wealthier planters, who have no interest in taxing themselves for a communal free public school, for the general good. Those planters educate their children under the care of private tutors, in private boarding schools, in colleges, or send them to the North. Teachers of both sexes are imported from New England, as such intellectual produce does not germinate and blossom in the slaveholding States.

Moreover, it is an inborn instinct of oligarchies, to hate light and civilization, to prevent them in any manner whatever from penetrating to the masses. The Southern oligarchies abhor culture of mind in the white population, no less than in their chattels. They scorn the intelligent operatives, mechanics, artisans, of the North. The enlightened white masses would cease to be the tools of the slaveowners, and slavery would be undermined, and then explode. It would take volumes to collect the contemptuous utterances of Southern so-called statesmen, orators, theorists, stigmatizing enlightened industry and its progress, united with the intellectual progress of working populations. Never did the most feudal, aristocratic, and benighted times in Europe witness such a hatred towards independent, industrial populations and communities, as is manifested by the Southern slave-masters. Not from these rulers of the destinies of the South, nor its laboring classes—of whatever color—is to be expected the fostering of culture, or any step for mental amelioration, and the material improvement so closely connected with it. Not in this way act the Governments, the superior classes in Europe. And in face of this thorough degradation of the white population of their own kindred, of the descendants of those who fought the battles of independence, the upholders of slavery dare to upbraid the civilization of those whom they call the "greasy mechanics" of the North, scrutinize the condition of the proletariat in Europe, and represent slavery as the only guarantee of prosperity to the masses.

Freedom, under whatever shape it manifests itself, is and always was repulsive to oligarchies. The Southern oligarchy hates its name and its substance, abhorring free labor, free schools, and men of every color who are elevated by them.

History fully proves that oligarchies are more fatal to society than even the most unlimited power of one man. Still more so must be an oligarchy founded exclusively on the most atrocious social abuse. Oligarchies based on a certain traditional right, on the possession and exercise of power, have had in their behalf the same traditional feeling in the masses, accustomed to be ruled for generations, accustomed to consider their rulers as exercising a legitimate power over them. But the slavery oligarchy is in principle and political relations not superior to the rest of the white population. It is only by using its wealth and influence for systematically debasing the whites, and retaining them in poverty and degradation, that the slaveholder can maintain over them his baneful preponderance.

Facts and not fiction prove how slavery denaturalizes, distorts the great principle laid down broadly and exclusively at the foundation of American society. Facts and not fiction evidence how directly it is opposed to the tendencies of the free civilized part of the American Union, as well as to those of Europe. The efforts of reason, of culture, of social morality, are directed towards generalizing, among the masses, self-respect, good breeding, honorable pride of labor, generous, elevated feelings, polish of manners; in one word, towards elevating the social level, the social tone; and thus towards diminishing even to its total disappearance the aristocratic, social and political distinctions. Slavery constrains itself to build up what is distanced, abandoned by the spirit of our age. But her productions are shams; her aristocracy is a counterfeit; her social polish only a coarse gloss.

Slavery is a curse more fatal to the master than to the victim. It deteriorates the mind, hardens the heart, and makes the slave-breeder perpetually false to the better impulses of human nature. A slave-owner is a good master, kind-hearted, patient, full of forbearance and care as long as the slave is abject, fawning, crawling, and submissive,—as long as he licks his chains, and the hand which forges them. But the slightest breath of manhood raises the anger of that kind master, in whose opinion the slave deserves condescension, good treatment, as long only as he acquiesces in being a brute, but becomes highly condemnable and is to be ferociously repressed as soon as he feels himself to be a man.

To the planter as a child, and afterwards as a grown up

man, in his daily domestic life, is wanting in his relation with the slave that which exclusively curbs and regulates the exuberance and the original force of human passions. It is the early, calm, omnipotent influence of a genuine moral culture, softening the savage impulses of our nature. He grows up upon the plantation surrounded by beings whom he is accustomed to consider below him morally and mentally, as forming a medium between man and brute, existing there to obey his bidding, to satisfy his will and pleasure. As a child, as a boy, he sees and hears instances of severity, nay of cruelty, modified mostly by the material interest for not weakening and disabling a necessary and costly tool. So he reaches the age of manhood, and the softening influences of reason, of the world without, begin to work on his mind, only when the first impressions are already deeply stamped, when they have penetrated his whole frame, and then may arise within his bosom a struggle between his better nature, and this falsehood of his condition in his domestic relations—at war with his position, his relations with the world without. In such moments sincere men among the slaveholders have condemned and deprecated slavery. But misunderstood self-interest, prejudices, false pride, generally maintain the upper hand. Men enjoying immunities must necessarily have prejudices, and prejudices pervert and overpower the mind. The slaveholder carries them within him, they bear heavily on all the relations of life, of a man, a citizen, a republican, a politician, a divine, a lover of study and science, or whatever other pursuits in life he may choose. And so slavery, originating on the American soil by an accident, in a mercantile speculation, about half a century ago, considered as an evil by the most patriotic men of the South, is upheld now as an offensive weapon against the moral sense of our age, against the general outcry of civilization. It is no longer an economical availability, and still less a social evil, but a high moral obligation, a social law, a nursery of freedom, an agency of culture. Few minds or hearts can resist such an unnatural tension. They lose elasticity, become incapable of any loftier impulse, whatever might be the otherwise generous propensities of those laboring under this mental disorder.

Beyond the regions blighted with slavery, the slaveholder comes in contact with a different social state, with other notions and convictions, with men more or less strongly condemning what he is bound to uphold. This necessity makes him uneasy. He feels that he carries a burden of moral and social condemnation; the best among them are always on the defensive, or in a state of a baneful, unwholsome mental irritation. Some of them speak then of slavery as of an evil inherited, which they are unable to avert, to change, or to modify. If such are their true convictions, then how can they harmonize with the dignity of manhood the upholding by their political vote, or even by silent acquiescence, those who proclaim slavery a good, a blessing, and who drag the legislative action of the States to strengthen and make the evil irremediable, or who direct intensely the efforts of the States, of the Southern populations, towards extending it over lands hitherto not blighted with the curse? If conscience speaks loudly in them, and they stifle it off through false shame, interest, or the spirit of party, then they willingly degrade themselves. Or if their manifestations of regret are insincere, if they are made only for the sake of appearances, to avert from themselves the disgust of others, to be taken for enlightened or humane, then they have no claim on respect and consideration. Either way, therefore, the best of them are forcibly dragged by slavery into hypocrisy, into a struggle with the better longings of human reason and nature.

Others again bear up against the accusations of the outward civilized world, and in their false pride harden their hearts, poison and corrupt their reason, their judgment.

For these and similar causes, slaveholders are inimical to the ideas of the age, are inimical to the loftier activity of civilization. They in general deny its usefulness, its necessity, and above all dread its general diffusion, not only in their own land, but even in other regions of the world,—prosperity, progress, onward march, diffusion of knowledge being their loudest condemnation.

Scattered among the mass of slaveholders there are men and women of culture and refinement, whose social qualities raise them to a level with the best of any society, whose feelings of morality and genuine honor elevate them above the muddy current into which fate has thrown their existence. Such persons inspire a deep sorrow, to see their noble faculties and impulses depressed or blighted by the emanations of a social and political state which sooner or later must unavoidably tarnish them. Such do not give the tone, either in social or political relations, to the immense majority of their fellow-citizens. Their influence or action does not come to daylight, nor manifest itself in legislative enactments, or other public utterances. They are subdued or overawed—and some of them end by howling with the wolves.

At the family hearth, slavery loosens and desecrates the family ties, the relations by blood; lust and lewdness display themselves unbridled. In those unchecked relations, matrimonial fidelity wholly disappears. The great numbers of mulattoes are living evidences thereof. Among the ancients, concubinage was not condemned either by religion, ethics, customs, manners or laws, as it is in Christian society. Then the traffic in slaves was not a business organized in the manner in which it exists now in the Southern States. By this organization the produce of blood is here brought into the market. Fathers thus sell their children; or at the best, brothers, sisters, sell the offspring of their common parent, and thus the trafficking extends among the nearest connections by blood.

The external manifestations of the influence of slavery on the slaveholders must be judged by the tone, the customs, actions, and the degree of mental culture, of the great mass.

Where public education is generally neglected, the members of a community possessing limited means, soon sink into a state of mental torpor. The small planter is secluded from the world, from social and civil softening influences. A domestic despotism, recklessness and self-will, become for him the attributes of self-government. The means of sustaining the feeble sparks of culture—if he has received any—are beyond his reach, and thus abandoned, he necessarily becomes imbruted. His habits and manners become fierce, brute force is substituted for law. Accustomed to subdue by violence every opposition of his chattels to his will, he carries into civility, into contact with society, the same indomitable and injurious vehemence. Thus are bred the perpetrators of those bloody assaults, of lynching and burning, deeds of which accounts are to be found continually in the Southern press. These men use bloodhounds. Honor in their comprehension becomes brutality, assassination and murder the manifestation of courage. Each of them carries the decision of law, the sword of justice, in his own hands, and deals blows at pleasure. In their brutality, their prejudice, their pride, they treat the laws with contempt, and thus justify the complaints of those more humanized among the Southern inhabitants, about the degradation of the public sense of morality, rendering impossible by juries and judges the conviction of criminals.

This great slaveholding mass produces and elects those legislators, for their States or for Congress, whose enactments—by their worship of ignorance and of darkness, and by their ferocity—outrage the comprehension, desecrate the name of law. These enactments, making bondage daily and daily more stringent and pitiless, or attempting its extension, are the best evidences of the moral ruin into which slavery drags its white victims. Before the tribunal of morality, of reason, of justice, and of history, the one who enacts such laws is lower in the scale of human beings than those against whom such laws are directed. Humanity must condemn any society which can only be maintained by increasing legislative, and therefore cool-blooded violence.

Where the immense majority of the population is enslaved, the one portion by law, the other by ignorance, where labor and industry are regarded with contempt, there agriculture principally absorbs the productive activity. The South, by the nature of its products, considers itself as a region exclusively predestined for agriculture. But slavery prevents the agricultural interest from keeping pace with the material improvements in that branch of industry. Generally, the ancient routine is preserved, the immense majority of plantations squander labor and time in using the worthless, old-fashioned implements of husbandry. Thus slavery is compelled to reject inventions which would make agriculture profitable. The lands in old and new States become quickly unproductive, exhausted by coarse, irrational husbandry. This is the general lamentation echoed in official and non-official documents. But nevertheless the planters, and the merchants who grow fat on the former, proclaim that the South ought only to base its prosperity on the exports of its crude products, that free trade is the only natural, economical policy of that region. The Southern planter forgets, or rather does not comprehend, that all the industries are blended, and progress hand in hand, that to exclude one blights most assuredly the other. The most industrious countries and regions of Europe, England, Belgium, parts of Germany, Normandy, Flanders, are likewise foremost among all others in agriculture. Free trade is the death of prosperity and progress. The human mind and intellect as well as the human body prospers in variety, in the manifold application of its faculties. Neither man nor nature is ruled by oneness and onesightedness. Matter adapts itself to multifarious productions and uses, when plied and directed by the intellect and the hand of man. Harmony of mental and material life in individuals, communities and nations, consists in the development of varieties, in the combination of various chords and tunes. A man whose mind is concentrated in one idea—whatever be its intrinsic value—destroys within himself the fulness of his nature. An operative using principally one of his limbs distorts it, and the harmony of his frame is destroyed. A country devoted to a single labor, working out a single branch of production, becomes impoverished mentally and physically. Its inhabitants sink in every respect, and become inferior to those who multiply and diffuse their mental and intellectual occupations, who vary to infinity their pursuits in life. The exclusively agricultural countries have been always inferior, and their inferiority is not limited to the laborers only—either free, serfs, or slaves, —but stamps the immense majority of the ruling class, be it noblemen or planters.

Serfdom, contempt for free labor and civilization, arrogant presumption and free trade, exclusively and absolutely caused the destruction of Poland. The Polish serfs, as well as those of Germany, Russia, and of some other parts of Eastern Europe, were of the same race, of the same blood as their masters or the nobility. There exists, however, the most perfect analogy between the social state, the political action and the reasonings of the slave-breeders, and that of the ancient Polish nobility. Poland was for several centuries nearly the only granary of Europe, above all of the northern part, as the cotton planter enjoys at present the monopoly of cotton. The Polish nobility imported most of the manufactured necessaries of life from abroad, instead of fostering industrial development at home. For centuries free trade flourished in the fullest blaze, and with it increased domestic misery, abjection and ignorance. Free trade impeded and prevented the sprouting, the growth of an industrial, active, intelligent national class; the few unavoidably necessary artisans and operatives were all foreigners. There was no native middle class of any consequence to stand between the serf and the nobleman, as there is none in the South between the slave and the master. The mass of the nobility, amounting to between two and three hundred thousand —and all in principle politically equal—constituted the political and civil nation, as is the case to a great extent with the aggregate of planters and slaveholders. The magnates possessed polish and culture; the immense majority of the small or poor nobility were a lazy, ignorant, pugnacious, boisterous rabble, although not murderers or treacherous assassins, not heroes of the cudgel. They were clamorous at political reunions and diets, virulently opposing reforms and progress, averse to recognizing human and political rights in others. They considered industrial pursuits and occupations as beneath them. They spoke with the same contempt of their intelligent, orderly laborious, progressive, enlightened neighbors, the Germans, as the slavebreeders speak of the Yankees, so far superior to them in every way. The Polish nobles boasted that the world would become starved without their cerealia, that they could buy for them whatever else they wanted, as the South boasts that the world will be naked without its cotton. The world went on; the German neighbor, Prussia—which as a state shot out of Polish imbecility—is to-day among the greatest and most enlightened nations; Poland, with its nobility, feeble and decrepit, dissolved in ignorance, has disappeared from the record of living nations. So mental and material degradation, the fruits of serfdom and of free trade, dug for centuries the abyss into which Poland fell.

The South begins to feel its degradation, its backwardness, its industrial and commercial dependence. It tries to remedy it by conventions and resolutions, that such or such a port or city is to become a Southern metropolis; that trade is to expand, navigation and industry to be created. But liberty, civilization, the free opening of all issues to human activity, respect for free labor, intelligent and educated populations, and not boisterous and foolish conventions, create trade, animate cities, raise manufactures, build ships, and evoking a higher life, evoke and fix prosperity.

Not conventions and resolutions, but freedom has made New York, Boston, Philadelphia, the centres of the commercial wealth of this hemisphere. Freedom erects cities as Cincinnati, Chicago, Milwaukee, and others, which, emerging as by a spell from nothingness, teem with industry, trade, grow with an unheard of rapidity; while Charleston and Savannah, old already by centuries, backed by the cotton-growing and slave-whipping South, situated near the ocean, see the grass growing in their desolated streets.

Despotism in its most implacable and virulent action, has now become the paramount creed of the upholders of slavery. Suspicious, uneasy, alarmed, exasperated, they, like all the tyrants, remorselessly proscribe, attempt to extirpate, to kill and destroy whatever has the slightest shadow of disagreement with the most frenetic conceptions, definitions and exercise of slavery. Under penalty of lynching, mobbing, imprisonment, expulsion, or assassination—applauded from one end to the other in the slavery region—no voice can be raised contrary to the institution. Its value, its good or evil is forbidden to be discussed, nay even the slightest doubt is criminal, is unpardonable. Identity of causes produces identity of effects. As the Neros, the Domitians, the Heliogobali allowed only one worship, that of their person, and of their will, so slavery requires from all within its area, to bend the knee and worship her. Minds, opinions, words, the secrecy of intercourse and of letters are overwatched; the closet as well as the pulpit, the sacred ceremonies of public religious prayer are put absolutely under the control of slavery. What else was done by the most abhorred tyrants and despots of all times, of all nations? Not in the fiction of a novel, but in inexcusable facts, in public speeches, in public acts perpetrated in cities and communities, in the numberless articles of the Southern press, are brought forth these terroristic principles, are recorded those saturnalia of slaveholding polity. For the first time the history of the human race will have to deeply imbrue in blood and shame the annals of a society, in which terror, remorseless espionage, inexorable hatred carried to homicide, became the supreme law, being perpetrated not by a single despot and his accomplices and mercenaries, but by whole communities.

In vain for slavery are the teachings of history, the fate of tyrants and tyrannies, the rapid fall and ruin of social systems, conditions and bodies, needing in self-defence to be upheld by stringent and atrocious laws, treading in their fury upon freedom, rights, and independent convictions. In the whole world's history never was oppression carried out more consistently, conducted with such reckless energy, cold blood, understanding and discernment, than that by Sulla in Rome, for the sake and in the name of the Roman patricians. But the oligarchical despotism for which Sulla acted could not stand; the patricians lost their power, and the hecatombs of people were avenged by their blood.

On such a social condition is supported what in the political struggles of America takes the name of the democratic party. But as Demosthenes said: "To a democracy nothing is more essential than a scrupulous regard to equity and justice." Here slavery extends its action beyond its geographical boundaries, and encroaches upon the domain of liberty. So it accomplishes the perversion of names and principles. The Southern, the slavery States, as a political party in the Union, form the hot-bed, the heart, the pivot of such a democracy. Never was misnomer more salient, never a confusion of truth and falsehood, of right and wrong, of justice and injustice more complete. A society wherein bondage, degradation, contempt for labor, for popular education are the cardinal strictures, is held up as democracy. Whereas the efforts of true democracy are uninterruptedly directed to emancipate, to enlighten man, to exalt him in proportion to his intrinsic worth, and thus to exalt labor, the true mainspring of democratic association and polity. Thus democracy, one of the highest and most salutary philosophical and social conceptions, identified, embodied in slavery, has become a social ulcer. The annals of the past, or modern European theories, would be searched in vain to elucidate how this most generous principle could be ever distorted to such an extent for the use of narrow, egotistical schemes and views. It was the lot of America to show how it becomes degraded in its substance, when reduced to merely a partisan denomination, a shroud extended over a socially and politically corroded body.

The confessors of the thus desecrated democracy, proclaim her to be conservative of darkness and slavery, of abuse and prejudice. But democracy in its genuine and pure nature, as it really constitutes the essence of American society, is neither conservative nor destructive. American democracy in its germ, in its growth and development, has been hitherto and is now integrally creative, self-improving and progressive. Such a democracy spurns the revolting association with slavery, deceitfully seeking a shelter behind the splendor of the name, as crime often assumes or borrows the semblance of virtue.

Mental sterility preëminently stamps the pro-slavery States. In the boundless expanse of the human mind, the slavery region alone gives no signs of a healthy, intellectual activity. It is a dark speck on the auroral horizon of literary America. Science, scholarship, mechanic inventions, poetry, arts, in one word, the domain of intuitions, of knowledge, as well as that of imagination, belongs almost exclusively to New England and to the other free States. The South is a withered desert. And as in the desert, only a few plants are brought forth by nature's creative power; so in the slavery land it is only a puny slave literature that thrives. Forcibly bent and circumscribed into a narrow and crooked orbit, the southern intellect has seemingly lost all susceptibility, it shrinks and wastes in its restriction. It is impossible to rise into the higher domains of science, to think, to combine, to embrace and diversify, when the power of independent investigation is thwarted in man by absolute, narrow, preconceived, and deeply imprinted notions. But the South is proud of not producing, of not possessing thinkers. Poets and artists can find no high inspiration and impulse in the clang of chains. In the feverish excitement which surrounds them on all sides, the inner world of imagination dissolves and vanishes. The pro-slavery or the southern intellect has only one issue open, is impressible but by one single phenomenon, directs its activity towards one single object, embraces and comprehends only one single problem, and that is slavery. Its forced literary efforts are like those of a paralytic for motion. Disgust and sorrow fill the mind in wading through such a miasmatic pool, in witnessing such a defilement of the noblest faculties.

European pauperism—this favorite contrast which slavery champions urge against their opponents—European pauperism has not stifled the activity of mind, has not dried up or cooled the heart-warmth of those devoted to intellectual or scientific pursuits and occupations. Where this social evil is the most deeply rooted, there has appeared against it the most vigorous scientific, philosophical, and literary reaction. Statesmen, moralists, theologians, economists, poets, artists, in one word, all those whom the all-embracing genius of humanity illuminates and incites in various ways—all those investigate, analyze the evil, try to find a cure, or at least an alleviation; others, by reality or fiction, depict its blighting influence on the poor as well as on the rich. Whatever in other respects may have been the depravation of those who have supported by their pen the abuses of caste or despotic rule, they have never sunk so low as to proclaim and elucidate scientifically the unavoidable necessity of the moral, mental and material degradation of the masses of the people, or of the paupers, to uphold it as an imperative condition for the proletaries, and for those in a position above them. European science, scholarship, and literature preserve and maintain the sacred rights of mental independent investigation. In the minds, in the souls of those devoted to them, the sciences hover above the world's casualties. Their disciples enter the sanctuary with minds purified from egotistical, partisan, degrading influences. They shield science from being forced to receive the watchword from reckless passions. The few who act differently form as rare exceptions in Europe, as do those in the Southern region who dare to maintain the independence of science and letters, against the all-crushing mental and material corrosion of slavery.

The recognition of slavery as a cardinal social and political element, has destroyed the true statesmanship which was once the glory of the Southern region. The men who engendered the revolutionary epoch and the independence of this country, did not belong to the range of pro-slavery convictions. Patrick Henry, Washington, Jefferson, and the other great patriots of that time, belonged to an anti-slavery epoch. Those men who, as patriots, statesmen, will shine immortal in the annals of our race, those pilots of the new-born nation among the breakers surrounding her first independent movements—these by their creed, their culture, their convictions, belonged to the general Christian, humane, and at that time European civilization. They had nothing in common with the modern exponents of the South. In common with the moral creed of the civilized world, they recognized in slavery an evil, a curse. They admonished their compatriots to arrest, if not to extirpate it. For them civic virtue and patriotism were not condensed into the belief in slavery. Its modern offshoots in the councils of their own States, or in those of the Union, are of a wholly different substance and mould. In vain one searches in them for broad conceptions, for an enlightened and warm patriotism, for generously elated and high-toned feelings, for wide-reaching ideas. Never in history can be pointed out such a rapid decomposition and degradation of the mental faculties, as well as of nobleness of convictions, as is found in the juxtaposition of the men of the anti-slavery times by the side of their actual successors. The race, the blood is the same;—but conditions, events have changed, defiled manhood and mind.

Such a degeneracy, unprecedented in its rapidity, more and more thoroughly permeates the Southern society. And no wonder. The first generation of the heroes of American independence encompassed in their minds the world, with its elevated aspirations. Their successors began to cut themselves willingly off from all communion with the generous and all-embracing interests of mankind, concentrating all their mental powers and material resources upon the organization of a social state and polity, outlawed by reason, by the moral sense, by the tendencies of the age. Quick and in widening circles extends the corrosion. Now the younger generation distances already in virulence and blind worship of slavery, those who first abandoned the glorious and luminous path of their revolutionary sires. Its exasperation against freedom and human rights, its hostility to discussion, its indifference towards ennobling and fructifying culture, increases in proportion to the space of time which separates it from the forefathers. Those drew their wisdom from the fountain common to the world's civilization. Now the deteriorated, secluded social organism makes public education more and more divergent from that of other civilized communities, more and more circumscribed, compressed. In this manner pro-slavery education is void of elasticity, of generality, of free choice, is trammelled in its expansion. The aim publicly asserted is, to elevate slave-breeders, slavery upholders. The avowed tendency is to turn all science upside down. The mental and moral training of the youth is to become in harmony with the social institution. A conclusion logical in itself, and therefore producing repeated appeals from divines, professors, politicians, and the press, for the production of new sources or books for tuition in sciences, history, religion and morality, all to be made in accordance with slavery.

Such a proceeding is not new in the history of the attempts and efforts to degrade reason, to blight heart and soul. It originated with the Jesuits. In order to deprave the youthful minds, the Jesuits, in their educational establishments, adjust the sciences to suit their purpose. Ethics, religion, history, positive facts and phenomena, truth recognized by ages, are perverted and form the venom instilled as knowledge. So they have poisoned generation after generation. But in the end Jesuitism, Jesuits, and their tuition are placed without the pale of civilization; and human reason, human freedom, overclouded, darkened and arrested for a time, emerge victorious from the deadly struggle.

Such are the characteristics and the criteria of slavery, as the element on which is built this social structure. Such is the condition into which it drags its supporters, its champions. Thus covered with sores, the Southern body politic loudly proclaims its superiority in all respects over the citizens of the free States, and, above all, over those of New England. The aggregate of habits, sentiments, creative, productive energies, of intelligence manifested by the freeman, by the New Englander, is in salient contrast with those in which, generally or habitually, etiolates the man of the South. There is not one mental faculty, not one attribute of genuine manhood, in which the Southerner is justified in claiming any superiority over the character of the masses of the Northern, Western, and Eastern free populations. Because the freeman or the Yankee does not spend his time in idleness, because on deference to the individuality of others he bases his own personal honor and security, and thus does not recur to the mean and brutal usage of concealed weapons, it is not a proof that he lacks genuine courage. A civilized man does not consider fighting as the paramount duty. His life, his activity is devoted to other pursuits. He prefers to study, to enlighten his mind, to work, to plough, to be occupied industrially in manufactures and workshops, to build towns, mills, railroads, farms, to live peacefully, raise well-bred and intelligent families; in one word, to honor humanity in a true manner, rather than by assailing, killing and murdering his fellow-men. The civilized man resents a personal, wanton outrage by the self-consciousness of moral superiority, of that of mind and intellect. All this does not exclude courage. The sons of New-England shed the first blood in the American Revolution. No chivalry surpassed the heroes of Bunker Hill. The Yankees numbered the most largely in the defence of independence, and they were the last to furl their flag in that terrible struggle. They never disgraced their country by cowardice. They are men with spirit, courage, endurance, and deep love of liberty, and they remain faithful to this their common mother.

New England, with the free States, and their antagonists, the Southern slave-holding communities, started as two mighty meteors from one and the same point; but each took an opposite course. The one ascending into higher and purer regions of light, freedom and culture; the other whirling down into the chaotic night of prejudices, abuses, and misconstructions of duties, obligations, rights and mutual relations. And the fallen, tarnished meteor, having lost faith in the original and common essence, envious of the superiority of the brilliant one, accuses it of fanaticism.

But what is fanaticism, and what makes a fanatic?

The initiation of human kind into an ascending and superior moral, social and political condition, has been always accomplished by self-conscious, unyielding minds, liberating themselves at their own risk and peril from mental or social bondage, liberating their individual deep and ardent convictions from subjection to established, worn-out notions or forms. Such fiery minds, identifying themselves and the world around them with the sacred and sublime ideas which they cherish, have been commonly called fanatics. Such fanatics have unhinged and moved onward the world and single nations. They have dragged human society out of the mire, and given to it a fresh and invigorating impulse. Such a state of mind is called a fanaticised one by those averse to any emancipation, amelioration or progress. Christ and the apostles were criminal fanatics to the orthodox high-priests, the Sanhedrim, the Pharisees. Fanaticism extends to all subjects which deeply move the human mind and heart. There are fanatics in religion as well as in patriotism, in the love of liberty, in science, in arts. Fanatics for the disenthralment of human reason, were the reformers of the 16th century. Fanatic for science was Galileo; for poetry, Tasso; for philosophy, Bruno, Vanini, Campanella. All those who sacrifice themselves for an idea, successful or not, an idea encompassing an emancipation of whatever nature, are considered by the vulgar mind as fanatics. Such, in the eyes of their adversaries, were the heroes of the American and of the French Revolution. So fanatics are now those who rise to oppose the progress, the extension of slavery; who devote themselves to rescue from ignorance, to redeem their kindred, their white countrymen and their former colaborers in the struggle for national independence.

Fanatics are those who above the transient conventions made between men recognize the prevalence of a higher law; a law which for the religious mind is of divine emanation, which for the moralist proceeds from the inward pure essence of our existence. But in pagan as well as Christian times, whatever might have been the conception of Divinity, and of the relation of man to it, whatever might have been the moral standard of society, the variously manifested but nevertheless uninterrupted and unequivocal tendency of legislators, and even often of despots, was to make the laws more or less harmonize with what was recognized as the higher law. And woe to the society or nation, when its laws oppose these higher sources.

Slavery with its withering breath reaches the hearthstone of the freeman of the Free States. It corrupts there in various ways the public mind and individual character. In the generality of men, passions, interests, ambition, often get the upper hand of the most generous primitive impulses and principles. Temptation often proves irresistible, and the rule of common sense as well as of morality is to avert, to keep temptation out of reach. Thus very naturally the better part of the people in northern communities shudder at the contact, and the deleterious influence of slavery upon their citizens. Thus very naturally the sense of the people craves to circumscribe slavery within absolute and limited precincts, to lessen its power in the general political relations which concern the whole Union. Many are the examples of men of the North who embraced the political career, pure and unstained, who would otherwise remain true and faithful to freedom—this vital principle of the American body politic—and to themselves; but who, hardened by political struggles, gnawed by ambition, give the lie to themselves, abandon and deny what once they recognized as the supreme good, and sell their conscience to the support of the pro-slavery party. The betrayed must mourn the loss and fall of one from among them, and they are justified in attempting to preserve others in future from pollution. And the only way to reach this aim is to render the slavery power less predominant in its action on the common fatherland. Manifold are the enticements which generally carry away man from the path of duty; and those growing out of the community between the free and the slave States are diversified in their action. To them some yield from debility of mind, some by the weakness of an otherwise good heart, others by want of character or obtuseness of intellect, others by fear, others again by egotistical calculation bearing on their ambitious schemes or on commercial pecuniary gains and advantages. And in this manner slavery most sensibly wounds, affects and vitiates the free communities.

The principle of justice, its character, its administration, becomes daily more and more denaturalized, alloyed, and perverted, by the alliance of freedom with bondage. Often does it happen that the Northern judge, when the interests of humanity and freedom clash with those of slavery, twists and tortures the law to wrest from it constructions and definitions favorable to the latter. Often the clearest principle of law, as established and consecrated by judicial science, as well as by the successive acquiescence and common use of civil society, if contrary to slaveholding interests, is made nugatory by the decision of a partial judge. The spirit of eternal justice is then banished from the law, and the dry and dead letter loads and overturns the scales.

Pauperism has not hitherto withered and blackened the sanctuary of justice in the majority of European states. When the two opposite interests—that of the poor and destitute, and that of the rich—are brought into litigation, the judge would rather put the most favorable construction of the law on the side of the poor. Above all France, Prussia, and several other German states, preserve unsullied the impartiality of judicial decisions.

On three cardinal columns reposes slavery in its own home. The ministers of various confessions, the press, and the public leading men—whose influence on the masses is proportional to popular passion, shortsightedness, indolence and ignorance—form this triad. They stimulate the pro-slavery ardor, they justify and reconcile it with the duties of man and of citizen; they blunt the consciences of the people and harden them against the outburst of generous, humane and religious feelings.

The ministers, those teachers of religion and morals, consecrate by the authority of their example and of their words, a state of society which is a continual outrage against both. In no other Christian country do the ministers of religion exercise such a wide-spread influence as they do over the people at large in the United States. But pusillanimity or worldly interests make them subservient to the imperious commands of slavery. Thus they have identified the cause of their God with the cause of bondage and of chattelhood. They sustain it in the pulpit and in various theological and would-be biblical writings and disquisitions; not to mention and enlarge upon the thorough absence of religious instruction among the slaves, about the immorality which must necessarily prevail among those victims, abandoned by God and man. Difficult to be sure it is for the ministers to speak and expatiate about divine love, mercy, and justice, before those to whom no love, no mercy, no justice is shown, to whom the quality of man is contested. At the marriage of the slaves the religious rite becomes degraded by the minister to a ludicrous formality, and often even this formality is authoritatively dispensed with, without arousing the admonition or the holy wrath of the divines. The promiscuity of sexes between the blacks is not only tolerated but stimulated by the masters, who do not care about the sacramental ceremony, provided that children are procreated and the stock increased. At the best, the master himself ties or unties the matrimonial knot among his chattels. The ministers are silent as to the birth of mulattoes, who necessarily must be the fruits of adultery; neither do they thunder in the name of God against the sale of those mulattoes by their parents or the nearest kindred.

Those privileged depositaries, and guardians of what they call the Word of God, torture it in order to make it bear witness in favor of the biblical justification of the enslavement of the colored race. Those apostles and expounders of the gospel forget the words of St. Paul to the Athenians: "That God has made of one blood all races of men to dwell on the face of the earth." On it dwells the black race. If that race might even have been doomed to servitude by the curse of Noah,—in the true spirit of Christian salvation, the black race was redeemed together with the white one, by the sacrifice on Calvary, from previous hereditary sins. If there is any truth in the theory of redemption, then the death of Christ atoned for the sin in

Eden, and for that committed on the slopes of Mount Ararat as well. Or if, according to the Southern science, the black race is different from the white, and inferior to it psychologically, then even the simulacreum of religion ought not to be thrown before it. If the Africans, children of the same God, descend from the same common ancestor as the planters, and are judged worthy to be embraced in the sacrifice of redemption, if before the majesty of God they are endowed with all human attributes, and deserve to be admitted into Christian communion,—then the more do they possess human rights and attributes in worldly relations. A religious Christian despoiling his spiritual brethren of their inborn rights, commits religious and moral fratricide, commits the deed of Cain, and the clergy which sanctifies such a spoliation take sides with Cain.

Moreover, in no way can American slavery be justified, and still less considered as being authorized by the Scriptures. Slavery among the Hebrews was different in its origin from that established here. Neither Moses nor the Scriptures maintain that such or such race is predestined to be held in bondage by another. The ten commandments do not mention slavery or slaves. Jews were slaves one of another; Hebrew servants were bought, as says the Bible. In Egypt the Jews had no slaves, but were enslaved themselves. When they subdued other tribes, or conquered them, they transformed their prisoners into slaves, as very often they in their turn were enslaved by the contrary fortunes of war. Nowhere does the Bible speak of slavery as of a social institution, but as of one of domestic economy. The character of slavery among the Hebrews was accidental and transient, as it was among all the other nations of that time. American slavery is a permanent, unredeemable, social state. Jewish slaves, of the same origin, at certain periods were liberated.

Lepers and leprosy existed among the Jews, and the Scriptures speak of it more than of slavery. Should it therefrom be concluded that the leper and leprosy have biblical authority for their necessary existence?

Slavery at the time of Christ and the apostles was of the same character as that above mentioned. Christ and the apostles considered it as a transient human evil, and they were devoted to extirpating the cardinal and permanent ones. Teaching brotherly love, equality before God, they undermined slavery. Christ, Peter, Paul, and the other apostles, were mechanical working-men, operatives, and thus paid tribute to free labor. The triumph of their doctrine in its highest purity, as conceived by them, included the cessation of all kind of social and domestic oppressions. Further, brotherly love, if realized, destroys war, and thus the nursery of ancient slavery would have disappeared.

The Roman clergy in America, by sustaining slavery in the most distant manner, act—even if possible—more revoltingly than the ministers of the other denominations. At the side of the original Christian doctrine common to all those confessions and denaturalized by them all, the Roman clergy recognizes absolute obedience to the hierarchy, to the orders issued by the supreme heads of that Church. Siding with slavery in America, the priesthood abandons the multiplied examples given by the clergy at the time of the invasion of the Roman Empire. Then the Church did not spare moral and material efforts, and used its powerful spiritual authority to diminish slavery, to foster the emancipation of slaves. Now the branch of the Roman Church in this country puts aside the various decisions of councils and synods, and flatly disobeys the positive admonitions and orders of various Popes, thus incurring directly or indirectly the penalty of excommunication.

The Roman clergy forget the explicit words of Pope St. Gregory the First, admonishing manumission: "Homines quos ab initio natura creavit liberos,—et jus gentium jugo substitüit servitutis;" that clergy deliberately oppose the pastoral letters of Paul III., of Urban VIII., of Benedict XIV., above all that of Pius II., who specially blames the conduct of those who reduce negroes to slavery. Finally, the clergy directly violate the prohibitions contained in the Encyclique issued in 1839 by Pope Gregory XVI., who is not celebrated in history for mildness, or for any liberal propensities. This most severe absolutist and reactionary Pope, "in virtue of his apostolic authority, condemns those who reduce blacks into servitude, or buy and sell them; and by the same authority he absolutely prohibts and interdicts all ecclesiastics from *venturing to maintain that this traffic in blacks is permitted under any pretext or color whatsoever*, or to preach or teach in public *or in private in any way* whatever any thing contrary to his apostolic letters."

The press of the pro-slavery States is a melancholy evidence how the most beneficial agency and lever of civilization and freedom may become a degraded instrumentality of blind and violent passions. It shows how the misused faculty of reasoning can become nefarious and pernicious when enlisted in favor of falsehood and outrage. The Southern press, the most unrelenting apostle of slavery, by its every-day action strengthens the prejudices and emasculates the minds of the credulous and uncultivated masses. If nothing else were at hand, in the Southern press one can study and become perfectly familiar with the intellectual aberrations in which slavery entangles and hurries away its confessors. Its perusal, repugnant in itself, is nevertheless the most instructive with regard to the deterioration of social morality and manly honor by the baneful workings of this institution. All its tenets are fully exposed by the Southern press. It not only mirrors the state of opinion, but it is as a focus from which radiate the most extreme and vehement incentives. It evokes, stirs up the most unbounded and hidden passions of those who look to her for direction and advice. It encourages all the violences offered to the laws of justice and civility. It preaches and incites to lawlessness, to the murder and assassination of those who consider slavery as a social and political evil, as an institution degrading more the master than his chattel. Thus even the murder of inoffensive teachers is at times held up to the Southern public as a signal service rendered to society. The press carefully nurses all the perversions of science, of polity, of public and domestic economy, administering poison daily and in large quantities. To its ebullitions are to be principally ascribed the low moral tone, the mental prostration of the Southern population.

The exceptions to this general character of the proslavery press are few and rare. Still fewer are the instances that the cooler and dignified organs sternly rebuke or repudiate fellowship with those who sacrilegiously prostitute the elevated mission of the press.

What must be the society in which such a press can spring up, and which endures, supports, and patronizes it?

The politicians, the public men, the statesmen of slavery, belong to the same category, and go hand in hand with the press. As if by reciprocal compact, they do the utmost, they vie with each other in distorting the judgment of their fellow-citizens. If some of them, as well as of the members of the press, are under what must be believed to be an insane exaltation, by far the greatest number foment deliberately the prejudices of the people, as an easier way to increase their personal influence, to secure the leadership in the district, the State, or that of the whole party. If ever history shall preserve their names from oblivion, it will consign them to irretrievable condemnation.

The significance of America in the development, in the march of the Christian world, is fully and exclusively embodied in the Free States. Humanity, history, philosophy, civilization, ignore absolutely or repudiate the slavery connection. Without the Free States, America would lose the brilliant halo which marks her as the harbinger of the future, as the foremost among the nations of the earth. The Slave States have hitherto passed unnoticed under the fascination emanating from the holy labarum unfurled and held in the hand of the intelligent, active, laborious, self-improving freemen of the Union. The Slave States, separated and alone, would sink at the best into absolute insignificancy, would become of less interest than are the Papuans or Polynesians for the great association of mankind.

If by an unforeseen calamity, Free America should become palsied in its onward course, if ever slavery policy should prevail in the councils of the united nation,—then her phenomenal apparition on the historical horizon will be an abortion, a social mistake. Then she will stand there branded for future generations and future ages,—the sign of disgrace burning for eternity on the brow of this fallen genius of humanity.

CHAPTER VI.

MANIFEST DESTINY.

Nations, like individuals, have destinies to fulfil. Seldom individuals, however, as well as nations, have had a clear comprehension of the task allotted to them. Only when their course was run could it be said—that their destinies were ascertained.

Hitherto, science, embracing in a general view and comprehension the tasks variously fulfilled by nations and by representative men, has explained their respective destinies. Science has unveiled mysteries, disentangled and elucidated combinations of events complicated, and for the most part otherwise incomprehensible; events by which have been unfolded the destinies, the mission, the character of various epochs and peoples.

Science has found out the meaning, and pointed out the influence of the various conquests and invasions on the general march and development of the human race; science has explained the existence of a Cyrus, an Alexander, and the insatiable conquering avidity of the Romans, and thus has mirrored their destinies. These various conquests have mediated the intercourse, and drawn nations nearer to each other. They were terrible and rude, but nevertheless they were the agencies and channels of civilization. They were a bond of union. Alexander opened the door to the hellenization of Asia, and centuries afterwards Christian doctrine and science profited by the unity of language prevailing since Alexander in those Greco-Asiatic regions. The Roman conquests, overhauling the world, brought and mixed together in the interests of general culture, nations scarcely aware of each other's existence. Roman unity facilitated the first steps of Christianity.

Science again, long centuries after the event took place, explained the mission and revealed the destiny of those savage barbarians, the destroyers of the Roman world. Clouded and veiled to the actors themselves was generally their true destiny; successive ages and generations have lifted the veil and assigned to their action its historical and philosophical significance.

It might seem therefore unjustified by the past, for a nation, scarcely equalling in existence the age of one individual, to proclaim already the consciousness of its manifest destiny. But few if any among the axioms derived or framed out from the history and fate of the old nations of Europe, find an application to that wholly new phenomenon which constitutes the American nation. Not one of the past or of the existing nations of the old world, started in social, political life as a self-conscious whole. They depended upon founders, heroes or chiefs, and thus for the most part they have been blind executors of the impulses received from those chiefs. Rome was led on by a consolidated patriciate having the paramount aim to keep down the mass of the Roman people, to keep it busy with wars. In the past the Athenian democracy alone had at times, lightning like, an insight into its manifest destiny. At such moments of revelation, Athens perceived that her mission was to democratize the Grecian world; that the interest of her existence was to be surrounded, not by envious, hostile vassals, but by freely acting and moving democracies. The aims, the undertakings, the ambitious views, the tendencies and attempts of the chiefs and leaders of nations, were rarely prosecuted by their successors, rarely lived through two generations. And when they did, it was rarely beneficial to the nations. The change of the person of the ruler, and still more so of a dynasty, was accompanied generally by a change, and by a new impulse to the internal and external activity of the whole nation. Thus nations continually directed, conducted, receiving the watch-word, have been unused to rely on themselves. They rather groped in the dark, and could never arrive at a clear individual as well as concrete comprehension of their destiny—of the *what for* and *whereto* of their existence.

True it is, that under these supreme, individual influences and impulses, there existed, more or less sensibly, a kind of under-current, divulging the true tendency, the character of an epoch, and of a nation, the more so when this nation stood on the foreground of history. This current, powerful at times, carried away the leaders who held in their grasp the destiny of the governed; but oftener these individuals, strong by the possession of power, and still more so by the patient submission, by the inherited prejudices, and even the affections of the masses, have thrown impediments or diverted the current from its genuine and normal course. So the predominant power of the Popes denaturalized, deteriorated, soiled the character, the exuberance and fulness of the mind of the Italians. So Charles V. and Philip II. arrested the tendency of the Spanish mind towards religious freedom of conscience; so Catharine de Medicis and her two sons succeeded in extirpating the religious reform in France, although the teaching of Calvin spread in its first period with ease and rapidity, showing by it that the masses of the French people were wholly accessible, and inclined towards the reformation.

From the time of its conception as a colony, and more so from its birth-day as an independent nation, the American people outgrew their swaddling-clothes. A principle called it to life, and each individual draws from this fountain, according to his power and capacity, impulsion, direction, and consciousness. The principle reveals to each one, the close connection of his destiny with the destinies of the whole, the nation, the state. This uninterrupted transmission, unchecked by events, is wholly beyond the reach of authoritative decisions, will, and influence; thus the horizon brightens and extends before the intelligent perception of each free individual, and he becomes conscious of the general destinies of the society with which he lives, moves, and acts. As small sources, brooks, and rivulets form a mighty river; as countless rays, united, reveal the brilliancy of the sun; so from countless individual convictions, tendencies, and actions, clearly appreciated and comprehended, independent but united, is formed the powerful current of national life, the luminous light projected on national destinies. The onward march of the people is not led by an individual, nor by any authoritative social body; the national activity and intelligence are neither stimulated nor directed by any power acknowledged as supreme. Each individual is as a ray plunging into the mist which envelops the future, and the millions of rays dissolve the cloud which overhangs it. The self-consciousness of a whole people more completely comprehends the problem, and works out its solution simultaneously, in the spontaneous action of freely associated, intellectual and material forces. And so the respective destinies, which at the outset of their journey could not have become manifest and visible to the nations of the past, are clearly discerned and manifest to the free, self-improving, self-directing American people.

The races and nations of the Old World reeled in darkness; often pushed here and there by availabilities and expediencies, by the egotistical aims of their chiefs, they pressed on each other in their passage through various states of society, as nomadism, savagery, barbarism; and so they do even now, in the state of what is called civilization. No steady purpose has directed them in their secular course. The settlers on this continent, above all the Puritans, at the first stroke of the axe and of the spade, in the first furrow of the plough, laid down the seeds whose growth has kept nearly equal step with the increase of material forces and resources. The nations of the past, in deadly struggle, disputed with each other soil, hearth, and food. Here immense primitive spaces invited, and for centuries to come will invite, the vivifying and reproductive action of culture and civilization. The then, as now, comparatively small number of aborigines repel civilization, and, to avoid it, deliberately select destruction. It was and is, therefore, clearly unveiled to every American, as his manifest destiny, to transform the wilderness into a fit abode for man. It is his manifest destiny to preserve in their purity the principles of social equality, freedom, and self-government, which nursed and rocked the cradle in infancy, which instructed the youth and inspire the manhood of the American people.

Until now, among the nations of the Old World, some believe that they have to settle old accounts between each other; and nearly all have imperatively to do this with their domestic oppressors. They have to extirpate and to change; so much dust of the past is still rising in clouds before the eyes even of the most keen-sighted, that the piercing into the future seems almost impossible. Social structures are tottering and crumbling. Every body, the man of the past as well as the man of progress, are awestruck by the to-morrow, which is dawning menacingly with destruction and desolation. American society, having started from a fixed purpose and principle, and moving on its broad orbit, sees clearly before her; and her to-morrow is not hidden by clouds and uncertainties. The few transient specks must finally dissolve; no gifted, selected prophet, but the whole intelligent people can distinctly see the brighter and brighter unfolding of its manifest destiny.

Expand civilization, extend culture and industry, stimulate intelligent activity all over the continent, and utilize its various and almost inexhaustible resources, together with the extension of those institutions to which the Americans owe their greatness, prosperity, and rapid progress, owe their lofty position among the nations of the earth; all this is a simple and natural revelation and development of the American destinies. Simple, likewise pure and natural, is the more or less ardent desire to make and see others participate in the good which one enjoys. In some respects, a similar desire has urged all apostles and firm believers, to spread their creeds. Such a feeling is easily awakened in the bosom of every American, and easily can we conceive his belief, that this task of extension, geographically and socially, is his manifest destiny. It is not the tendency in itself, but the ways and means of its realization, which in some cases is to be condemned.

The genuine Yankee, that embodiment of intelligent activity, penetrates everywhere, and becomes the bearer of a new word. He brings civility, culture, restless but productive nimbleness, shrewdness, clear-sightedness, industry and order, inseparably combined, and, above all, so to say, the innate power and faculty of social constructiveness. Wherever he sets his foot, a new creation seems to sprout out of the soil. Wild nature is combated and overpowered, culture dawns, trade stirs up the indolence of the native, Indian or white; new products, that is, new wealth is created;—and the lazy existence of the inhabitants enters in this manner upon a new and re-invigorating phasis. Thus the Yankee, the man of the Free States, the child of free labor, of the free comprehension of life, becomes, in the new region entered upon by him, the apostle of a new social creed, the creator and dispenser of new powers, new faculties, new enjoyments.

The Spanish American, in that respect an image of the modern planter of the slave States, started with enslaving the Indians, and did not learn the secret of civilizing industry; did not learn how to become great, powerful, and rich, not by oppression and spoil, but by labor, association, and industrious activity. Thus in general the creole population becomes impoverished, and sinks into degradation. The exception of a small number of wealthier and more polished individuals, forming a distinct class, weakens not the rule. The creole population at large has hitherto showed itself wholly unable, by its own efforts, to utilize the rich natural resources of the regions which it occupies. From the start, the Spaniards have not understood how to colonize, but only how to be tyrants and to plunder. Their progeny and descendants have inherited their aversion to labor. These natives, disciplined in indolence and aversion to civilization by priestly and monkish example and rule, are inwardly corroded, and cannot keep pace with the American. They must in the long run succumb, and dissolve in the great genius of the man of the North, who knows how to overpower and tame the wilderness, to lay down immovable foundations for powerful States. This man of the North, settling or spreading in those regions, meets with impediments thrown in his path by the opposition of darkness to light, of morbidity to vigorous health. In his clear, quick, and appreciative comprehension, he has only in view what the country explored could become, if recast socially by him, and thus electrified and evoked to a new, vigorous life. He knows that, if he enriches himself, he contributes also to increase the prosperity of the community at large. Opposition, obstacles, stupidity, irritate him. The torpor which prevails in men and their institutions, the prejudices which counteract his otherwise beneficial activity, at last make him ardently desire to bring all the external conditions into harmony with the new destinies, of which he is even, sometimes, the unconscious initiator. . So step by step arises the wish for the annexation of the land to his great commonwealth—sure as he is to confer in this manner upon the new member a higher social and material condition. He desires to accomplish this by pacific and intelligent conquests. And American conquests do not create dependencies and colonies, but free and sister States.

Such is the high and pure development and working of manifest destiny. It has however its low and impure expression. This second one pours out from the unbridled coarseness of that section, which directs all its efforts to the extension of slavery. For the Slave States' manifest destiny consists in propagating the cancer which is eating them up. Not liberty, industry, culture, order, are to be brought to other regions; but subjugation, and the clank of chains, the curse and the groans of victims. Not the laborious, the civilized, the industrious, but the idle, the reckless adventurer, the rough and ignorant, are the bearers of this kind of destiny. Not the factory, the mill, improved agricultural implements, the school, the law, are to be transplanted; but the arbitrary will of the master, the slave-pen, the domestic, internal slave-trade, ignorance and misery. The originators and the carriers of such-like gifts are not men bound upon the honest pursuits of life, but are recruited among the social offal, among vagrants, among the impure and corroded agglomerations of large cities. Such apostles of manifest destiny are condemned and execrated by the men of the Free States, by the immense majority of the intelligent, honest, and laborious population. Against such invaders and violators, humanity and policy, America and Europe, the Christian and the pagan world ought to unite.

Unhappily this worst feature of the working out of manifest destiny, is a consequence of a hitherto prevailing historical development, carried out to its ugliest extremes. It is stimulated here by free and self-governing institutions, which leave the individual uncontrolled in his actions and pursuits. Nearly all the invasions and conquests on this continent were originally the result of an adventurous enterprise. The authorization given by kings or popes does not change their filibustering character. Columbus alone set out, not for conquest—but, as it is known—in search of a way to the East Indies. But after him—the Puritans excepted—all the other discoverers and conquerors of America, North and South, were exclusively impelled by greediness for gold. All started in this pursuit with the idle purpose to quench this thirst without any regard to ways and means, to become speedily rich at the cost and by the oppression of former occupants. When force could not avail, cunning was resorted to; but the chief object was always extortion and subjugation. What difference is there in reality between Walker and some other modern filibusters, and Cortez, Pizarro, Raleigh, and even the Cabots and the rest? Only the epoch in which they live differs; but the character of their action, its motives are one and the same. A lucky adventurer becomes a hero; and often a hero, when unsuccessful and fallen, passes for an adventurer. Filibustering seems to such an extent inborn in the nature of the American, and to prevail in the course of American events, that it was a kind of filibustering expedition from New-England itself, which transformed the Dutch New-Amsterdam into the modern New-York.

On the whole, however, this filibustering, grovelling excrescence in the political condition of America, has been hitherto checked by the far more powerful soundness of the national character. It was more in words than in action, and not to conquests of a filibustering character, that the American republic owes its rapid, and almost miraculous extension.

Its ways and means are original, and, up to this time, unused in history. They differ from all the modes of extension used in all other epochs, and by all other nations or sovereigns; they are truly American, and constitute a cardinal difference between the history of the States of the Old World, and that of the United Republic.

It is a common-place saying, thrown out by the partisans of absolute and monarchical governments in the face of republics and democracies, that these are always aggressive and greedy of conquest. With the exception of Rome, history does not justify this saying, by showing aggression exclusively on the side of republics. All the monarchies, of whatever age, nature, and form, have been always warlike, conquering, and aggressive. All of them extended their possessions by invasions and conquests, and uninterruptedly imbrued the annals of the human race in blood. Republics have been few, democracies still fewer; and any one, even superficially familiar with history, ought conscientiously to acknowledge, that they have been less aggressive than monarchies.

Still less are justified the modern European assertions, made by governments and political writers, concerning the insatiable desire to extend the American nation. In face of their past history, as well as of their present uninterrupted proceedings, it does not behoove any of the European states to upbraid America. Not by war and violence, but by agreement and purchase, the American Union reached the Gulf of Mexico and the Pacific, everywhere introducing civilization, industry, and culture. Even the acquisitions made by the war with Mexico, have been paid for; an action unknown and unwonted in the history of any other victorious nation or government on earth. No one at that time anticipated the riches of California, and European states have no reason to complain, that they see that once savage and abandoned region, transformed into an orderly and flourishing State. While America purchased and extended itself over the wilderness and unpeopled solitudes, England almost daily overthrows and absorbs organized, populous, and rich empires in India, extending over thousands of square miles, and with millions and millions of population. English conquests are destructive; American purchases and annexations are organic and creative. Therein lies the whole differenee. England extorts tributes, imposes heavy taxes, presses down and impoverishes the natives :—America promotes new life, not for her own sake, not for her exchequer, but for the benefit, advancement, and interests of all other nations. France and Russia extend their dominion, the one in Africa, the other in Asia; and their conquests, in their civilizing purpose and character, as well as in that of the regions over which they are extended, have a certain similitude to the American annexation. If other European states and sovereigns do not engage in warfare and conquest, it is not the will, but the possibility which is wanting. Each of them has invaded, conquered on a small scale, as much as it could at given circumstances and epochs. Austria, Prussia, Piedmont, would readily absorb their neighbors, if they were not mutually checked by each other, or by other states. Among them all, America alone can proudly raise its brow, and not shrink from historical and political comparisons.

The consciousness of carving out the manifest destiny of this continent, inaugurates a new distinct policy for America, in her relations with others, above all with European governments. The technical name of this policy, called the Monroe doctrine, is only its partial enunciation. In its full comprehension, this policy is the utterance of maturity and manhood, is the fulfilment of the historical mission.

This continent ought to be independent and sheltered from any direct, that is, governmental, or indirect, political and diplomatic influence, to be exercised in any way by European powers. It is natural to the free Union, to look for an end of the colonial dependency of any region on this continent upon what is called the mother countries; it is natural to see the Americans extend their flag, to shield other States here from the baneful breezes of European policy. The European monarchies, based all of them without exception on prerogatives and privileges, surrounded by various kinds of aristocracies, are conjured not to allow a republic to start among them, to preserve the royal and aristocratical brotherhood untouched. It is natural and logical that this commonwealth wishes and tends to be surrounded by a cluster of sister democracies. It is logical and natural that it tends to see the whole continent fully emancipated. No dependency ought to exist. The natural bonds between Europe and America are only those of commercial intercourse and exchange, and of ideas and notions; all on the footing of absolute political equality. The supremacy of Europe over the internal affairs of this whole continent must and ought to have an end. It is natural and logical for the United States, that, embodying a new and higher social principle in its vigorous growth and expansion, they should assert their rights, and speak to the old world peremptorily in the name of the new one. The American Republic does not interfere with the annexations and extensions carried out by various European powers on the other parts of the world;—but it is her most sacred duty to repel any encroachments of Europe on the soil of America, as well as to repel the intervention of European policy in any relations, domestic or external, of the North or South-American States. It is duty and right to put a term in the name of this new world, to the arrogant and unjustifiable assumption of European monarchical governments, to regulate in any way the affairs of this hemisphere. The real supremacy of Europe in the arts, in several branches of manufactures, industry, science, and literature, will by itself preserve its influence. This supremacy, of which the European people are the creators, is independent of the action on it of the governments. These civilizing and pacific channels alone can unite the two worlds. Europe might still serve in many mental and intellectual respects, as a master to America; nevertheless the action of the currents is reciprocal. But the governments of Europe are not so constituted as to exercise any beneficial influence on this continent. Against them alone is to be directed, in its fullest meaning and extent, the Monroe doctrine. The European governments, on the contrary, in questions of general policy, must yield to the principles asserted by the American Republic. This irrefutable influence of reason, as proclaimed by America, has already enforced upon the European powers the modification of the maritime laws concerning neutrals. Before long, Europe will be obliged to recognize the superiority of the principles laid down by the United States, and accept in full the law of absolute respect by belligerents of all private property on the high seas, a principle put forward and urgently advocated by the American policy.

From whatever point of view we regard the question, Europe has not a right to interfere on this continent. Only, if America should tread down the sacred principles wherein she originated; if America should swerve and abandon the luminous orbit of freedom and civilization, pervert her character, and use her power for extending and implanting slavery in regions where it does not exist, or where it has been already abolished; in one word, if extension of the Union should become synonymous with bondage and chattelhood, with the slave-trade; then only, as the positions would thus become reversed, and Europe defend a holier principle, her intervention and her defence of sacred human rights would be justified before the tribunal of justice, morality, civilization, and history.

Europe ought not to have any footing on the American continent. Justly, likewise, the European powers will never allow to the American Republic to acquire any foothold in Europe. In this respect, both the continents ought to be absolutely independent and free of each other. Under no pretence, American interference with European internal affairs, with wars or revolutions, would be justified. Principles and example are the only agencies—moral ones—of the action of America on the old world. No other republican propaganda could justly be put forward; and if attempted, then the governments of Europe, of whatever character, free or absolute, ought to coalesce and repel the intrusion.

The emancipation of European nations must be worked out from within themselves, and with the ideas, notions, and material means that exist among them. Their condition is a volcanic one—eruptions will succeed one another—perhaps for a long time, before a brighter future can dawn upon that part of the world. Whatever may be this future, and its final organism and form, it must be constructed and shaped from existing data and elements, and not in imitation even of the American social development.

As has been mentioned in previous chapters, the European nations have few if any elements of self-government. The comprehension of its principles is not familiar even to the most advanced reformers. Self-government, to be beneficial, can only be handled by masses in an advanced state of civilization, like those of New-England and of some of the other Free States. Otherwise it is a dangerous and damaging experiment. Already its functions begin to be distorted and desecrated, by the weight of the ignorant and barbarian masses that pour in here from the old world. The future of Europe is thickly veiled; it is a problem whose solution belongs to new men, to new generations. America cannot even render the service of a midwife or nurse in this painful delivery. The European nations are in a peculiar condition; various ideas and conceptions of future reform and reconstruction ferment in their brain; and out of them, in due time, under propitious circumstances, will emerge the word of regeneration. No action of America ought to precipitate the advent of that hour. Forced deliveries bring forth generally sickly abortions. If the European peoples are unable by themselves to break their chains, to raise by themselves a new social structure, no helping of America can be of any real utility. The populations of Europe outnumber ten times that of the Union; an American expedition to support any nation, will be like adding a drop to the Ocean. If the European nations rise simultaneously against their present rulers, then they ought to be strong enough to expel them; if each will try single-handed, then the allied kings will be strong enough to repel and annihilate any armed intervention from America. The European nations are divided into two camps; and their oppressors are supported by the natives themselves. It was not any foreign help or intervention that strangled liberty in France and Germany, but domestic troops. Frenchmen fought against Frenchmen in the streets of Paris on the 2d of December. Prussian troops quietly put down the liberal movement in Berlin, and fought in Dresden and Baden. Austrian troops stormed Vienna for their Emperor. As long as these central nations of Europe are unable to disenthrall themselves, the smaller ones will be oppressed and depend upon the fate of the greater. France and Germany reorganized, oppression in Italy ends as by a spell.

Europe is not wanting in sinewy arms to fight her battles, nor in implements of warfare. Arsenals and manufactures are teeming with weapons sufficient to arm the whole active population. All the material means are possessed by Europe in proportions far surpassing what America could effect as an ally of the struggling nations. Men, arms, money—European capital flow continually to this point. The continent of Europe possesses immense accumulated wealth in gold and silver. It is the problem of the revolutionist, to get hold of these resources. At the present moment, in the banks which sprout out in all points of Germany, in imitation of the American system, there lies deposited in bullion far more than in all the chartered banks of the United States. Sums large enough to vivify any revolution. Taxes now levied by rulers can be turned into the revolutionary chests. What paltry aid could America contribute in comparison with such resources, and of what small use could this aid be?

America is admonished by some revolutionary apostles

to pay her debt, contracted by the succor tendered her by France against England. But America had at that time neither arms, sufficient men, nor money. All these objects are now abundant in Europe. The conditions are wholly different, and it is no ingratitude in this country, if she does not arm in favor of political parties struggling in Europe. The liberals, the reformers are seemingly in minorities; otherwise they would not want any support. And if they cannot succeed without foreign help in establishing their principles, how will they maintain themselves when this help shall retire? It is therefore in no way the manifest destiny of America, to interfere with European broils, or to propagate revolutions on that continent.

The European and the American social worlds ought each to run a distinct and separate course, in special orbits, without interfering with each other. Like the celestial bodies, they could be under the influence of combined attractions, and like them they ought to move in the social space, without clashing with and impeding one another. Civilizing and commercial interests alone are to intertwine them. Both have the same problem before them, namely, to secure the greatest attainable freedom and material happiness to the masses. The solution of the problem, it is likely, will be worked out differently by both parts of the world, as both find themselves in different conditions. The human race for ages aspires and tends to the realization of justice and reason; sages and legislators have had the same aim, but their conceptions and comprehension have differed. From Zoroaster, Pythagoras, Plato, Solon, down to Fourier and to our times, the great object of social organization has been to secure to men and harmonize moral and material welfare. This harmony was, above all, the aim of Christ, and is the tendency of well understood Christianity. Through John, his most beloved and most spiritual disciple, Christ said, "that his kingdom"—that is, the kingdom of love and justice—"is not *now* of this world." Christ therefore did not exclude from happiness the material existence of man, but comprehended the earthly, material kingdom united with the spiritual, moral, or heavenly one. Man's happiness in this world, that is, Christ's kingdom, could not have been based on the material misery of humanity, or of its greatest number. Christ therefore foretold the realization of this harmonious union, when the seeds of fraternity and love sown by him should have purified man's nature. That man is to be in full possession of moral and material development, enjoyment, and beatitude on this earth, Christ taught in the daily prayer, still repeated by millions and millions of the Christian world. The kingdom of God is to come to man; that is in the conditions of his existence here below; and not that man, miserable, poor, destitute here, but transformed by death, is to go hereafter into the kingdom of heaven.

The European nations gravitate—very slowly, it is true—towards a general amelioration of their social, moral, and material condition; but the American commonwealth can by no material fact or action advantageously accelerate the European movement. The American destiny and duty is to watch over this continent, to accomplish by peaceful means its emancipation from European rule. Colonies and dependencies must sooner or later disappear from the new world. European governments will be obliged by the force of events to resign all supremacy, and give up their possessions on the American continent. The now independent Union contributes more to the prosperity, to the industrial and commercial development of England, than could ever have been done by the colonies. The same will be the case with Canada, when it has once outgrown the European governmental swaddling-clothes. As has been said before, there still exist, and will exist for a long time to come, various moral and intellectual accomplishments, securing a partial leadership to Europe. Both hemispheres have a great deal to exchange peacefully, and to learn from one another.

It would seem that any forcible transmission or propagation from West to East is contrary to the laws, to the tendencies of nature. Science and history show that, since the formation of the present earthy surface, the vegetable kingdom, animals, man, and ideas, have marched from the East towards the West. Such was the principal current of the migration of the historical races, and in their train that of useful domesticated animals, of seeds and plants. In the East were born the religious and philosophical ideas which animated the Christian civilization. As the Greeks drew from the East the primitive rays of culture, enriching and multiplying them in their own exuberant individuality, so the post-Roman Europe gathered the remains of Grecian civilization; and on Aristotle, Plato, and the other lights of the classical world, were nursed those minds which begat in all its variety the modern European social and philosophical culture. The American social state sprouted out from rudiments brought from Europe; purified, to be sure, and recast, remodelled, under the pressure and action of new conjunctures and causes.

Hitherto the West has never strongly reacted on the East. Alexander's empire dissolved as soon as built; the Seleukides, the Ptolemies became absorbed by the Eastern luxurious life, and a mongrel, feeble Greco-Asiatic culture issued from these violent nuptials. Rome, after conquering the East, broke down under the effeminacy resulting from this conquest, and finally the East separated. The Popes of Rome could never subdue the Eastern Church; the efforts, the devotions, the sacrifices of the Crusades dissolved in nothingness. Napoleon unsuccessfully battered the East through Egypt and Russia; and even recently the efforts of Europe to break through the Eastern spell were foiled before Sebastopol.

Europe has received all the animals and useful nutritious seeds and plants from Asia, and transferred them to America. Coffee, sugar, cotton, those rich staples are of Eastern origin. Even the bee, whose original home is the western slope of the Ural Mountains, thrives here, when it cannot in any way be propagated east of the above named mountains. The original products of the American continent have not contributed largely to the benefit of Europe or of the East. Aside from a few medical plants of real utility, of a few spices, of caoutchouc, the great staples introduced to Europe since the discovery of this continent consist of potatoes and tobacco, both of rather dubious qualities in regard to their utility and influence on the domestic, economical and sanitary condition of the European population. The exaggerated culture of the potato has, it may be, occasionally preserved the people from famine, in various European countries; but it has also often occasioned it. Some attribute to the potato the extension of the scrofula among the continental populations. Above all, however, the culture of the potato has enormously increased the production of alcohol, and thus intemperance, and all its retinue of misery, destitution, crimes and vices, have been facilitated and increased over the greatest part of Northern Europe—as Germany, Sweden, Norway, Russia, Austria. Tobacco, having become almost a necessary of life, even for the poorest, without any nutritious, but with rather a deleterious influence on the health,—is therefore an unproductive, and in many ways an impoverishing discovery. Maize, or Indian corn, is traced, by some scientific investigators, to Asia, whence it might have been brought to this continent at some remote period. In the south of Europe, maize has long been known and cultivated, although not on a large scale—wheat being preferred. In Italy, Southern Germany, the Slavonias, the Danubian Principalities, and in Southern Russia, maize is called Turkish wheat, or *cucuruzza;* in Greece it has the name of *arabositi*, or of Arabian wheat or corn.

The animals of this continent are useless for Europe. The breed of the alpaca was tried in Europe, but unsuccessfully, while the sheep spreads here with the same facility as in the old world.*

A community and a political state originating in principles of reason and of peace, ought not, it would seem, to breathe the martial spirit which prevails in America. This anomaly, however, is the result here, as elsewhere, of feelings—probably inborn generally in human nature—

* It is curious to observe to what extent the Americans identify themselves with the animal and vegetable kingdoms belonging to this continent, and existing prior to its discovery. They generally consider as a slight to their country any mention of the superiority of European animals or vegetation over those of America. They defend it against the charge of diseases, whose origin science or history attributes exclusively to America when she was possessed by the Indians. It is generally maintained that syphilis was unknown to the old world previous to the discovery of America. The Spaniards took it from the natives and brought it to Europe. It is said that from Spain it came to Naples, Italy, and France, receiving the name in these two last countries of the Neapolitan disease, as it was and is still commonly called in Germany and in the whole North the French one. Mr. Prescott, the narrator of the reign of Ferdinand and Isabella, relying on some doubtful and obscure quotation and authorities, is glad, as he says, to prove that syphilis was known in Europe two years previous to the voyage of Columbus, and that the Indians and their continent can be whitewashed from the slander.

or which otherwise became natural to man by being impressed on his mind through the uninterrupted action of long ages and countless generations. Military glory, military achievements, have always dazzled the imagination of the masses. Even the soundest and most clear-sighted intellects usually succumb to the charmer, and become lost in the admiration of bloody laurels. From the hour of the first association of man, from the time of the first social structures, patriarchates, empires, kingdoms, or republics, the history of the world re-echoes the war-strife, and its great heroes are conquerors, and the world-unhinging captains. It was and is firmly rooted in the minds of even eminent moralists and philosophers, that war is the necessary baptism of a self-asserting nation, that war is a powerful agency in the service of civilization. Contrary convictions pierce slowly, and toilsomely they come to daylight. But a very long time will run before peace and not warfare shall become an absolute social and political fact, a historical law. The American Commonwealth inaugurated itself among the nations of the earth by the baptism of blood. After the first and glorious victory, the old enemy, envenomed by defeat, taunted the young nation. It was difficult for England to renounce the idea of her ephemeral military superiority, and she thirsted for an occasion to revenge the affront. In 1812, unjustly assailed, the Union learnt that it ought always to be prepared to meet and repulse unscrupulous enemies. "Quivis pacem para bellum," is an ancient saying; and America must be armed for emergencies. But America will never assail Europe. In the present condition of general policy, some of the European powers, however, might in extreme cases, throw the torch of war upon the shores of America.

A free man feels the value of liberty, and is always

ready to defend it heartily, without compulsion. But will and devotion are not sufficient; drill and skill increase a hundredfold the powers of defence and action. The organization of national militias, principally in view of repulsing a foreign enemy or invader, nourishes and stimulates the martial predisposition. And well it is that in the present condition and relations with other powers, this spirit is entertained. It is even shameful and ridiculous to see youth, preposterously imagining itself to be something better than the great bulk of the people, to see this sham aristocracy declining to partake in the duties and exercises on which depend the peace, the immediate destinies of the fatherland. As long as justice and reason shall not absolutely rule the various political, external, nay even internal relations, war must always be possible. Declining are the destinies of a country, which is obliged in case of emergency, to recur to mercenaries, even if recruited among its own population. A small standing army might not prove thus fatal, but the experience of ages teaches that such armies finally become tools for oppression. Free states, republics, have tended towards destruction, when wealth and effeminacy dissolved the martial spirit—when the rich and poor youth avoided the civic military duties, and when mercenaries stepped into their place. So Thebes, and above all Athens, after the Peloponnesian wars, saw the ancient spirit slowly expiring among them. The Athenians became disused to arms—unable to cope with the trained Macedonian bands—they recurred to mercenaries, and the last hour of Athenian and Grecian liberty was marked on the dial of ages.

There is no danger that the preservation of the martial spirit, in the free and civilized States of the Union, will degenerate, and become tantamount to a savage, reckless spirit of assault, invasion, and piracy. The population of those States value the worth of civilization, of peace and its blessings; they prefer the quiet pursuits of agriculture and industry, the family hearth, to the roving idleness of military bands and expeditions. Not among the intelligent freemen are such bands started and recruited. Slavery institutions, promoting idleness and contempt for labor, inculcating from childhood perverted notions on the duties and relations of a member of society, breed individuals who contract habits that fully qualify them to be food for gunpowder. Among the populations of the Slave States, as well as among the scum of large cities, individuals therefore can be easily found who are ready to risk their charmless life in the invasion of other pacific nations. Such a spirit has nothing in common with that noble martial one, which is vivid in the men of Free States, the noble defenders of their homes and liberties, but not savage aggressors on those of others.

America as a nation is so situated that her extension, even if aimed at indefinitely, can be accomplished more easily by peace than by aggression. The band of the federation is limitlessly elastic. To it gravitates—at present it may be imperceptibly—the North and the South—Canada as well as the republics of Central America. That the result of such union will be the successive disappearance and dissolution of the creole race in its own shiftlessness, is almost indubitable. In Louisiana, Florida, the original native elements, living on equal rights with the new comers, preserving their respective idioms in all the every-day and domestic relations, vanish or are absorbed, dissolved, by the preponderating influence of the language used by the law, in politics and in business, used for general and public education, as they are absorbed by the influx of new occupants. The same will occur with the Spanish inhabitants of the central states or of Cuba, if they shall enter the Union. They will yield the path to the northern man, (not however to the slavery extenders and pirates,) to his superior activity, industry, culture, robustness of mind and of body. And those among the natives who may be able to keep step with the men of the North, will merge in the new culture and language, and only the family names will tell of the original difference. It is this certainty of absorbing by the superiority of intellectual muscle, other populations coming in contact with him, that increases in the American of the North his faith in the manifest destiny. By this superiority, and by peaceful arts, industry, commerce, he attracts; by them he increases the national wealth in colossal proportions; and can buy lands, paying for them millions, as he did to the Indians, and annex. Canada, united already by identity of birth, of language, and of interests, must finally by her own free choice throw away her royalist livery, and become an independent and self-acting member of the federation.

The preservation of the martial spirit is not therefore an agency or a lever for the fulfilment of manifest destinies—as those destinies are not pregnant with the curse and calamities of war. War is inborn among the nations of past and of modern Europe, it exhausts their material resources, demoralizes their respective populations, disabling them for freedom and for its acting soul—self-government. War in the life and development of America is an excrescence on the social body, an excrescence produced by an irritating action from without, or by the fermentation of the impure elements created inwardly in the body by the deviation of a part of the nation from the fundamental principles of reason and justice, from which America draws her life.

The European nations and governments can only be

losers by carrying a war against the American republic. This conviction they acquire daily. They and not American industry and commerce will suffer losses and stagnation; an industry which the American consummation thus eminently contributes to nourish. England stands foremost among the European powers, which from tradition and false policy, is more prompted than others to interfere with matters concerning this continent, and thus create complications which could reach so great irritation, as to require forcibly to be cooled by war. But even in England, opinion, enlightened by material interests, supports the efforts of the friends of reason, civilization, and humanity, aiding them to smooth difficulties and solve them in a peaceable way. The results of a struggle between the two nations would be calamitous beyond calculation. Nevertheless such a struggle, if protracted for several years, would end in the prostration of England, and in the thorough industrial emancipation of the United States. All the branches of domestic industry, most of them having at home inexhaustible resources in the necessary raw material, being thus stimulated by the exclusion of foreign imports, would take wing, and free the country for ever—even for times of peace—from external competition and overflowing. To be sure, the influx of English capital would have an end; but comparing the sums exported from the United States in gold to pay for foreign, above all for English merchandise, this capital remaining at home, put in circulation and employed productively, would compensate for the English investments. Domestic wealth would increase with the expansion of domestic industry, and new capital would be created. The continental system, during the reign of Napoleon, has after all eminently contributed to develope industry in France and Germany. The United States, possessing inexhaustible iron ore and coals, nevertheless cover the soil with imported rails, laid often over regions where crude iron, left idle on the surface, stares in wonder at such a waste and neglect of domestic means. Prussia, after years of protection, is ready now to compete with England in iron, and Prussian competition will be limited only by the insufficient quantity of raw material. America could light furnaces and sink shafts, equalling at least in number those in England, and America imports iron wares. Furnaces kindled in America would extinguish those burning in England for the American demand; and English miners and workmen after a war would be obliged to emigrate to this country, following the demand for their labor and skill. The same would be the case with many other branches, which once developed during the war, would for ever exclude England from the American market.

England *per contra* would be unable to find any where the sufficient quantity of cotton for her mills—which would become stopped by a war, and the operatives thrown upon the streets. Thus by a war the demand for labor would increase in America, decrease in England. In peace English industry depends in a great measure on this country. Nowhere can England find such prosperous consumers, and who demand such large supplies. England exports more to the United States than to all Europe, with her more than two hundred millions of population. From whatever aspect it is considered, England alone would be a heavy loser by a war.

America's expansive tendency and internal development would not be arrested by a war. The losses in men and capital would become speedily compensated. European powers, as well as European nations, daily and daily more clearly understand, that the prosperity of that hemisphere increases with the preponderating influence of North

America. England gets more than the lion's share of the gold from California, transformed as by a spell from an unknown solitude into a flourishing community, by the expansive energy, the activity, the constructiveness of the freemen from the free States. The creative and untiring activity of these genuine Yankees covers the pestilential marshes with railroads, clears the forests, subdues wild nature, and aids the surplus of European populations to take possession of those primitive, or badly cultivated regions. The free North Americans are alone born to start, to create, to organize and direct new communities, and thus to facilitate the efforts of Europeans. They alone possess the required self-consciousness and energy, and above all the inborn faculty of social organization. By the extension of American freedom Europe becomes benefited, and new and prosperous marts are opened as outlets for her industry.

War will not therefore prevent the progress of America, and is not necessary to forward the fulfilment of her manifest destiny. Not war alone, however, requires human sacrifices. Fate or providence demands from man to pay with his life every initiation, be it a warlike or a pacific one. This terrible law towers over the destinies, the progress, the mental, moral and material development of our race. The turning up into culture of new soils, poisons and kills the first cultivator. The richer, the more exuberant is nature, the deadlier the strife, the more destructive her powers of defence, the greater the number of victims. But the death of the fallen in those battles of exploration and culture, is productive of good to their immediate followers; and labor, capital often seemingly lost and ingulfed in such civilizing enterprises, are generally retrieved by those who follow in the cleared up path. Many hundreds of thousands of men, and millions of capital and material destroyed in wars, remain for ever lost and unproductive. With the money, the material and the labor of men destroyed in the last Eastern war, the whole of Central America could have been transformed into a healthy, flourishing habitation for a free, active, industrious, and vigorous race; her mountains, marshes and rivers been intersected by easy ways of communication, and the tropical region finally conquered for the free labor of the white man.

CHAPTER VII.

FOREIGN ELEMENTS.

FREEDOM and social equality, freedom enjoyed by man's labor and industry, the security of his earnings from governmental exactions and taxes, the facility of acquisition of land and property, the continually increasing demand for labor, skill, industry, these constitute the magical attractions exercised by America over the old world. From all regions of the old continent, as from so many human rolling cataracts, partial currents separate, setting forward toward the West. Individuals, families, and it might be said, populations from whole communes and districts wander in search of an amelioration which Europe can in no way proffer or secure to them. Every race, nation, tribe, lineage, generation, every language and idiom, from the South and the North, from the East and the West, sends forth its sprouts, and the thus ethnologically and geographically checkered Europe, becomes transferred to this country.

Two currents, however, pre-eminently pour in large masses of immigrants, so as to absolve or render comparatively insignificant the increase of population from other nationalities. Ireland and Germany form the principal nurseries which send here the greatest mass of new-comers, out of whom are composed these cardinal foreign elements, whose influence and weight must necessarily be felt on the psychological, social, political, and material development of America.

Considered from the purely material standpoint, foreign immigration supplies a want and a demand which never could have been satisfied by an ordinary increase of the original population since the constitution of the nation; and without which the Union, under any circumstances, could never have reached so rapidly its present prosperity and elevated position among the nations of the earth. The foreign influx fertilizes in various ways, and fosters the growth of America. Increase of population, increases production and consumption. Labor increases the general capital and wealth, to a hundredfold in this country; labor, as represented in artisans, mechanics, operatives, daily laborers, workingmen, by whose hands railroads and channels, mills, furnaces, industrial establishments are completed, cities erected, prairies broken, forests cleared. Whatever might be the unquestionable power and skill of the Americans, without the bulky supply of hands coming from Europe, material impossibility, the want of sufficient labor would have prevented or delayed the accomplishment of the industrial, commercial and agricultural wonders which amaze and perplex the old Europe.

To obtain and secure the above-mentioned results, all the diversified imports of populations from Europe contribute variously and in proportion to their special numbers, and mostly in harmony with their previous occupations and vocations. Before, however, a complete amalgamation of those elements with the intellectual and political life of America can be thoroughly accomplished—an amalgamation only possible in a long process of time—

these elements necessarily affect in various ways the function of American institutions and of her internal, social, and political condition.

The English and Scotch who come to this country, find themselves among homogeneous elements. United by blood, creed, language, understanding already the rudiments of liberty and its working on society and on the individual, they are normally prepared to learn and receive the higher degrees of initiation into the rights of social manhood. They do not generally occasion any confusion in the existing conditions, but fall in with ease into the great, social, developing movement. Not so the mass of Irish. Issuing from a state of barbarism, nay from that of savage brutism, in which twofold oppression and tyranny have kept them for long centuries, the mass of Irish immigrants is unable to acquire a perception and insight into the new, and for them unwonted and unthought of existence. Of course there are exceptions, numerous and highly honorable. Many Irishmen bring here cultivated minds, others, so to say, dissolve in the American life, abandon, at least to a great extent, the clannish connection and discipline, and in various pursuits of life count among the best and most useful members of the community. But these exceptions—rather limited in proportion to the mass, do not change the nature, the character of the Irish immigration of these last twenty-five years.

European history in its manifold compound of nations and states, does not know an Irish nation. The Irish never formed one. By no event, by no line are they recorded as a state, in the general movement of post-Roman or Christian Europe. They never possessed any form of a judicious and independent civil government, never gave any such manifestation externally in contact or relations with other nations and states. All the criteria which constitute a nation, a political, intelligent, internally fruitful nationality, have never existed or come to light on that island. Neither are the Irish a fair sample of the mighty Celtic race. Accepting even in the fullest signification the theory of races, they may be compared to a powerful tree with a cluster of branches. Some of these branches bear fruits, some remain unproductive, verdant to a certain degree, but never blossoming, and dying out fruitless. Such a branch are the Irish, in the historical development of the great Celtic stem. The Irish improve when denationalized psychologically and physiologically; when brought into new social conditions, and crossed with other races. They alone among the whole Celtic race are intemperate. Intemperance, now almost innate to the Irish, might have been the result of degrading oppression, and might have been to a certain degree a result of the contact, the intercourse with English and Anglo-Saxons, as intemperance forms a prominent characteristic of the German race, and was recorded by Tacitus, though so friendly to them. The bumper does not occupy such an eminent position in the heroic and chivalrous lays and legends of the various Celtic families, as it does among the German ones. The tyranny of the English conquerors, unparalleled in history, maintained for centuries by a heartless, despotic misrule, plunged the various populations and tribes of Ireland into a mire of social degradation. Generations after generations grow therein. Violence and hatred, disorder and lawlessness have formed the only social links and currents, surrounding and inspiring the Irishman from the cradle to the grave—becoming thus inborn to the people, they compose the salient features of the so-called Irish nationality. The feeblest sprouts of orderly self-consciousness seem to have been crushed out for a long time, if not for ever; and social and political psychology often doubt the possibility of their recovery.

No less destructive to the character and the faculties of the victimized Irish people at large, has been the influence of Romanism. The experience of ages, the lessons from history establish beyond dispute how Romanism, and above all since the reformation, when Jesuitism became its soul and its moulder, how Romanism has fatally affected and degraded the nations submitted to its sway. It is its character and nature to prevent the enlightenment of man in general, but above all to intercept the rays of light, and turn them from the masses. Its enmity to reason is indisputable and recorded by every country, on every page of the annals of human progress and development. In order to exist, to prevail and domineer, Romanism fosters and entertains the darkest and most degrading superstitions; combats with all the weapons of passion and prejudice: self-consciousness, self-judgment, thought and mental emancipation, those primordial conditions of social and political liberty. If at times Romanism has seemed to support free, and even republican or democratic institutions, it is only when by their help it could rule supreme over society, and retain the people in mental stupor. On such conditions, Romanism once wandered hand in hand with some Italian republics, and in our days is an intimate ally of several Swiss cantons. But mental liberty and Romanism cannot live well together. So teaches its own history and that of human culture. Therein Romanism stands reeking with the gore of martyrs. It has cheerfully consecrated all the murders and crimes perpetrated against those who have tried to emancipate man, who have denounced the allegiance to religious or civil tyranny. Never in any land has Romanism recognized the rights of a citizen, the rights of society, as at least equal to those of the Church, but has always contrived and still contrives to trample on, to subdue, to make them wholly subservient. When it could do it safely, Romanism has never hesitated even to destroy all other rights, for the sake of its own supremacy. The Romish surplice is not stained but dipped and kept in blood. Not in any single instance has Romanism disapproved the atrocities of the civil power, when perpetrated against liberty. And hence for the sake of civil and religious oppression Rome, the hierarchy, the popes, bestowed their blessings on the exterminators of the Albigenses; they kindled the fires of the inquisition; they blessed the murders of St. Bartholomew's night, those committed in the Netherlands, in Germany, in England, in one word, in every nation of Europe, in every region of the globe. Romanism, when its conservation is at stake, is meek only when it is wholly unable to shed blood or persecute. It is unchangeable, it cannot be modified and never was so in reality. As it has acted once, so it will and must act for ever; not the will but the power is wanting now. Its cardinal rule is to save the souls in its own manner, and according to its peculiar comprehension, and for this salvation to tread down, to destroy family, society, freedom, consciousness in single individuals as well as in whole nations.

The Irish are the fullest and ripest productions of Romanism, combined and harmonizing with their inborn characteristics. No other nation on the earth, neither the Italians nor Spaniards equal the Irish in this respect. Romanism in Ireland took under its wing the nationality;—it appropriated to herself all the powers of mind and soul, whatever may have been possessed by the Irish tribes, and for centuries ruled them with limitless power and influence. The priestly training to which this people was submitted for generation after generation, and to which alone it was and is now tractable, extinguished every aspiration after culture, brought it to hate and repudiate even the slightest intercourse with the spirit of ages moving around them. The priests nursed bravely the sloth natural to a degraded people. There is little if any difference in the mental faculties and development between the Irish, as described by historians at the end of the sixteenth, seventeenth, eighteenth centuries, and those whom the last quarter of a century has poured on the American shores. In this element Romanism here finds its cardinal support, and through the Irish it eats its way into the heart of the American social and political institutions.

Wherever Romanism gets a foothold, its tendencies and workings have been and are always identical. It is to envelope society in its anaconda-like folds, to subdue, to govern it surreptitiously, if it cannot do it openly. Towards this aim it directs all its efforts, uses all influences, slow but unrelenting as time in its destructive action. Romanism in America remains true to its nature; it is not different here from what it was always and every where. Romanism alone, of all European importations on the American continent, becomes not ennobled, ameliorated by transplantation. True it is, that the priesthood shows externally various signs of devotion to freedom, and to institutions existing here; but if such demonstrations may be sincere with some few, the whole hierarchy recurs to them as far as it is needed to influence and to delude public opinion, to seize and secure domination over a credulous and submissive flock. How is it possible to believe Romanism sincere in the love of freedom, self-consciousness, and independent judgment, all of which, united or separated, work the destruction of Romanism. It yields now to circumstances, watches them, and turns them to account with unflinching consistency. Romanism flirted with the French Republic in 1848, but it secured the election of Louis Napoleon; applauded, consecrated the deed of the 2d December, and saluted in *pontificalibus* the Empire. When it cannot rule alone, Romanism sides always with despots and absolutists.

The pious tendency of Romanism, as avowed by its leaders and chiefs, is to Romanize the population of America; or, in other words, to subvert the corner-stones of the institutions, poison the life, and destroy the destinies of America; in one word, to Irishize the Republic. The populations once become devotedly Romanist, the spiritual supremacy of the hierarchy and of its head, the pope, will become a fact firmly fixed in their creed, in their consciences. The philosophers and casuists of that sect have clearly and repeatedly established in theory, and as repeatedly the popes have attempted to establish it as a fact, that as matter is submitted to the spirit, and the body to the soul, so temporalities are inferior to spiritualities. A power supreme, therefore, in the spiritual order, *ipso facto* is supreme in temporal or worldly affairs; that is, in all matters concerning society, its government, its institutions. This deduction, logical in itself, is the credo of Romanism, a credo paramount to all the other confessions; for it Romanism works, and to its realization it directs all its forces; this is its beginning and the end of its spiritual and temporal life and activity.

But self-government, reason, must then disappear before the advent of Romish theocracy. In Europe, for centuries it has been checked by the equally ambitious and grasping royalty; but here it avails itself of the principles of freedom, of the non-interference of government in religious matters, of the latitude thus offered to its dark and tortuous under-dealings. It hopes and expects a final victory. It is opposed here by the force of light and reason, by that of the beneficial example of advanced culture and emancipation. But powerful as are these divine agencies, no less powerful are those of the genius of evil, acting on deeply rooted prejudices, on bigotry, on mental obtuseness and degradation. The strife between the good and the evil principle is not new. It has been carried on under various manifestations, from the earliest existence of the human race. The force of truth—it is a gloomy avowal—often succumbs under the pressure of falsehood;—otherwise progress would not be so difficult and slow. Undoubtedly Romanism cherishes the hope, by identifying itself with republican self-governing institutions, and by directing them cunningly, to reconquer on the American soil what it has successively lost in Europe; although it begins slowly to recover there from some stunning blows, and again restores intolerance, inquisition, persecutions. These dreams of supremacy once realized, Romanism believes it to be as easy a task to erect scaffolds, to kindle pyres for religious and political heretics, or throw them into dungeons in the name and with the co-operation of a Romanized, Irishized, and fanaticised people, as to do this in the name of a pope, a king, or an emperor. The spirit of intolerance moves uninterruptedly over Romanism its heavy and crushing wings.

Doubtless all these aims, schemes, and efforts, of whatever nature and character, are repulsive to the genuine American mind, to the heart and the understanding of populations nursed and bred by reason, freedom, and self-consciousness. Romanism therefore takes care to maintain the compactness of the Irishry, to surround it with the opaque wall of prejudices, to preserve its power over them; in one word, to have in hand a bigoted and devoted mass in the midst of the American population. Romanism watches over the Irish with the utmost care, and continues the work of mental enslavement. The hatred stimulated in Ireland against the English oppressor, is turned and entertained here by the priesthood against the light of reason and self-judgment. Romanism steps between its Irish tools and the regenerating action of the social institutions here. Romanism is the conductor through which they penetrate to the Irish, and they are thus administered in a wholly perverted and adulterated form. These immigrants, coming to a social state based on culture and on emancipation of mind, remain nevertheless in the most absolute unconsciousness and dependency. Their political convictions are administered to them ready made, as faith and communion. Whatever might have been his original unfitness to comprehend the order into which he is transplanted, it might be hoped that the Irishman, surrounded by sound sense on all sides, would finally be enabled to comprehend and appreciate liberty, the conditions of self-government, the necessity of self-improvement. But all this reaches him through the priestly exegesis, and as much of it as is judged suitable by the exegete. He spares no sacrifice to raise and maintain between his tool and the American heretic, a line of hateful demarcation. For this, Romanism insists clamorously on the separation of public schools, that its pupils might not be contaminated, that is, enlightened, and thus the power of Romanism be undermined and destroyed. Even in many European states, such arrogant demands of the clergy, if made, are not conceded. The education of the people, one of the sublimest results of American social progress, as all other fruits of liberty, is to be desecrated by the hands of Romanism. These fruits are to become a dispensation, of which the priesthood are to be the dispensers.

Socially and politically, the Irishry forms a state in the state, mostly impermeable to higher and civilizing influences. It acts blindly under the orders and under the guidance of the clergy, without discernment, without appreciation, without comprehension of the rights acquired by the rehabilitation of the dignity of man. The Irishry thus becomes a cudgel in the hands of leaders and intriguers. True it is, that the discipline of political parties often reduces to a nullity the will and self-choice of others, better prepared for political life. However, such a result is preceded by public discussion, by which, after all, self-consciousness can be stirred up and maintain its rights. But no such influences act on those guided by the priesthood. All is mysterious and secret. They follow orders given as a case of conscience, and cannot safely swerve therefrom.

The Irishman, on coming to America, finds already a bond in the common language, this powerful agency of assimilation. The process of his merging in the American life condition, and nationality, is therefore immensely facilitated, and his human and political education ought to be easily accomplished. He ought to plunge into the new and pure current, wash away, dissolve, his inborn crudity and shiftlessness, and become born anew. This however is prevented, palsied by the religious prejudices which are kept alive by Romanism. On the other side, a no less mischievous action is exercised on the mass of the Irishry, by those of its representative men who act and write, apparently, independent of Romanism. Those Shans prey on the excited feelings, on the recollections of sufferings and outrages, wherein consists the Irish nationality. As if such or any other nationality could be transplanted into new and different conditions, as if it ought to be nursed, cherished, and sustained. The Irish, like all other immigrants, ought to become Americans; that is, enter a higher social state than that abandoned in the old world, adapt themselves to it, by divorcing from the past, its interests, hatreds, or even dear delusions. But the mass of the Irish is maintained by its priesthoods, as by its Shans, in a constant state of irritation. For them their new country is always in the second line behind the reminiscences of the Green Island. It would seem that, without being henceforth truly Irishmen, they unwillingly become Americans. The exchange is, however, mostly advantageous to the new-comer. The mass of the Irishry bestow upon the society which receives them open-handed, drunkenness and ruffianism. The records of criminal cases, of assassinations, as well as of all kinds of offences, show that the greatest number in any American community is perpetrated by the Irish. The Irish prefer in general to hang around cities, to depend upon daily accidental earnings, rather than to scatter over the country, and turn to agriculture. In this way, they are individually more easily controlled by Romanism. In cities they form massy receptacles of ignorance and crime, which overshadow better humane qualities. Priestly rule and English oppression, both have thus shaped out the Irish character. Such are now its prominent features. Those brought into a daily and manifold contact with the Hibernians, and with the colored population, almost unanimously give the palm for intelligence, honesty, cleanliness, aptitude to work, and good-breeding, to the colored people. And it ought to be considered, that the African ancestry of the American colored population was brought from the Western part of Africa, inhabited by tribes considered as the inferior strata in the black race.

Such is the substance of one of the foreign elements which exercise already a powerful influence on the operation of political institutions. It bands votes together, and throws them preponderatingly into one scale, thus falsifying the genuine manifestation of the sense of the really enlightened population. In the recent election of President, the Irishry, its priests and Shans, sided with the propagators and apostles of slavery. As if they wished to show their regret in being themselves disenthralled. Dissecting the vote thrown for the two candidates throughout the whole Union, it will be found, that the really numerical majority of civilized, moral, and enlightened Americans, was on the side of freedom. Where the voice of reason reached the masses, the people answered to the call. The Irishry, in immense throngs, threw its weight on the other side. It swelled the numbers, and constituted the majority. With it coalesced what in sociological and philosophical appreciation forms the offal of cultivated societies; as broken ambitions, financial oppressors and suckers of the people, monopolizing bankers, haters of liberty, jobbers in money or in convictions, pusillanimous pessimists, and, in one word, all those who, in all political conditions, in all states of society, in all epochs and governmental forms, constitute the most corrupt portion—constitute the bars and impediments to progress, who lower the moral and intellectual tone of large or small communities, whether republics or monarchies, aristocracies or democracies.

Time, by its slow working, the irresistible action of social light and truth, may dissolve the coarse crust, stir up and evoke to germination the Irish mind, which is now, for all nobler and civilizing influences, in a state of torpor. But this process of dissolution, purification, and regeneration, is counteracted by a vigilant opponent, nestled in the interior, and watching over all the issues and communications. As in the junction of two rivers, the waters of the one often preserve for a long space the turbid color of the muddy soils through which they have passed, so the Irish current discharging itself into America, shall long be discernible by its impure exhalations. Nothing in the whole creation is more antagonistic, than Romanism and the luminous and sacred principles which constitute exclusively the fulness of the social life of America. Even liberty, all-healing and all-reinvigorating as she is, cannot regenerate at once; she recoils at first, impotent, from these Romano-Hibernian minds. They are even still more blinded by her glare. So the full blaze of light, poured suddenly, destroys the visual organs of one from whom the scales have been torn away, so the best and most nutritious food must be scantily administered after protracted starvation.

The immigrants to America are received without any restriction, with the most unparalleled social, political generosity. The whole sanctuary of institutions is thrown open, is accessible to them. The liberty of action, enjoyed without limit by the American, is conferred on the new-comer. His mental and social sores and ulcers are cared for, and this alike by the political institutions, and by private sacrifices. The humane establishments, public charities and private benevolence here surpass most of the like institutions in Europe. Those entertained by the States or by the communes are the result of the popular will, the people furnish the means for their support; and by their side there exist innumerable charitable establishments, results of private munificence, care and devotion. This constitutes one of the loftiest and warmest features of American society. These charities grow out of inward generous impulses. All the social shadowings participate therein, the men furnish money and their time, the women of the wealthier classes their care, tutorship and instruction, to the poor. The large cities, where pauperism and destitution are the most prevalent, go foremost with their devotion and example. All these establishments are principally beneficial to the foreign-born population, grown up as well as children, more in proportion than to those born on the American soil.

Schools for tuition, and finally participation in political life, that is in the highest and most free development and exercise of individuality, with the above named humane and charitable establishments, compose the boons that are proffered by Americans to the mass of foreign population that pours in among them. It was to have been expected that those new-comers would heartily accept the gifts, and apply themselves diligently to merge and fuse with the great national current. But the reverse takes place. They separate, and do their utmost to preserve and increase this separation. They enter into political activity, not as Americans, but under the name and watchword of distinct nationalities, that are strange to the soil. This arrogant and offensive putting forth, provoked naturally a reaction in the feelings of the people. If this movement called the Know-Nothing or American party, with the aim of limiting the political rights of the new citizens, is considered as a monstrous excrescence in the free institutions; in justice it must be said, that it results from the action from without, which, disordering the normal operation, evoked this violent erruption. The movement was originated not by theorists and speculators, but among the people; it is the expression of aversion to the doings of the banded nationalities and to religious intolerance, as well as of anxiety. The popular feeling was wounded. As the provocations from Romanism were more direct and immediate, the counteraction was originally directed towards that. Then it increased in its proportions and overhauled the whole foreign element, menacing it in the enjoyment of political rights. Intriguers, schemers, seizing upon this movement, envenomed and perverted it; but its logic remains intrinsically just. It is a violent attempt, perhaps, but nevertheless a salutary one, to force the immigrants to merge and to become recast in the nationality which is readily and heartily opened to them, to put an end to the influence over them of Romanism, and of the spirit of petty, puny national seclusions. It is an attempt to prevent the American soil from being cut up and checkered according to idioms, consanguinities and prejudices, as is the case for instance in Hungary; it is an attempt to destroy one of the most dangerous barriers to the general harmonious development and onward movement of the country.

The originators of American independence threw the country open to all comers, without regard to the origin of race, religion, or any such distinctions. They did not judge it necessary to throw impediments in the path of the immigrants. They themselves were not imbued with any prejudices of race or religion. Even Anglo-Saxonism was unknown to them; their large minds were not accessible to narrow limitations. And finally, they saw the necessity of increasing the population, as the only way to subdue the wilderness of the country. Man prospers and increases in numbers only in culture and civilization: animals, on the contrary, propagate and thrive in the savage wilderness. America wanted culture, wanted hands. Further, these immortal founders had one paramount creed—this was freedom and equality. They enthusiastically believed in the miraculous power of principles, whose electric touch was at once to transform and assimilate the immigrants. They did not foresee that immigrations might acquire such gigantic proportions, that the unchecked current might carry and deposit on the American shores masses, overtaxing the normal and regular powers of absorption by reason and light. They could not foresee that Romanism would ever try to raise menacingly its head, or what is still worse, to set busily at work to palsy and annul the beneficial action of American principles. They could still less foresee that the new-comers would attempt to form separate bodies and corporations—to form states in the great State under the plea of religions and nationalities. They could not foresee that the school-house, considered by them as the preëminent agency of fusion, and of moral improvement, would be avoided, prohibited on account of dogmatic squabbles, or that the regular movement of institutions should become distorted by the deadly might of ignorance thrown therein by foreign-born populations.

The recent American movement, however narrow and distorted it may be deemed; when judged impartially, is less narrow and abnormal than the wilful seclusion and formation in separate bodies of the Romano-Hibernians, or of the German nationalities or *Landsmannschaften*, amidst a powerful, flourishing, civilized and well-organized nation. This American movement is likewise more logical and less narrow-minded than that called Anglo-Saxon, based upon imaginary physiological, innate predispositions and distinctions, unsustained either by science or history. The former is a child of events and conjunctures. The Americans recognize, generally, that all races are adapted to liberty, but that they ought to pass through a preparatory apprenticeship, if they are not born on the American soil, that is, if they have not been nursed from the cradle by American principles, have not breathed the bracing air pregnant with them, nor been trained in liberty and self-government by daily intercourse and action. Anglo-Saxonism necessarily annuls the influence of education, example, principles, all of which are powerless to create the cranial bump in which is located the faculty for freedom and democracy. Whatever may be the ulterior results of the American movement, it has successfully prevented the separation of common public schools according to confessions, as was claimed by Romanism. Thus they have rendered a signal service to future generations, to the cause of freedom and reason, to the highest interests of the commonwealth, securing at least a part of the youthful mind from being delivered to the poisonous action of separatism. At the present moment, Romanism by its assumption and arrogance disturbs the harmony of several European countries, even absolutely Catholic ones. Wherever it can do so, Romanism attempts to get hold of public education. Belgium is at present agitated violently by the struggle between the encroaching Romanism and the spirit of liberty of instruction. Austria has delivered herself, hands and feet tied, to education by Romanism. Darkness is there as triumphant as it was before the reforms introduced by Joseph II. Baden, Switzerland, are agitated violently by the aggressive spirit of the Romanist hierarchy, which tries likewise to create agitation in the Prussian provinces peopled by Catholics, as well as those on the banks of the Rhine and in the dukedom of Posen. In both these regions principally the nobility sustain Romanism in the attempt to seize the public education. For securing his presidential election in 1849, and for siding with him after the destruction of liberty in the night of the 2d December, Louis Napoleon remunerated Romanism by giving to it a preponderating influence over the public instruction, by allowing the establishment of schools wholly in the hands of priests and Jesuits. This was granted under the pretence of liberty of education invoked by Romanism. Now Louis Napoleon begins to be aware of the danger in having conceded so much, and thrown into the hands of the priests the education of the people.

During fourteen centuries, Romanism almost exclusively, and since the Reformation, the other creeds and denominations have shared with Romanism the supreme direction of the Christian public education. If the past generations, or the present one are degraded, as the Roman priesthood, and the pious ministry of some other confessions assert, the fault is with the tutors. It proves that the confidence of the human race in the clergy of all faiths, as ministers of education, has not been justified, and that education is to be wholly transferred into other hands, that another spirit is to preside over it. This change the American people—religious as it is—have alone understood how to carry out. The clergy has not power to interfere with the public common schools.

The restrictions on the time in which full citizenship is to be acquired, and with it the faculty of exercising political rights, and of entering the public service, as claimed by the Americans, are already contained in the Constitution. According to it, naturalization can be acquired only after a certain number (5) of years of sojourn and apprenticeship. The question started now relates to an extension of the term. The greater or restricted facility for foreigners to become citizens or subjects, and public servants, of other states, vary in Europe mostly according to the nature and the form of governments. In the absolutist monarchies the facility is generally the greatest. The will of the sovereign admits at once a foreigner into the public service, and thus incorporates him among his subjects, his nation. Of old the admission by sovereigns of foreigners to elevated public and military offices was a usual and common occurrence. Many such foreign seekers of fortune served several courts, several governments in succession, and thus enjoyed privileges, rights and prerogatives, equal to those of all other subjects. It is the liberal governments that put various restrictions on the acquisition of citizenship, or on the ability to enter the public service. Such legal restrictions exist in England; they were introduced in France after the great revolution. In Switzerland every legally and politically organized commune can confer the right of citizenship, admitting any one as its member. The same exists partially in Prussia, but the admission or naturalization thus acquired must be confirmed by government, besides the sovereign having an unlimited right to naturalize or admit into the public service.

The same policy prevailed in the ancient world. It was easier to become a Persian or Macedonian subject, with all the rights and privileges of official servitude, than to become a citizen of Athens, Thebes, Sparta, or of any free city of Greece. Roman citizenship, originally was a boon acquired with difficulty; and in the mediæval free cities and republics, naturalization, that is the admission to the enjoyment of the full rights, privileges and immunities of liberty, was less easily acquired than from sovereigns. Generally, free communities seem to have been more jealous in this respect, and to have maintained a defensive position against foreign-born comers.

Next to Ireland, Germany contributes most considerably to populate America. The Romanist part of this German influx, albeit in many respects, such as intelligence, skill, orderly habits, laboriousness, aptness to tuition, is superior to the bulk of the Irishry; and equals it, with few exceptions, in bigotry, credulity, and submission to the priesthood. Still the majority of German settlers are akin to the natives in religious convictions. Some of them practically, others in general outlines and conceptions, are already familiar with the partial rudiments of social liberty. Numbers likewise have been through a mental training, and their intelligence variously schooled, already in process of germination at home. The Germans bring into America not only rough labor, as do the Irish, but are skilful working-men, operatives, artisans and artists, intelligent and laborious agriculturists. As such they contribute eminently to break up and put into culture the virgin soil; they contribute in various ways to the rapid increase of American prosperity. The internal trade as well as the foreign importing and exporting commerce, is increased by German capital, laboriousness, activity and steadiness. Most of the maritime and commercial cities of America count numbers of Germans among their principal trading houses. In one word, in every practical pursuit the assiduous German industry is easily to be distinguished.

Moreover, for the last ten years, the German immigration is, on the average, superior in mental and material quality to its predecessors. Formerly the great throng of immigrants consisted principally of the most mentally and physically impoverished portion of the population in Germany. The better ones among them, the apparently improved, were really as coarse as the others, and generally unfit to truly appreciate the new conditions which they found here. For most of them these conditions were summed up in one, paramount to all others: that of making money rapidly and by all means. Of late years the German immigration has consisted of individuals often enjoying a certain degree of prosperity in their humble spheres at home, as farmers, established artisans and mechanics, numbers of whom have come here supplied with moneyed capital, and thus at once in every respect augmenting the general wealth of America. Political revolutions, as well as a general dissatisfaction with the present state of their fatherland, and the despondency which grows out of it, has forced many and many to take up the wanderer's staff. Thus individuals and families have turned their steps towards this country, searching for the amelioration of their social, political and moral, more even than that of their material condition. In this manner numerous highly educated and enlightened Germans, thoroughly familiar with various scientific and practical pursuits, are scattered over the whole free area of the Union. These mental forces and resources are valuable acquisitions and gains for America; in the course of time they will fertilize, facilitate and aliment the avidity inborn to the Americans, for enlightenment and information.

If the Irish spade has contributed principally to cut canals and build up railroads, the German plough, upturning prairies, the German laborious husbandry, the German diversified and improved industry, and finally the German thorough and serious learning, and assiduous and studious habits, ought to contribute eminently to render the improved means of communication beneficial and profitable.

The German, like every immigrant from the European continent landing on these shores, in the difference of language meets at once the greatest impediment to assimilation. To a certain extent, therefore, he is forcibly reduced to an almost exclusive association with his compatriots. By natural attractions, the new-comers group together, and the groups increase in numbers and proportion. Those clubbing together form more and more compact masses, above all in large cities. The German life, in all classes, with its easy, simple, sociable, communicative habits and manners, has a charm of everlasting attraction, and the charm becomes stronger in a foreign land, amidst a society at the first sight rather formal, stiff, cold, and gloomy in all its manifestations. The mannerism prevailing here must appear somewhat unsociable to the simple-hearted Germans. It is therefore natural, that the German population should cherish these domestic habits, should live in them, and not be eager to exchange them for those which prevail around them. Thus the gap of separation becomes broader and broader. Besides, the Germans bring with them certain social and religious notions and conceptions, more elastic in some respects than those which are cherished by American minds, and are tenaciously attached to them. To such belong toleration, and even indifference in many religious performances, like the observation of the Sabbath, which for the Germans, as for all Europeans, is a day of sociable and mirthful repose and intercourse.

However, the restraint imposed by the so-called American strict and religious observation of the Sabbath, may be, in principle, wholesome and necessary. In a society organized on the principle of self-control and of self-government, where preventive and repressive powers, external and governmental, do not really exist, but ought to be rooted in every individual, to be alive in his conscience; such a society cannot too often be admonished, and have them refreshed in his mind and memory, of the social and moral purposes and duties of the civilized, onward striving man. The Sunday performances as observed in America, may be considered therefore as constituting a mental discipline, directed towards regulating and giving a sound and pure impulse to the actions, the convictions of the community. Individuals and families absorbed day after day by the hardening material pursuits of life, have often no time to gather up their consciences, to embrace in a general view the multifold combinations of moral and civil obligations to themselves, to their neighbors, to society. This is generally done on those religious Sabbath gatherings; and their influence must, after all, improve the people, and thus correct many shortcomings proceeding from an incomplete or adulterated mental culture.

In these daily increasing German groups rather than communities, containing elements and resources of internal vitality, arose the tendency to preserve their distinct nationality, and to assert it. Such a feeling in a German can easily be understood. The German nationality has a completeness in its various domestic, social, and high mental developments, some of them of warm coloring, and of unsurpassed beauty. These hearty features in the domestic life are worthy of preservation. They become inborn to the German character. Not less easily is it to be understood, that the cultivated Germans in America should attempt not only to preserve, but to nurse and entertain in full blossom, a language—this cardinal national distinction—whose variously developed literature, accumulated learning, and scientific treasures, form a fountain from which other nations draw deeply, and largely borrow. But nationality cannot prosper when transplanted to a new soil, in a society fully developed, and having its own powerful vitality. A German literature can no more sprout out here, than can a new, thoroughly German nation. Both can thrive only in the fullest independence; they require free air and untrammelled space. A language, to leaf forth and flourish, must expand in all the directions of activity. It must be the language of public and political life, of laws, of general, and not only of domestic intercourse; it must be the paramount instrumentality of mental culture. All these unavoidable and life-giving conditions cannot be enjoyed here by the German nationality, and by the German language. The Germans, pressed by the irresistible current of events, must adopt the language of the country to which they come; and to participate in its development, they must master it mentally and practically. They must adapt themselves, and merge in the powerful social current, and not square themselves against it. Only the Germans are the losers by attempting to maintain, what in itself is not maintainable, what does not find any firm basis, what always must float on the surface, what must dwindle in itself; in one word, a distinct nationality, a distinct language. In such a manner they may form puny confraternities, but never a nation. Thus, willingly secluding themselves, instead of coalescing with the native-born population, the Germans have not hitherto acquired the signification and influence which their mental culture ought to have secured to them, in the yeasty undulations of American intellectual and political life. In those arenas German names are unknown to American scientific, literary, or political records. Few Germans are in a position to participate in the legislative bodies, even in States where the German populations are settled in large numbers; not one is heard in the councils of the nation, where Frenchmen and Hebrews raise their voice. The Germans of Pennsylvania and Maryland, although for a century established there, have kept aloof from the national current; nevertheless they have not preserved their own language, their nationality, but only a coarse compound of both.

A mass of German intellect thrown on the American shores, during the last ten years, craves for congenial activity and occupation, and for means to utilize the stores of knowledge acquired by studies in their mother country, and increased by study and observation in their adopted one. Numbers of those highly cultivated individualities look to the press in their native tongue, as the medium of usefulness to themselves and to their compatriots. When such a press aims to explain and elucidate to those unacquainted with the English idiom, the institutions, the character, the cardinal conditions, of the nation and society in which they are to merge; when this press does it without admixture of conceptions, notions, and appreciations, applicable to European conditions, almost virtually different from the American ones; when it enlightens German readers about the difference of destructive European, and constructive, genuine American democracy—not that sham and nominal one—then the German press is of incontestable utility. But the tenacious encouragement to uphold what is called a distinct German nationality amidst the mighty and rapid growth of the American one, can never, and in nowise, prove beneficial to the German settlers.

For all the above-mentioned reasons, separate German schools are not only unnecessary, but must prove injurious to the rising generation. Such schools can never be better than the American common public schools and establishments, and must contribute to strengthen and entertain the separation; disabling rather than enabling the German youth to become, in the fullest comprehension, citizens of America. Separate German schools, and still worse, separate gymnasia or universities, would prove as mischievous as those claimed by Romanism on religious grounds. Both the one and the other stimulate estrangement and prejudices, and prevent the fusion of the various compounds, whose destiny is to melt and dissolve into one great harmonious nationality. Out of the fusion of various faculties, passions, feelings, intellectual powers and predispositions, characteristics of mind and of soul, as well as of the combination of physiological differences, completing each other, must necessarily be obtained a richer, fuller, and higher social as well as anthropological product.

Of all nations, the Americans are the least exclusive, and the least antagonistic or refractory to a fusion with any other race, tribe, family, coming from Europe, settling and taking roots among them. There are comparatively more intermarriages between Americans and the Hebrews, than in any European country. Thus the native-born Americans show by long and daily practice, that not the law of an exclusive race, but the combination almost of all, is to regulate the occupancy, the future development of American destinies. The Americans, or if one will, the original English settlers, for centuries amalgamated with the Irish in large proportions; the German influx, mixing, penetrating, spreading among the American population, will enrich these populations with various mental germs, add new and warming rays to their domestic hearth.

The German mind is of a depth and versatility unsurpassed by that of any other nation. Not a branch of human knowledge and science, wherein the Germans have not been in the first line. Kepler was the forerunner of Newton; Leibnitz his rival. The German erudition bears the palm above all others. The German metaphysics alone penetrate unknown spaces of mind, wherein the English or French mind shudders to follow. This does not prevent the German mind from ranking foremost to-day in all the branches of exact and natural sciences. Liebig, Müller, Ludwig, Gausz, the lately deceased mathematician, Buch, Alexander v. Humboldt, Moleschott, and hosts of others, lead the van in astronomy, chemistry, physiology, and all the sciences. The German practical technical schools are the model to all others. German industry, artisans, mechanicians, vie with those of England. Further, the German mind is a mixture of deep earnestness hearty merriment, and of poetical aspirations; and the admixture of all these qualities will give a higher tone, a necessary and needed elasticity to America. None as the Germans understand how to intertwine the domestic, the family hearth, the daily tasks of domestic occupations, with cheerful, lovely, poetical ingenuity. This artless impulse is inborn to them; is not a painfully acquired taste. The German household deities will dispel the artificial shams and the stiffness that often darken the American roof, cheering it by simplicity. Tenderness of mind (*gemütlichkeit*), moderation, frugality, contempt for external, empty show, are the graceful realities in the cortege of German family life;—they smooth and facilitate sociable intercourse. Scrupulous exactness in the fulfilment of the task, distinguishes the German mental or mechanical laborer among those of all other nations. These and the like qualities, fused with others that are salient in the Americans, will enhance their value. That is what the German brings and exchanges for being taught how to exist free, self-conscious, self-governing, and self-improving.

There are to be found among the mass of the Germans coarseness and brutality, drunkenness and lawlessness; but neither in such intensity, nor in such thoroughness, as among the Hibernians. And the Germans atone, by good, for those black stains which here and there darken their character.

The Irish and the Germans, with the smaller affluents of the great Teutonic family, such as Swiss and Scandinavians, spread over the land, and strike their roots in the bosom of the American people. They become its intrinsic compound, in larger and larger proportions. Psychologically therefore, as well as physiologically, they influence the powers and the formation of a new population, above all in the West, in whose morally and physically untrammelled spaces, the American historical and humanitarian signification will become completed, the future elaborated and fulfilled.

CHAPTER VIII.

EDUCATION OF THE PEOPLE.

For past centuries and even now, Europe educates certain classes of society, rather than the masses of the people. America, which in reality has no classes—as all such distinctions here are absolutely conventional, and thus absolutely fanciful and illogical—but a people—America inaugurated for the first time in the history of culture, a people educating itself. The educational system, its conception, tendency, agencies and execution in America and Europe are the most conspicuous features in the chain of superiorities and of differences between the new and the old continent and society.

Nearly every European state has a different system of spreading a certain rudimentary instruction among the masses of the people. All of them differ in principle and in working, from what is done and carried out in the American free States. All of them have in view to provide the people with limited elementary instruction, scarcely sufficient for the practical, or rather the mechanical use of every-day life, rather than to stir up, to stimulate the intellect, to develop and make it susceptible of a higher impulse. The tuition in the European primary schools, generally ends with teaching to read and write, and the first rules of arithmetic, but there does not exist, as in the American townships and villages, an uninterrupted and closely connected or ascending chain of general instruction. Europe has cared little to possess enlightened masses.

When, after the terrible tempest which marked the commencement of the middle ages, some of the European nations began toilsomely to dispel the darkness which enveloped them, the most rudimental instruction was limited to a comparatively few. The difficulties to be overcome were numerous, and for various reasons instruction was inaccessible to the mass, and thus limited to a class of the nation or of single communities. Public instruction preserved for centuries this character of exclusiveness or limitations, and even yet has not wholly thrown it off. General and higher information or intellectual education is still beyond the reach of the masses, even in states prominent for their educational establishments, as are Prussia and some other parts of Germany, Sweden, Belgium, Greece. Various reasons contribute to make the access to them difficult, if not wholly impossible. In old times the children of the lower classes, of the peasantry and laborers, often only by accident received primary instruction from a parish priest, or from a monk. And out of such accidents there emerged a Luther, a Keppler, and several of those names immortal in the records of human progress. But the mass remained in ignorance. In modern times poverty, often indifference, prevents the immense majority of the lower classes in Europe, from resorting to educational establishments, from which they are no longer excluded by social or political limitations.

The cardinal hinderance, however, in Europe, proceeds from what so distinctly and in the original source and germ separates the two social organisms. In Europe the education of the people is the task of governments acting from above; in America the people cares itself for it, and has the whole subject in its hands. The educational system in the American public common schools, is the highest triumph of democracy and of self-government. The European nations expect every thing to be done by their governments, and are satisfied with crumbs thrown to them. The English nation, enjoying self-government in several minor combinations, does not understand how to derive therefrom this self-improving energy, so strongly inborn among the Americans. The English people has not raised itself to the elevated condition of bringing within the reach of the masses a thorough elementary education. If the English do not expect, as the nations of the continent, to have the work done by the government, they look to the patronage, to the stimulus from the powerful and influential landed aristocracy, and as often to that of the church. The example of America stirs up England. Scotland, although covered with primary schools, has nothing which can compare with the common schools of this country. All over Europe the tuition succeeding to the first rudiments, can only be acquired in superior schools, located in larger boroughs and cities, and supplied there by the government. Thus the access to them is almost impossible to the children of poor laborers, of agriculturists, to the immense majority of the peasantry. An American town or village corresponding to an European borough, has several primary schools, and generally one of a second degree, and then a high school, within the reach of all the inhabitants of the township, where the children of both sexes can successively acquire a certain store of various general information, by which they can be fairly piloted through after life. Among the immense majority of the European masses, a kind of mental collapse follows the sparse instruction received in the village or some other primary school. The freeman of America, even in the most humble worldly condition, is accompanied generally through life by the thirst for spreading and increasing the information once acquired in the schools of his village or town. As the ancient mediæval cities and boroughs were studded with turrets and gates, so the American town or village is surrounded with common school-houses, over which towers the high school, at the side of private establishments for education. For the same amount of population, the proportion between the facilities existing here for the use of the people, and a European country enjoying even the best educational system, can be fairly put as four to one. The inhabitants of the American township create, vote and pay their schools, and increase their number, when the European centralization—it can be said—only niggardly supplies the like wants of the people. An American community of twenty-five hundred or three thousand inhabitants spends cheerfully three thousand dollars to pay the expenses, and the salary of the teachers of its schools; a corresponding sum is scarcely bestowed on the same object by a European government, in cities with from ten to fifteen thousand inhabitants. The school fund in the like American villages, absorbs about one-third of the communal taxes and expenditures, and this item leads the van in the communal budget; in that of European governments it is generally at the end of all the others. Large cities here devote larger sums to educational purposes, than do whole provinces of the most civilized character in Europe. The whole money spent yearly for schools, academies, colleges in the United States will almost surpass what all the European governments, put together, devote to the same object, the population of Europe being more than tenfold greater than that of the American Commonwealth.

In Europe the village schoolmaster was of old, and is still to a great extent, the personified mental misery, material poverty, and often an object of ridicule. In France the position of schoolmasters is in every respect deplorable; their dependence upon the government absolute. In Prussia and several parts of Germany, the situation of this most beneficial class of the community is comparatively ameliorated. Generally they go through certain studies, preparatory to a vocation, which is lasting during good behavior and the will of the government. But nowhere in Europe, governed, directed, conducted with ribbons, does the woman present so generally the cheering sight of becoming the first tender and devoted nurse of infantine intellect in the elementary common schools, as is the case in those of America. The like occurrences in Europe result rather from accident, but are not a deliberate aim. Here the young woman prepares herself freely by study, to supply this demand, largely made on her by the community. It is one of the noblest tasks of her social condition; and thus the American woman, from among the humblest strata of the people, is one of the principal sources and agencies of the incontestable superiority in the intellectual development of the American over the European masses. For women and men this function forms mostly a transition to other social duties and pursuits. Schoolmasters are among the most eminent men of America in the literary and in the political career. For the intelligent farmers, artisans, all kind of operatives, as well as for the wealthy merchant, the professional man, a female school teacher is often the most desirable wife.

Fresh from schools and colleges, girls and young men devote the first years of their matured activity to teach in public common schools. They fulfil this task with the unshaken confidence of youth in its energies. Not yet withered by disappointments and mishaps, they generally for a time only, and thus cheerfully discharge this function. By this—so to say, initiatory step—into the hardships of life, other broader prospects and expectations are not darkened or cut off, but on the contrary brighten and unfold. In Europe the village schoolmaster is either a poor weather-beaten and used-up wanderer through life, or as schoolmaster, excluded from all other prospects and hopes, he becomes a narrow-minded disciplinarian, going mechanically, without love or attraction, through a weary routine.

On the common schools, more than any other basis, depends and is fixed the future, the weal and the woe of American society, and they are the noblest and most luminous manifestations of the spirit, the will and the temper of the genuine American communities and people. They are the results of its self-respect, of the comprehension of its duties. The people feel that self-government cannot go on with ignorance; that education is the granite rock on which reposes the political organization. Even children are aware and feel the vital necessity and influence of knowledge; that it opens and facilitates success in all pursuits and undertakings. Children and adults feel that to be well informed, is to fulfil a moral duty towards themselves and towards society. Information becomes to them as necessary as air and daily bread. This makes the people bestir themselves cheerfully and busily to procure and sustain the schools. Legislative bodies, as well as town and communal meetings, impose taxes on themselves unhesitatingly for educational purposes. The European masses have not a general thirst for knowledge, deprived as they still are by various reasons, of large and untrammelled openings and issues into the great current of life. They are not yet generally actuated by the consciousness and self-respect, resulting from political as well as from social liberty. They have not the consciousness that the destinies, the prosperity of society, of the country, the normal and orderly action of the governmental organism depends upon their mental elevation. In Europe hitherto every thing, even the diffusion of knowledge, is comparatively circumscribed, centralized. Although most of the governments are aware that it is better and safer to rule and govern over the intelligent, than over the ignorant and brutes, they still labor under the misconception that the instruction of the masses, in order not to prove dangerous, requires to be limited. Their object is to form useful but ductile and obedient subjects, but not self-relying, independent men, investigating, judging and appreciating their rulers. Long protracted and various social, political and governmental depressions have resulted in the certain and almost chronic indifference of the masses to any instruction beyond the often coarse rudiments of an elementary one. The best methods and systems will be inefficient until the spirit shall awaken and stimulate the man from within. Inward impulse secures better results than any governmental compulsion. Whatever grows by itself, by its own vitality, is generally healthier and stronger than what depends upon the external care of often strange and unfriendly coadjutors.

Century after century has multiplied the various treasures of science, learning, and knowledge. But during ages of accumulation and transmission of all those mental riches, they did not produce anywhere in Europe a well-informed, mentally developed, intelligent people—except perhaps the Florentine democracy on the eve of its fall. Notwithstanding the great beacons of knowledge and science illuminating ages and generations, notwithstanding the matchless universities, the numerous and well-organized gymnasia, the limitless learning of numerous individuals in every State, in every nation, the masses of the population have remained and remain still mostly in darkness and ignorance, even in the so-called most favored European countries. Information is not domesticated among them.

Europe possesses great savans in all branches, certain informed and polished social classes, but separated by a broad intellectual gap from the immense majority of the people. England, with her brutalized populations in the mining districts, with her ignorant small farmers, laborers, and working-men, does not distance continental Europe, but stands behind many parts of Prussia and Germany. America, fresh and new on this arena, cannot vie with Europe in the number or quality of those giants of science, learning and philosophy. America has not the facilities consisting in libraries, in higher establishments, in traditional, uninterrupted transmission, and can admit without shame that it is thus outnumbered by the learned class in Europe. But in proportion to her population, America can with noble pride point out to the mass of well informed people, by far outnumbering any corresponding number in Europe. Numerous here are those dilettanti of knowledge, who, aside from the practical pursuits in industry, commerce, or any profession, follow some scientific and literary speciality, not sparing time and cost to satisfy quietly this intelligent attraction. Europe, however thickly planted with cities, boroughs, villages, has the intellectual level of her populations far below that of the free America. If this country has no such eminences as Europe, her plains are not as low, dark and shallow. For example, five million Americans—the Slave States of course excepted—will be better informed, instructed, and behaved, than an equal number of Europeans from any country whatever. Europe, with all her cities, boroughs, palaces, castles, villas, has not such villages, and even log-houses, eagerly intercepting and harboring the rays of civilization. Broad light or cheering dawn radiates over the American horizon; the several popular revolutions, reforms, as well as the *tutelary, paternal* efforts of European governments, have not yet dispelled the thick and heavy mist enveloping the intellects of the European masses.

Not those luminous representatives, rising as brilliant stars over the general darkness and ignorance, constitute the true glory of our race, or secure its happiness; it shall then only become a reality, when *all*, even the humblest and smallest, shall bathe in light, and their mental stupidity or incapacity be relieved. When the masses, and not only minorities or few, shall reach a higher moral, mental, and scientific development, then alone progress shall become a social truth. Not single individualities, not minorities, are to ascend, but the greatest number. Excrescences, hump-backs, and monsters, form comparatively rare occurrences in the realm of material creation; care and culture can often rectify what accident, but not an absolute law, has vitiated. The same law of normal healthiness prevails in the mental and moral world. Germs of mental powers, the aptitude for their multifold development, growth, and scientific humane application and utilization, are inborn substantially with the generality of human beings; in congenial conditions, those germs become the agencies, impulses, and lights of human actions. Whatever may be the assertions of moralists, philosophers, sociologists, and theologians, dividing the race religiously and socially into flocks and shepherds, establishing the necessity of supreme, independent authorities, and demonstrating the utter incapacity of the masses to an enlightened spontaneity, and to an unconditional progress, intellectual absolute inferiority, incapacity, and ignorance, are diseases, and, as such, an abnormal state; and thus they are the condition only of a few; at the utmost, of considerable minorities. It is not on account of any inborn inability, that the masses have been hitherto groping in the dark, and require tutorship and direction; that they must be stirred up, incited, often dragged, to acquire knowledge; but the faulty social order generates stagnation, crushes out or checks the civilizatory spontaneity of the masses. By the action of this perverted order, numberless minds and intellects have been and are continually murdered; and over the masses was pronounced a condemnatory verdict of imbecility. So it has been from of old, through centuries and generations. America made the first lift, the first effort to restore to every individual the use of his mental faculties, bringing within his reach the fertilizing means of instruction. The spark latent in every human creature can thus enkindle, the dignity of humanity become redeemed in the masses. The common schools are the noble initiators to this new and better era. Whatever may be the imperfections and hinderances in their action, those will be corrected or overcome; but on the extension of such schools depend the true progress and the all-embracing civilization of the people.

The aim of the various degrees of common schools is to form enlightened members of the community, as well as skilful, well informed, practical artisans, operatives, mechanics, agriculturists. In this view, instruction extending the horizon of thought, giving ballast to the mind, like ethics, history, literature, ought to go hand in hand with the teaching of all the branches of the exact and natural sciences; on the knowledge of which eminently depends any success in the every-day undertakings, occupations, and pursuits of life. Those last branches seem hitherto to have been rather pushed into the background; but their union with the former completes genuine civilization, fixes the material and social prosperity of the whole country. Every mechanical pursuit is a science in itself; such a pursuit, to become really productive, ought to be carried out scientifically. Education ought therefore, at the start, to familiarize with the scientific elements, whose application and further development are to become the every day's task of life. What is done already in Europe on a small scale, must be enlarged, made truly popular in America. Germany possesses technical schools, wherein artisans and operatives receive the necessary instruction for their various callings. France has in Paris and other cities schools for artisans and trades. England, where the true education of the masses is scarcely in an embryonic state, England has several schools for grown-up artisans and mechanics, where drawing and some other objects of immediate practical use are taught. But all that is done in Europe has the character of restriction; accident brings the working-man into contact with localities possessing the like establishments. The American common-schools, those intellectual nurseries of the whole people, ought to bring to the home of each one, and within the range of all, every department of necessary and useful knowledge.

New England was and is the centre, from which the common schools spread over the other parts of the country. New York, Ohio, vie to-day with her—so justly deserving the name of the brain of the Union. The younger Free States of the West, a political and intellectual progeny of the East, through common schools lay the corner-stones of their social structures;—in the same way as the Southern States base these structures on slavery. New England is the animating spirit of civilization, not only by her example; but her children of both sexes spread as teachers over the whole area of the Union. If it is a business, a way of earning subsistence, it is the most useful and beneficial one for the American community at large. Those shoots of the Eastern, Northern, and Western Free States, penetrating into the South, and there establishing schools and classes, prevent the utter ruin and degradation of the white population. The intervention of these missionaries of knowledge arrests the Slaveholding South on the verge of an abyss; it prevents it from collapsing into the total ignorance and barbarity, into which it is irrevocably dragged by the cherished institution.

The common schools are the result, the creation of the democratic spirit of America, and therein is the source of their incontestable superiority over the European educational establishments, which are consecrated to what is called in Europe the common people. But the superiority of the workings of the democratic spirit can be verified, even in America, by comparing the common schools with the superior colleges. These colleges were mostly founded during the colonial period, in strict imitation of the like establishments in the mother country. The common schools, on the other hand, originated in the wants and necessities felt by the people, are the creation of its will; they are born and evolve from new and different events and conditions. Thus, while the higher establishments still preserve their original scholastic and English character, the common schools, a genuine domestic growth, are the product of American civilization.

The colleges in America, being corporate bodies, and mostly sectarian institutions, are thus exposed in various ways to becoming narrow-minded and exclusive, as are almost always close societies, whatever be their character and name. Such associations easily become stiffened and retrograde, as their nature, like that of corporations, is rather to contract than to expand, their views often being governed by petty interests or individual animosities. Neither the sectarian spirit nor corporations can ever be equitable and all-embracing. Examples thereof abound in Europe as well as in America, in matters concerning knowledge, sciences, ethics, politics, as well as other more practical and daily purposes. Here, of late, the pressure of public opinion, the direct interference of the will of the people, have in many occurrences corrected the evil, have instilled a purer and more elastic spirit into the corporations, which direct and absolutely rule the colleges, corporations, which, contracted by dogmatic or political prejudices, do not give the necessary free scope to science, to investigation, and judgment, and have often appointed professors, not on account of their scientific, but of dogmatic or partisan merits. Therein corporations rival often in illiberality the most absolutist and retrograde government in Europe. It would therefore be desirable, as being more in harmony with the broad foundations on which reposes the American civility, and with the object of truly popular civilization, that the colleges should recast, and come more directly and fully into communion with the needs of the people, and be more directly controlled by it.

The Gymnasia, and above all the universities of Europe, although under the control of governments, are in many respects superior to the American colleges, which, like the European universities, are to bestow the final superior instruction. The American colleges can be only considered in general as a mediating degree to a higher universary instruction. They are scholastic in their method, and lack the free spirit animating the Universities of Continental Europe. The European Universities, for centuries of their existence, were the foci in which new and large ideas in philosophy, science, even in religion, were elaborated. Thus centuries ago the University of Paris was the arena of the struggle between the nominalists and realists, a conception which, under various changes, modifications, and names, still divides the philosophic world. The Sorbonne of Paris systematized Romanism. The Italian, and the German Universities, cast into the world many luminous conceptions, gave many solutions, philosophical, learned, and scientific. The American colleges, although possessing men of eminent learning and great mental accomplishments, have not exercised such an influence on the social or scientific progress of the country, have not projected any striking light on philosophical, scientific, or social problems. In America, as in England, almost every great movement and progress has been accomplished independent of the learned and collegiate corporations. When aristocratical notions, when the division of society into classes, ruled with almost omnipotent sway over the European nations, the universities almost alone represented and even practised the free and democratic idea. The American colleges, reverberating English immobility, have a tint of an aristocratical and exclusive, and often arrogant character. I do not affirm that the Universities of Europe always were liberal, or that they have not often shown a spirit of persecution. Unhappily their history proves that they at times have been animated by this hateful influence. They had their luminous and dark days, and those are on record. Thus, for example, the university of Tübingen, the greatest Protestant authority at the birth of the reformation, which for this reason ought to have been progressive in all scientific conceptions, that university protested against the system of Copernicus, as contradictory to biblical and classical authorities; and the faculties of Tübingen persecuted Kepler with great animosity, not because he practised astrology, but because he accepted and developed the Copernican system. Jenner and Fulton were likewise condemned by scientific corporations, whose nature in general is clannish, attached to established systems, and averse to new, routine-breaking inventions and impulses.

The American colleges attach, if not an exclusive, at any rate an overwhelming weight and significance to classical studies, as if the whole range of human culture were principally encompassed in ancient languages. They labor under the conviction that a dead language, to be acquired after much toil by study, nevertheless forms a better discipline of the mind than the vernacular one, in which the ideas are born and clothed, in which the intellect works and utters itself. The philosophical, scientific and social progress of our race is at present manifested and embodied in the modern languages; the most perfect classic scholar will be wholly ignorant where the world stands, in all that is useful, practical and moral, in his day. One of the results of this preponderance of classical studies is that the collegiate youth is more familiar with the facts—and not even with the true spirit—of the history of Greece and Rome, than with the literature, with the political history, with the history of the culture and progress of European nations, with which that of America is more immediately connected, and from which it directly descends. Classical studies, and above all that of the Latin language, were paramount in Europe at a time when the Catholic Church adopting it was the paramount dispenser of knowledge; it can be said that at that time the Latin was almost a living language, used not only in education, but in literature, in governmental judicial acts, and often in daily common intercourse. Learning, education, were then almost entirely restricted to a limited number, and formed a privilege of difficult access. The vernacular languages, in all scientific pursuits, were then in the state of inferiority, were only dialects. All the conditions favorable to the supremacy of the Latin disappeared every where, and never were extended in America, who, herself the offspring of new ideas, in the highest education of her children ought to take a course more in harmony with the claims of the spirit of the age, with the social and practical requirements of the people. The classical studies are to become accessory and ornamental, and the whole range of the modern civilization, with its languages, history, literatures, exact and natural sciences, ought to form the basis of public education.

European governments pay a due homage to the superiority of the democratic principle, as manifested in the common schools of America, and thus confirm their comparative superiority over the various colleges. Several of these governments continually investigate and by every means apply themselves to gaining an acquaintance with the system, the method, and their so successful execution in the United States. They attempt to imitate; but a dead skeleton in their hands without the animating spirit cannot give the same fruits as here. But no one of the European governments pays any attention to the organization of the American colleges. They know that they belong to the past —and of the past, Europe after all has the good and the evil, inferior, but likewise superior educational institutions.

The new Free States in the West, erecting superior educational establishments, enlarge the conception, and are in a fair way to make these establishments truly popular institutions. The new academies and colleges, as well as those erected of late in the State of New York, are created by the people, and not submitted to close corporations. Although they retain some of the deficiencies of the old colleges, they in many respects approach nearer to the European universities. The fresh and healthy spirit, independent of old routine, prevailing in general in these new States, makes it probable, that at no distant time the West may perfect these higher establishments, and make them correspond, as well to the democratic spirit and to the wants of the people at large, as do already the public common schools.

Public lectures number among the agencies and means for nourishing intellectual activity, and diffusing various general knowledge. Cities, towns and villages thus enjoy a pastime, a mental recreation, both useful and laudable. One part of the population, prepared by former studies or readings, and having thus sharpened its intellectual appetite, is supplied through lectures with new facts and notions, and enabled to keep pace with the general run of events, with the literary and scientific evolutions, which they are prevented from following in any other way by the daily hard or assiduous occupations of life. To the wholly ignorant a lecture brings new food, opens a new world, often stirs up the mind, and awakens the inclination for information. From the oldest times public lectures were delivered in Greece and Rome, by philosophers and rhetors; as they were also by professors of universities in the mediæval as well as in modern times. The professor, remunerated for other labors, generally offered one lecture gratuitously. The access to these somewhat exceptional lectures, was in principle free to all, but the topics were rarely interesting or attractive for the mass of poor and ignorant people. Besides, such lectures were delivered in so-to-say secluded spots, generally in capitals, the larger cities, or in those possessing universities. It is only in America that, stimulated by the inborn craving in the Yankee for information, lectures have become a popular institution, a social necessity, and a profession.

Started up by the example of this country, England has extended the usage of lectures, known there long ago, but never used as a general popular measure. Now the nobles begin to lecture for their tenants. It is a step, but a restricted one. The spirit of aristocracy will exercise a censorship over the choice of the topics. It will be one of *bon plaisir*, and very likely conservative of the rights of the better classes. The lecturing in America is carried out with a method and continuity evidencing that not an artificially created demand, but a vital necessity of the masses is to be satisfied.

On the continent of Europe, popular lecturing is almost unknown, and in the present mental and political condition of the masses, it is impossible. American lecturing is the fruit of freedom, and its demand reveals the existence of a people prepared to hear, a people already enlightened. Uncontrolled freedom like that exercised and enjoyed here is nowhere to be found on the continent. Here the people, its sense or taste, public opinion, control the lecturer; in Europe for such an exercise governmental authorization is imperatively required. The few scientific, practical lectures delivered in large cities for the use of operatives, are made mostly by the provision of government, without having the character of popular measures. The millions and millions of inhabitants of the smaller cities, towns and villages, have never brought within their reach this mode of instructive entertainment. And in truth these masses are still kept in such ignorance, so uneducated, that lectures would be for them neither attractive nor profitable. The European governments know too well, that the only welcome lecturer to the masses of cities, as well as of the country, would be the men who might speak to them of their wrongs, injustices, and various social, governmental, and administrative oppressions and exactions. On such topics, and on the means to get rid of the evil, or to have it at least corrected, the European masses crave to be enlightened. Their immediate interest bears on their immediate sufferings. Literary, artistical, scientific, encyclopœdical disquisitions, so acceptable and beneficial here, a brief analysis of passions, characters, men, things, of social and governmental problems,—this average of sound nourishment sucked in from lectures by the American country people, would be neither understood nor wished for by the mass of the people of any European country.

Lecturing in America has become a trade, a business more or less profitable, according to the capacity of the lecturer, his literary, scintific or political notoriety, according often to the excitement and even the infatuation of the moment. In the immense extension which lecturing has now acquired, much abuse can exist, much common-place may be enlarged, diluted, and thus served out to the often too confiding public. But even the poorest lecturer throws into the mind some incentives, obliges his hearers to exercise the power of thinking and judging. He evokes inward doubt, criticism, and thus often the wish to become better informed. It is always an intelligent occupation to listen to a lecture, to concentrate attention on even a seemingly if not really serious object; and every friend of progress ought to wish that the European populations might reach such a degree of mental development, that even mediocre lectures might be attractive and profitable to them.

Libraries, public and private, the diffusion and use of books of every kind, facilitate the mental progress of the people at large, supply its intellectual cravings, and complete the democratic education, which constitutes the superiority of free, self-improving, self-relying America, over the states that are submerged in European authority.

The accumulation made through centuries by government, disposing of large means, has formed in the European world those great depositories of the productivity of the human mind, with which the American public libraries of course cannot compare. In this country the beginning was small, and comparatively recent; but the extension of libraries keeps pace with the rapid increase of general prosperity. Private munificence or associations originally founded the public libraries here. The various colleges, endowed in this way with libraries, or increasing them by their own means, or by public subscriptions, although unable to rival the libraries possessed by the European universities, evidence the early and earnest solicitude of a society and of individuals depending upon themselves, to provide the community with means of education. Now, in many States, the legislatures, those organs of a self-governing people, extend their support to existing libraries, and create new ones, principally in view of the normal education of the masses. The public common schools possess libraries, and their stock increases yearly, by the care of the popular government, by the care of the communes. In this way millions of books are put at the disposal of the masses in the Free States. School-books embracing various subjects of instruction are the most numerous products of American typographical industry. None of the villages, and not many towns and boroughs in Europe possess public school libraries, they have no such fountains for the supply of their intellectual wants. Neither the care of governments, nor private solicitude, extends to that branch of the diffusion of knowledge. Where such resources exist they are neglected and considered as the last of all the necessary provisions. In the Free States, some few of the more recent ones excepted, in New England, New York, Ohio, and all the older States, there is scarcely a farm, or even a log-house, without books; nothing but the utmost poverty prevents a family from surrounding itself with these household goods, well used and highly valued, and almost wholly unknown to the millions and millions of European rustics, operatives and working-men. In this respect, not any European country, not even Germany or Prussia, can compare with the Free States of the Union. The Slave States in this as in all other points of civilization, carefully and proudly nurse their utter inferiority. This use of books by the masses explains, aside from the extension of the press, the consumption of paper, yearly surpassing in America that of France and England put together.

Private collections of books are more numerous and more extended among the population of the Union, than is the case comparatively in Europe. In every European country can be found larger and more complete libraries, owned by certain individuals in aristocratic castles and palaces, by rich parvenus, and a few others, than among private persons in America, but these special, individual collections are surrounded by millions of men uneducated, unlettered. The diffusion of books among the American people constitutes one of these rare occurrences in the comparison of the two worlds, where there is less show and more reality on this side than in many other conventional terms of comparison. Where the genuine democratic spirit is at work, there no shams are possible.*

* Among the private libraries in America, the one collected with the most masterly choice is that of the Rev. Theodore Parker, in Boston. Without having large sums at his disposal, Mr. Parker is always in advance of every public library in America, he is the first to enjoy the last sterling publications concerning history, philosophy, theology, that are issued in Germany, England or France. Each

If higher scholarship, exquisite finish and refinement in arts, scientific supremacy, have hitherto been the incontestable patrimony of Europe; all this is chiefly concentrated in a comparatively few bright eminences. America has enkindled light on the plains where undulate the great and real waves of mankind. Europe has polished classes; learned societies; but with less preponderating individual learning, America, the Free States—stimulated, led on by New England, by Massachusetts—they alone possess intelligent, educated masses.

work in his collection reveals the earnest, studious and progressive mind,—holding communion with the most luminous, learned and advanced spirits of his epoch.

CHAPTER IX.

THE PRESS

THE independent press is the high pontiff of our epoch. Light and freedom are the elements of its life, of its function. The press, in its true and normal comprehension, is to become more and more emphatically the most spontaneous utterance of the human spirit, with its manifold thoughts, impressions, feelings, faculties and passions. In the press re-echo the most delicate, energetic and subtle powers of our minds, and its destiny is to warm and enlighten, to radiate in all directions and to penetrate into the most secret recesses. The more society shall free itself from prejudices and from deference to the so-called, time-honored, various authorities, the more must grow and expand the influence of the press, entering and transfixing all the social crevices and fibres. The mission of the press is to be the chivalry of the age. She is to dissolve prejudices, disentangle the truth, elucidate if not solve daily social, political and administrative problems, defend the oppressed, the poor, bring to daylight abuses, discuss with conscientious independence the acts, not only of those to whom society in any way or manner intrusts the regulation of its affairs, but even of private individuals when their actions bear upon the community. On account of the daily increasing power of the press, it is her sacred duty to keep always elevated before the public a higher standard of morality, and direct towards it the public opinion. It is her function to remind men of rights, to keep communities in the path of duty, and unflinchingly adhere to what she recognizes as true and elevated. The press may err, but her errors are pardonable when they originate in a mistaken judgment, and not in a premeditated treason to her own convictions and faith.

The growing influence and power of the press are proportional to the increase of freedom and civilization among nations. This is an indisputable fact, and many are the reasons which account for it. The press is the most rapid way of initiation to life, to its exigencies, causalities, activity, to its daily occurring phenomena. It is accepted, valued and submitted to as a spiritual chain of daily communion between personally unknown but mentally united, associated individuals and numbers, and gives them the security not to stand alone, to have convictions shared, to be linked with many in tendencies, aims, purposes. So the press serves as a sign of mutual recognition for those who are separated by space, even by time. Freedom and publicity are the cardinal conditions of a higher development of the individual, of society, of communities. The sunlike publicity and expansion of the press, constitute and explain one of the reasons of its power.

Every new idea, notion, opinion, fact, moral or material conception brought forward, inaugurated in the world to assert its existence, has used the means of publicity, extant at the time of its appearance. The word spoken by the prophets and masters, by philosophers, and even by bards, by apostles and other teachers, was the most immediate and direct way of bringing forth and diffusing among men the fruits and results of mental activity. The printed word stepped in and became the channel and agency of teachings, communications and discussions. Books, pamphlets then became the most appropriate modes of publicity and mental intercourse. Finally, in most such cases the press becomes the vigorous, rapid organ, inherits and extends the activity of its forerunners. Nowadays, religion and science, ethics and politics, all the useful innovations and inventions in the realm of mind or of matter, in one word, the whole productivity of the human spirit gravitates towards the press, and searches for an opening in its issues. There the various oscillations, darings and hesitations of the human mind become easily and broadly reflected. The progress of the press is therefore marked by the slow but uninterrupted mastery over all the other means and ways of communication and publicity. The press welcomes every idea, every utterance and conception, nurses them carefully, tenderly, preserves them from death and destruction, introduces them into the world, prepares the ways and facilitates their reception. The press continues and in most cases completes the education of the masses. It is the oil which sustains the flame. Its providence-like vigilance wins the confidence of those who by their daily pursuits, or by the tendency of their minds, are prevented from watching over their own and the common destinies and wants. Towards her therefore turn opinions for steady direction and for enlightenment. Man in general dislikes to submit to being admonished, directed, or sermonized by special individuals, or at least to avow such positive submission to any one, be it ruler, priest, moralist, or any other adviser that may be singled out. In the moment of her action the press is a moral, impersonal agency, acting on the reason of each individual, and thus finds an easier access to the public mind. The well-advised submits almost unconsciously to her suggestions. Every body is aware that behind a newspaper there is one or several individuals, whose opinions or judgment the paper represents. But as their communications reach the public in writing, the reader forgets the individual behind his reasonings and his article becomes more easily accessible and impressive ; he matures and deliberates more independently on what is suggested, or what is acceptable to his individuality and reason, than could generally be the case in oral, personal explanations. The more energetic and rich is the spontaneity of a press, the stronger and more deeply penetrating her influence. When she understands her true dignity and influence, the press is the most independent among the now existing social powers. It can be said that, like nature, the press is to be henceforth eternally creative and productive. She initiates, evokes to life the activity of all, aids discoveries, popularizes them; she presents the arena on which ideas and conceptions become purified; where opinions, convictions meet and clash against each other; and where the only forces and weapons to be used ought to be information, mastership of subjects, comprehensiveness, logic and dialectics. The one who commands such allies is sure to overpower his antagonist, however animated and protracted may be the struggle. Few who stand without the arena of the press, are aware how much conscientious study, investigation and thought are often devoted to its productions. Ideas, conceptions, rich, useful and advanced, lie entombed, scarcely appreciated beyond the moment of their perusal, often misunderstood and not appreciated, without even a grateful reminiscence from those benefited by them. Often numerous sparks of genius are thrown out and scattered, stirring up, illuminating others ; each of which, if carefully amplified and extended, could alone suffice to secure the celebrity of a name.

The press is one of the youngest powers and components of society. Its significance extends more rapidly than that of all its predecessors, and hence the press has its enemies, detractors, and traducers. Its lot in this respect is in common with all the other social phenomena, and with all new inventions, which in the succession of time have appeared, dispossessed, or weakened the powers firmly established, and for longer or shorter periods ruling without contest over the whole, or a part of society. Every new phenomenon, as an idea or as a fact, is necessarily in strife with the past, which proclaims the menacing new comer to be mischievous, destructive, and subversive. Often eminent, generous, and partly, at least, progressive minds, with difficulty accept a new creation, which disturbs their repose, their preconceived ideas, and forces on them a change of judgment, a modification in their appreciation of ideas, in the comprehension of existing and acting agencies. The history of human events, of human culture and progress, is a continual record of such changes, evoking opposition; men in the aggregate, as well as single individuals, reluctantly submit to changes. Thus for example, Erasmus while applauding Luther, was still devoted to the party which was assailed by that audacious reformer. The assaults, the discredit which the champions of the past, of its secret proceedings, of the darkness, sheltering abuses and ignorance, attempt to throw on the press recoil and vanish, and even the most inveterate enemies recognize and submit to its increasing, all-embracing, and wholesome action. The press is resisted, outraged, vilified or undervalued by those only, who shrink from light, who prefer benumbing cold to the intellectual warmth which daily expanded by the press. Her power grows in proportion to the difficulties and impediments thrown in her way. Militant against abuses, often against the shrivelling and rotten past, the true condition of the press is to be the beacon for the present, the harbinger of the future. She becomes daily more and more the compass, as well as the expression of the moral tone of society, and is so even in the appreciation of her enemies, of tyrants, absolutists, conspirers against justice, reason and progress; all of whom hate but bow to her, and according to the old saying, *odit dum metuit*. Thus her supremacy daily becomes a reality; and shaking all other powers and influences, she will soon stand paramount to all, crushing out her most fierce antagonists.

This formidable lever and social ferment becomes of beneficial or evil boding, according as it is wielded by pure or impure minds. The press is like a two-edged sword, cutting out abuses, or inflicting poisonous wounds. Like almost every thing in the mental and in the material world, the press has thus a twofold character, and oscillates between good and evil. It can therefore have and often has a demoniac, degrading or destructive influence. But publicity and freedom carry within themselves a cure, and in normal conditions of society, when violence and reckless passions do not darken the minds, do not pervert public opinion, when the press stands face to face with free communities, the bad and impure one will be shortlived, will find no support, and die in its own mire.

America is at present the only country where the press now exists in partially normal conditions, where it is a truly social and popular institution. In Europe the press is not a necessity of life for the great masses; it does not reach them. The press is fettered by the government—or deliberately fetters itself, being devoted to the interest of a certain class, and embracing the real interests of the people only in generalities. Switzerland, Belgium, Holland, Piedmont, Norway, Sweden, scarcely constitute exceptions to this general rule. These countries enjoy a liberty of the press such as is not conceded to the other continental nations; larger than in Prussia, Saxony, and other German states. They make great improvements likewise in their common schools, thus advancing the education of the genuine people. Cheering as is such a progress, it does not however influence directly the great bulk of the masses on the continent. The progress and improvement effected in those smaller states, may be compared to one accomplished on the extremities, when at the same time the trunk is itself not affected thereby. This trunk is formed by the populations of France and Germany, adding to it Spain, Portugal, Italy, and the Austrian possessions. Exclusive of Russia and of Turkey, the continental population of Europe amounts to more than one hundred and sixty millions. Scarcely one fifth of this number enjoys a more or less free press, and still smaller is the proportion of the continental population which considers a free press as a vital necessity of existence. A genuine, free and independent press must have to deal with a free and enlightened people. To that the press is to look for intellectual and material appreciation and support. There must be a reciprocal action between the people and the press. One of the principal material conditions of the existence and the extension of the press is cheapness. It must be accessible without inconvenience to the smallest means. Not the specific quality, the conventional standing of the readers, but the quantity of sober, laborious masses constitutes the true public and the true value of a press. Not a lump of gold thrown by a government, by a class, or by few individuals into the conscience of the writer, constitutes the true prosperity of the press, but the small change flowing uninterruptedly over its counter.

A cheap and independent press is a recent experiment in England, not very likely to succeed at the outset, for the want of people or masses prepared to need it and to support it, as is the case in America. As for the continent of Europe, above all in France and Germany, a genuine popular cheap press cannot exist, for various reasons already pointed out.

The American journalist must strike a cord vibrating freely and powerfully in the masses; he must carry away his public; he must either find access to the popular mind, insinuate himself honestly into it, or overpower the public by his superiority. There must exist a mental attraction between the two; the press must inspire, awake, incite, push onward the mass, but it must likewise in a certain manner harmonize with the moral and social tendency of the people, which otherwise would abandon repulsive advisers. The cheapness of the press, and the large number of readers give the assurance of always finding a public, and also that even the dimmest shadowing and mark of opinion will be uttered, elucidated with the utmost independence. All these reciprocal conditions for the existence of a press equal to her mission, can be found only among intelligent masses, among a people in the full meaning of the word. And such a people hitherto exists nowhere in Europe, or if it exists it is in such small proportions that those data disappear in the general appreciation. Even in England the press has been to the most recent epoch a luxury not within the reach, not within the appetite of the people at large; not an attraction for it. In England—as is the case with the so-called independent press in some states of the continent—almost the whole press is in the hands of cliques, using it for certain direct purposes. Thus it becomes the organ of these individual aims and schemes, and the, what are called in Europe, better classes, forming almost exclusively the clientage of the press, are after all commonly led astray. But the independence, the vast number of newspapers, the competition, the watchfulness over each other, the aggregate of various opinions re-echoed in the press, all these combined conditions result in elucidating all questions from all possible sides, in bringing all the facts in their true light to the knowledge of the public; and further, in facilitating to any one with a little assiduity, an acquaintance with the state of public opinion on general or special objects and occurrences. In England with the freedom of the press, but without a people educated and prepared for its enjoyment, not possessing numerous country papers, supported and used by the masses; a skilful or bold writer, himself a toady or the tool of a clique, or of a man, deludes or bewilders the people, twists reason, facts and logic to serve his own· purposes or those of his employers. The schemes of these men are represented as truth. Besides, the majority of the English press addresses itself to classes, but seldom, very seldom to the people itself, as the only national element. The English press mentions the name of the people, to be sure, but speaks of it only in generalities, not in that broad and direct sense, as is the case in America. Whole districts, communities and townships in England, as well as on the continent, exist without having any newspaper, any organ of publicity. Therein England is under the influence of centralization, as are the other European states. Almost every township and more populous village in the free States of the Union has its organs, whose circulation is independent, and does not interfere with that of those larger papers published in the capitals of States, or in the larger cities.

The American does not limit himself to reading one

paper, to knowing only one side of an opinion, or of a question, but generally tries to acquire many-sided information. In Europe the partial public reading the papers, is mostly satisfied with the organ of its party; listens to one bell, and follows blindly its directions or insinuations. For an American, rich and poor, the press is the salt of his existence; the European laboring man is generally indifferent or wholly unacquainted with this intellectual condiment. The American people at large shows a degree of mental fitness, superior to the immense majority of their European kindred, in supporting and thus in securing the existence of an independent press; and in justice the inferiority of Europeans in that respect corresponds to the inferiority of their social condition and institutions, to the all-withering influence of governments, of whatever name and nature; to the still preponderating division into higher, aristocratical, burgher, and lower classes, of which the superior and directing classes are averse to this most nourishing fruit of reason and liberty. The genuine American people, the intelligent, working masses, require in the press a strong mental food, and they are able to digest it. The people likes an open, unhesitating, plain enunciation of principles and of appreciation. It demands from the press an onward impulse, aside from the discussion of daily occurrences. If the self-styled better classes in America, the men of narrow minds and large fortunes, shrink occasionally from a press like this, the true people, the people at large, support more heartily that paper which has the strongest and purest mettle.

The concentration of power, of intelligence, of wealth, the central action of government, the gathering to the centre of social classes, and of interests general and private, constitute the great preponderance, the paramount influence of the European capitalists over the country in political, social, conventional, as well as in real interests, in customs, manners, and all the innumerable relations of the kind. In America the great and most generally felt influence of the city of New York, that commercial emporium of the new world, emanates and spreads over all the Union, from the independent newspapers published in the metropolis. This influence reaches villages, and the most distant log-houses, and penetrates to the minds and convictions of millions, more directly and more thoroughly than that of any other social or monetary power in America.

Such a press—unhappily for the European masses, but happily for their rulers—such an independent press does not yet constitute the daily mental nourishment of the European millions. Europe being in a state of continued open or subdued ebullitions, the press often loses its energy and elasticity, in attempts to conciliate antagonisms, or to compromise principles. This kind of press is the only one acceptable to liberal European governments, but such a press is always in a false position, is always subdued in its tone, and lame in its movements. It is even repulsive to the people at large, which by the agency of such a press does not acquire the taste for public organs, and is not interested in their prosperity. Even the most free European countries, as Sweden, Norway, Piedmont, Holland, Belgium, Switzerland, have not reached the elevated degree of culture that causes their people to consider the press, the newspaper, as indispensable to their daily existence. As observed already, local papers in the villages and boroughs of England, France and Germany do not exist, and those received from other quarters are a luxury reserved for the few, but without any attraction for the many. Nowadays, when new communes are established on the virgin soil of America, the printing office of a local paper rises as soon, or even sooner, than the school-house. The settler, that pioneer of civilization and culture, after his daily hard struggles and labor, looks to the press, to the public organ, for relish, for encouragement, and for cheering consolation.

The indestructible vitality of the press is evidenced in Europe by the fact, that with all the restrictions, impediments, thrown in her way, notwithstanding the bitter and unrelenting hostility with which she is surrounded, she nowadays can no more be destroyed, as a social abstract principle, or as a positive fact, than could be destroyed the creative power of nature. Even the fiercest despots are obliged to keep her alive, often to appeal to her; they chain and muzzle, but cannot wholly suppress and strangle her. It is beyond human power to arrest its action, and the most powerful in Europe, Czars, Popes, Emperors, Kings, Aristocrats, and all other social compounds or impurities, dread her attacks. No one is so high as not to be sensitive to even her feeblest pulsations. Only those who are wholly insignificant mentally and socially, affect to mask their dulness by a so-called contempt for the verdicts of an independent press.

The American press—excepting that portion of it which is polluted by slavery, and that other portion which arrays itself wilfully in its defence, and fights its battles in the area of freedom,—the American press, in its productivity and circulation unrivalled by European countries, reflects all the degrees of social and mental progress spread and elaborated by the population. Some of its branches and shoots may be less energetic, less keen and clear-sighted, command a less extensive information, knowledge and scholarship; but by far the immense majority exercise a wholesome influence. By far the immense majority answer to the mission of public organs in the wider or circumscribed circles of their activity. In general, these organs and flambeaus, lighting the march of the people, according to their individual comprehensions, make efforts to point out the right way, to direct towards a higher moral and social goal. Considering the number of papers published in the United States, considering the absence of any restraint, the various countless interests, great and small, passions, excitements, irascibilities, and wranglings; the American press nevertheless redeems and dispels all the slanders directed by retrograde spirits against the, according to their assertions, irremediable abuse, licentiousness, and immorality of a press wholly free, and established for the exclusive use of the masses. In the position reached to-day in America and in Europe, most of the papers of this country, in truthfulness, purity of convictions and honesty, can fairly compare with their European kindred, to whom, by the combination of various governmental and social relations, scrupulous honesty, independenee and truthfulness become often almost impossible.

The ulterior destiny and significance of a free, enlightened and independent press, is intimately interwoven with the progressive moralization of society. The press is to become the paramount umpire, to prevent civil and unjust foreign wars, pacify irritations, suppress abuses, make them recede, and to a great extent disappear before the ever-pouring light of publicity. No question can be so complicated and explosive as not to become disentangled, mollified, in the free unprejudiced handling of it by the press. The envenomed question of slavery never could have reached such a degree of unscrupulousness, if the South had possessed a free press, if every opinion disagreeing with slavery had not been suppressed, menaced with murder, by the violent and lawless pro-slavery partisans. The time may come, when society in both hemispheres, and even in its actual phases of development, will accept the press as the sole omnipotent authority.

CHAPTER X.

THE PULPIT.

RELIGIOUS liberty, the absolute separation of Church and State, has become realized in America far beyond the conception, and still more the execution, of a similar separation in any European Protestant country. This separation, and the political equality of all creeds, constitute one of the cardinal and salient traits of the American community. The equality of creeds in principle and in application, is not limited to the various Christian sects and confessions swarming over the Union; but partially in the sentiments of the people, as well in the spirit as the letter of the political institutions, it extends to other creeds. The Jewish confession, as in England and several European countries, does not disable its members from the enjoyment of any political rights; and there is no word in the constitution, by which any other worship, even a heathen one, could be legally proscribed. Not in indifference to religious convictions originated this religious liberty, but in the finally well understood and well applied principle of the freedom and equality of moral as well as of political rights.

Religious freedom and independence were almost paramount to all other aims and objects, which were had in view by the primitve emigrants to America. Puritans,

Huguenots, Irish Presbyterians, Quakers, came here with the purpose of establishing and enjoying the freedom of religious convictions. Thus this principle from the start was one of the cardinal germs and principal corner-stones of American civility. Intolerance, persecution, stained, however, even here the first pages of the Puritanic establishment. It was the momentary victory of the dark spirit of the past, overpowering at times the bright coruscations of truth. But bigoted ferocity finally yielded before the light of reason, before the vital and all-absorbing force of principles.

With the freedom of conscience, the pulpit constituted in the American social birth and growth, one of the most active and powerful moral and social elements and agencies. In the formation of nations and states, the germs, of whatever character and nature, that are once laid down at the foundations of society, and forming the sources of its further development, preserve their vitality. They penetrate deeply, act and influence powerfully, the moral or the political unfolding and march. History is full of evidences of such vitality. The pulpit, therefore, which in the American primitive formation was such a cardinal and efficient element, of the same character as was the authority of a legislator, of a hero, a king, a caste, in the formation of ancient society or of European nations; the pulpit preserves here naturally and logically its uninterrupted action and influence upon the religious and the social man, both as a member of a religious communion, and as a citizen.

Religious influence has always made itself sensible, and mostly with great effect, in human affairs. It is a predisposition, a natural bent of the human mind, of human feelings. It is a positive, irrefutable, historical as well as psychological fact. Hierophants, high-priests, augurs, Brahmas, and uncounted other names, representing this religious element in the formation of societies, evidence—it may be even for our times—its still unavoidable necessity. Any one, even half-way familiar with history, knows to what extent the three greatest historical nations of antiquity, Persians, Greeks, and Romans, have been religious; and what a preponderating influence worship exercised in their political, domestic, and national life. Among the principal reasons of the condemnation of Socrates by the Athenians, was his real or supposed disregard of gods. Even St. Simonism, this most powerful new social conception for the remodelling of society, and whose axioms and ideas, thrown into European culture, ferment therein more vigorously than those of other socialist doctrines, most of which have been engrafted on St. Simonism, this St. Simonism, albeit accused of materialism, asserts the religious idea to be the most elastic and durable social cement. The American populations, the descendants of the various primitive settlers, as well as the more recent immigrants, all are still eminently and in majorities, under the influence of religious ideas and feelings.

In the American community, the pulpit is an undeniable social element; it has grown with the community, it is a part of its free life, more so than in any European nation; it has participated in all the social or rather political transmutations and transitions. As the Church is wholly separated from any interference of the State, and its whole administrative organization is in the hands of the people, the pulpit belongs to the primordial manifestations of the self-government of the people. In the enjoyment of the plenitude of its right, the people by its choice, or by its deliberate, self-decided submission to the influence of the pulpit, authorizes its influence, authorizes its tendency to harmonize the inward with the outward man, to bring into union the worldly political acts and laws with the inward conceptions and aspirations of men's better moral nature.

Whatever may be the individual opinions or comprehensions about the value and the interference of the pulpit in human affairs, the American pulpit is firmly rooted in the public life, is one of its freely, publicly, and independently operating vital agencies; and for the most part, it is a civilizing and moralizing one. The American pulpit, on the average, remains not behind, but progresses with the epoch. It throws often new and fresh light on questions of the moment, as well as on those penetrating deeply and lastingly into the destiny and development of the community. It seizes and considers often such questions boldly, going to the bottom, pointing to the substance of their signification, showing their immediate bearing on the conscience and on the religious feelings of man. The open intervention of the pulpit in problems concerning the social, internal questions of a country, questions on which depends the peace, the moral progress of men—as bad and immoral laws form immoral men;—this intervention, rooted from the start in the American social formation, is at least as logical and natural as the generally commended intervention of the clergy and of the pulpit against a foreign invader or enemy. And often the danger for the moral man—this principal object of the solicitude of the pulpit—is more imminent and destructive from foul internal legislation, or from a defective civil or political condition, than from external invasion.

In an absolutely free country, as is America, all the human potencies are called to act, and, binding with each other, to contribute to the progress of the individual, of the community; the pulpit, as an open manifestation of such a potency, as the expression of higher aspirations, has a duty and a right to perform, in uttering its opinion or its advice, on concerns where the social dignity and worth of man and of communities are at stake. For a sincerely religious man, enjoying his full and independent powers and activity, the supreme or divine precepts believed by him, ought to direct his public and civil actions towards the goal of higher morality; and the pulpit, as constituted and developed in the American social relations, and in the spirit of truly understood Christianity, is or ought to be one of the most watchful sentinels and finger-posts towards social amelioration. But such a character and such an influence can only be recognized and used by the pulpit in a social state, and in a condition of perfect liberty and equality, where violent passions, egotism, individual interest, do not pervert and corrupt minds and convictions; where society exists and moves in normal conditions, or at least approaches near them. These conditions, for various reasons, do not exist in the political and social state of Europe: many and multifold are the sources of this dissimilarity, and paramount to them all is the union or the mutual independence established for so many centuries between the churches of various denominations and the State, nearly in all countries and nations, a relation becoming thus inborn, inherent, chronic to European social organization. Social and political revolutions bear therefore in Europe equally on Churches as on States or governments to whom the Churches are wedded. When restorations of ancient abuses—called the ancient order of things—take place, among the restored objects counts always the power of the Church, be it a Romanist or a Protestant, and the one generally not less obnoxious than the other. The pulpit in Europe cannot acquire this free, independent expansion, and the civil significance that is possessed by the American pulpit, born and nursed among new events and conjunctures. Nearly all the European churches, confessions, pulpits, and confessionals, in Protestant or Romanist nations, are interested in the worldly powers, side for or against the special governments, according to their special relations with them, be those governments absolute, constitutional, or republican. So it is in France, as in England, in Germany, Prussia, Holland, as in Austria, in autocratic Russia, or in of late democratized Switzerland, where, as for example in the Cantons of Geneva, Vaud, Neufchatel, and others, numbers of the protestant clergy took a stand against the new governments, established in 1848 by the people on the ruins of the ancient privileged burghers, patricians, and various puny local oligarchies. The American clergy and pulpit is not linked with a past, as no such one exists for American society, or at least not one inimical to progress. The American clergy or pulpit has not linked its destinies with castes, governments, and power-holders, nor has it ever been—in the Free States—their servant or accomplice. It has nothing to dread from new ideas, or even from new social transformations. It can therefore freely discuss the principles on which society reposes, without falling under the reproach of submissiveness, egotism, or servility.

The average of those devoted to the pulpit in various confessions, represents comparatively the greatest mass of learning, scholarship, and diversified information in America. The Unitarian confession, although the smallest numerically, possesses the most elastic and all-embracing minds. The various American theologians, if generally not equal to the great giants of theological dogmatism and criticism in Germany, can nevertheless compare with them favorably; and, for the variety of their literary attainments and productivity, they surpass the mass of the clergy of any European country. They are studious, laborious; and depending for support upon their parishioners, they are their pride, and must endeavor to maintain their conspicuous mental standing, in order to answer their expectations, or else a successful competitor may conciliate the favor of the religious congregation. Living and depending on a community among which is spread a certain degree of general culture, the pastor naturally attempts not only not to remain behind its average, but to preserve a certain superiority in harmony with his leading position. Most of these incentives do not exist in Europe, where the favor of government is to be courted, or where the communities in the country are generally less advanced and less interested in the various—even in what is called superficial or encyclopedical—activity and manifestations of the human mind. The political development and progressive amelioration of society in its legislative concerns, is of equal interest for the American clergyman, with theological, dogmatical niceties; he observes them with care and devotion. He does not wish to hinder and encumber the social progress, but to preserve to it—what he believes to be—a Christian character.

Men originally prepared for the pulpit, after having abandoned the theological vocation, are found in various mental, literary, and political functions, among the most eminent on the American horizon; as, for example, the highly accomplished scholar, the elegant and truly American orator, and at times the sagacious statesman, Edward Everett, Bancroft, the historian, Sparks, the indefatigable compilator and writer of American historical documents, and independent philosophical minds, as that of Ripley, of Emerson, of James, the brilliant rhetorician, and many others. A transition from theological studies, from the pulpit to other worldly pursuits, to political life, is easier generally in America than it is anywhere in Europe.

The Romanist clergy, numerous in America, and in

its immense majority composed of Irish, does not constitute in the average, an aggregate of superiority in variety of information and mental culture, as is the case with other confessions. Some prominent individuals scattered among the mass do not change the general character of inferiority. Many are the reasons which account for this. Romanism, and principally its clergy, all over Europe, is inferior in all the branches of human learning and science to the aggregate of various learning, mastered by its philosophical or doctrinal opponents, and generally possessed by the laity. For the last few centuries, and above all, as now reduced to the defensive, clerical Romanism has lost vitality, productivity, expansion and elasticity. Before the Reformation its power was rarely if at all questioned, it ruled nearly paramount in the domain of mind. It was then for the most part friendly to sciences and scholarship, as the danger from knowledge was not thus imminent and immediate. Romanism partly preserved this elasticity even in the first ten years of the Reformation, then not yet conscious of its future civilizing power. Thus, for example, the system of Copernicus was originally better treated by Catholics than by Protestants. The inquisition, the Popes, began to condemn it when they found that this would suit their policy, when they saw the danger of any innovation. About the time when Galileo was shut up in dungeons—but uttered his celebrated *e pur' si muove* —an Augustine monk, Didacus Stunica, in Spain, writing commentaries on the book of Job, declared the Copernican system to be the only true one. In the 15th, 16th, and even in the beginning of the 17th century, there was hardly, besides the court of Rome, any other spot in the world that could exhibit such manifold efforts in literature and art, so much racy intellectual impulse and enjoyment, and an existence so much engaging the various powers of the mind. Now, neither the court of Rome nor its clerical legions extended over Europe, are in the first ranks of the intellectual, scientific, and learned world. The American catholic clergy shares the common fate, but in a larger degree, and is inferior to its European confraternity. The greatest number of them seem rather indifferent to enlightening themselves, or to lessening the ignorance of their rude flocks. It seems to be of small or secondary interest to them to have enlightened congregations. They aim rather at preserving and nursing the mental stupidity for the greater glory of Rome and for their own security. Some do this it may be said innocently, not aware of a better aim, but the hierarchy has fixed and well defined purposes. The hierarchy wants among its ordained officials, as well as among the flocks, submission, willing and pliant tools, and not self-conscious individualities. The means of education for the Romanist clergy are inferior in every respect to the like establishments in Europe. The very insufficient diocesan seminaries are generally directed by Jesuits. The history of this militant, aggressive order, so unrelenting in the prosecution of power, shows that one of the cardinal objects in education is to prepare and drill the mind to an absolute dependence, to crush out, extinguish any spark of self-judgment, not only in the laity but likewise in the clergy, and above all in the secular clergy. In this spirit is directed the public education in the jesuitical establishments, as well as in the seminaries. The pupils of each must be so shaped out as to remain for life unshaken in their faith in the supremacy of the fathers. A secular priest, who after all is to be let loose into the world, entering a community breathing self-consciousness, self-reliance, where the power of reason is recognized as paramount; such a priest, thrown among such temptations, must be penetrated through and through with the conviction of his inferiority, that he must always seek and cling to the decision of his tutors and masters, that he must remain for ever a tool, unaware of his individuality. He must never be able to appeal to his own reason, judgment, and mental initiative. So his general information is limited, mangled, defective. He is inspired and wholly schooled to be distrustful of the light of his own reason, as well as to suspect learning and knowledge when illuminated or vivified by it. He, as well as the flocks confided to his care, must never discover that reason and mind alone constitute the difference between man and brute; that if there is any truth in the supposed or admitted likeness between the Creator and the creature, this likeness is absolutely spiritual, based on the faculty of reason. The priest and the flock must never discover that reason and mind are the highest gifts, and that faith at the best is only the corollary of a mind actuated by reason.

The Romanist clergy is unrelenting in its activity—rather a mechanical one—under the direction of the hierarchy, under the inspiration of the Jesuits. Some halo of devotion and self-sacrifice surrounded and embellished years ago the labors and life of the secular Romanist clergy. They shared the poverty, the gross abjectness, of their parishioners, and still, in many instances, their material destitution equals the mental one. With the material progress and conditional prosperity of the Romanist population, a sensible amelioration has taken place in the worldly situation of its clergy; but the mental emancipation of flocks and shepherds is for a long time out of the question.

CHAPTER XI.

THE AMERICAN MIND.

The genuine American mind is the sum of various components, intuitive as well as objective in their source, and in their operations. Various inward and external combinations, events and conjunctures, have added to the English substratum, new, diversified, spiritual, and so to say, corporeal terms and substances. In its present stage of development, this alloy reveals an inward struggle between the substratum and the affluxes. This progress of effervescence, and the consequent internal and external phenomena, taken in general outlines, constitute the dissimilarity of the American mind, from the special characteristics of the mind of each European nation. The contending forces in the American mind manifest themselves in various ways, and in efforts for asserting individuality, originality, and an independent mode of perception. Nevertheless the substratum maintains its ground, yielding slowly and stubbornly to the pressure of the elements which accumulate upon it. In the oscillations produced by this struggle, originate those contrasts which mark more or less distinctly the intellectual manifestations.

The American mind tends pre-eminently towards the objective, at times however being given to the subjective, even to abstract speculation. It is singularly impulsive and receptive, seizes eagerly upon the most antagonistic objects, and embraces them with considerable elasticity. Expansive, and at times daring, it is less disciplined and subdued by routine, than is the case with the English mind. Hitherto the American mind has not reached the elevated stand-point of an absolute, intuitive individuality. Stimulated by the fulness and vigor of intuitiveness, but open to the breathing influences of outward nature, to the ever freshly pouring combinations of events, the mind ascends slowly, step by step, into the expanding region of normal self-consciousness. It is inquisitive, analytic, dismembering, and still eager often to discover, to comprehend a general law, to accept general formulas and axioms, and to submit to them. It grapples willingly with difficulties, but is not however always enduring or patient enough to overcome and subdue them, above all when the difficulties are founded in merely abstract, speculative combinations. Evoked to self-conscious activity, the American mind was thrown at the start into a stern and rough medium, and cut off from the motherland; it was obliged to direct all its intensity to struggles with nature, with destructive matter, was forced to choose and decide swiftly, to act, and not to remain in musing contemplation.

Immediate practical results are more attractive for the American mind, although not exclusively, than the charms of imagination. In its intellectual, positive turn, it yields easily to the pressure of outward events and combinations. Intellect finds more food, more stimulus, in externalities, and therefore it overpowers the spirit, the imagination, as well as the tendency to abstract, interior contemplation. Of great mobility, expansive but not deep, the American mind as yet seems unable to seize thoroughly and penetrate deeply into the infinity of intuitive ideas, engrossed as it has hitherto been by sensations. The social condition, the primitive state of nature, opening uninterruptedly her wider and wider circles before the Americans, challenge and attract the intellectual powers, carry away the activity into one general, explorative, mechanical, commercial current. But then even, a certain inborn elasticity redeems and saves it from utter degradation. And so, notwithstanding this seemingly all-absorbing commercial propensity, the mind of the people at large does not become eaten up or narrowed, as is the case, for example, with the immense majority of the various commercial classes in Europe. The so-called petty shopkeeper spirit does not prevail in America to the same extent as in most of the European parent countries.

Excitability, omnipotent in the American character, scarcely affects the activity of mind. The keen internal perception of the object strongly resists excitability or nervousness, and dispels the mist that has been aroused. If the Americans do not resist but yield to the current of excitement, it is more from want of independence, than from want of a sound, internal, mental judgment. Comparatively rapid and comprehensive in assimilation and combination—far more so than the English—the American mind seems to be indifferent to method; at the same time, by a striking contrast, the intellect is disciplined by it in most of its mechanical dealings with the realm of matter. Though not absolutely rigorous in its operations, the American mind is earnest, giving fixity and ballast, and forming a counterpoise to the often febrile unrest of character.

The various peculiarities of the American mind, the outbursts of its originality and independence, are manifested more generally and freely in the people at large, in its promptings and impulses, than in those which are commonly considered as the representative minds, the literary stars, or any other exponents of the spiritual or imaginative faculties. Among the people likewise, as for example among that of New England, that of the West, gushes out and is domestic the rich vein of humor, which constitutes a trait of originality, distinct from the English humor, and from that of other European nations.

Taken in the whole, in its substance, the American mind is eminently a progressive one. If it is as yet comparatively deficient in absolute philosophical comprehensiveness, if it assiduously elaborates the special and the single, by this process it gathers and prepares materials, to become co-ordinated and then fused together. The eternal spirit which watches over the progress and the development of mankind, alternately evokes to prominent activity the various powers and attributes of the mind, bringing them into full play, and making them preponderate, the one over another, according to the given conditions and necessities. Observing in mankind the march of mental culture, there is clearly perceptible an alternated but uninterrupted putting out and holding back of the various mental powers, the intuitive and the intellectual playing into each other. This assimilation and fusion at the given moment of the life of individuals, as of a whole people, constitute a complete real progress and civilization. Almost every mental and intellectual phenomenon corresponds to a philosophical and social claim of our being, and solutions are obtained by their harmonious interweaving. Then again new problems arise, requiring new combinations and fresh efforts. Exclusive idealism and exclusive positivism, bear the mark of onesidedness and uniformity, and are not virtually progressive. A wheel can stand still, can turn backwards, but its normal function is to move onward, and carry onward all its composing atoms. So it is with the mind; it embraces subject and object and moves on, because movement and progress are the sole conditions of life and of development; they alone are creative.

The powers of the intellect have been exclusively put into requisition and taxed from the first signs of vitality made by American society. As a people, as a nation, the Americans have not traversed the same successive stages as other peoples and nations. It can be said, that America has had no childhood, no juvenility. She was not lulled at the cradle with the legend, with the mythic song, with the murmur of tales. The Americans matured at once, and at once wrestled with stern reality. The lay, the popular minstrel, are wanting in their existence. The lay, the song, pour out of the heart and the unruffled feelings of a people. They flow from the näive faith, and the imaginative, undefined, tender longings of childhood and of youth. Thus the lay becomes impressed on the heart, it penetrates soul and imagination. Where it has once resounded, there it never dies away, and can disappear only with the disappearance of the human family from the earth. The song sways over the heart, undulating it softly and playfully between deep earnestness, and sweetly moved feelings. The song softens and appeases the most bitter and burning pains of heart and soul, as the embrace of a mother solaces and appeases the suffering and weeping child. When the thorny and withering contact of the world stifles the purest pulsations of one's nature, when it fills the existence with bitterness and despair, the heavenly charm of song warms it again to hope and to life.

Almost every European people lives upon popular lays; they form the most precious and inexhaustible treasure of the domestic hearth. Whether by the stern severity of the Puritanic rule, regulating and absorbing feelings, impressions, emotions, or by the arduous hardships of existence pressing pitilessly on the primitive settlers north and south in the United States, the vein of popular song was cut through and dried up. From the first day, it nevermore gushed anew. Unwonted, nay unknown to the American people, to the American hearth, is the soothing worship of national and domestic legends, tales, traditions, recollections. Reveries rocked not the people; miseries and sufferings, longings and love, found no vent in songs and melodies, those holy transmissions from the youth of a nation, treasured not in the dead leaves of books, but everliving in the memory of successive generations. The bards of such-like spontaneous outbursts sprouted nameless from the people; they left their songs resounding in the hearts and in the air, but their names remained unknown and never have been catalogued. The lays, like the art of writing, were not born in factories, nor did they appear as mediators of commercial intercourse. There must have been powerful or soft emotions, to be sung in ecstatic inspirations, and emotions and actions to be preserved from oblivion; their memory was to be transmitted to coming generations. Thus appeared unknown minstrels; thus unknown is the name of the first inventor of writing. The lays of unnamed minstrels repeated by the people, inspired a Homer, an Ossian, or the Niebelungen; the song of the people being one from among the many ever-enduring sources of poetry.

Poetical feelings and aspirations are, however, inborn in the human mind, in human nature. Poetry,—that sublime and purest reflection of the spirit, elevating man above the animal world,—poetry is distributed, although not equally, in all human beings. Few souls are wholly bereaved of this spark, kindling up in youth, and often in mere mature age, in love, in actions of sacrifice and of struggles, in noble passions, in longings, in aspirations towards an ideal, in efforts to elevate oneself above the troubled and depressing turmoil of life. How often is the simple life of a devoted woman—a wife, a mother, a sister—an uninterrupted current of unconscious poetry. True poetry is not necessarily self-conscious, self-concentrated. True poetry is not absolutely an art, but rather an ecstatic prompting of the soul, and does not always consist in the musical combination of words, in the harmonious, cadenced expression of emotions; but it makes life itself harmonious under all circumstances. The highest poetry of life is manifested in action. If, however, almost all beings originally possess such a poetic spark, not in all does it survive the terrible contact with the outward world. In most it becomes soon exhausted, it dies out. In some chosen souls alone the spark kindles to a life-giving flame; inspired by genius, they soar above creation, and immortality receives their name. In them poetry is the highest art, and the highest completion of their existence. Even sufferings and trials often increase the flame, opening new veins in their inspired souls, sufferings and trials being to them as the sledgehammer which crushes glass, but forges steel into a sword.

There must have been poetry of action and of endurance in the American primitive life, as there was in the sacrifices of the Puritans, although it found no vent in songs and other productions. The poetical spark slumbered during the colonial time. Colonial existence seems never to have been favorable to any kind of poetical effusions. So the ancient colonies of Greece, in Italy, Sicily, Marseilles, repeated the songs of the mother country, but no fresh genuine strain flowed from them. It might even have been also, that the climate here, assimilating and identifying to its influences the new comer, repressed at the start the poetical effluence. No spring, but rapid transition from winter to summer; so the individual here passes from childhood at once to manhood; so the people unknown, unconsidered yesterday, took at once, in full activity, its place among the oldest and grown up nations of the world. Among the people of the Old World, even material poverty, transformed into a chronic normal state, sometimes formed a source of poetical inspiration. There the youth of the poorer class, in forced self-contentment, abandons himself often to reveries or to the inward life of the heart, to soft, lovely emotions; here the child in the cradle, the tender youth, have striven and strive to free themselves from the withering embrace of poverty, plunge at once into the current of the prosaic but active world. Not spring but autumn charms and attracts the Americans; not the bud—as is it the popular song—but the ripened fruit, the carefully worked out art, characterize American poetry.

As soon as independence was asserted by the nation, the activity of mind became evoked in all directions; poetry and literature began to be a domestic American product. Lyrical poetry preëminently pours out abundantly, in powerful streams and often full of grace, freshness and charm. The lyric productions of acknowledged American poets, men and women, as well as many accidental effusions, can fairly stand beside, and some above the lyricism of other nations. Many of the little fiery or graceful poems, that have been evoked by events of national, domestic character, bear the mark of originality.

Generally, however, their literature, with its poetical and ephemeral creations, is not original in conception, not stamped with individuality, to the same degree, as are the life of the people and its political institutions. Emancipated as a nation, the Americans remain mentally, by their literary productions, in the colonial dependence upon England. They have outstripped the Old World in most of the productions of intellect, in mechanical arts and inventions, impressing on them, to a certain degree, the stamp of originality; *per contra* in literature, they with difficulty take an independent start. Many are the natural as well as the conventional reasons and causes which account for the phenomenon, that in reality there does not exist—a few productions excepted, as for example Longfellow's Evangelina—an original American literature, but only an imitation, or a continuation of the English literature. Hitherto literature seems rather to be engrafted on, than to sprout out of the vitality of the nation.

It may be considered as trivial, and in itself not worth mentioning, but nevertheless a regret presses on one's mind, that with such countlessly accumulated elements for originality in every direction, no new language could have been created in America. When the Latin world succumbed, out of its linguistic ruins emerged the Italian, the Spanish, the Portuguese, the Provençal, and the French idioms; the two last (the Provençal through minstrels) contributing again, with the Latin and Saxon, to shape out the English. All these offshoots of the Latin developed themselves, to a certain degree, independently. The parturition was difficult, and its process took centuries. Dante complained of not having a literary national language; but he became the god-father of the idiom used by the people, lifted it up, and purified it, and the Tuscan was created. By the formation of the above-named sprouts from the Latin, new agencies for the expansion of the inborn productivity of the human mind were brought forth, and the world endowed with new characteristic literatures, reflecting the mental, the imaginative, the social peculiarities of those various nations. Such newly formed languages are generally richer in words than is their matrix; but they are poorer in grammatical forms.

The English colonists in America, although immersed in a new world of intuitions as well as of facts, impressions, emotions, but neither politically nor mentally severed from the mother country, did not attempt to assert a social, and still less a literary independence. They were not yet *a people;* and it is only in *a people*, in its distinct, independent existence, that the urgings for self-consciousness in mental, social, and literary creations are revealed. They dared not to overstep the authority, or—what very likely they believed—the propriety of the English language, and increase irreverently, by new linguistic combinations and creations, the original parent stock. They unconsciously submitted therein to the all-powerful authority of the masters, using old names, for daily newly appearing mental and material phenomena.

Languages, those great arteries of mental vitality, repose not on authorities;—they were not taught by any primitive creator or inventor; but their creative essence and force are in the people, and a distinct language is the cardinal assertion of independence. Hitherto, all the great nations of mighty and lasting historical significance, have had a distinct language. The American nation appears the first on the social and political horizon, as yet deprived of this symbol of individuality. Independence must exist within, in the thought, and then it becomes asserted outwardly, in all the intellectual, social, and physical or material manifestations of an independent people. An innate relation exists between thinking and speaking; and the completeness and fulness of this relation reveals and points out, in the crowd of nations, the historical people. To speak an original, one's own language, is to have an original, individual manner of thinking, instead of borrowing other people's comprehensions, ideas, and utterances. To speak an original language, is to have independent, individual intuition and conception; because to speak is to manifest the inner thought. Language is the manifestation of the spirit *geist* which animates man. Freedom is the characteristic and the element, as well as the attribute of the spirit, in contrast to nature or matter. Language is the fullest utterance of the spirit; it pours out from the intuitive freedom, and evidences that freedom is man's destiny. The development of the spirit and of language generally traverse identical stages, both being manifestations of virtual individuality. The spirit and the language are the highest and purest essences of man's mental activity. Language has to answer to the demands of the mind; it is therefore ever-living and ever-moving, and not made once in time, to last for all eternities. Language ought to keep pace with the expansion of an onward, striving people. Words break out from the inward man, and their generator is life, and not dictionaries and authorities. A people in the condition of normal and healthy growth and development, extending its faculties of comprehension, increasing its multifarious mental productions, expanding its aspirations, multiplying its mental and material wants, and the means and resources for their satisfaction—such a people must unavoidably want new expressions, and it creates them. Such words are the spontaneous revelations of the immanent spirit. The substratum of the Amercan people, in its unrelenting activity, makes use of such creative force. This people moves on a separate, almost limitless orbit, and develops its individuality among the new mental and physical phenomena therein encountered. The people is not disturbed by models or traditional authorities, but creates new words for new ideas, conceptions, objects, emotions, and bestows on them the right of citizenship. Already many of the same words and expressions have different meanings in America and in England. The vocabulary of Americanisms forms a thick volume. The Americanisms will increase, will become sifted; and from the lips of the people, they will indubitably pass into books, in spite of their so-called barbarism, and become used by refined literators. Their origin, the power creating them, are the same as were those of all pre-existent languages, and words that are now sustained by authorities, and included in dictionaries.

The American literators, being brought up and nursed on English models, entertain for these authorities the most filial deference. They look up to them, rather than to the living fountain within themselves, and in the people. They are less daring than the people amidst whom they move, and who attempt continually to rival old models, to surpass them, to strike in every direction an independent vein, dissimilar to the English. The highest aim of literators is to imitate, to approach those examples, to remain within the boundaries traced by those whom they recognize as their masters, to win their approbation. The majority, above all, of the elder, leading literators, almost in all branches, who publish their labors, count upon the circulation in America, but turn nevertheless their mind towards England, wherefrom they are anxious to receive the supreme consecration, the knightly accolade. England is for them the supreme judge of the correctness and purity of the language, of the form, the style. This pupil-like deference to that distant authority, must influence and cramp the spontaneity of their mind, of their imagination, always on the alert not to commit a breach upon the proprieties of conventional or established English rules; not to be self-relying, young; not to use words or images, not to introduce forms, unknown in dictionaries and in time-honored authorities. For many of the literators, the utmost possible nicety, the fidelity to English models, to English authorities, the finish of the form, becoming in this way the main object, the substance, the conception, the idea, are often and unavoidably either sacrificed or pushed into the back-ground. In most of the authoritative American writers, there can be detected a certain uneasiness in handling the language, as in a dress not fitting them exactly; they seem to tread down with hesitation and uncertainty on unsafe ground. Few only seem to break, self-asserting, through the bar, and take an independent, individual course. In reading lengthy English works or reviews, one sees minds perfectly at home in the use of the language. They handle it with ease and boldness, seem to appeal to the inward fountain for words and expressions, impressing the reader as being careless of the assent or approbation of tutors. The English writers seem to enjoy independence; the critics enter more resolutely in general into the intrinsic value of the production, without paying so much consideration to the artificial smoothness of the form, as is the case in literary and critical America.

The unequalled actual productivity of the German mind, as well in quality as in quantity, is to a great extent facilitated by the absolute independence of the writer upon authorities and dictionaries. The only authority to which a German submits, is the intrinsic nature and character of the language, as felt by himself; the toilsomely elaborate form, the nicety of style, will never cramp the run of an idea. This independence is more pre-eminently asserted in all productions of a so-called serious character; of course, in poetical or ephemeral literature, the rules of art are strictly observed. But there is scarcely any German writer, even of secondary name, who does not appeal to his innate creative power for bringing out new words or turns of expression, answering to new demands of his mind or of his imagination.

The mental dependence upon England is so wide-embracing, that even in the judgment of the most cultivated Americans, familiar with the literatures of other European nations, as well as with their development, march, and history, England still represents the whole of Europe. So when, in any matter whatever, they look for a term of comparison, or seek to elucidate a problem, either scientific, literary, or social, by correlative facts existing in Europe, they generally limit their assertion or comparison to England, firmly believing that it is the same as if they were drawing the necessary evidences from any other European nation. Few hitherto can clearly realize and comprehend the immense difference existing between the social and mental culture, the customs, habits, modes of life, on the Continent of Europe and those of England; few are acquainted to that extent with the historical and chronological development and concatenation of various sciences and learning, as to be aware that, in this transmission and development, many of the sciences have originated or have been carried forward elsewhere than on the English soil. The people at large are less under the influence of this mental mirage, and in the thus extensive intercourse with Europe, are less ruled and influenced by the reverence for England. But as the faithful wander to Mecca and Rome, paying their worship to the pope and cardinals, so American literators of every degree and hue visit and pay homage almost exclusively to their English models and masters.

Literature being a reflection of the modes, the habits of life, as well as of a certain current of notions and ideas, its character, even in serious productions, corresponds to the character, nay, even to the locality, of the people.

American literature was started, almost born in New-England, and has been developed principally in Boston. The authority of Boston, which prides itself on its close resemblance to some secondary features of the English life, as well as on its literary deference to England, has checked, in the otherwise independent mind of the people of New England, the impulse of originality and of individuality But emancipation dawns. The people at large more and more diverges from Old England, and carries away literature. Further, the West elaborates a new social and mental life. There the man must fall back upon his inborn resources and faculties; the inner and the outer world equally inspire and urge him to individuality, to independence. The mind and imagination have no bounds there. Elements of the most varied and strongly dissimilar character, mingle and fuse with each other in the West. Their shock and fusion will produce new luminous sparks, new phenomena. The West seems therefore destined to mark a new epoch, to give a new and original start to American literature.

The American mind, the American people, has the greatest capacity of consummation, a capacity unequalled and unparallelled by any other people in the history of the human race. The very considerable literary home production in America is increased by the English literature, and by translations from other languages. The people at large, and not only certain portions of them, read; and thus there exists an inexhaustible demand for new products. Almost all the branches of mental and intellectual activity, good, bad, or indifferent, find issues, and are absorbed by the reading public. There are large masses, however, of either poor or illiterate, and scarcely rudimentally instructed whites in the Slavery States, who are not attracted to mental occupation, or who cannot buy books. Not less considerable is the mass of illiterate Irish, who therefore do not contribute to stimulate the demand for domestic or imported literary productions. The Germans, amounting likewise to several millions, confine themselves mostly to German literature. About sixteen millions of inhabitants in the United States—principally of the Free States—constitute the kernel of the population, which absorbs domestic and English literature, and foreign imports. Not any European country, not even several of the most civilized ones combined, and accordingly greatly outnumbering America, proffers in proportion so large and remunerative an outlet for literary productiveness.

The mental pursuit of book-writing preserves the prominent characteristic of all other pursuits in America. It is principally, if not exclusively, an object of material gain, and the aim is the sale. Such is the case even with productions of serious scientific purport or contents. European *savants*, in giving to the world the fruits of their —often life-long—protracted speculations, investigations and studies, yield more to an inward, moral desire to reveal and throw into the world a new generating idea, by which others may become enlightened, or stimulated to a new and fresh activity. They have in view scientific and literary fame, more than the pecuniary advantages to be obtained from their arduous labors, all serious, scientific books of whatever range meeting generally with a rather limited demand. In America, even productions in that department are in proportion by far more remunerative.

Theology and history stand foremost among the more elaborate indigenous literary products. The numerous various confessions, the unlimited religious freedom, and the innumerable independent spiritual communities and associations which it creates, the religious element still powerful in the composition of American society, the mental and social standing and influence of the clergy, sufficiently explain this prolificness. .

Mythical traditions, legends, lays and tales, preserved religiously by oral transmissions, have been the living fountains of history for all nations. America, born in positive times, and in the epoch of print, could not surround her cradle with such dim but venerated recollections. But for that, the May-Flower, or even the vessels which brought to these shores Smith, Raleigh and the other first settlers, might have rivalled the Argo in their mythical halo. But for that, the daring discoverers of the buffalo tracks in the undulating lands of Kentucky, in the prairies of the West; Fremont, the pathfinder, upon the Rocky Mountains, such men might stand before posterity as a Hercules, Theseus, or Odin. The recollection of the deeds of the past, charms and attracts the human mind. Man likes to tear them from oblivion. This tendency of the mind is evidenced strongly in America. With eager diligence the Americans make up the deficiency of not being covered by the myths and the dust of many centuries, by chronicling the most minute details of the action of the first settlers, the records of the first settlements, and of the establishment of towns, cities, colonies, and their expansion into States. Thus every village, nay, almost every spot has its positive history, its chronicler. Those simple accounts, how society, how communities, communes were born and organized here, how natural, simple causes, and the combination of events with human activity, human social and material wants, almost insignificant at the start, in their subsequent normal concatenation, have expanded and founded States and a nation—these facts by inference aid to explain the origin of elder and ancient nations, which is wrapped in mist. Human nature, human tendencies, cravings and urgings, although not uniform, are in substance alike; their workings, manifold in their outward results, are evolved from similar foci. Several of the events, among which America was conceived, and her cradle was rocked, when duly weighed and illuminated, partly serve as a thread amongst the mythico-historical mazes of the long by-gone times of the ancient world.

Unable to ascend back into the night of times, or wrap themselves in myths as a nation, the Americans seek a compensation in individual genealogies. As the ancient families of classical or modern Europe trace their origin to gods, demigods, monsters, giants, heroes, so the Americans delight to jump over the honorable, laborious reality, which marks their existence as Americans, and to deduce their mythical genealogical trees from English, Saxons, Norman nobility and gentry, ascending even directly to castles in Normandy; or from the fishermen, hard-working and trading *mynheers* of the Zealand sands and marshes, transformed in their imagination, into medieval knights. In perusing these accounts, one finds that—whatever may be the opinion of English heraldists and peers to the contrary—English aristocratic lineages do not run the risk of becoming easily extinct, as they branch off into numerous American families. This in itself childish and innocent desire, evidences that man placed in the most opposite conditions, is prompt to overlook his own intrinsic, individual worth for an ephemeral, far-fetched one.

Genealogy and chronicling, or diligent and laborious collecting of biographies, facts, documents, and sources are not the only features of American historical literature. Philosophical comprehension and criticism illuminate this field. So Bancroft has distinguished himself by the genuine historical intuition, with which his mind traces out the knots of the historical net. Seizing these knots, he disentangles the threads, follows their windings, points out how they again interweave, and how they continually complicate and branch off. A lover of freedom, but so to say, coldly, elaborately enthusiastic, Bancroft shows his mastery in the delineation of historical events, of historical characters. Hildreth, an earnest, positive, sober narrator, advocates the universality of human rights, and thus points out luminously where and how in her short historical existence, America has deviated from the bright and all-embracing principle of freedom, once laid down as the corner-stone of her social structure. So is Motley inspired with a noble and ardent hatred of oppression and tyranny; in him the fiery passion for liberty illuminates and warms his studies and researches, giving insight into the true character of those historical personages—hitherto misunderstood or overrated—around whom were grouped the events of one of the most ominous epochs in the history of the emancipation of Europe and of the Christian world.

The industrial and mechanical arts which bear directly on the necessities of existence, and urged by these necessities have generated the most multifarious results. They have reached in America an expansion almost unrivalled by any other European nation. All such inventions, answering to immediate demand, become a specialty with the Americans. They directly increase the material wealth, the forces and the power of the nation, producing the expansion of prosperity among the masses of the people. Democratic in their nature, origin and results, benefiting thereby the greatest number, they stand foremost in popular appreciation, and excite general and intense interest. In harmony with the state of society, and with its urgent necessities, they constitute the salient feature of the American mind. And so it happens that millions will pass unnoticed a work of the Fine Arts, when an industrial and mechanical invention would throw them into a feverish excitement.

A taste for the fine plastic arts, a sense of the harmonious, the beautiful, of refined elegance—inborn, it may be a love, in man, when considered in the abstract—often lies dormant in the deepest recesses of the mind of the masses. In general those senses require certain social conditions, a certain state of culture, to be awakened, to bud, to blossom and to give fruits. It is likewise generally asserted, that nicety of taste can be acquired only with difficulty, as the feeling for the beautiful is not one that can be called forth by instruction. Those who find in the law of races the solution of mental and social phenomena, concede that neither the so-called Anglo-Saxons nor the English are pre-eminently distinguished in the plastic arts, or in genuine artistic perception. This deficiency extends even to carriage, dress, etc. It is maintained that the taste for the Fine Arts in the English, is the result of education, of wealth, instead of being inborn, as it is for instance not only in those born plastics, the Italians, but even in the Netherlanders, the Flemish and various Germanic or Romanic families. English parentage, the very natural favor bestowed on purely mechanical and industrial arts, as immediately productive—the paramount necessity of struggling with nature, and tearing from her life and situation; the dollar and cent value which is bestowed finally on every product of the mind, in virtue of which the thinker, the artist is considered by many, and above all by those who in their opinion are of the better and wealthier sort, only in proportion to his gains; all this together would seemingly array and does partly array a sum of odds against a truly artistic taste and development in America. Nevertheless, there is manifest a powerful attraction towards the plastic and Fine Arts, evidenced by the comparatively large number of individuals devoted to artistic pursuits.

The natural and progressive development of a people is generally slow; and the æsthetic one—when not favored by special combinations—is the slowest of all. Freedom's paramount power, at times more intensely stimulates in a people the taste for the beautiful, evokes the longing for art, or enhances and generalizes it. Freedom creates or opens new arteries for the creative currents of mind and of imagination. So freedom can spread in the masses refinement and æsthetic taste. A truly independent people, fully enjoying and developing its individuality, becomes alive to the beautiful in Art. So the Athenians, the purest democrats of the Ionic family—had the most refined artistic perception and taste among all the Greeks. The realm of the Fine Arts is the realm of the absolute, independent spirit. Art in its highest conception and manifestation is the product of self-determination in the artist and in the people. Originality is the essence, and imitation is timidity. Originality consists in the difference of the apperceptive powers of one mind or soul from another. Character, originality and independence constitute individuality. Art, therefore, in order to have a broad and luminous signification, ought to be above all intuitive. Various are the reasons and the impediments accounting for the fact that hitherto American Art has not had a thorough stamp of intuitiveness and originality. The reasons are to be found in the nature of existing conditions, in the artists and in the media wherein he lives and moves.

Architecture was the first in the genesis of the arts. Necessity as well as higher aspirations were its generators. It had therefore no original type. In its higher conception and execution it was the symbol uttering a religious feeling. As such the architectural art was first monumental, and then it became applied as a domestic, as a household one. It would seem that the religious symbol, as represented by architectural creations, undergoes various modifications; but only at distant epochs and under a special condition of the mind and soul, both of them become creative, and bring forth new symbolic utterances. Monumental, religious architecture in America cannot inaugurate a new conception, but has to combine, adopt and imitate. For the Protestant churches of congregationalist, rational, democratic Ameriea, the Greek style, with its streams of light, its serene symmetry, like reason lying at the bottom of religious America, seems more appropriate than the gloomy, sullen, bodeful, awe-inspiring religious architecture called Gothic, Norman or romantic. The absolutely awkward spires or towers so greatly relished on American churches, have no symbolical meaning; they do not embellish nor do they give a distinct, imposing, or graceful physiognomy to the monumental architecture of the country.

The various original styles of monumental and religious architecture do not absolutely indicate the character of a people, but have often depended probably on the kind of soil on which they were started and erected; on the climate, the quality of existing materials, and their adaptation to the original conception and the object in view. The inferences in regard to the character of a people drawn from its symbolical monuments, are not at all conclusive. Gloomy, imposing religious edifices are not an evidence of an identical character of the nation or tribe by which they are erected. There is nothing more serious and grave than the Egyptian religious monuments; but the frescoes on the walls representing their habitations, with the light, graceful columns, the vine garlands overhanging the houses, place their domestic architecture among the neatest and lightest, and such must have been the inmates of the houses in their daily life and intercourse. One of the most ancient tribes of Greece, the Tirynthians, although they are counted among the originators of the heavy cyclopean edifices, were very fond of laughing, and other Greeks considered them a silly people. The church architecture adopted or rather preferred in America, does not in the least reveal any of the peculiarities of the American mind and character.

Civil, monumental and domestic architecture have an immense field open before them in America. They, to a certain extent, tax the creative power of the artists, for whom the peculiarities of the climate, the social conditions, the ways and habits of life ought to form the determinating characteristics of American architecture. If it should be difficult or impossible to originate a distinct American style, the selection from existing styles, their modifications and adaptation to the nature of things which prevail here would create almost a distinct art. False pretensions, trumpery in drawing and in materials ought to be avoided. Gaudy shams, florid additions delight in the showy, at the expense of the truly elegant and tasteful, ought to be shunned. The art or the artist ought to resist and correct the desire of making an unnecessary and indiscriminate display of wealth, or of pushing aside symmetry for the sake of premature combinations, represented as originality. Generally, architecture has no field at present for new creations. Only a thorough transformation of society would start a truly original architecture.

Sculpture and painting have their ideals and types in the intuitive revelations of the spirit, and in the reflection of nature. Their various productivity is limitless in prin ciple and inexhaustible. In sculpture and painting, improvement and individuality ought therefore to be attainable by the American artists. Intense vitality animates the genuine American people; taken together in all its characteristics, peculiarities and modes, it is full of energy, prompt in action, and on a larger scale than were even the Athenians. In the deep, broad, overflowing land, the whole current of people, the artist ought to search for types, models, and inspirations. There is the space for artistic genius.

Genius reveals itself intuitively. It bursts from the recesses of the mind and rushes to communion with eternal nature. The harmonious blending of this impulse with the objective world, turns inspiration into reality, and art is born. Genius and talent elaborate art. Genius reveals and creates, talent reproduces with more or less finish external perceptions. Both therefore in various gradations constitute the artist. The loftier and purer are the inspirations of the artist, the more fully and perfectly he brings out the various manifestations to plasticity from the depth of the human spirit and soul; a depth which he can only fathom by the force of his individual mind. The plastic work of art takes the middle ground between the immediately sensual and the ideal conception. Thus the mere strict imitation of nature is not the exclusive scope of art, but to evoke, to incite all the countless emotions of which man is susceptible, to robe them with corporeal realization. Man and his nature are the object of art; man as he feels, lives, acts, as he is impressed, nay, even surrounded by the world without. In painting, but above all in sculpture, only one moment in a given action can be selected, seized and fixed; and all the secondary parts and details are to be brought submissively but harmoniously into accord with that paramount moment. The problem to be solved in sculpture consists in sinking and fixing into the statue the spiritual essence of the being, to bring this essence into such accord with the body, that the reflection of the spiritual becomes expressed and conspicuous in that special form and part of the body which corresponds to the passion or emotion to be represented. The transient and accidental in all the other parts or members of the statue, ought, so to say, to dissolve, to disappear in the paramount aim, preserving nevertheless in the whole the marks of individuality. The vitality, elasticity, and freedom of the sculptured body depend on the precision, and on the conscious elaborate finish, of every single part thereof.

Regarded under the above aspect, sculpture can be uninterruptedly creative. Even in Europe—where art for many reasons has collapsed into routine—art makes efforts to unshackle itself from the onesighted comprehension of the antique or classical, and of its slavish imitation, avoiding likewise being carried away into the infinite of romantic exaltation. Both these directions have been run to their utmost limits and consequences, and the problem of our epoch seems to be, to bring into accord, inspiration, imagination, with nature and study; the contemplation of nature resulting without contempt of classical art. When the above problem shall be solved, the epoch of self-consciousness in art will become inaugurated. The works of art have to reflect the endless agitations, emotions, and play of our imaginative and sensitive faculty. A genuine artist must have the full consciousness of his creative power; he ought to dominate above the vacillations of his own imagination, as well as to be free from slavish deference to classical models and their imitation. He ought to stand firmly on his individual mental and even domestic ground. Such artists alone have initiated new epochs and schools.

To reach such height ought to be the aim of American art.

Palmer, the child of the people, receiving from it his inspirations, seems to approach the threshold of such a new era. His works have the marks of the above-mentioned tendency of the century, as well as of the country and of the people. In him the intuition of genius reveals the new road, which is pointed out in Europe by criticism, reflection and study. His works are truly American. His ideal of beauty is not limited to the Greek or classic type. He shows himself to be an individuality, and not a coerced imitator. The supreme beautiful is always a compound of invention and imitation. So are always born—and so has Palmer created them—the highest poetized realities. Art is to be the free but inspired interpreter of nature, of the living model; the expression of the sentimental, of the beautiful, of the vivid, soft, deep, or intense emotions of the soul, does not necessarily require to be encompassed by what is called perfectly classical features. Nature revelling in diversity of traits, exhibits herself with charm in the so called incorrect facial outlines. A deviation from the absolutely classical type enhances, gives freshness to the works of art.

Painting more fully embraces man and nature than sculpture, and commands a greater variety of material faculties to reflect, to reproduce inward emotions and outward impressions. Its cardinal element is light—(as shadow is only its diminution)—or idealized matter. The creative power of this art embraces a wider sphere, by bringing out more completely and saliently the inmost emotions of the soul. The individuality of the artist has innumerable ways and unlimited material resources to assert itself, and this accounts for so many and various schools of painting. Landscape painting has not its fountain in intuition, inspiration, but wholly depends on material nature, and on the endless combinations of her various images.

Painting is largely and diligently cultivated in Amerca, but hitherto has not risen to a self-determined artistic individuality. Europe proffers to the American student her most accumulated treasures for study, and there he disappears in the labyrinth of master-works, schools and various attractions. And thus American art is yet either wholly in infancy or limited to imitation. Its development is constrained and spasmodic, and although some distinguished talents sparkle, no native genius soars, marking the dawn of a genuine national art. In certain conventional social conditions surrounding the artist at home, and partly rooted in the artists themselves, less even than in the dispositions of the people at large, or in the prevalence of a democratic atmosphere, we are to look for the reasons of this rather unsteady and unpropitious course. Portrait painting—a few historical compositions excepted—is, if not the paramount, at any rate the cardinal and all-absorbing productiveness of American artists. It carries them away. But not from portrait painting emerged the immortal masters, who have given the character to art, and elevated it to a heavenly spiritual perfection. Corregio, who stands unsurpassed and alone, was not a portrait painter. Van Dyke's portraits, as well as those of all the great artists, occupy the second range in the appreciation of their various productions.

Portrait painting being the most remunerative in America, it therefore attracts naturally the artist. It is in accordance with the general character of society—above all of that portion which possesses the means of remuneration. The demand for portraits increases with increasing prosperity and wealth, and answers to the inborn and justifiable vanity of our nature. But in this rapid production, inspiration—if there was any in the artist—dies slowly out, and even the principles of art become—often unconsciously—neglected. Difficulties grow more and more before him, who in proportion loses the means to overcome the hinderances, loses his intuitive insight in art. One can observe in the successive exhibitions of the American artists, how year by year most of them become less and less skilful in combining in just proportions art and truth. A good portrait painter is to bring out what is characteristic, without running into caricature; he is to vail—without seeming effort—that of which only a glimpse is to be had. Beyond the inward sentiment in the artist himself, there exists no rule to fix the proportions between sincerity and artifice; and this sentiment, if not nursed carefully in the soul of the artist, in his feelings, shrinks and becomes extinguished. To be sure, faithfulness to the original is to be found, is to be felt deeply by the gazer. The works ought to be true, but without excess. Style, or what is even still worse, the affectation of one—which exercises such havoc at present every where—ought not to destroy or overshadow the mental expression in the original; precision is not to run into dryness, nor what in nature is elastic, to become mellow under the brush. Portrait painting, as observable in the exhibitions, descends by degrees into a mechanical task. The majority of artists delight in the facility of production, and lose the feeling of the exquisite, their brush loses the habit of correctness, and thus instead of reaching the graceful, they arrive at stiffness. They slowly fall into poverty of intention, into meagreness of design, and occasionally into a harshness of tint, at the side of which their other faults vanish. They seem often to have lost the faculty to fix the measure of the relations of contrasts, forgetting that a tint faultily selected, falsifies and destroys the effect of the surrounding tints—though selected with taste and skill. Arrived at this stage, art and artist are only imitators and counterfeiters of masters and schools; the ideal of art vanishes from their mind. The feeling of the beautiful in art disappears, in proportion as the artist loses sight of the ideal and drops into imitation.

The generality of American artists crowd mostly to the commercial metropolis, attracted there by the greater opportunity to find demand for profitable work. They return from Europe with the dim idea, that a large American commerial and populous city can proffer to them the elements, the means, nay the atmosphere so necessary to their further artistical development, to their inward artistical existence. But in neither respect does an American commercial metropolis bear any resemblance, or contain the same various social, civilizing and modelling elements as the European capitals, or as once did the cities of Italy, Belgium, the Netherlands, or Germany, celebrated in the history of art. The American cities are not centres, where the whole life of the people condenses, reflects itself, radiating therefrom again. Their tone and their influences are almost exclusively those of business and money-making; and as such they affect the artist's existence.

The highest European social circles consider the artist among their gracefullest adornments. The aristocracy of genius, or the talent of the artist, at any rate finds more easily a deferential place amid the aristocracy of Europe, than among the would-be aristocracy of an American commercial metropolis. Besides, without that social circle, the artist finds in the European cities variegated, picturesque, suggestive excitements, ebullitions of life in all directions, and attractive or instructive associations. All this combined puts into shadow the sameness which prevails in

American cities, acts powerfully on the artist, excites and expands his mind, spreads fresh and various food for his imagination. The exchange of impressions, ideas, ripens to revelations in works of art. So the poet of history, Goerres, inspired Kaulbach, and many great works of art have been generated by the like mental intercourse and influences.

Italy, that sacred and privileged land of art, the Italians its born worshippers, are not fit standards for comparison. But the Belgian, Dutch, and German cities, where the arts flourished, were likewise, as are the American cities, prominently the seats of industry and trade; and nevertheless the arts found in them their shrine. Rich and poor were attracted towards the artist, he was surrounded with enthusiastic respect. There the artist felt his existence interwoven with that of the people. His standing in the palaces or in public squares was among the foremost. It does not seem that the American artist finds here this warm atmosphere, so necessary to his existence and expansion. His studio counts not among the prides of the city, and of its inhabitants. Art is looked at and liked, but not worshipped. The existence of an artist is not an entity in the American life, in the American social relations. Very few only among the wealthy classes, or those who enjoy leisure, find time to throw a glimpse on art and artists. Most of them believe that, paying for a picture or a bust, they completely fulfil their duty to society and art. That kind of society demands of literature and from art, to be entertained, amused. It is even sensible to the glory spread by them over the nation; but it does not understand how to surround the artist in every day's intercourse with cheering and refined consideration. That society does not imagine, that a large remuneration is not sufficient to nurse the tender growth of art, among a stiff, discolored, conventional world, an imitation of all imitations.

Such seem to be the social influences of an American metropolis on the artists; if otherwise, why are the best and most eminent among them continually oozed out from their country? why do those who remain collapse, while a progressive sinking is visible in their works? The air, therefore, of American cities acts slowly, but it seems to depress and wither them, often without their being conscious of it. Most of the artists continually seek a more congenial atmosphere. Almost all their best productions have been composed or executed in Europe. While they dwindle at home, they reinvigorate in the distant pilgrimage. Thus, among others, the masterly historical paintings of Leutze are executed in Europe.

Not in Europe, however, can be created a genuine American art. There the artist stands on foreign soil, and is lost among the schools. Art must have, as it has always had, its own national ground and fountain. A mental, spiritual, as well as a material communion, must exist uninterruptedly between the artist and the people. So it was in Athens, so in modern Europe, wherever art has flourished, and wherever schools or particular *genres* were created. The true artist grows and expands on domestic soil, ought to breathe domestic aroma; and then only he gives to art the national stamp. The artist residing in Europe, or even in such American cities as do not mirror the life of the people nor its physiognomy, will never create a distinct American art. The Madonnas of Raphael have a Florentine and Roman type. All that surrounds them is Italian, and represents the minutiæ of the Italian life. Da Vinci, Titian, preserved to their masterpieces the Lombard, the Venetian character. Zurbaran, Murillo, etc., are Spaniards in their Madonnas, their saints, angels, and

Christ children, as well in the street boys and beggars. The splendid carnation of the pictures of Rubens reproduces the Flemish type. The Holbeins, Dürer, are eminently German. All these examples show that art remains always faithful to the character of the nation in features and types, as well as in the paraphernalia. The Netherland school was born out of the independence of the nation. In all its branches, composition, portraits, or landscape, it is the most faithful reflection, not only of the lineal features of the Dutch, but of their modes of life, manners, habits, customs, dresses, various social distinctions, of the festivals and occupations of all classes of the people. So was formed the character of the Netherland school and *genre*. It became distinct and original by remaining faithful to the people.

Art cannot acquire expansion and splendor if it is a luxury enjoyed or understood only by few. Poetry, literature, as well as art, ought to plunge into the daring and vigorous life of the great body of the people, and not plash in the vapid air of cities, in their conventionally distorted societies. The artistic feeling in the American people must be formed independent of the aristocratic one. To create such a feeling seems to be the mission of a genuine American artist. Artists created tho love of arts in the people of Athens, Italy, Belgium, Holland, etc. A Pericles cannot emerge out of the American institutions. A church, like the Catholic corporations, aristocracies and sovereigns, are impossibilities here and art must prosper without them. Artists creating a national art will create a feeling, a sense and an interest for art among the people; in the people alone he will find lavish and hearty patronage.

Music has its fountain in our soul, is the purest and loftiest expression of its various emotions. The Germans believe music to be the poetry of the soul. Among the genuine Americans, music, however deeply felt and valued, seems nevertheless to be an acquired and cultivated taste. The musical sense is touched, incited from without, but bursts not spontaneously from within. There are no domestic popular melodies resounding from the chords of the heart, vibrating with the various emotions, as there are no national dances, the one and the other revealing an inborn musical sense. The acquired, the cultivated taste, spreads elaborately in cities and villages, in rich parlors and in cottages. Those re-echo the fervently studied, mostly operatic Italian airs, or at times English ballads. Difficult, ungrateful and almost impossible must prove the attempt of an American musical genius to create a specific American art. He cannot make vibrate what does not exist; he cannot evoke from within himself, nor become inspired, nor move and draw from an inward genuine national melodial flow, which is not running in the utmost depth of feeling, not caressingly undulating in tunes. He cannot strike such sympathetic chords in the breast of his compatriots, as do in their homes the Italian, German or French composers.

Aside from what in their compositions is a creation inspired by the intuitive art in its expression of general human emotions, passions, or longings, those composers strike peculiar accords, combining, re-echoing, modulating feelings and sounds almost innate in the various nations among which they live. So for example, Meyerbeer re-echoes the chant of the Hebrew synagogues; Gottschalk, the American composer, owns his all conceded originality to having struck the rich vein of the Negro melodies. Music very likely will for a long time, if not for ever, remain a studied, borrowed, and therefore artificial taste and want for this country.

CHAPTER XII.

CUSTOMS, MANNERS, HABITS, ETC.

Social conditions variously influence and model customs, usages, habits, and manners. In Europe, the distinctions which have existed for centuries, the different social conditions, pursuits, and daily occupations of each social stratum, have shaped out a variety of customs peculiar to each class. At the side, therefore, of certain national habits, common to all—nobility, burghers, the lower classes, composed of operatives, laborers and peasantry—each of them has certain characteristic usages. No such social subdivisions and distinctions having existed in America at the start, nor existing now, the customs, habits, usages of the Americans are more uniform than those of European nations. Little if any difference exists therein between cities and villages, between what is customary in the dwellings of the rich in commercial cities, or plantations, and in the cottages of artisans and farmers. These habits, notwithstanding their modification by wealth or by attempted assimilation to the modes of life of the aristocratic and superior European classes, in their generality are similar to the mode of life among the small European burghers (*petite bourgeoisie*). They are similar in their general character and their minute shadowings, as the mode of life of the first settlers was necessarily a transmission and a continuation of the life of the small burghers artisans, or yeomen, from whom most of the settlers draw their honorable origin. Domestic, family, household virtues were once in Europe called specially the burgher's virtues; they consisted in quietness, sobriety, order, laboriousness, morality. Such was and must have been preëminently the American domestic life and intercourse. Luxury, lavishness, expensiveness, are only comparatively recent acquirements, overhanging the traditional customs.

The ceremonies used at festivals, weddings, receptions, and various other occasions, in even those habitual social intercourses among the wealthiest who are most apt to imitate the European higher classes, differ nevertheless almost wholly from those in use among them; bear the strongest resemblance to the usages which are considered in European higher society as obsolete, but which are religiously preserved in some corners, in second and third rate cities, by their burgher inhabitants. The highest burgher classes of the Old World, composed of bankers, capitalists, money makers, or *financiers*, wealthy industrials, and professional men, since the great French revolution mix more or less freely, and stand almost on an equal footing with the ancient nobility. Their manners and customs are nearly the same, and small existing differences can be detected only by a well experienced eye. The customs and manners common to them are rarely transplanted into America, and are not indigenous to the country. Besides, new exigencies and modes, special and peculiar to the American conditions of society and life, have operated on the social intercourse. And thus an immense difference exists between the conventionalities by which social intercourse is regulated in Europe and in America. However complete the knowledge of the like conventionalities and habits acquired among the best and most finished society in Europe, one might still stumble often here, as many such conventionalities have a totally opposite signification in their bearing, as politeness and impoliteness, in America and in Europe.

Notwithstanding the already acquired and rapidly increasing wealth and prosperity of the people, there exist only a few individuals and no classes of leisure, and their influence on social life and its usages has hitherto been in general imperceptible. In Europe the aristocracy, that is, a whole class of families living by the labor of others, have formed, for uncounted centuries—Greece and Rome included—the pivot of social relations, their apex, as well as the nursery of refined customs and usages. In America individual labor and occupation have been imperative necessities of existence, as well as the means of social distinction; they have therefore influenced and shaped out to a great extent American customs and usages, stamping on them in many respects a distinct mark. This land, this society proffers no space, no inducements, no charm for an intellectual and still less for a social leisure. Production, activity are enjoyments, and existence becomes a burden, and deteriorates morally and materially without a serious pursuit, without daily work and occupation. In European societies persons of leisure or of idleness plunge into various excitements; many of them refined, but often mischievous to themselves and others. America proffers only somewhat gross or coarse pastimes for such a class; most men retiring from active or business life, after a short time return to it indirectly, and continue to dabble in money-making. Thus generally when Europeans chatter, the Americans sign bills, stocks, or—as it is said in common parlance—shave.

The active, busy, industrious, and in all conditions of life, hard-working Americans do not surpass, however, in endurance of toil that immense portion of European society, which in all social gradations is likewise obliged to earn a livelihood, either in an elevated or in the lowest social condition. That the European men of business, of every profession, the officials, artisans, operatives, laborers —when not utterly poor and destitute—find almost daily a few hours to devote to leisure, to sociability, and even to amusement, results from a certain superior method in the distribution of their hours and occupations, and from the habits thus acquired.

The myriads of various officials, high and low, are at work more hours daily than are the men in corresponding stations in America. The wheelworks of the governmental machineries are more complicated; on account of centralization they embrace far more objects, and cover far more extensive space. The countless threads of the government and of all the branches of administration, penetrate in most minute ramifications the whole social structure, cross and combine with each other, and depend wholly upon precision in their working and rotations for preventing accumulation, interruption, stagnation. The various official correspondences, even of the inferior officials, are very complicated and extensive, and the superior, therefore, as the inferior, spends more time at his desk than his American colleague. The responsibility, the discipline, the absolute dependence on the chief or superior, the continually increasing competition, by far surpassing the demand, the almost insurmountable difficulty in finding a new occupation, position, nay the means of sustaining existence, when those once possessed are lost; all this summed up together, obliges the European officials to be to the utmost precise, diligent, and assiduous in fulfilling their daily tasks and duties.

The man of studious pursuits, the savans, the professors at universities and gymnasia, above all in Germany, generally cover a more extensive as well as a deeper ground with their labors and investigations. They are surrounded by numerous competitors and critics; and either if dependent on government, or on the public favor or assent, they must maintain by the utmost efforts and diligence, their scholarship and their scientific name, on both which depend their mostly scanty means of daily existence. The hours devoted daily by a professor in Europe to teaching and lecturing, generally equal and often outnumber what in similar conditions are devoted here. The principal income of a professor depends upon the fees received from the students. Often several professors lecture on the same subject in the university; or a professor who has acquired fame in a speciality, attracts pupils in hundreds from all Germany. The students have mostly the free choice of university and of professor, and thus is created and maintained an uninterrupted rivalry and competition, by which science and her worshippers are equally benefited. All this taxes to the utmost the time and the mental capacities of the professors and savants, whose productivity, as is evidenced by their various publications and contributions, on the average surpass those of American scholars and men devoted to the various scientific professions. In spite of all this accumulation of labor, the European savants in general, and in particular the far-famed German professors, those mines of learning and productivity, spend almost daily a couple of hours in sociable relaxation, conviviality, or genial conversation. All such pastimes are nearly unwonted, or rarely enjoyed by the American learned brotherhood.

Artisans, shopkeepers, tradesmen, merchants, bankers, in general all business men, in Europe as in America, must rely alike upon skill, shrewdness, acuteness, and aptitude for their pursuits. But as Europe is the centre of commercial, banking and industrial activity, production, and expansion, the commercial combinations are more wide-embracing and complicated there than in America. This alone obliges the European bankers, the chiefs of industry, and commercial men, to devote their intellect more intensely to various and accumulated operations. Besides, in Europe the crowd is dense, every spot is occupied, and he who falls is downtrodden, and usually has no opportunity to rise again and to gather new forces. On the continent, the failure of a commercial house generally disgraces the name of the party, his family, his children, and is often followed by suicide. Thus the existence of a man engaged in a regular honest business, is a struggle for honor, for life and death. Here, on the contrary, an individual, unsuccessful in any branch or line, rises as quickly as he fell; dusts himself off, and rushes again into the same or another enterprise, without any great injury to his name or credit. An American changes place, and even occupation, pursuit, trade, running from one extreme to another, with a rapidity and ease neither thought of nor possible in crowded Europe. For these reasons, European merchants, bankers, and business men ought apparently to be more overworked, and have fewer hours to devote to social intercourse and even amusements, than the Americans. But the contrary is the case. In European capitals, in large and small cities, that class of men participates in all large and small, in public and private amusements and gatherings, for which the Americans generally either have no taste or no time. And nevertheless, the American seems to be always in a hurry and excited; at his meals, in his study, and at his counter. For example, in the morning hours, when the New York business population, old and young—and all is business in New York—pours out into the main artery, in Broadway, and descends hurriedly "down town," nothing in the world could stop or divert the torrent. Even if Sebastopol had been in their way, those men would have run over it at one rush.

The unsteadiness, however, which prevails in all American conditions and pursuits, renders it very difficult and thorny to the American business men to attend to the superintendence and direction of details in the management of their various interests. Although the business of the European is more complicated and more extensive, it can be more easily organized, brought into a methodical and regular activity, and thus be more easily superintended. In Europe the subordinate clerks have not as many various and free openings before them as in America; and thus they remain in their condition often for life; they acquire the necessary routine of each special house; win the confidence of the employers, and become faithful and trusty workers. Often in Europe the existence of a clerk and subordinate is intimately interwoven with the existence, the honor, the welfare of the house; he becomes a member of the body, a bone of its bones. In America men change continually as their prospects brighten, and thus the chiefs of commercial houses must continually and laboriously train new subjects, and exercise a more strict vigilance upon them and their daily work. Such a continual effort must be more exhausting, than are the intense and wide-reaching, but methodical and calmly conducted, operations of European mercantile and banking houses. This daily fatigue and exhaustion may account for the fact, that generally very few men of mature age are to be seen in social circles and places of amusement.

Artisans, operatives, workingmen in overpeopled Europe, have far smaller gains and wages than the same classes in America. To make their living, they must therefore work longer and harder. The small workshops open earlier, and the operatives are more hours at their task in Europe than in America, and so are generally mechanics at out-door work. The various tools used by Americans being, however, more perfect and handy than those used by the majority of Europeans, the former no doubt accomplish more work in a given time than the latter. A European village, farm, and field are likewise already animated while the American one still slumbers; and generally only the darkness of night stops the toil of a European farmer, field-laborer, or journeyman.

Economy in general prevails not among Americans to the same extent, as it does among those various European classes, who are obliged to live by their labor, of whatever nature,—the superior social crust, formed of various elements, aristocratic as well as bourgeois, alone excepted. In America, labor is almost always productive—matter, nature is exuberant, and the general rise of every object so continual that the value of land, of products, etc., double quickly, almost as by their innate movement. No one seems to think about the necessity of saving, or of husbanding material resources. The Americans economize forces by their labor-saving machineries, which have been contrived by necessity,—but in handling the primitive matter and produce, they waste it with a lavishness unknown to Europeans, who are short of space, overburdened, compressed by vicious, social organization, and crowded upon one another.*

* The creative forces of nature seem likewise not to be carefully husbanded. Among other striking proofs of it is the destruction of the forests by use and misuse, by the axe, and by fires. In some time the climate may become affected by this destruction, as there exists no other barrier to break the northern and north-western winds and storms, freezing the country and covering it with snow almost in one day—from a Siberian to the Italian, nay to an African latitude. Colds and snows are always more violent in the prairies, on account

The dwelling houses of the masses of Americans, their food—at least the provisions for it are better and more plentiful—and their external appearance in dress, is also more decent and neat than that of Europeans. Palaces, refinement, splendor, finish, elegance, luxury, taste, and genuine fashion are at home in Europe, and remain there unrivalled. But they are the lot, the patrimony only of certain classes. The average of Americans are better housed and fed, are far better and more substantially dressed than the average of Europeans. Homespun has almost disappeared, and the consumption of various articles by twenty odd million Americans surpasses that of one hundred millions of Europeans. Peasants, villagers, almost all the laboring populations in Europe are generally poorly and cheaply clad; suits of clothes among them are hereditary, and women often principally wear those of their grandmothers. If America is deprived of the picturesque costumes to be found among European nations, she has far less tatters—and generally only imported beggars. The European populations enjoy, however, in one respect an incontestable superiority. The disgusting habit of tobacco chewing, which is so common in all social positions in America, and its so repugnant results, are almost unknown in Europe, chewing being limited, with rare exceptions, only to sailors and to the lowest and poorest inhabitants of maritime cities.

The love of show and of shining, of keeping up external appearances, and of thus winning consideration, is carried by the Americans to a degree unusual in Europe, and above all on the continent. *The coat makes the man*, is proverbial here. The love of external show, a social weed

of their denudation. So the destruction of forests in the mountainous parts of France occasions frequent and violent inundations; and now it is almost too late to stop the freshets and repair the mischief.

generating many evils, and in its various ramifications destructive of easy, unpretentious, sociable life, seems to spread more luxuriantly in the city mansions of the wealthy than in the cottages of the people. Among the masses, it has partly its source in a misapprehension and perversion of the notion of democratic equality, and, in its more intense development among the superior crust, it is one of the signs of a disease, eaten deeply into all degrees of English society, and inherited partly by Americans. Snobbism, one of whose numerous symptoms is to attach more value to outward distinctions than to the inner worth of an individual, and to reflect a borrowed lustre; snobbism, in its fulness and completeness, is nearly unknown to any class of continental societies, and no other language has an equivalent for it. Snobbism, however, generally loses its hold on the great current of the American people; those only are strongly affected by it, who attempt or think to rise conventionally above the mass.

The always hurrying, excited, busily occupied Americans have no time to imitate and to learn, from those who are regarded as standards, the daily use of those most minute details and rites of courtesy, whose scrupulous observation and exchange cement social intercourse, and smooth the asperities arising from the division of European society into classes, annulling these divisions with the level of politeness. The thoroughbred European aristocrat is generally the most scrupulous in observing towards his equals, and still more towards his inferiors in a social point of view, those highest degrees of masonry of good-breeding, in which few seem to be initiated here, or to the fulfilment of which either time or habit is wanting. In other respects, when the Americans are in a normal state, as is the majority of all social positions of the people, good-breeding prevails, and hearty, intentional politeness marks their address and intercourse. Intentional coarseness and rudeness are rare and exceptional among the masses; and their easy, off-hand, straight-forward manners are neither ill-bred, derogatory, nor offensive. Democracy teaches self-respect to everybody, in respecting others. The straight-forward address of the man of the West, as well as the often spoken of curiosity, inquisitiveness, of the American people, of the Yankee in particular, are neither offensive nor rudely intrusive. Only snobs, filled with superciliousness and affectation, shudder at them. But disgusting is the mixture of assumption, constraint, stiffness, affectation, fidgetiness, which by many are put on as good-breeding, or as refined demeanor, making them in turn rude or obsequious, as if momentary and feverish obsequiousness were courtesy or good-breeding. The inquisitiveness of the people at large is often a childish, naïve curiosity, striving for information. The Yankee always tries to increase his stock of knowledge; and, after all, even the cunning mixed with it is rather amusing than otherwise. Moreover, man is normally communicative and easy; closeness, secrecy, are an artificial state. They are a deviation from our nature, imposed by necessities, by a perverted social organization, but they are not innate. The people at large, practising and observing politeness in their own way, seem not to wear a heavy harness, while often for those who believe that they constitute a superior and distinct class, politeness is not an innate or daily habit; but they put it on as a Sunday dress, or tight boots, becoming stiff, uneasy, and hurrying to throw off with joy the uncomfortable gear. The man of the South, possessing generally many amiable social qualities, is on the average more easy, elastic, urbane, and scrupulously observant of conventional relations, than is often the man of the Northern States.

Now, as of old, hospitality constitutes one of the noblest features of human society. In America, as every where, it has various characteristics and modes. Much of it is spurious, and much genuine. Houses thrown open, or dinners served up in rich private halls, with the purpose to overpower the visitor with costly furniture, plate, or wines, to earn his applause after such display, and have thus one's own vanity gratified, constitutes not hospitality. Practised in this way, it loses aroma and the convivial character, being marred by a kind of mercantile calculation. It is no more hospitality, but a speculation, a debt paid or contracted purposely, towards those who are in a position to repay it here or eventually in Europe. So the conspicuous social circles generally *pay* visits, while in Europe every body *makes* them. The genuine European aristocracy, as well as the wealthy classes, mixing with it, and largely practising hospitality, do not make it depend upon debt and credit; the favor, the honor, the pleasure bestowed, is mutual between the host and the guests. Hospitality and social intercourse generally spread a real charm when disinterested. Exchange of ideas, genial intercourse, stand higher than a simple exchange of dinners.

Unassuming, hearty hospitality more easily warms the roofs of the rich, who do not pretend to whirl in the vortex of society, and it is largely observed among the various quiet, industrious, professional, laborious classes, as well as in cities and villages.* American characteristic hospitality, as practised by single families and individuals, as well as by entire communities or associations, administer-

* Such hospitality among many other instances I have especially witnessed and experienced from C. C. Felton, professor in Cambridge, Mass. He counts among the most eminent scholars of this country, and could occupy a no less distinguished position for learning every where in Europe; as to hospitality, his is almost of the Homeric stamp.

ing to the individual sufferings and wants of thousands and thousands brought to this country,—this hospitality equals, if it does not surpass, what in this way is accomplished by any other nation.

In cities as well as in the country, in streets as in the fields, in mansions as in cottages, in large or small gatherings, the Americans show a different aspect and physiognomy from Europeans. Rather dusky than radiant, but rendered nervous by the struggle to enjoy naturally the moment, and by the fear of hurting imaginary propriety, they give the impression that they either do not care or do not understand how to win from life the cheerful, congenial, exhilarating side. At such moments the pang of severe duty seems to furrow their brow, rarely and only occasionally irradiated with impulsive joyousness. The European masses, bending under heavy burdens, are more impulsive to merriment, than the far happier and more prosperous Americans. Glee smiles from under misery, and the Europeans are always ready to transform the minutes of respite into a gay repose. Song and dance are the friendly fairies of their toilsome existence. From North to South, from the Atlantic to the borders of Asia —when extreme misery has not dried out the last drops of vitality—the workshops of the operatives, the suburban streets and gardens, the farms and fields, at dawn and twilight, re-echo with national or love songs, peculiar to each country. As neither the lark nor the nightingale, so almost never human song resounds in American fields, gardens, or groves. Cheerfulness is a spontaneous impulse, is catching with Europeans of all classes. Americans—on the average—seem not to possess the rich gift of extemporizing pleasures. Their enjoyments must be prepared, deliberated, but do not flow from the drift of the moment. Dance is for them a study, instead of being a smiling attraction, an unconscious rapture. It reflects a mental sultriness, has the appearance of a nervous excitement, of a laborious muscular effort and task. Often likewise easy, cosy talk in their gatherings is superseded by speeches, by exertions to produce an effect, to bring out themselves rather than to enliven, to charm their companions. The art or gift of conversation, so general in Europe, is not yet domesticated in America.

Americans stand out the best in the simple domesticity of family life. It is the only normal condition growing out of their earliest traditions and habits; it is their uninterrupted inheritance. The domestic hearth, the family joys and hardships must have formed almost the exclusive stimulus of existence, for the first settlers; therein they concentrated all their affections and cares. Out-door variegated attractions, comparatively recent here, and previously accidental, from time immemorial almost are innate to European life. Religious convictions, local impossibility, the limited means of the colonies, prevented them at the outset and for a long time afterwards from recurring to public joyful gatherings, from creating the like various pastimes and forming the habit and possessing out-door sociable attractions. The day spent in hard labor or in professional duties, was cheerfully ended in the family circle. Even now, notwithstanding the rapidly increasing wealth and expansion in large cities, out-door pleasures seem rather exotic to the American life. At any rate far more so in America than in Europe, the family hearth is about the only preventive against gross and often degrading recreations; it alone assuages the tediousness and burdensomeness of existence even for the rich, who often find that it is almost easier to make a fortune than to know how to use and spend it.

American homes are warmed by parental love The

relations between parents and children, harmonizing in their outward manifestations, with certain conditions and modes special to the development of American society, being misunderstood or not thoroughly examined by several European writers and visitors, have created the erroneous opinion of the want of parental feeling. At the outside, however, the reverse is apparent; less filial affection, or at least a less demonstrative one from children towards parents, seems noticeable; less so than is customary in Europe. Family ties seem to be looser, because generally Americans bear small affection to the spot of their birth; young members leave it or change with indifference, and parents do not make undue sacrifices to keep their children around them. Events providentially enforced upon Americans this unconcern, otherwise the task of extending culture and civilization would not have been fulfilled. Fortunes and means of existence were small among the settlers, but the space, the modes to win a position by labor were unlimited, and thus children began early to work and earn for themselves. Thus early they became self-relying and independent, and this independence continues to prevail in filial relations. Parents then, as now, worked hard and accumulated for their children. But the facility of early becoming artisans of their own destinies, of securing independence by labor, activity, and intelligence, in times and conditions when no other pastimes were possible, matured and emancipated children from parental authority and domestic discipline. For centuries and centuries in Europe, conditions, positions, occupations, pursuits, labors have been hereditary, families have been riveted to one spot; generation after generation living in the same precincts of a wall, in view of the same parish spire, under the same roof, in the same workshop, laboratory or study. Generation succeeded to generation, with out breaking the family group, without loosening the parental discipline. American parents, allowing an almost unlimited choice to their children, spare nevertheless no hardships and pains to bring them up, and to educate them according to their conception of what is the best and the most useful for the mature duties of life. Parents love their children as dearly and intensely here as in Europe, but exercise less control, less authority. Further, in Europe parents part with a share of their property, in order to facilitate, in various ways, the establishment of their children; in America, where labor is the corner-stone of society, where originally the fortune of the parents was limited, but a boundless facility existed for every beginner to acquire one, parents could not endow their children. This wholesome habit being still common, is no evidence, however, of a want of parental love.

American parents are far more forbearing, nay meeker with their children than are those in Europe. What here results from freedom or a yielding disposition, to the European comprehension appears as irreverence. A slight or no constraint is imposed upon children in America; and as childhood—in virtue of a cardinal animal law—is eminently imitative, their good-breeding depends upon the bad or good examples which in various quarters are freely set before them. Children accustomed to the utmost familiarity and absence of constraint with their parents, behave in the same manner with other older persons, and this sometimes deprives the social intercourse of Americans of the tint of politeness, which is more habitual in Europe.

In America children generally lead and regulate their parents, in the choice of social intercourse, and in most of the relations and modes of life. Many are the reasons which account for this seeming anomaly. Nothing is traditionary here, as in Europe, and still less so are positions, luxury, refinement of habits and modes of existence in whole classes or single families; parents, therefore, who started in life with small means—and such a start has always been common—acquired fortune, but had no time to acquire external refinement, to study and to master the conventional knowledge of society. They feel the deficiency, and to make it up they surround their children with all external signs of prosperity or wealth, and wish them to possess that art which they want themselves. Through and in the children parents enjoy wealth and standing, becoming thus docile to their impulsions or advice. The simplicity, the frugality of the parents, contrasts often even disagreeably with the prodigality, the assumptions, self-assertion, and conceit of the children. In European domestic life the children even of the highest aristocracy, are educated with more comparative simplicity than is the case in America. Parental authority extends over the grown up, and they always occupy the background in all relations of conventional intercourse with society. In America, parents, as well as persons of mature age, are seemingly overruled by the younger generation. European youth of both sexes, of all social positions, from the wealthiest to the poorest, from kings, aristocrats, down to the lowest plebeians, in all feelings, emotions, as well as in worldly concerns, remain children longer than they do in America. Here they mingle with society, with life, almost from the swaddling clothes. And so young unmarried girls give the tone to all those social gatherings, which in Europe are under the exclusive sway of married women, of matured men. The American custom and combination is more normal and natural in itself; and it corresponds to that bourgeois construction of society, which lies at the bottom of the American social life. Of old, among the European bourgeoisie and the laboring classes, convivial gatherings had pre-eminently in view to amuse young people, to bring them together, to facilitate marriages. Those who have already made their choice and settled for life, abandon the gay foreground of the scene, to attend to more serious duties. Such was likewise the social custom of the colonists, and such is that of their descendants. In abstract comprehension, dissipation and even the innocent admiration commonly paid to married women, and their forming the pivot of social whirling, are as many dissolving ferments of the actual state of society, wherein the unmarried girl is the natural centre of attraction, and one of its elementary and cementing forces. Gatherings organized in this manner lose, however, the charm depending upon the contact of various ages; and youth, uncontrolled and paramount, becomes regardless of the pleasure of others, pushing aside, and often, without the least restraint, whatever stands in its way. Society in America has thus a physiognomy of freshness, together with a tint of harshness—being in turn attractive and repulsive.

Even in the serious decisions of life, children in America enjoy a fulness of independence, not customary in Europe. They make freely the choice of their intimacies, then of their church, of their politics, their husbands and wives. On the average far more marriages are contracted in America without the consent of parents, than in any of the European social classes. Aside from the prevailing looseness of what in European customs constitutes the parental authority, the facility with which one can create here for himself a position, and secure the material means of existence, makes the choice less dependent on parental will or advice.

In the country, in villages or farming districts, marriages are contracted with less regard to fortune, than is the case among the richer portion of the inhabitants of cities.

In civilized, Christian nations, woman's influence is almost paramount on manners, habits, customs; on their polish, refinement, gentleness; on their interweaving and regulating social intercourse. Such influence is normal and natural; it is in harmony with the pure manifestation of the human spirit, and of its creation-ordering laws. Man is the acting principle and force, woman the inspiring, quietly efficient and softening element, the ethereal aroma filling the space. Man and woman complete each other, perfect the creation in its material or animal, as in its spiritual and mental revelations. The faculties, passions, emotions of man and woman have one and the same focus and germ; they are equivalent in principle and in origin. Their impressibility may be differently graduated, the intensity, expansion and power of mental perceptions and faculties become differently developed, urged, and uttered. The combination of these differences runs out into the harmonious accord of man and woman as mental creations, as the combination of various deep and high tones vibrate and dissolve into a musical harmony. Certain capacities may be more efficiently developed and salient in woman, others in man; these superiorities balanced against each other raise both to the same level. It is beyond contestation that woman is endowed with a certain intuitive perception, with observation, penetration, and appreciation of various mental and psychological phenomena, differing, and in many respects superior for their acuteness and delicacy to that of man. As moral beings they are on an absolute equality. Nature alone has pointed out and defined certain distinct functions for each, but again equal in both, and resulting in the harmonious and full combination of animal and of social, of intellectual as well as of material development and life. Those limits drawn by nature, constitute alone the apparent—not at all the essential—inferiority of woman; beyond these, duties and rights are equal, and the right of woman to self-determination in no way in principle is inferior to that of man. To both applies the same conception, comprehension, and scale of the moral and immoral, of right and wrong, of just and unjust, of allowed and forbidden, of legal and illegal, of indulged and condemned. Modifications, changes, and different applications of those rules to the one, to the detriment of the other, are essentially unjust, and originate in abuse. Any such superiority apodictically asserted is illogical and abnormal.

Psychological passional attractions combine and overrule the relations between man and woman, wherein the purity of the woman exalts often and purifies the man. Where corruption gnaws, as a general rule the first sting, the first venom, the first dissolving shock, originated with man. In the present prevailing social structure, based exclusively on family, woman, as wife, mother, or sister, is the hearth-stone, woman is the sacred fire, projecting warmth and charm over the inner sanctuary.

In the social combination of America, woman as woman, independently of any social, conventional distinctions of wealth or poverty, independently of personal attractions, is surrounded with more considerate and respectful deference than was ever the case in Europe. The source of this feeling may be either pure and psychological, or wholly material. It may have been that the scarcity of women among the first settlers, and their thereby enhanced moral and material value, or the loneliness of the existence of isolated colonists, made dearer to them their delicate, and in their condition specially life-cheering companions. But whatever may have been the primordial reason of this respect paid to women, it softens and dissolves many asperities in the habits of men, and evidences a higher general tone of civilization. In all social, domestic relations and combinations, the woman in America moves in an atmosphere under certain aspects more elevated and tender, than she does in many corresponding relations in Europe. In the American villages and farms, even among the poorest laborers and workmen, woman is emancipated from the field or garden labor, as well as from any outdoor toiling in husbandry; while in Europe generally she shares all the heaviest burdens of labor, exposure, and hardships. Those relative conditions prove at any rate a more elevated degree of refinement in the domesticity of Americans, than prevails among European masses. For centuries of serfdom and degradation, the man as well as woman of the people were dragging the same yoke, toiled for the master, as do the slaves in the South. Serfdom and statute-labor disappeared, but in the small households woman's field-labor still remained one of the pivotal forces of husbandry; and, lashed by poverty, she toils as hard now as she did of old. In the American city life, the marketing, the providing for the wants and necessities of the household, is generally within the range of man's domestic duties, while in Europe these cares devolve generally on the wives of artisans, merchants, tradesmen, officials, and on those of all kinds of professional men. Only wealth and elevated social position exempts the wife from the fulfilment or superintendence of this domestic duty, and throws it into the hands of menials.

The external physical appearance of the mass of American women, evinces a prevalence of feminine beauty, but likewise evinces a kind of democratic standard salient in the comparison which may be made with Europe. In the mass, the Americans look is neater, handsomer, and, in all conditions, of a less decided ugliness, than those on the other side of the ocean. But, likewise, it is difficult to find out in this mass those classical, perfect beauties, pure, symmetrical, in all their traits, members and proportions, expressive of inner emotions and of physical perfection. Such women are encountered in every European nation, in almost all numerous gatherings, either of the higher or lower classes. Europe abounds and runs out into the two extremes; between them stands the average of American women.

Rigidity, constraint, even to stiffness, a certain *géne* or nervousness, are the more prevailing external aspects of the American women, than the easy, unconcerned grace peculiar to the women of the Old World, of Europe as well as of Asia. The American woman has the appearance of coldness, founded in notions, principles, as well as in the temperament; she seems not to be exposed to the ebullitions of blood, to those violent emotions common to the women of the Old World, in all nations and latitudes, in all conditions, in palaces and huts, in cities and villages, ebullitions rendering them volcanic and passionate. The American and the European women are daughters of the same moral, Christian, social creed and conceptions. The same principles of morality and duty are instilled into the one and the other, with equal purity, with equal intensity. But numberless mental and physical temptations, mostly here unknown, unwonted, or only in the bud, are thickly strewn on the path of women in Europe, inflaming the air in which they move, which they breathe. There and here social verdicts originate in like purity of conceptions and convictions, being however at times more forbearing, more indulgent, in the elastic Europe, than in the more inflexible America. In virtue of the democratic essence permeating society here, nobody with impunity can offend the public sentiment, or stand so high as to almost force on society at large his bad example. The contrary is the case in Europe, divided for centuries into summit and plains. Torrents descending from elevations overflow and carry away low grounds. Finally the climate affects the senses differently, it is supposed, in the New and in the Old World. These may be the cardinal reasons that the American woman is not often thus exalted passionately to that extent as to overstep the limits traced by the social comprehension of morality. In general she is, therefore, a surer guardian of the domestic hearth and of its purity, than is in many cases the European, surrounded by inner and outer urgings and temptations, with inflammable blood, with burning heart and soul. The European woman errs and falls, but often likewise she glowingly redeems her fall by the heroism of love, devotion, and expiation. Vanity, curiosity, idleness and unrest, are among the salient tempters which often carry away and destroy the American woman; but the tragedy of passion glides rather along her breast, of passion raging, tearing, and consuming the existence of Europeans.

The intellectual education of the American woman, especially in the Free States, averages a higher degree than in Europe, even in countries considered as foremost in civilization. The girls participate in all the blessings of the common public schools, and in all the establishments of education scattered broadcast over the free country. The culture of the mind is superior and more generally diffused among women than it is on the average among men. The majority of them devoting themselves early in life to practical pursuits, as operatives, artisans, farmers, laborers, merchants, etc., find their time wholly absorbed, and lose often the scent of study; while the women, as wives and girls, have comparatively more time to devote to study, to nurse and entertain the germs laid down in their minds in the schools. Lecture-rooms in cities and in villages are generally more thickly filled by women than by men. American women, as was pointed out in another chapter, form the numerous tender and devoted class of elementary teachers; they largely participate in the literary movement. They are distinguished by the highest accomplishments of soul and mind, in learning, poetry, art. So the powerful authoress of "Passion Flowers," * by her philosophical as well as poetical spirit; so the lofty, genial, soul-teeming, dramatic artist, Matilda Heron. Scattered throughout all positions of American society, are women who are models of intellectual clearness and soundness, of gentleness of heart and manner. Women take an elevated, noble, large view, and a warm, intense interest in all social questions. Any reform for the better enlists them on its side. Temperance, anti-slavery, every cause of liberty and humanity, is enthusiastically countenanced by them. If legally, directly they do not bear on the like questions, their influence as wives, mothers, sisters, and beloved, is powerful, and almost always elevating, ennobling to the man. Public opinion, if not the law, the social habits surrounding women with truer and more respectful deference than in Europe, accords them more space, liberty, and a larger part in all serious aspects of life. And generally, public opinion, in all its bearings, when duly comprehended and appreciated, is neither contracted, oppressive nor tyrannical here. It expands as does the boundless space, as does the inexhaustible principle of free development of individuality almost unrestrained here, and paramount to all mental and social considerations. Only public opinion must not be confused and lowered to the puny verdicts of small coteries or cliques,

* Mrs. Julia Howe.

jealous, narrow or envious, pressing hardly on the weak-minded, but harmless, and vanishing before the self-relying.

In the immense majority of American women, when not marred—as is the case in certain positions—by attempts at a kind of shabby genteel notions, the genial soul-life breaks mightily through the apparently inflexible crust, spreads over the surface, giving a soft tone and expression to manners, ideas, and conventionalities. Then in them, as in all truly highbred natural European women, the contrast between innocence and prudery, between genuine inborn gentleness of manners and affected composure, is preëminently discernible. *When not laboring under efforts at representation*, when truly and frankly natural, either as the devoted wife and mother, or as the independent, self-confident, and in her purity and innocence, proud girl, the American woman is hearty, simple, affectionate; her impulses are generous, spreading amenity over conventional intercourse and relations. The normal state, the pedestal, the frame wherein the American woman of every social position, rich or poor, stands out the best, is the simple informal intercourse, more than representation, or the taking of postures or airs, be it in gaudy crowded saloons, in luxurious boudoirs, in country life, or in the simple cottage.

Among all classes of society, and preëminently among women, considerable confusion seems to prevail in often mistaking the conventional ladylike manner for true genuine womanhood. The word lady is all-powerful, and all-powerfully used and misused in America. It is applied not to mark a certain distinct position, but extends to morals, character, dress, behavior, occupation, pleasures. It has almost superseded the use, the signification of the word woman. In its thus generalized sense, it is applied with equal right and logic in the parlor as in the kitchen, in the mansion as on the farm, to the luxurious and the idle, as to the laborious and the plain. But by its shabby genteel sense, this lady and ladylike character stands often in the way of truthfulness and nature, stands in the way even of accomplishing many social, conventional, as well as real duties,* besides generating shams, affectations, and all kinds of spurious displays, defacing genuine reality. It is as an acid, destroying the suave perfume of ingenuousness, discoloring the freshest tints of a richly blossoming flower. The misuse overflows all the strata, and spreads even in literature,† while the word *gentlewoman*, the noblest in the English language, and unequalled in any other, resuming all the purest qualities of the soul, of the heart, combining them harmoniously with external gentleness of demeanor, is unheard in conversation, and has scarcely penetrated into literature.

Artificiality, internal or external, in notions or in half-formed manners, stiffness denoting or covering mostly fragmentary crumbs of breeding, lame imitations, make not a woman, not even a lady. The best manners are simple, not attracting notice, not striking by any extreme. High-

* A farmer in New England, questioned by me about the number of cows kept on his farm, answered, that he could keep twice as many, but that his ladies (wife and daughters) objected to it on account of the increased work in the dairy. I could not abstain from saying, that he would be better off if he had in his family true women, instead of ladies.

† Even Motley in his history could not avoid the contagion. In relating the defence of a small Dutch city besieged by the Spaniards, he extols the devotion, the sacrifices made by the *ladies*. Who ever used this word speaking of the women of Carthage, Numanea, Saragossa, etc.? Or who will speak of Imogen, Portia, Desdemona, Juliette, Rosalinda, or even of lady Macbeth, as of the ladies of Shakspeare?

toned, well-bred, elegantly accomplished women are not stylish, have no style at all. *Stylish looking*, an appellation profusely applied in America, would be considered the poorest compliment, if not an offence, in Europe.

The scrupulous observance of rites regulating social courtesy, their exchange, and that of these unavoidable conventionalities, cementing, facilitating, and smoothing daily intercourse between individuals as well as between families, not only in relations between equal, but between most distant and distinct positions; all these in Europe are generally watched over, directed, and maintained by the man. Acting and representing the head of the family, as husband or father, it belongs to him to give the example, to him the prize for urbanity, for good breeding, to him the blame for omissions, lesions, deviations from or breach of established, and in their nature, easy and elastic rules. Almost as generally the contrary is the case in America. The wife, the mother, often advised by children, is the mainspring, the *anima movens*, of all sociability. She is the arch on which the law reposes, and on her depends its fulfilment. The husband, the father, acts under her advice; he is the deacon where she is the high-priest. The woman, wife, mother, or even daughter, exercise in all these worldly relations an omnipotence and latitude nowhere conceded to them in Europe. The woman, therefore, in America, and more preëminently than in Europe, constitutes the charm, the attraction of sociability, animates, sustains integrally its current. To her the incense and tribute, but with her likewise the responsibility when the charm is dispelled, rites omitted, courtesy ruffled and bruised, and intercourse rendered knobby and unattractive.

CHAPTER XIII.

COUNTRY AND CITY.

In America, the country and city as constituent social, political elements and agencies, stand in an inverse relation to each other from that in which they stood in the ancient and in the European world. Their respective significations are different, and the difference runs through almost all the fibres of their multiform development, is visible in all the lights and shadows of general, political, social, as well as of domestic life and intercourse. Country and city in the greater part of their mutual relations affect and react on each other by different currents from those in the Old World, and are to be judged and appreciated by new and original criteria.

The ancient world was essentially municipal in all its social, political, legislative, and governmental structure. It was so, taking the world in its original, strictest, Roman or Latin sense. Within the walls of the city was concentrated the whole human multifarious development and movement. Light, culture, civil and political rights, were embodied in the cities, or intrinsically depended on them. Without its walls, the space was a social vacuum, life in all its humane elevated manifestations evolving from the city. The society which emerged out of the ruins of the Roman world changed integrally at the start its social pivot, transferring power in all its character and ramifications to the independent nobility and knighthood, scattered over the country; but this was another feature of privileges enjoyed comparatively by few who were masters of the whole land, and of the, in all respects, disfranchised masses. Soon, however, the city, by various means, either as the residence of royalty, as the capital of the State, as one of the powerful compartments in the feudal edifice; as the creator and agent of culture, industry, and commerce, and by numerous other ways, the city recovered its signification, acquired rights, stood next to and rivalled the nobility, and in several cases absorbed it. Amidst all these changes and fluctuations, no country existed, politically or socially, with free self-asserting populations, with equal rights to all other portions of the nation. America inaugurated such a one. The country and its inhabitants are on an absolute parity here with the city. The relations between the one and the other depend on free intercourse and attractions, they result from the nature of things, from their respective as well as their relative occupations. Uninterrupted but free currents circulate between city and country, carrying and exchanging forces and products, and combining production and reproduction.

Democracy, decentralization, emancipated man, space, localities, have created those new and equal relations, formerly unknown in Europe. In various preceding chapters have been pointed out the preëminent features and influences which constitute the difference between the European and American cities, principally of capitals, their different action on the country, as civilizing, as political or governmental agencies. No such distance separates country and city in America as existed and partly now exists in Europe, stamping the one with real or conventional inferiority in comparison with the other. No city, as was always the case among the European nations, rises above the country, or impresses upon it its own stamp, in language, manners, customs, habits, notions, conceptions, impulses, aspirations. No positive relations constitute a capital and a province, making the one wholly dependent on the other—no social provincialism in reality lowers the country in comparison with a large city.

The apparent social superiority of any American commercial metropolis consists more especially in a certain external, material perfection and polish, a result of the accumulation of wealth and capital, facilitating and stimulating acquisition, continual renovation, or imitation of foreign models. The extensive trade, the uninterrupted movement creating intercourse with foreign and distant regions, brings into exchange their various creations, and the cities are the first to assimilate and to transmit them to the country. But they do not acquire thereby any supremacy similar to that of European capitals. The American metropolises act rather as mediators towards the country, mediators between the foreign and the domestic. The commercial cities are no foci or exclusive depositaries of light and culture, where from those elements radiate and spread over the country; nor are they types—as are the capitals in Europe, with royalty, nobility, and concentration as well of wealth and of culture—after which the intellectual, moral, and material life, and the modes, the refinement, and tastes of the country at large are exclusively developed and fashioned. Therefore provincialism, in its extensive and manifold meaning, does not characterize the stand-point of the country, in relation to the city or capital, as it does in Europe.

The city of Boston alone possesses a certain tradition of supremacy, of a similar kind. This was once real in many and various aspects. Boston, for a long time, was the real capital of a State, and the mental one of all New England, of whose wide expanding character Boston was partly the generator, partly the exponent, and has thus, in many ways, marked and influenced the North, its development, and the history of the Union. Now, however, the spirit which animates New England has risen above that of the city, which has seemingly lost much of its ancient influence and leadership. Nevertheless, Boston is still, to a certain extent, the centre, and radiates still the character, the convictions, the spirit, and the peculiarities of the surrounding country. Philadelphia never impressed deeply on Pennsylvania the character, the convictions of her founders—the peace-loving, rational, and discreet Quakers; and it does so still less now, when that spirit has almost wholly disappeared from her social character. New York likewise does not mirror the character of its own State; and, with all its real, assumed, or conceded pre-eminences, New York is no more exclusively a heart of the country, of its multifarious and energetic vitality, than are the other large cities.

Commercial concentration and supremacy do not bestow on American commercial cities a paramount position, a regulating power over all social and political relations; and no comparisons in this respect can be established between them and certain historical cities of Europe.

The great Italian cities, Venice, Pisa, Genoa, Florence, and many others, were independent sovereignties; their leading inhabitants, a part of their populations, were real sovereigns, legislating and acting for themselves, aside from being merchants, or industrials. Many of the leading families belonged by birth and tradition to the feudal nobility, and were depositaries of real power. For all these reasons the name of merchant-prince was bestowed on them. Likewise some among the foremost German Hanseatic towns were sovereigns. At one time, Lubeck was the most powerful state on the Baltic shores, warring, making treaties, influencing the destinies and the Governments of Sweden, Denmark, and of some smaller German principalities. The American commercial metropolises, whatever may be their expansion, and the influence derived from commerce and wealth, in all other aspects are dependencies of their respective States. If comparisons are to be established, then, for example, New York cannot be compared in a social, political, or any conventional point of view, with London, or Paris, etc., nor even with any of the capitals of the second order. It cannot be compared, in that respect, with the past condition of Italian cities, or the few towns of the Hanseatic League.

The city of New York acquires and extends daily a commercial signification and influence, which make her already the commercial metropolis of this part of the globe. Under this cardinal, as under several secondary and collateral aspects, New York, in character, in resources, in original, as well as in the alluvial elements of its population, which is eminently cross-bred from all nations and states, in its ways and means of activity, in the variety of its small and great combinations and features, New York eminently differs from the commercial metropolises of ancient and modern times. New York is a world in itself, with numberless small circles, with elevations and depressions, constituting its distinct and special features. By its population, New York occupies the third place among the cities in the Christian world. Its commerce expands over the globe, its own capital, or that attracted by its mediation, is felt in all the arteries between the Atlantic and the Pacific. Nearly all its outward outlines and tendencies are broad and public-minded; they denote greatness in the aggregate, and nevertheless New York is eminently provincial in all social aspects, when compared to European capitals. The most diversified extremes meet in New York. Gigantic in its commercial and industrial pursuits, and in all relations depending thereon, and stamped by littleness in most of its daily and life-interweaving conventionalities, relations, intercourse; full of the genuine democratic essence, at the side of an equally strong sham one, and with some of its crusts agitated by the most convulsive attempts at forming an embryonic aristocracy; sound, as well as even febrile activity, parallel with stupidity and stagnation; light pouring out in streams from the press, from the more or less perfect scientific, literary, and educational establishments, and dark mental shadows overhanging summits and lowlands. A vigorous, rapid, often reckless run onwards, and a very strong retrograding tendency; all-embracing in trade and speculation, and in social relations cut up into sets, separated into parcels by the most artificial notions. Nowhere, even in any second and third rate capital of Europe, has society the aspect of falling into so many various, puny, parishional distinctions. An agglomeration of social offal, flowing in from almost all parts and races of the globe; then a genuine, large, sound, substantial, intelligent, active population; forming a compact substratum, on whose surface rise and swim, in shape, character, tone, and color, the most curious, socially-artificial efflorescences. Many others are the contrasts within the city itself, and in its relations to the country.

In the commercial cities of the Free States, attempts are made at establishing a kind of conventional, artificial, parlor, and church-pew aristocracy, at imitating the aristocratic demeanor, at borrowing from Europe, and becoming tamed by petty aristocratic notions. The disease catches not, however, the sound substratum of the same cities, nor the country, in its broadest sense. Such attempts, insignificant and valueless, would scarcely deserve to be noticed, but for their completing the salient features of difference between the old and the new, between America and Europe; for their contributing to elucidate the soundness of the democratic essence, deeply and thoroughly penetrating the country; and finally, because by their mirage those aristocratic shams sometimes mislead in the appreciation of the intrinsic worth of American society.

Aristocracy, as a conception or as a social fact, wraps itself generally in the prestige of past grandeur. Ancient families live on traditions and recollections of national, as well as of domestic greatness; on those of power and influence exercised over the nation, the society, and transmitted, inherited, from generation to generation. Descendants are proud of their ancestors, and consider them as superior beings They do not blush for nor disavow the occupations, the pursuits of their forefathers. With the exception of a few well-known families of historical revolutionary renown, some few others descending from officials of the colonial times, and still fewer of a wholly fortuitous, or rather conventionally conceded distinction, the pretenders to aristocracy in the American society descend, in an overpowering majority, from originally poor but honorable traffickers, artisans, farmers, or professional men. *Noblesse oblige* was the device of the ancient nobility all over Europe. It obliged to imitate the gallantry, the noble deeds of ancestors. The American aristocrats might imitate theirs in simplicity of manners, soundness of sense, and the absence of conceited assumption. In reading the names in the cemetery of a New England or any other ancient inland village, or even the sign-boards over the stores, or the shops of artificers, of country-towns, almost all the names will be found which, from one end to the other of the republic, resound in trade, politics, literature; which occupy the various leading positions in every commercial metropolis; all this bearing testimony to the humble and equal beginning of all the families. Alike humble but honorable was the origin of the American descendants of the Huguenots. Very few, if any, French nobles emigrated to the Carolinas in the 16th century, during the reign of the Valois. It was mostly artisans, small traders, operatives, whom Coligny directed to America. The nobles remained at home to fight the battles of the reformation. Not one of the aristocrats of America, who does not believe himself superior to his fishing, trading, farming, hard-toiling ancestry, whose start was small, and so were the modes of life, the houses, and households, and the trade. Such was the condition of the Puritans, Planters, Quakers, Knickerbockers. New Amsterdam was comparatively a small, uninfluential, trafficking spot. Mostly poor people from Holland, among them Hebrews, emigrated to America in the 17th century, and have been the primitive founders of the Knickerbockers.* The new men and families whom, for example, the Knickerbockers, the descendants of the Quakers in Philadelphia, or the Bostonians, Baltimoreans,

* The descendants—now aristocracized—of those primitive settlers and seekers of fortune possess a rare inventive power. One of them, whose grandfather's land in the suburbs of New York, occupied as a gardener, where is now one of the most aristocratic avenues, told me that the founder of his lineage on this continent was heir to a dukedom in Holland; but an uncle and tutor of his, likewise a sovereign duke, seized the heirdom and sent the youth to the American colony. The narrator forgot that no such family name is to be found among the feudal records of Holland, and that feudalism was overthrown in the 17th century, and such highhanded and treacherous proceedings almost impossible in Holland, or at least would have been mentioned in her history. Others tell stories even more improbable, about their Dutch, Scotch, English, Irish, etc., illustrious origin.

and other like parishioners, consider as not up to them, started from the same point as did the sires of the others. The difference is not in the nature of their pursuits, not in the ways and means by which positions have been acquired then and now, but exclusively in chronology. The new families and men carry on a more extensive business, have a larger and more comprehensive range of notions, live in larger, more comfortable and elegant houses, and larger households and retinue surround them than did the old citizens; the new have equal or more culture, polish, and more means to procure it, than had the old city-founders and parishioners. The puny spirit of provincialism, of parish distinctions, is nursed, entertained, by all these petty assumptions, whatever might be their origin and their name. Provincialism is their principal inheritance. The so-called old families give the character of littleness, which is so salient in the social relations and intercourse of what is styled the "best" society of American commercial cities. Little, if any, difference in good-breeding is to be detected between the "good," the "best," the "exclusive," or with whatever else denomination the tenants of an imaginary superiority try to distinguish themselves, and what they call the new men and families, on whom they look down and try to keep them at bay. The difference, if existing, is not always and altogether on the side of the "best," clustering as representatives, and forming the ornamental portion of the conventional social structure, as it does the highest society in every European capital. At the side of these "aristocratic" and "choicest" in America, exist families of deserved consideration, forming smaller groups, enjoying quietly and substantially their wealth; intelligent, natural, unassuming, and thus attractive and inoffensive. Among those, as well as in general in the country, are to be found real distinction, ease, gentleness of feelings, simplicity in demeanor, constituting genuine good-breeding, and extensive and various information. Even good blood—that aristocratic criterion—and often spoken of in America, good blood—if it should be noticed—runs purer in the country than among the "best" of the metropolis. Aristocracy has not generally originated in stores, counters, or in the gutters of cities. European aristocracies never had, and have not now, their roots in cities, not even in capitals, but in the country; and the high society in Europe is such in reality, forming the apex of special but real rights and privileges, of power, of abuses and prejudices, out of which is built up the European social edifice. As no such clear distinct landmarks exist here, artificial ones are created out of thousands of ridiculous imaginary distinctions, based on or deduced from the kind or nature of the commercial or industrial undertaking, pursuit, or trade; definitions and distinctions—in their hair-splitting niceties—mostly unintelligible to the ritualists and expounders themselves.

The noblest feature of a genuine aristocrat is, that, proud of his individual dignity, his birth, and blood, he feels himself no more honored by contact with royalty, than he is compromised in his standing and dignity by contact with the poorest laborer. But the American imitators, surrounding themselves with whimsical fences, are continually on the alert, nervous about not losing their respectability; true imitators therein of English snobbism. From behind those strongholds, they defend jealously and spasmodically their assumed positions, dreading the approach of any new face, always on the defensive against new-comers, intruders. All this contracts, narrows the social intercourse, makes it uneasy; it contracts the minds of those living under the like misconceived and trying conditions. All of them vegetate mentally on personalities and petty interests. Wide-reaching, general events and objects, agitate and engross not these circles, as is the case in European high society. Even a third-rate capital or watering-place of Europe is superior in this aspect to any set of the "best," the "purest," the "choicest," here. Literature, arts, political problems, solutions agitating the state, the country, all events calling or concentrating attention, are more vividly felt and spoken of by men and women in the country, and in the cities, by those groups not claiming aristocratical distinction, the sets of the "best" exercising none, or, at the utmost, very insignificant influence on the public judgment and opinion.

This, in many respects, abnormal and unnatural social confusion, perverts, nay caricatures relations, which otherwise might be large, expansive, and truly high-toned. So the wealthy merchant, who, in his business place is all-embracing, public-minded, generous, and expanding, contracts and narrows as soon as he returns into the region of his daily social intercourse. The merchant princes of Italy, were as large-minded in sociability as in their commercial or political combinations, conceptions, actions. The merchant princes considered it as the greatest honor to throw their palaces open and fill them with scholars, artists, literators; with men of intellectual standing and distinction, of whatever kind and nature, they rivalled each other in attracting such guests. No merchant prince of an American metropolis or any of the "bests" is attracted, or finds enjoyment in the like associations. And, should it ever be so, he or his family would not dare to imitate the Italian and European models, and break through or overstep the range of puny notions, to risk artificial respectability, and undergo the disapprobation of the little world around them, and in which everybody looks up continually to somebody else.

In Boston, however, social relations, courtesies, and considerations are, at times, regulated by deference to mental and intellectual worth: above all when political prejudices, passions, or even hatred, do not cloud the sound sense of those who constitute the upper social circles.

Not the aristocracy of these cities, but those moving without its dwarfish orbits, and above all the inhabitants of the country, from one end to the other, and belonging to all conditions, render homage to mental power and distinction. The literator, the poet, the artist, the savant, is always surrounded in the country, in towns, villages, with consideration, excites, attracts interest, and deferential curiosity, while the nabob, who throws into nervous excitement the "best" in the metropolis will remain unnoticed. The same "best" circles of the commercial metropolis preserve and nurse still the feeling of colonial inferiority towards England—a feeling which does not in the least exist in the country. An occasional arrival of a Lord, of any Englishman of note,* and often of one who in his own land had not even a glimpse at society, will throw the "best" into a state of ecstatic excitement; while the inhabitants of the country remain unconcerned thereat.

Such a development of the social relations of a portion of American society is the more to be regretted, because the

* During the last misunderstanding with England on account of the fisheries, one of the members of the house of Baring Brothers, from London, visited America. The excitement among the "best" was intense, as nearly all the commercial houses in America depend upon the credit of the London banker. In Boston, in public speeches the office of a diplomatic, high, and confidential mission, was attributed to the traveller, who, by his sensible conduct, gave no occasion to so much imaginary distinction, and declined all such allusions and honors. The sensible people in cities and the country kept perfectly cool, quiet, and unconcerned. Such, or similar occurrences, are repeated again and again.

same man and woman who are spasmodic when in their aristocratic toga, are pleasant, easy, sociable, when they lay it aside. Then they are susceptible and accessible to all the generous impulses of the people. The aristocratical imitation is the shadowy side of the character in the daily relations and social intercourse. The radiating side shines when the same people are seen in their true American nature. Thus, for example, a woman, a girl, ridiculously fastidious, affected, and therefore highly aristocratical in her own estimation, in the evening, has sometimes spent the morning nobly in teaching, superintending some ragged school, or in some charitable and humane occupation of the kind. Nevertheless, the vanity and affectation which infect those regions seems to spread in wider and wider circles, penetrates deeper to the core. It begins to operate on the infancy. Thus children get old, withered, and distorted notions in their little heads. Thus early in youth ingenuousness is nipped in the bud, and the germ of gentleness tarnished if not wholly destroyed.

The country is little or not at all exposed to such like aberrations and deviations. Assumption and aristocratic attempts are difficult, and cannot find there a propitious soil. In the country, the normal elements of American society are purer, and have an easier and simpler action. Families, occupations, are all honorable—groupings by sets difficult. All are equal and independent in their contact, in their relations. The cities draw from the country nearly all the elements of real or fancied supremacy. The country and not generally the cities, and still less their various "sets," bring forth those vigorous minds, which in literature, in trade, in industry, in politics, in the press, in professional or commercial pursuits, marks, develops, and expands the destinies of America.

Among the conspicuous American cities, the city of

Washington has the purest and broadest national, distinct American character. Not being commercial or industrial, it does not possess large wealth, and wealth is not an influential or swaying social ingredient there. Neither has Washington the relation to the country in which stand the respective capitals in centralized Europe. Washington, however, truly and largely reflects the democratic element of America—the democratic character of the people, of the institutions, and the essence of democratic urbanity. Social relations and intercourse are regulated and depend mostly upon the intrinsic value of man, or upon what as such, is conceded or recognized to the individual. Neither wealth nor any fictitious assumption or arrogant claims of superiority of blood or birth, are omnipotent or influential. Not these give the tone to society, and no local petty influences direct it. Men coming from all parts of the republic, independent and equal to each other in their public character, give and preserve to society the broad republican features and space wherein every one moves freely and finds his absolute or at least his relative appreciation. Politics being the cardinal element, the eminent political leaders form of course the cardinal points of attraction. Such leadership, from whatever light it may be considered, is always an evidence of certain individual superiority and ability. A man of learning, a literator, known in any way by his mental and intellectual accomplishments, an artist, will be met with more courtesy in Washington than the man of wealth, who shakes the exchanges of the commercial metropolis, or the leaders of their "best," "purest," and most "exquisite" sets. Gorgeous display is valued at its worth, imposes not oppressingly on relations and intercourse, and these, in general, are easy, elastic, and with a tint of more genuine refinement and better toned than in any other American society. The conversational topics are diversified on account of the variety of interests, notions, comprehensions, meeting, crossing, or running, agitating, at the side of each other. Courtesy, inborn or conventional, must prevail, resulting from the relations of mutual independence between the legislators and the administration, and from the broad basis on which a society so variously composed, stands and moves.

Of late, savage violence has stained bloodily and darkly the social relations in Washington. The disgrace came from and attaches to that part of the republic in which a perverted social order perverts public opinion, generates a political fury, superseding culture, civility, and self-respect by the ferocious self-will of the individual. Such occurrences cannot in justice be considered as the true exponents of the social tone in this political and eminently American metropolis.

As the large commercial cities do not exercise a social or conventional supremacy, or affect in such aspects the tone of the country, in the same way they are not the fair exponents or reflections of the prevailing morals. Cities, always and every where, contain inducements, excitements, to moral degradation, corruption, dissipation and dissoluteness, and the American cities do not differ much in that respect from those of Europe. The country alone in many respects has hitherto preserved a superiority over the prevailing morals throughout Europe.

Where the democratic principle is playing in its fulness, America generally outshines Europe in culture, manners, good-breeding, mental superiority. The country, with its towns and villages, and with the laborious, enterprising, intelligent and self-improving population, the sound substratum in the cities constitute integrally the higher development by which the scales of comparison turn in favor of America. The attempts made by certain portions of society to secede from the normal American element and spirit, to assimilate themselves, to imitate in various ways European aristocracies, are altogether abortions. Such copies are mostly inferior to the originals, and notwithstanding their wealth or superficial varnish, they are thoroughly inferior to the mass of the American people. Undoubtedly this mass possesses more varied culture of mind, more true refinement than those social efflorescences. Undoubtedly likewise, the European aristocracy, together with all its ramifications, embracing the official, financial, commercial, and industrial highest classes, is superior in mind, in scientific and literary information, as well as in exquisiteness of manners to its American imitations.

In the masses, and therefore principally in the country, are salient the luminous and all-embracing results of American civilization, while in Europe hitherto only certain classes, and generally the cities constitute the civilized aggregate. The decline of American culture and social progress, with all its mental, moral, and material features, will begin when the interests of the city and country, instead of harmonizing, shall be at variance; when the country shall be sacrificed to the claims or interests of cities; or when, by a mistake or a curse, the power of legislations shall rise and extend the influence of great commercial cities, and push into the second line that of the country.

CONCLUSION.

THE great life of the people, the unsullied democratic substance, alone generates all the bright and vigorous aspects in the development of America. Beyond, shadows rise and deepen. Whatever breathes the spirit which animates the people, grows and expands; what deviates, separates, fails to emerge, and is not tempered therein, shrivels, corrugates, becomes inefficient, incomplete. This law is absolute. It controls social problems, political and legislative solutions; it prevails in education, literature, poetry, arts, industry; it is felt in habits and customs, in the relations which constitute the daily, private, social intercourse.

Liberty fills the space, and therein—as the ethereal bodies in celestial immensities—individualities find their scope less restrained than in any human institutions hitherto known. Each individuality grows self-asserting, according to its vitality and fecundity, each moving freely on its freely selected orbit. Liberty and equality are forces which impel in America varieties of human families and characters to combination and union, precursory of the unity towards which gravitates mankind. Not the flock-like agglomeration of samenesses and uniformities, but the free harmonious combination of varieties is the key-note of social unity.

The progress that has hitherto been accomplished by

America solves the question between authority and liberty, as elements paramount and integrally constitutive of human society. America incarnates liberty, Europe authority. America evidences—contrary to time-honored and still generally asserted axioms—that liberty in superseding authority does not disorganize society. Authority, in its various modes of comprehension, as principle and agency, is the substance of the dominant ideas and actions for Europe, even for the reforming, revolutionary portion of it. Here authority is wholly subordinate to liberty. In her all-embracing, all-creative activity, liberty alternates between lights and shadows, as did, as now does, authority. Short and dim are the shadows of liberty, but protracted in time and deep in tint, where authority is in the ascendant. It is now undeniably evidenced, that in the normal condition of man and society, liberty is cohesive and constructive, and more so than authority. Here liberty alone cements the social structure, it is a central hearth, towards which gravitate elements, passions, interests, activities, once judged irreconcilable in their character and nature. Until the apparition of the American social state, the like elements have been considered as chaotic, dissolving, disorganizing, fit only to be compressed, to be held sternly, and directed by authority. Liberty, not authority, gathers, classifies, combines, adjusts, imparts to them healthy vitality, regulates their orderly association. So almost boundlessly enlarges the range of action of the American people.

The subjugation of authority to liberty corresponds with the dualistic essence and action of the laws of the universe, in their moral and physical functions. Spirit rises above matter, ethical laws finally operate over the physical. Liberty, essentially a moral law and force, absorbs authority, which, even in its most philosophical and exalted conception, resolves itself into material substance.

With liberty, therefore, as sole compass and pilot, society can traverse the inner and outer breakers and perils, without shaking in its foundations, disjoining and falling to pieces. Guided and inspired by liberty, America moves with stately impetuosity, and shall so move undisturbed in her luminous onward course.

THE END.

MISCELLANEOUS—Continued.

Atlas. Appletons' Modern Atlas of the Earth, on 34 Maps. Colored. Royal 8vo. Half bound, 3 50

—— **Cornell's New General Atlas.** 1 handsome vol. 4to..... 1 00

Attache (The) in Madrid; or Sketches of the Court of Isabella II. 1 vol. 12mo..... 1 00

Baldwin's Flush Times in Mississippi and Alabama. 12mo. Illustrated................ 1 25

———— **Party Leaders.** 12mo. ....Cloth, 1 00

Barker (Jacob) Incidents in the Life of. 8vo. 2 portraits. Cloth, 1 00

Barth's Travels in Africa. (in press.)......................

Bartlett. Personal Narrative of Explorations in Texas, New Mexico, California, &c. &c. Maps and Illustrations. 2 vols. 8vo......................... 4 00

Bartlett. The same, in half calf extra 7 00

———— The same, in full calf extra 8 00

———— The same, cheap edition, in 1 vol., bound................... 3 50

Basil. A Story of Modern Life. By W. Wilkie Collins. 12mo. ....Cloth, 75

Benton's Thirty Years' View; or a History of the Working of the American Government for thirty years, from 1820 to 1850. 2 very large vols., 8vo. pp. 1527, well printed, Cloth, 5 00
Sheep, 6 00
In half calf or half mor., 7 00
In full calf, 8 00

Abridgment of the Debates of Congress, from 1789 to 1856. From Gales and Seaton's Annals of Congress; from their Register of Debates; and from the Official Reported Debates, by John C. Rives. By the Author of "The "Thirty Years' View." Vol. I. (to be in 15) preparing. Price per vol. 3 00

Beyminstre. By the author of "Lena." 1 vol. (in press)........

Bridgman's, The Pilgrims of Boston and their Descendants. 1 large vol., 8vo.....Cloth, 3 00

Butler's Philosophy of the Weather, and a Guide to its Changes. 12mo..........Cloth 1 00

Brace's Fawn of the Pale Faces. 12mo.............Cloth, 75

Brownell's Poems. 12mo. Boards, 75

———— **Ephemeron; a Poem.** 12mo............Paper, 25

Bryant's Poems. New edition, revised throughout. 2 vols. 12mo. Cloth, 2 00
Extra cloth, gilt edges, 2 50
Morocco, antique or extra 6 00
Half morocco, gilt, 4 00
Half calf, antique or extra, 4 00
Full calf, antique or extra, 5 00
" In 1 vol. 18mo.....Cloth, 63
Gilt edges, 75
Antique morocco, 2 00

Bryant's What I Saw in California. With Map. 12mo..... 1 25

Burnett's Notes on the North-Western Territory. 8vo. Cloth, 2 00

Burton's Encyclopædia of Wit and Humour. Illustrated. 1 large vol. 8vo. (In press.)......

Calhoun (J. C.) The Works of (now first collected). 6 vols. 8vo. per vol............................ 2 00

———— Sold separately:
Vol. 1. ON GOVERNMENT.
2. REPORTS & LETTERS.
3, 4. SPEECHES.
5, 6. REPORTS & LETTERS.
Or, sets in 6 vols. half calf, 20 00
" " " full calf, 24 00

MISCELLANEOUS—Continued.

Captain Canot; or, Twenty Years of a Slaver's Life. Edited by Brantz Mayer. 1 vol. 12mo. Illustrated..........Cloth, 1 25

Chapman's Instructions to Young Marksmen on the Improved American Rifle. 16mo. Illustrated..........Cloth, 1 25

Chestnut Wood. A Tale. By Liele Linden. 2 vols. 12mo...Cloth, 1 75

Clark, L. G. Knick-knacks from an Editor's Table. 12mo. Illustrated................ 1 25

Clarke (Mrs. Cowden). The Iron Cousin. A Tale. 1 vol. 12mo......................Cloth, 1 25

Cockburn's (Lord) Memorials of His Time. 1 thick vol. 12mo. Beautifully printed..... ...Cloth, 1 25

Cooley, A. J. The Book of Useful Knowledge. Containing 6,000 Practical Receipts in all branches of Arts, Manufactures, and Trades. 8vo. Illustrated.
Bound, 1 25

Coit, Dr. History of Puritanism. 12mo ....Cloth, 1 00

Coleridge's Poems. 1 neat vol. 12mo. ....Cloth, 1 00
Gilt edges, 1 50
Morocco antique, or extra, 3 50

Coming's Preservation of Health and Prevention of Disease. 12mo................ 75

Cornwall, N. E. Music as It Was, and as It Is. 12mo.
Cloth, 63

Cousin's Course of Modern Philosophy. Translated by Wight. 2 vols. 8vo........Cloth, 3 00
Half calf, 5 00
Full calf, 6 00

Cousin's Philosophy of the Beautiful. 16mo........Cloth, 62

Cousin's Lectures on the True, the Beautiful, and the Good. Translated by Wight. 8vo.
Cloth, 1 50
Half calf, 2 50
Full calf, 3 00

————**The Youth of Madame De Longueville.** 1 vol. 12mo........................Cloth, 1 00

Cowper's Homer's Iliad. Revised by Southey, with Notes by Dwight. 1 vol.............Cloth, 1 25
Gilt edges, 1 50
Antique or extra morocco, 4 00

Creasy (Prof.) Rise and Progress of the English Constitution. 1 vol. 1 00

Croswell. A Memoir of the Rev. W. Croswell, D.D. 1 vol. 8vo...................Cloth, 2 00

Cust (Lady.) The Invalid's Own Book. 12mo.......Cloth, 50

D'Abrantes (Duchess.) Memoirs of Napoleon, his Court and Family. 2 large vols. 8vo. Portraits...................Cloth, 4 00
———————— The same, in half calf extra or antique......... 7 00
———————— The same, in full calf extra or antique.......... 8 00

De Bow's Industrial Resources, Statistics, &c., of the United States. 8vo. 3vols. bound in 1 vol..............Cloth, 5 00

De Custine's Russia. Trans. from the French. Thick 12mo.
Cloth, 1 25

Dew's Digest of Ancient and Modern History. 8vo. Cloth, 2 00

Don Quixote de La Mancha. Translated from the Spanish. Illustrated with engravings. 8vo.
Cloth. 2 00
Half calf, 3 00
Full calf, 4 00

MISCELLANEOUS—Continued.

Drury, A. H. Light and Shade; or, the Young Artist. 12mo. ......Cloth, 75

Dix's Winter in Madeira, and Summer in Spain, &c. 12mo. Illustrated......Cloth, 1 00

Dumas (Alex.) The Foresters. A Tale. 12mo......Cloth, 75

—— **Philibert; or, the European Wars of the 16th Century.** 12mo....Cloth, 1 25

Dumont's Life Sketches from Common Paths. A Series of American Tales. 12mo.....Cloth, 1 00

Dupuy, A. E. The Conspirator. 12mo......Cloth, 75

Dwight's Introduction to the Study of Art. 12mo.....Cloth, 1 00

Ellen Parry; or, Trials of the Heart. 12mo......Cloth, 63

Ellis, Mrs. Hearts & Homes; or, Social Distinctions. A Story......Cloth, 1 50

Evelyn's Life of Mrs. Godolphin. Edited by the Bishop of Oxford. 16mo......Cloth, 50

Ewbank. The World a Workshop. 16mo......Cloth, 75

Fay, T. S. Ulric; or, the Voices. 12mo. ......Boards, 75

Farmingdale. A Tale. By Caroline Thomas. 12mo......Cloth, 1 00

French's Historical Collections of Louisiana. Part III. 8vo......Cloth, 1 50

Foote's Africa and the American Flag. 1 vol. 12mo. Illust. Cloth, 1 50

Fullerton, Lady G. Lady Bird. 12mo......Cloth, 75

Garland's Life of John Randolph. 2 vols. in 1. 8vo. Portraits 1 50
Half calf, 2 50
Full calf, 3 00

Gibbes' Documentary History of the American Revolution, 1781, 1782. 1 vol. 8vo. Cloth, 1 50

—— The same. 2d vol. 1764 to 1776. 1 vol. 8vo......Cloth, 1 50

Ghostly Colloquies. By the Author of "Letters from Rome," &c. 12mo......Cloth, 1 00

Gil Blas. Translated from the French by Le Sage. Illustrated with over 500 spirited engravings. 1 large vol. 8vo......Extra cloth, Gilt edges, 3 00
Half calf, 3 50
Full calf, 4 00

Gilfillan, Geo. Gallery of Literary Portraits. Second Series. 12mo......Cloth, 1 00

Goddard's Gleanings. Some Wheat—Some Chaff. 12mo. Cloth, 1 00

Goethe's Iphigenia in Tauris. A Drama in Five Acts. Translated from the German by C. J. Adler. 12mo......Boards, 75

Goldsmith's Vicar of Wakefield. 12mo. Illustrated. Cloth, 75
Gilt edges, 1 00

Gore, Mrs. The Dean's Daughter. 12mo......Cloth, 75

Gould's (W. M.) Zephyrs from Italy and Sicily. 12mo. Colored plate, 1 00

Grant's Memoirs of an American Lady. 12mo......Cloth, 75

Griffith's (Mattie) Poems. 12mo......Cloth, 75
Gilt edges, 1 25

Guizot's History of Civilization. 4 vols. 12mo.....Cloth, 3 50
Half calf, 8 00

—— **Democracy in France.** 12mo......Paper, 25

MISCELLANEOUS—Continued.

Gurowski's Russia As It Is. 1 vol. 12mo................Cloth, 1 00

Hall, B. R. The New Purchase; or, Early Years in the Far West. Illustrated. 12mo. Cloth, 1 25

Harry Muir. A Scottish Story. 12mo..............Cloth, 75

Hamilton's Philosophy. Arranged and Edited by O. W. Wight. 1 vol. 8vo........Cloth, 1 50

——— The Same, in full calf, 3 00

Heartsease; or, The Brother's Wife. By the Author of "The Heir of Redclyffe." 2 vols. 12mo. Cloth, 1 50

Heir of Redclyffe (The). A Tale. 2 vols. 12mo...............Cloth, 1 50

Heloise; or, The Unrevealed Secret. By Talvi. 12mo..... Cloth, 75

Holmes's Tempest and Sunshine; or, Life in Kentucky. 12mo.......................Cloth, 1 00

——— **The English Orphans.** A Tale. 12mo. Cloth, 75

Home is Home A Domestic Story. 12mo.............Cloth, 75

Home; or, The Ways of the World. By Mrs. Reeves. 1 vol. (In press.)........................

Household Mysteries. By the Author of "Light and Darkness." 1 vol. 12mo...................... 1 00

Hunt's Pantological System of History. Folio, ...Cloth, 3 00

Iconographic Cyclopædia of Science, Literature, and Art, Systematically Arranged. Illustrated with 500 fine steel plate engravings. 6 vols. Half morocco, 40 00

——— Or in full morocco,..... 50 00

——— Or in separate divisions:—

The Laws of Nature; or, Mathematics, Astronomy, Physics, and Meteorology Illustrated. With an Atlas of twenty-nine steel plates, containing twelve hundred illustrations. 2 vols.........................Cloth, 5 00

The Sciences; or, Chemistry, Mineralogy, and Geology Illustrated. With an Atlas of twenty-four steel plates, containing one thousand illustrations. 2 vols. Cloth, 3 00

The Anatomy of the Human Body; or, Anthropology Illustrated. With an Atlas of twenty-two steel plates, containing six hundred illustrations. 2 vols. Cloth, 3 00

The Countries and Cities of the World; or, Geography Illustrated. Including a Complete German and English Geographical Glossary. With an Atlas of forty-four steel plates, containing Geographical Maps and Plans of Cities. 2 vols..............Cloth, 5 00

The Customs and Costumes of People of Ancient and Modern Times; or, History and Ethnology Illustrated. With an Atlas of eighty-one steel plates, containing fourteen hundred illustrations. 2 vols............Cloth, 8 00

The Warfare of All Ages; or, Military Sciences Illustrated. With an Atlas of fifty-one steel plates, containing fifteen hundred illustrations. 2 vols...Cloth, 5 00

MISCELLANEOUS—Continued.

The Navigation of All Ages; or, Naval Science Illustrated. With an Atlas of thirty-two steel plates, containing six hundred illustrations. 2 vols. ....Cloth, 4 00

The Art of Building in Ancient and Modern Times; or, Architecture Illustrated. With an Atlas of sixty steel plates, containing 1100 illustrations. 2 vols....................Cloth, 6 00

The Religions of Ancient and Modern Times; or, Mythology Illustrated. With an Atlas of thirty steel plates, containing eight hundred illustrations. 2 vols....................Cloth, 4 00

The Fine Arts Illustrated. Being a Complete History of Sculpture, Painting, and the Graphic Arts, including a Theory of the Art of Drawing. With an Atlas of twenty-six steel plates, containing five hundred illustrations. 2 vols. Cloth, 4 00

Technology Illustrated. Being a Series of Treatises on the Construction of Roads, Bridges, Canals, Hydraulic Engines, Flouring and Spinning Mills, and on the Principal Proceedings in Cotton Manufacture, Coining, Mining, Metallurgy, Agriculture, &c. With an Atlas of thirty-five steel plates, containing 1,100 engravings. 2 vols....................Cloth, 4 00

A very few copies only remain of the above. Early orders are necessary to secure them.

IO. A Tale of the Ancient Fane. By Barton. 12mo. Cloth, 75

Irish (The) Abroad and at Home, at the Court and in the Camp. 12mo.........Cloth, 1 00

Isham's Mud Cabin; or, Character and Tendency of British Institutions. 12mo. Cloth, 1 00

James, Henry. The Nature of Evil, considered in a Letter to the Rev. Edward Beecher, D.D. 1 vol. 16mo. Cloth, 1 00

James, G. P. R. and M. B. Field. Adrien; or, The Clouds of the Mind. 12mo. Cloth, 75

Jameson (Mrs.) Common-place Book of Thoughts, Memories, and Fancies. 12mo....................Cloth, 75
Half calf extra, 1 75

Johnson, A. B. The Meaning of Words. 12mo........Cloth, 1 00

Johnston's Chemistry of Common Life. Illustrated with numerous woodcuts. 2 vols. 12mo.
Cloth, 2 00
In sheep, 2 25
In half calf, 4 00

Juno Clifford. A Tale. By a Lady. With illustrations. 12mo. Cloth, 1 25

Kavanagh, Julia. Women of Christianity, Exemplary for Piety and Charity. 12mo. Cloth, 75

——— **Nathalie. A Tale.** 12mo....................Cloth, 1 00

——— **Madeleine.** 12mo. Cloth, 75

——— **Daisy Burns.** 12mo. Cloth, 1 00

——— **Grace Lee.** ..Cloth, 1 00

——— **Rachel Gray.** 12mo. Cloth, 0 75

——— The same. 6 volumes. Half calf, 10 00

Keats' Poetical Works. 1 vol. 12mo....................Cloth, 1 00
Gilt edges, 1 50
Antique or extra morocco, 3 50

MISCELLANEOUS—Continued.

Kirkland (Mrs.) Personal Memoirs of George Washington. 1 vol. 12mo. Illustrated..................(In press.)

Kœppen. Atlas of the Middle Ages. With copious illustrative Text. 4to............Half bound, 4 50

——— **History of the Middle Ages.** 2 vols. 12mo. Cloth, 2 00

——— **Atlas to do.** Cloth, 2 50

Kohlrausch's Complete History of Germany. 8vo. Cloth, 1 50

——— A New Edition. Illustrated.........Extra Binding, 2 50

Lamartine's History of Turkey. Vol. 1. 12mo. Cloth, 1 00

Layard's Nineveh and its Remains. 1 large vol. 8vo., with all the illustrations............Cloth, 4 00
Half calf, 5 00

——— The Same. 1 vol. 12mo., without the illustrations....Cloth, 1 00

Lee, E. B. Life of Jean Paul F. Richter. 12mo.......Cloth, 1 25

Leger's History of Animal Magnetism. 12mo.......Cloth, 1 00

Letters from Rome, A.D. 138. By the Author of "Clouds and Sunshine." 12mo......Cloth, 1 00

Life and Correspondence of Judge Iredell.......(In press.)

Life's Discipline. A Tale of the Annals of Hungary. By Talvi. Author of "Heloise," &c. 12mo. ....Cloth, 63

Lindsay. Poems by Walter M. Lindsay. 16mo......Cloth, 75

Lord, W. W. Poems. 12mo. Boards, 75

Lord, W. W. Christ in Hades. 12mo.....................Boards, 75

Macaulay's Essays, Critical and Miscellaneous. Best Edition. 5 vols. small 8vo. Cloth, 3 75
Half calf extra, 8 00
Full calf extra, 10 00

Macintosh, M. J. Two Lives; or, To Seem and To Be. 12mo. Cloth, 75

——— **Aunt Kitty's Tales.** 12mo......................Cloth, 75

——— **Charms & Counter Charms.**.................Cloth, 1 00

——— **Evenings at Donaldson Manor.** 12mo....Cloth, 75

——— **The Lofty and Lowly.** 2 vols. 12mo....Cloth, 1 50

The above, in uniform sets, 6 vols., half calf extra,...................10 00

McCormick's Visit to the Camp before Sebastopol. Neatly illustrated. 12mo...Cloth, 1 00

McLee's Series of Alphabets, designed as a Text-Book for Engravers and Painters of Letters. 4to.........Cloth, 2 00

Mahon's (Lord) History of England. Edited by Professor Reed. 2 vols. 8vo............. 4 00

Manzoni. The Betrothed Lovers. 2 vols. 12mo...Cloth, 1 50

Margaret Cecil; or, I Can, Because I Ought. By Cousin Kate. 12mo...............Cloth, 75

Marrying Too Late. By Geo. Wood. Author of "Peter Schlemihl in America," &c., &c. 1 vol. (In press.)

MISCELLANEOUS—Continued.

Marsh's Theory and Practice of Bank Book-Keeping and Joint Stock Accounts. 1 vol. 4to. Printed in colors........... 4 00

Maxims of Washington. Selected from his own Writings. By Rev. J. F. Schroeder, D.D. 12mo. Cloth, 1 00
Gilt edges, 1 50

Meek's Red Eagle. A Poem of the South. 12mo...........Cloth, 75
———————— or, in extra cloth, gilt edges,.................. 1 00

Memorials of the Dead in Boston. 12mo...........Cloth, 1 50

Michelet's History of France. 2 vols. 8vo................Cloth, 3 50

———— **History of Roman Republic.** 12mo.........Cloth, 1 00

Milledulcia; a Thousand Pleasant Things Selected from the "Notes and Queries." (In press.).........

Milton's Paradise Lost. 18mo. Cloth, 0 38
Cloth gilt, 50

Minnie Myrtle. The Iroquois; or, Bright Side of Indian Character. Illustrated. 12mo. Cloth, 1 00

Montgomery's Sacred Poems and Hymns, for Pablic and Private Devotion. 12mo. Cloth, 0 75
Morocco antique, or extra, 2 50

Moore, C. C. Life of George Castriot, King of Albania. 12mo.........................Cloth, 1 00

Moore's (Frank) Songs and Ballads of the American Revolution. With Notes and illustrations. 12mo. ....Cloth, 1 00
Or, in morocco antique, 3 00

Moore's (Thos.) Memoirs, Journals, & Correspondence. Edited by Lord John Russell. Nos. I. to XI. Complete. In paper, each, 25
Or, in 1 vol. cloth, 3 00

Morse's General Atlas of the World. Containing seventy Maps, drawn and engraved from the latest and best authorities, with Descriptions and Statistics of all Nations to the year 1856. 1 vol. 4to, half bound, ... 9 00

Morton Montagu; or, Young Christian's Choice. By C. B. Mortimer. 12mo........Cloth, 75

Napoleon. The Confidential Correspondence of Napoleon Bonaparte with his Brother Joseph, some time King of Spain. 2 vols. 12mo.....Cloth, 2 00
———————— The same. 2 vols. Half calf, 4 00

Napoleon, Life of. From the French of Laurent de l'Ardeche. 2 vols. in 1. 8vo. 500 cuts, some colored. ....Im. morocco, 3 00

Newport Illustrated, in a Series of Pen and Pencil Sketches. 12mo. Cloth, 50

Norman Leslie. A Tale. By G. C. H. 12mo............Cloth, 75

Nursery Basket (The). A Hand-Book of Practical Directions for Young Mothers. 18mo.....Cloth, 38

Oates, Geo. Interest Tables at 6 per cent. per annum. 8vo.............................. 2 00
———————— Abridged Edition,... 1 25

———————— **Interest Tables at 7 per cent. per Annum.** 8vo.............................. 2 00
———————— Abridged Edition, .. 1 25

MISCELLANEOUS—Continued.

Osgood. The Hearth-Stone; or, Home Truths from a City Pulpit. 12mo............Cloth, 1 00
Gilt edges, 1 25

——— Illustrated new edition,. 1 25
Gilt edges, 1 50

——— **Mile-Stones in our Life Journey.** 12mo. Cloth, 1 00
Gilt edges, 1 25

Parkyn's Savage Life in Abyssynia. With illustrations. 2 vols. 12mo......................Cloth, 2 50
Ditto, cheap edition, in 1 vol. Cloth, 1 50

Pell's Guide for the Young. 12mo.......................Cloth, 38
Gilt edges, 50

Perry's Narrative of the Expedition of an American Squadron to the China Seas and Japan, performed in the Years 1852, 1853, and 1854, by order of the Government of the United States. Compiled from the Original Notes and Journals. By Francis L. Hawks, D.D. 1 vol. 8vo., with numerous illustrations......Cloth, 5 00
Half calf, 6 00
Full calf, 7 00
Morocco, 8 00

——— The Same, carefully abridged for District School Libraries and Young People. 1 neat vol. 12mo., illustrated. (Just ready.)

Phœnixiana; or, Sketches and Burlesques. By John Phœnix. Illustrated. 12mo. Cloth, 1 00

Pinkney's (Wm.) Life. By his Nephew. 1 vol. 8vo.......Cloth. 2 00

Pickell's New Chapter in the Early Life of Washington in connection with the Narrative History of the Potomac Company. 1 vol. 8vo.
Cloth, 1 25

Porter's (Miss Jane) Scottish Chiefs. A Romance. New and handsome edition, in 1 large vol. 8vo., with engravings...Cloth, 1 50
In extra roan, marb. edges, 2 00

Prismatics (Tales and Poems) By Richard Haywarde. 12mo. Illustrated........................ 1 25

Republic of the United States: Its Duties, &c. 12mo. Cloth, 1 00

Reid's New English Dictionary, with Derivations. 12mo.
Sheep, 1 00

Robinson Crusoe. Only complete edition. Illustrated with 300 Cuts. 8vo..................... 1 50
In gilt edges, 1 75
Half calf, 3 00

Rogers. Recollections of the Table-Talk of Samuel Rogers. 12mo..............Cloth, 1 00

Roe, A. S. James Mountjoy; or, I've been Thinking. 12mo.....................Cloth, 75

——— **Time and Tide.** 12mo.........................Cloth, 75

Reuben Medlicott; or, The Coming Man. 12mo....Cloth, 75

Sampson's Brief Remarker on the Ways of Man. Essays and Sketches of Life. 12mo. Cloth, 1 25

Scott's Lady of the Lake. 16mo........................Cloth, 38

——— **Marmion.** 16mo. Cloth, 37

——— **Lay of the Last Minstrel.** ....Cloth, 25

Schwegler's History of Philosophy. Translated from the original German by Julius H. Seelye. 12mo.................. 1 25

MISCELLANEOUS—Continued.

Select Italian Comedies. Translated. 12mo..........Cloth, 75

Sewell, E. M. The Earl's Daughter. 12mo........Cloth, 75

——— **Amy Herbert. A Tale.** 12mo........................Cloth, 75

——— **Gertrude. A Tale.** 12mo.........................Cloth 75

——— **Laneton Parsonage. A Tale.** 3 vols. 12mo. Cloth, 2 25

——— **Margaret Percival.** 2 vols..........................Cloth, 1 50

——— **Experience of Life.** 12mo........................Cloth, 75

——— **Walter Lorimer, and other Tales.** 12mo. Illustrated. Cloth, 75

——— **Katharine Ashton.** 2 vols. 12mo................Cloth, 1 50

——— **Journal Kept for the Children of a Village School.** Cloth, 1 00

Shakspeare's Dramatic Works and Life. 1 vol. 8vo. Cloth, gilt edges 2 00

Soyer's Modern Domestic Cookery. 12mo. ....Bound, 1 00

Southey's Life of Oliver Cromwell. 18mo........Cloth, 88

Southgate (Bishop). Visit to the Syrian Church. 12mo... 1 00

Souvestre's Attic Philosopher in Paris. 12mo..........Cloth, 50

——— **Stray Leaves from a Family Journal.** With illustrations. 12mo...........Cloth, 75

Sprague's History of the Florida War. Map and Plates. 8vo. 2 50

Spectator (The). A new edition, carefully revised. 6 large vols. 8vo. Fine bold type. ....Cloth, 9 00
Half calf, 15 00
Calf, 20 00

——— A smaller Edition, in 4 vols. 12mo. ....Cloth, 3 50
Half calf,
Full calf,

Spalding's History of English Literature. 12mo.......Cloth, 1 00

Squier's Nicaragua, Its People, Antiquities, &c. Maps and Plates. 2 vols. 8vo. 4 00

——— The Same. 2 vols. in 1. Cloth, or imperial morocco, 3 50

Summer Land (The). A Southern Story. By a Child of the Sun. 1 vol..................Cloth, 75

Sweet, Dr. Treatise on the Diseases of the Chest. 8vo. 3 00

Tappan's (Prof.) Logic. New and entirely revised edition. 12mo. Cloth, 1 25

——— **Steps from the New World to the Old, and Back Again.** 2 vols. 12mo.....Cloth, 1 75

Thorpe's The Hive of the Bee-Hunter. 16mo. Illustrated..........................Cloth, 1 00

Taylor's Manual of Ancient and Modern History. Edited by Prof. Henry. 8vo.......Cloth, 2 25
Sheep, 2 50

——— **Modern History.** separate........................Cloth, 1 50

——— **Ancient do. do.** Cloth, 1 25

Thackeray's Dr. Birch and his Young Friends. Square 12mo............................ 75

MISCELLANEOUS—Continued.

Thackeray's Popular Works. 12 vols. 16mo......Red cloth, each 50

——— The Same. 12mo. Extra brown cloth, each, 63

——— The Same. Bound in 6 vols..............Rich blue cloth, 6 00

——— The Same. Bound in 6 vols...............Half calf extra, 12 00

——— The Same. Bound in 12 vols...............Half calf extra, 15 00

Thiers' French Revolution. New edition, with steel engravings. 4 vols......................Cloth, 5 00
Or, in sheep, 6 00
Half calf extra, 10 00

——— A cheaper edition, in 2 vols. 8vo. ....Cloth, 3 00
Sheep, 4 00

Tuckerman's Artist Life. Biographical Sketches of American Painters. 12mo............Cloth, 75

Virginia Comedians (The); or, Old Days in the Old Dominion. 2 vols. 12mo....Cloth, 1 50

Ward's English Items. 12mo. Cloth, 1 00

Warner's (Miss) The Hills of the Shatemuc. 1 vol. 12mo.. 1 25

Warner (Miss A. B.) My Brother's Keeper. A Tale. 12mo.......................Cloth, 1 00

White (R. G.) Shakspeare's Scholar. 1 vol. 8vo.....Cloth, 2 50

——— The Same. In half calf extra, 3 50

——— The Same. In half mor. extra. 3 50

Whitehead's Contributions to the Early History of Perth Amboy and Adjoining Country. 8vo. Maps and illustrations....................Cloth, 2 75

Williams' Isthmus of Tehuantepec, its Climate, Productions, &c. Numerous Maps and Plates. 2 vols. 8vo.....Cloth, 3 50

Wilson's Elementary Treatise on Logic. 12mo.........Cloth, 1 25

Winkles (The); or, the Merry Monomaniacs. 12mo...Cloth, 1 00

Woman's Worth; or, Hints to Raise the Female Character. By a Lady. 18mo..... Cloth, 38

Warner's Rudimental Lessons in Music. 18mo. ..Cloth, 50

Wordsworth, W. The Prelude. An Autobiographical Poem. 12mo. .... Cloth, 1 00

Wanderings and Fortunes of German Emigrants. 12mo. Cloth, 75

Yonge's (Miss) Works.

——— **Heir of Redclyffe.** 2 vols. 12mo.......................Cloth, 1 50

——— **Heartsease.** 2 vols... 12mo.......................Cloth, 1 50

——— **The Daisy Chain; or, Aspirations.** A Family Chronicle. 2 vols. 12mo.........Cloth, 1 50

——— **The Castle Builders.** 12mo.....................Cloth, 75

——— **Richard the Fearless.** Cloth, 63

——— **The Two Guardians.** Cloth, 75

——— **Kenneth; or, The Rear Guard**............Cloth, 75

——— **Lances of Lynwood.** 16mo. ....Cloth, 75

SCIENTIFIC WORKS.

Appleton. Dictionary of Mechanics, Machines, Engine Work, and Engineering, containing over 4000 illustrations, and nearly 2000 pages. Complete in 2 vols. large 8vo. Strongly and neatly bound.................... 12 00

——— **Mechanics' Magazine & Engineers' Journal.** Vols. I., II. and III. for 1851-'52-'53.....................Cloth, each 3 50

Appletons' Cyclopædia of Drawing, for Engineers, Mechanics, and Architects. Edited by W. E. Worthen. 1 vol. royal 8vo..............(In press.)

Allen's Philosophy of the Mechanics of Nature. Illus. 8vo.............................. 3 50

Arnot, D. H. Gothic Architecture. Applied to Modern Residences. 40 plates. 1 vol. 4to. 4 00

Artisan Club. Treatise on the Steam Engine. Edited by J. Bourne. 83 plates, and 349 Engravings on wood. 4to........... 6 00

Barnard's Theory of Landscape Painting in Water Colors. With 24 colored plates. Extra cloth gilt, 5 00

Bartol's Treatise on the Marine Boilers of the United States. 8vo.....Cloth, 1 50

Bassnett's Theory of Storms. 1 vol. 12mo................Cloth, 1 00

Bourne, John. A Catechism of the Steam Engine. 16mo. Cloth, 75

——— **Treatise on the Screw Propeller.** New Edition. 1 vol. 4to.. ....Cloth, 9 00

Cleaveland & Backus's New Work on Cottage & Farm Architecture. 1 handsome vol. 8vo. With 100 fine engravings. Extra cloth, 2 00

Coles' Contractors' Book for Working Drawings of Machinery. Folio..........Cloth, 10 00

Comings' Class-Book of Physiology. 12mo............ 1 00

Downing, A. J. Architecture of Country Houses. Including Designs for Cottages, Farm Houses and Villas; with remarks on Interiors, Furniture, and the best modes of Warming and Ventilating. With 320 illustrations. 1 vol. 8vo.................Cloth, 4 00

Field's City Architecture. 1 vol. 8vo. With 20 engravings. Cloth, 2 00

Fry's Complete Treatise on Artificial Fish-Breeding. 12mo.......................Cloth, 75

Gillespie's (Prof.) Practical Treatise on Surveying. 1 vol. 8vo. With many engravings..... 2 00

Griffith's Treatise on Marine and Naval Architecture; or, Theory and Practice Blended in Ship-Building. 50 plates...................Cloth, 10 00

Green & Congdon. Analytical Class-Book of Botany. Illustrated. 1 vol. 4to.... 1 50

——— **Primary Class-Book of Botany.** Illustrated. 4to... 75

Haupt, H. Theory of Bridge Construction. With practical illustrations. 8vo...........Cloth, 3 00

Henck's Field-Book for Railroad Engineers. 1 vol. 12mo. Tuck, 1 75

www.ingramcontent.com/pod-product-compliance
Lightning Source LLC
LaVergne TN
LVHW021142110826
845150LV00005B/1100